VIRTUE AND DESPAIR

VIRTUE AND DESPAIR
IN THE PRESENT AGE

& OTHER ESSAYS

by

Kenneth A. Hammond

Printed by Createspace, An Amazon.com Company
Charleston, SC

ISBN-13: 978-1545258989
ISBN-10: 1545258988

Set in 10/11 pt. Garamond

For my Dad,
Robert George Hammond
June 27, 1926 — April 8, 2006

&

To S. Cainneach [Kenneth] of Derry Colmcille*
Abbott / Namesake
Calendar Feast Day, October 11th

*Adhamhnán's Life of Colum Cille

Scio opera tua: quia neque frigidus es, neque calidus: utinam frigidus esses, aut calidus: Sed quia tepidus es, et nec frigidus, nec calidus, incipiam te evomere ex ore meo. Quia dicis: quod dives sum, et locupletatus, et nullius egeo: et nescis quia tu es miser, et miserabilis, et pauper, et cæcus, et nudus.

APOCALYPSIS Caput III: 15-17, Latin Vulgate

I know thy works, that thou art neither cold nor hot, I would thou wert cold or hot. So then because thou art lukewarme, and neither cold nor hot, I wil spew thee out of my mouth:

REUELATION Chapter III: 15-17, KJV 1611

I know your works: you are neither cold nor hot. Would that you were cold or hot! So, because you are lukewarm, and neither cold nor hot, I will spew you out of my mouth. For you say, I am rich, I have prospered, and I need nothing; not knowing that you are wretched, pitiable, poor, blind, and naked.

REVELATION 3: 15-17, RSV

CONTENTS

Preface

The book that proceeds here is a compilation of my *spoils* in graduate school. It is, I think, the reward of many years "hard-labor"; a yeoman's academic effort, really.

Hundreds on hundreds of books read and countless hours of study in the completion of dual Masters of the Arts degrees in Theology, Philosophy/Religious Studies, is what is on display for the readers' indulgence.

PART ONE of this book is my re-polished Master's Thesis written at *Washington Theological Union* in DC (2009-2012). It was more than two years in research and writing. After careful consideration with my thesis director, I finally submitted it for the M.A. degree as two separate research papers (rather than the 70-100 page draft in hand). My vision of the thesis had not yet come together in the right way and *WTU* was "closing-up shop" due to financial difficulties. Instead of being a purist about it, I agreed with my then director that meeting the deadline was more important . . . so as to reach graduation in 2012; the second to last year before the 45-year-old Roman Catholic seminary's close.

And so, to get it into workable shape, the middle section on Kierkegaard was left out, while two individual papers were made of the first and third chapters. I have since revisited it, made it beautifully complete after some years of reflection since, and finally "put-it-back-together-again" like *Humpty-Dumpty* himself.[1] Materials from later research have been added in generously after the fact. I am satisfied with the finished product as it is presented in this book.

PART TWO of this project is a collection of essays written throughout the course of 4 years of graduate study. They are dense and technical at times—for the layman. However, the essays picked can be understood as peer-reviewed in that they were all graded and commented on by my professors. Every professor I have studied with is a recognized and respected intellectual with a doctorate in his or her field.

Feast of the *Annunciation*—March 25, 2017.

---

[1] *See* Lewis Carroll, *The Complete Works of Lewis Carroll* (London: The Nonesuch Press, 1989 [1939]).

Although he was made by God in a state of holiness, from the very onset of his history man abused his liberty, at the urging of the personified Evil. Man set himself against God and sought to attain his goal apart from God. Although he knew God, he did not glorify Him as God, but his senseless mind was darkened and he served the creature rather than the Creator. What divine revelation makes known to us agrees with experience. Examining his heart, man finds that he has inclinations toward evil too, and is engulfed by manifold ills which cannot come from his good Creator. Often refusing to acknowledge God as his beginning, man has disrupted also his proper relationship to his own ultimate goal as well as his whole relationship toward himself and others and all created things.

In iustitia a Deo constitutus, homo tamen, suadente maligno, inde ab exordio historiae, libertate sua abusus est, seipsum contra Deum erigens et finem suum extra Deum attingere cupiens. Cum cognovissent Deum, non sicut Deum glorificaverunt, sed obscuratum est insipiens cor eorum et servierunt creaturae potius quam creatori. Quod revelatione divina nobis innotescit, cum ipsa experientia concordat. Nam homo, cor suum inspiciens, etiam ad malum inclinatum se comperit et in multiplicibus malis demersum, quae a bono suo creatore provenire non possunt. Deum tamquam principium suum saepe agnoscere renuens, etiam debitum ordinem ad finem suum ultimum, simul ac totam suam sive erga seipsum sive erga alios homines et omnes res creatas ordinationem disrupit.

GAUDIUM ET SPES

PART I
INTRODUCTION:

Indubitably this is not bestseller material, *but* I can only think with the venerable Henry Adams that, "The difference is slight, to the influence of an author, whether he is read by 500 readers, or by 500,000; if he can select the 500, he reaches the 500,000."[2] So, that I am understood is more important to me than mass-market.[3] The *penultimate* consideration is perhaps simply to share my thoughts and ideas with others.[4] To reap a profit in more than money by means of reproducing my efforts in graduate school is a just and good instinct, one can imagine. My intention is not to be overly pedantic, precocious, pretentious, or even sardonic— Grimly jocular, full of bitter mockery, cynical (esp. ~ laughter). This is years of research and hundreds of books read . . . my best efforts.

As I look back now (upon the occasion of self-publishing a first "major work") on the early germination of my writing, I can see all the way back to my elementary school years where my love of writing first started. Like Sherlock Holmes everything to me is, in the end, "elementary my dear Watson."[5] Or, like T. S. Eliot: *in my beginning is my end.*[6]

> Time present and time past
> Are both perhaps present in time future,
> And time future contained in time past.[7]

---

[2] Henry Adams, *The Education of Henry Adams: An Autobiography* (Boston and New York: Houghton Mifflin Company, 1918), 259.

[3] Kierkegaard stood against the mass market media, as do I. *See* Søren Kierkegaard, *The Present Age and On the Difference Between A Genius and An Apostle*, trans. Alexander Dru (New York: Harper & Row, 1962); Vance Packard, *The Hidden Persuaders* (New York: David McKay Company, 1957); & C. Wright Mills, "Man in the Middle: The Designer," in *Power, Politics & People: The Collected Essays of C. Wright Mills*, ed. Irving Louis Horowitz (Oxford, UK: Oxford University Press, 1963), 374-386.

[4] Paul Fussell, *Class: A Guide Through the American Status System* (New York: Summit Books, 1983), "VII Speak, That I May See Thee."

[5] *See* Sir Arthur Conan Doyle, *The Adventures of Sherlock Holmes* (New York: Barnes & Noble Books, 2004). [ERRATUM: never in the written stories].

[6] T. S. Eliot, *Four Quartets* (New York: Harcourt, 1943), "East Coker."

[7] Ibid., "Burnt Norton."

The first two things written that I remember were my 3rd grade war stories *Blood Battle* and *Guts n' Glory*, both exceedingly gruesome and full of bloody butchery galore. My first bound-book was "published" in 4th grade. It bore the catchy title *The Scales of the Sewer Snake* and was soon to be followed by its sequel *The Executor*. These books too were at turns violent and ambitious for a boy at the tender age eleven.

Moving-on . . . in high school my first "poem" of any note was written in a creative writing class. A kind of Taoist proverb that I can recite here in its entirety as a retrospective:

SAMSARA

Coming
    Going
Stopping
    Starting
Running
    Waiting
Crying
    Parting
Pride
    Anger
      Pain
      and Suffering

Always preoccupied
Never satisfied
Always sinking
Never thinking
about the day
everythings gone
you are by yourself
and you can no longer run

making plans for the
      future
forgetting to live in the
    present
reality is never the fantasy
pointless disappointment

Stop
smell the flowers
Stop
see the trees
Stop
hear the birds
Stop
watch the leaves
turn from green to gold
fall off and
become covered in snow
the spring sun rises
again they grow
An invisible dance
clouded by illusions of
permanence
under a tree sit
Bring the Mind home
rest in the infinite.[8]

- KEN HAMMOND

It's no Kahlil Gibrian to be sure.[9] In fact I can't help seeing this admirable attempt in the vein of one of novelist Walker Percy's side-characters Lewis Peckham. Percy by way of the protagonist [Will Barrett] in the novel *The Second Coming*:

> Lewis showed him [Barrett] some of his poetry
> once. *It was not good.* There was one poem called
> 'New Moon over Khe Sanh,' which was typed in
> the shape of a new moon:

---

[8] My short little poem *Samsara* was "published" in the very same GHS literary journal as the long-dead Truman Capote. *See* Truman Capote, "Swamp Terror," June 1940, *The Green Witch*, Commencement Issue, Greenwich, CT, Beinecke Rare Book and Manuscript Library at Yale University. And *see* Truman Capote, "Miss Belle Rankin," December 1941, *The Green Witch*, Greenwich, CT, Beinecke Rare Book and Manuscript Library at Yale University. *See* Etienne Gilson, *The Christian Philosophy of St. Thomas Aquinas* (New York: Octogon Books, 1988) 100-101, for an explanation of infinitude as such.

[9] Kahlil Gibrian, *The Prophet* (New York: Alfred A Knopf, 1998).

The
> *rounds*
>> *incoming*
>>> *bright silver*
>>>> *of moon reflected*
>>>>> *in foul funkhole*
>>>> *bright silver of*
>>> *metal destined for*
>> *my brain is no*
> *Carolina*

moon
no[10]

(end quote) That poor old Lewis' poem is shaped like a *new moon* which also resembles the shape of a *boomerang* was probably not his intention. More to this effect, Percy [in Barrett's narration again] gives this succinct description of Lewis Peckham's character:

> He [Peckham] was a discontent golf pro. He looked like a Cherokee scout but his family was old-line Tidewater and he played golf at the University of Virginia. He was an unhappy golf pro. *Maybe books had ruined him.* What a shock to learn from this grave silent man that he wrote poetry in secret! Imagine Leatherstocking a poet. Lewis knew a great many things, could read signs like an Indian but unlike an Indian he did not know what he could not do. He thought he was a good poet but he was not. He thought books could tell him how to live but they couldn't. He was a serious but dazed reader. He read Dante and Shakespeare and Nietzsche and Freud. He read modern poetry and books on psychiatry. He had taken a degree in English, taught English, fought in a war, returned to teach English, couldn't, decided to farm, bought a goat farm, managed a Confederate mu-

---

[10] Walker Percy, *The Second Coming: A Novel* (New York: Picador, 1980), 150.

seum in a cave on his property, wrote poetry, went broke, became a golf pro.[11]

In light of types like Peckham I am wary of the above pitfalls in spreading an ambition too thin or laying on a literary palette too thick. It is not to be a dilettante like Peckham that one should look out for. That being said, these are my pearls after years of high-minded study and graduate scholarship. And we can look to the flowery embellishments of 1611 King James English to remind ourselves, "Giue not that which is holy vnto the dogs, neither cast ye your pearles before swine : lest they trample them vnder their feete, and turne againe and rent you." (MATTHAEUM 7:6)

To be sure, some of this is my own personal scribble for edification. Inside jokes and ironies that only I myself know, but I will assure that everything in my work is genuine, serious, and "right-on" by my own wits. No ambiguities, puns, misleading obscurantism, et cetera, is my intention ever, if rarely otherwise. I am writing here on serious subject matter. It is sensitive to those who care about it, myself included. Albeit a lot of what is written here is too heavy, specialized, or scholarly (for non-experts).

I am also gravely cognizant of the sin involved with accidentally sending others down a wrong path while writing publicly on the topics of religion or theology. I admonish the reader that I am not approaching this written document under any professed authority, nor am I pretending to. However, I fully acknowledge the rightful claims that some such authority may have in these matters, especially, say, things too high for my aspiration . . . or beyond my depth to broach. I respectfully defer in such instances to those more learnéd than I.

In matters of religion the adherent can leave me aside for needful corrections by my betters in the Roman Catholic Hierarchy, for instance.[12] I ask forgiveness for any "pontifications" made

---

[11] Ibid.

[12] *See* Joseph Cardinal Ratzinger with Vittorio Messori, *The Ratzinger Report: An Exclusive Interview on the State of the Church*, trans. Salvator Attanasio and Graham Harrison (San Francisco: Ignatius Press, 1985). In II. BRETHREN, BUT SEPARATED then Cardinal Ratzinger states: "Genuine Catholicism is a highly sensitive balance, an attempt to unite aspects of life which seem to contradict one another and yet which guarantee the completeness of the Credo. Moreover, Catholicism calls for an attitude of faith which often conflicts with today's dominant view . . . For

in false-consciousness here, e.g. things written that are merely an echo of what can be heard better elsewhere. Nonetheless, *Our Lord* does tell us that even the Scribes have a part to play in the Kingdom. What else are our *treasures old and new* or what else can *treasures old and new* be?

> *"Have you understood all this?" They answered, "Yes."*
> *And he said to them, "Therefore every scribe who has been*
> *trained for the kingdom of heaven is like the master of a*
> *household who brings out of his treasure what is new and*
> *what is old." When Jesus had finished these parables, he*
> *left that place* (Mttw 13:51-52).

In the first part of this book what follows is a long address at the revisions or "correctives" being made in Roman Catholic Moral Theology since the era of Vatican II. We tackle explicitly Catholic materials that have long been in development. Under the discernment of the *Holy Ghost*, the Clergy are still outstanding in their judgments on some of these live-matters of doctrinal development. My input is modest. By adding Kierkegaard and Percy to the fray I hope to contribute a unique voice readable by others already working on this—that is, through the authority of the institutional church.

---

the modern man in the street, the most obvious concept of the Church is what technically one would call *Congregationalist* or *Free Church*. It implies that the Church is a changeable form depending upon how men organize what pertains to faith. Consequently one has to adapt as far as possible to the demands of the present moment . . . today many people can hardly understand any more that behind a human reality stands the mysterious divine reality. And as we know, this is the Catholic understanding of the Church, and it is far harder to accept the one we have just outlined, which is not simply *the* Protestant understanding but one that has developed within the phenomenon of 'Protestantism'." Ratzinger also notes here as to Rome's refusal to allow intercommunion (e.g. the possibility of Catholics participating in the Eucharist of a Reformed church, or vice versa), that . . . "Even many Catholics regard this refusal as the final fruit of an intolerance that ought to belong to past history. Many people say to us, 'Don't be so harsh, so anachronistic!' But it is not a question of intolerance or of ecumenical reticence: the Catholic confession is that without the apostolic succession there is no genuine priesthood, and hence there can be no sacramental Eucharist in the proper sense. We believe that the Founder of Christianity himself wanted it this way."

I am writing without seeking the *nihil obstat* or *imprimatur* (albeit this is the kind of thing that that is sought for) and I am professedly indulging my liberty to speculate on dogmatic matters (hopefully not for the sake of "freethinking" alone). Knowing full-well the acceptable methods of the Roman Catholic system of theology, I look to keep these Magisterial parameters at least loosely in mind, by the grace of God. With Kierkegaard I can say I write *without authority*.[13] Perhaps there are moments of genuine light here, but surely the office of Apostleship is beyond my ken.[14]

"A Pinch of Spice!" is what Søren calls it. The correctives I offer are no more than a tiny itty-bitty tiny-tiny little teeny-weeny *pinch of spice* in the scheme of things, but an (I think) indispensable aspect of the whole; that is to mean the whole in its integral totality of *wholeness*. So, enough with caveats and disclaimers . . . I open this book on *Virtue and Despair*, sin and love, with Kierkegaard as to his metaphor of cooking. I quote:

'The Sacrifice', the Corrective

> As a skilful cook says with regard to a dish in which already a great many ingredients are mingled: 'It needs still just a little pinch of cinnamon' (and we perhaps could hardly tell by the taste that this little pinch of spice had entered into it, but she knew precisely why and precisely how it affected the taste of the whole mixture); as an artist says with a view to the colour effect of a whole painting which is composed of many, many colours: 'There and there, at that little point, there must be applied a little touch of red' (and we perhaps could hardly even discover that the red is there, so carefully has the artist suppressed it, although he knows exactly why it should be introduced) . . .

---

[13] Søren Kierkegaard. *The Point of View For My Work As An Author*, eds. and trans. Howard V. Hong and Edna H. Hong (Princeton, NJ: Princeton University Press, 1998).

[14] *See* Søren Kierkegaard, *The Present Age and On the Difference Between A Genius and An Apostle*.

. . . A little pinch of spice! That is to say: Here a man must be sacrificed, he is needed to impart a particular taste to the rest.

These are the correctives. It is a woeful error if he who is used for applying the corrective becomes impatient and would make the corrective normative for others. That is the temptation to bring everything to confusion.

A little pinch of spice! Humanly speaking, what a painful thing, thus to be sacrificed, to be the little pinch of spice! But on the other hand, God knows well him whom he elects to use in this way, and then he knows also how, in the inward understanding of it, to make it so blessed a thing for him to be sacrificed, that among the thousands of divers voices which express, each in its own way, the same thing, his also will be heard, and perhaps especially his which is truly *de profundis*, proclaiming: God is love. The birds on the branches, the lilies in the field, the deer in the forest, the fishes in the sea, countless hosts of happy men exultantly proclaim: God is love. But beneath all these sopranos, supporting them as it were, as the bass part does, is audible the *de profundis* which issues from the sacrificed one: God is love.[15]

---

[15] As quoted in Walter Lowrie, *A Short Life of Kierkegaard* (Princeton, NJ: Princeton University Press, 2013 [1942]), 259-260. Or, the original is in Søren Kierkegaard, *The Moment and Later Writings*, trans. Howard V. Hong and Edna H. Hong (Princeton, NJ: Princeton University Press, 1998), 422-423.

CHAPTER I

IMPORTANT THEMES
IN CATHOLIC MORAL THEOLOGY

for thy heart is not right in the sight of God.

Of Simon Magus the sorcerer, THE ACTS 8:21

That particular actions derive their character as parts of a larger whole is a point of view alien to our dominant ways of thinking and yet one which it is necessary at least to consider if we are to begin to understand how life may be more than a sequence of individual actions and episodes.

Alasdair MacIntyre, AFTER VIRTUE

The state of sin is a worse sin than the particular sins; it is the sin . . .

The line Shakespeare gives Macbeth (III, 2) is psychologically masterful:
Sündentsprossne Werke Erlangen nur durch Sünde Kraft und Stäke

Søren Kierkegaard, THE SICKNESS UNTO DEATH

Can. 7. If anyone says that in the sacrament of penance it is not required by divine law for the remission of sins to confess each and all mortal sins which are recalled after a due and diligent examination, also secret ones and those that are a violation of the two last commandments of the Decalogue, as also the circumstances that change the nature of a sin, but that this confession is useful only to instruct and console the penitent and in olden times was observed only to impose a canonical satisfaction; or says that they who strive to confess all sins wish to leave nothing to the divine mercy of pardon; or finally, that it is not lawful to confess venial sins, let him be anathema.

CANONS AND DECREES OF THE COUNCIL OF TRENT

1. *Context:*
A Brief Account of the Story of Sin,
Forgiveness and the Catholic Church

Centuries ago sin was treated simply as an act, often disconnected from the whole life of the person.[16] In response to this depiction of sin, contemporary Catholic moral theology tends to speak of sin as a rupture in a relationship that ought to exist between a person and God, others, himself or herself, and the created world.[17] The juridical perspective based on acts and rules alone, although valuable, is incomplete. Legal codes alone do not fully account for the context of individual actions, the interior depths of the human subject, or the inherent complexities of the human condition. The moral life is about seeking moral goodness, not just right actions. Sin involves the whole person, not just acts in isolation.

The history of moral theology, as a theological discipline, is intimately tied-in with the practice of the "Confessional" in the Catholic Church. From the earliest Apostolic period sin was understood in the context of the Bishop's power to "loose and bind" the sinner while effectively reconciling or excommunicating the penitent from the Christian community.[18] One of the first major challenges the Church faced was the question over the forgiveness of sinners who desired to rejoin the community after grave transgressions. For those who had fallen away or committed the serious sins of apostasy, murder or adultery, there was a natural feeling of righteous indignation on the part of the faithful toward the supposedly humane approach of treating sinners with *too much* mercy.[19]

In particular, at the height of the controversy in the third and fourth centuries many of those who had suffered under the Roman persecution became outwardly resistant toward the penitents

[16] Peter Black, C.Ss.R. and Kevin J. O'Neil, C.Ss.R., *The Essential Moral Handbook: A Guide to Catholic Living,* Revised Edition (Liguori, Missouri: Liguori Publications, 2006 [2003]). A good general "plain-vanilla" outline of Catholic moral teachings.

[17] The broader context of this approach to moral theology is in Todd A. Salzman, ed. *Method and Catholic Moral Theology: The Ongoing Reconstruction* (Omaha, NE: Creighton University Press, 1999).

[18] John Mahoney, *The Making of Moral Theology: A Study of the Roman Catholic Tradition* (Oxford: Clarendon Press, 1987), 1-2.

[19] Ibid., 3-4.

who returned when the persecution had subsided. For instance, the eminent theologian Tertullian believed the practice of readmitting apostates after persecution so unjust that he could not countenance maintaining communion with the Catholic Church for the sake of the said issue. Nevertheless, sin, in all its many forms, eventually did find a channel of forgiveness for all those who repented with an outward sign of sorrow and who sought reconciliation through the practice of penance in the early Church.[20] For no less of an authority than St. Augustine there was only one truly unforgiveable sin, that is, the final hardness of heart when faced with the eternal salvation offered through Christ Jesus.[21]

In Apostolic times the penances for sin were incredibly severe, often taking long periods of either individual chastisement or public humiliation. Upon the invasion of the barbarians and the collapse of the Roman Empire, the practice of public penance eventually became unsustainable. It was not until the Celtic monks from the Irish monasteries began the long fought battle for the Catholic soul of Western Europe in the ninth century that the practice of penance was renewed in the form of what became private auricular confession.[22]

Initially, for the monks, private confession was only practiced in the context of a personal spiritual relationship between a religious superior and his subordinate. For the most part the intention behind the private form of auricular confession was, presumably, the healing of the wound [gratia sanans] left from the sins of the guilty. Eventually the practice gained wider currency in the populace at large and soon standardized penitential literature surfaced in order to satisfy, in turn, the demand for ascribed penances amongst the faithful. The "penitentials," as they were called, were books that provided lists and classifications for all manner of sins, as well as the appropriate penances designated for each particular case or circumstance.[23]

With the passage of time and the development of the more highly cultivated Europe of the later Middle Ages the image of

---

[20] Ibid, 2-5.

[21] Ibid., 3.

[22] Thomas Cahill, *How the Irish Saved Civilization: The Untold Story of Ireland's Heroic Role from the Fall of Rome to the Rise of Medieval Europe* (New York: Doubleday, 1995), 106-107.

[23] John Mahoney, *The Making of Moral Theology: A Study of the Roman Catholic Tradition*, 5-17.

spiritual healing from holy "roaming" (nomadic) monks became superseded, naturally enough, with the idea of the juridical court and the priestly caste of Apostolic judges, mostly in reflection of the eventual political organization of Christendom. [24] With the growing establishment of the solidifying Church, the Fourth Lateran Council in 1215, at the very height of the Mediæval World, prescribed mandatory annual confession through the appropriate apostolic channels, essentially making the requirement of private confession universal.[25]

After the elaboration of the Western canon law beginning with Pope Gregory VII, and the solemn re-definitions of the Council of Trent during the Counter-Reformation, the Catholic Church, for all intents and purposes, enshrined the practice of approaching sin as a juridical (albeit spiritualized) transaction between the confessor and the penitent.[26] Without fleshing this aspect of moral theology out too much, suffice it to say that the juridical court imagery and legal understanding which became so entrenched during the post-Tridentine period had several important flaws.[27]

First of all, moral theology, as the academic and clerical discipline came to be known, was divorced from the fundamental integrity of Scholastic theology. For example, on the one hand, the Scholastic triads of "grave matter / full knowledge / full consent" and "moral object / intention / circumstance," respectively, continue to have perennial value as hermeneutical tools.[28] They provide valuable insight with which the category of sin might be interpreted and dealt with in view of the consistent traditional moral teaching of the Catholic Church since the High Middle Ages.

---

[24] Harold J. Berman, *Law and Revolution: The Formation of the Western Legal Tradition* (Cambridge, MA: Harvard University Press, 1983), 165-181.

[25] "Lateran IV" in *Decrees of the Ecumenical Councils*, ed. Norman Tanner, S.J. (Washington, DC: Georgetown University Press, 1990), 227-273.

[26] The old Tridentine Liturgy—*See, The Latin-English Booklet Missel for Praying the Traditional Mass*, Commemorative Edition in Thanksgiving for Summorum Pontificum (Glenview, IL: Coalition in Support of Ecclesia Dei, January, 2014).

[27] John Mahoney, *The Making of Moral Theology: A Study of the Roman Catholic Tradition*, 22-27.

[28] Peter J. Kreeft, *Catholic Christianity: A Complete Catechism of Beliefs Based on the Catechism of the Catholic Church* (San Francisco: Ignatius Press, 2001), 183 & 197-198.

However, reducing moral theology to the adjudication of penances in the context of the Confessional, that is, essentially separating it from the depths of spiritual theology and the full rigor of the scholastic system, is wholly inadequate in terms of the integrity of the discipline *in toto*.[29]

British Jesuit John Mahoney puts it succinctly in pointing out the central difficulty with pre-Vatican II moral theology. He writes:

> . . . it led to an approach to the moral life as discontinuous; 'freezing' the film in a jerky succession of individual 'stills' to be analyzed, and ignoring the plot. Continuity was discounted, or at most only a 'circumstance' and the 'story' of the individual's moral vocation and exploration either unsuspected or disregarded . . . reaction to this dissection of the moral continuum into disjointed instances has led to a development of a principle of moral totality, where responsibility is considered to arise at least as much from appreciating the sweep and pattern of the whole picture as it is from the individual brush strokes or coloured dots which go to make it up.[30]

Keeping in mind the above shortfall with the legalistic approach and the appropriateness of placing moral acts in the context of personal and communal narratives the concept/definition of sin is explored in greater depth in what follows.

2. *Legalism:*
An Inadequate Approach to Sin

Many moral theologians today recognize the need for the continued renewal of their subject-matter both within the Catholic Church and for the Christian community at large. In particular,

---

[29] James A. Coriden, *An Introduction to Canon Law* (Mahwah, NJ: Paulist Press, 1991). An excellent introduction to the context of Canon Law.

[30] John Mahoney, *The Making of Moral Theology: A Study of the Roman Catholic Tradition*, 31-32.

"legalism," in the sense in which the term has often been used, is a harsh pejorative for those who in the name of the "letter of the law" give into a creeping "Pharisaism." The Pharisees were notoriously self-righteous in following the letter of the law, but the spirit *mystified* them when confronted with it in the person of Jesus Christ. In fact, their sin was the worst of all, that is, spiritual pride.

One can imagine the depth of the sin that warranted such an attack as this: "Woe to you scribes and Pharisees, hypocrites! For you are like whitewashed tombs, which outwardly appear beautiful, but within are full of dead men's bones and all uncleanness" (Matthew: 23:27).[31] Moral theologians Dietrich and Alice von Hildebrand further explain:

> Pharisaism implies an existential hypocrisy, a constitutive hypocrisy. The Pharisee is possessed by the spirit of the lie. The Pharisee described in the gospel is mainly preoccupied with the ceremonial of the law. He is an enemy of the 'mystery' of God. He ignores the 'spirit' everywhere and reduces everything to the fulfillment of the letter.[32]

The above condemnations are severe. However, they provide an accurate picture of the religious hypocrite. Throughout the Church's history the approach toward morality has, at times, tragically tended toward the direction of "dead letter obedience," instead of the living faith of the total person committed toward an integral and true religious calling.[33]

The total commitment of the person to Christ, that is the interior life of the *Spirit*, as well as the virtuous life, was attended to by the Roman Catholic Church primarily in the spiritual theology

---

[31] All Scriptural citations are taken from the *Revised Standard Version* (Catholic Edition) unless otherwise noted.

[32] Dietrich von Hildebrand and Alice von Hildebrand, *Morality and Situation Ethics* (Quincy, IL: Franciscan Press, 1982), 27.

[33] Fyodor Dostoevsky, *The Brothers Karamazov* (New York: The Modern Library, 1996). *See* the "Grand Inquisitor" chapter for Ivan Karamazov's parable of a this-worldly Roman Catholic Church that rejects Jesus Christ returned in favor of maintaining the political order through an "immanentization of the Eschaton" (to use Eric Voeglin's paraphrase of Joachim of Flora). *See* Eric Voegelin, *The New Science of Politics: An Introduction* (Chicago: The University of Chicago Press, 1952), 110-117.

of the Church. The Catholic practice of morality was almost entirely viewed in terms of external conformity to rule. For example, there was a two-tiered approach to the spiritual life. The laity were expected to follow the Ten Commandments alone, while the clergy and religious orders were called to live the life of the Beatitudes [beatitudo]. This can be seen as what sociologist Charles Taylor has called the "multi-speed" social system, where different orders are held to higher (faster) or lower (slower) moral and religious expectations.[34] In other words, "in a large house there are utensils not only of gold and silver but also of wood and clay, some for special use, some for ordinary" (2 Timothy 2:20). So too, as to the pre-Vatican II dispensation the personal call for holiness among the laity was, in some ways, neglected.[35]

The complexity of the notion of sin is evasive in theory, let alone trying to discern its action in a living human being. In short, universally binding moral codes, although important, nonetheless are not enough when approaching the concept and meaning of sin. Moral theologian Germain Grisez in his book *Christian Moral Principles* has pointed out four important flaws with the so-called "legalism" of pre-Vatican II moral theology.

For Grisez, the classical pre-Vatican II approach to moral theology specified many rules for moral behavior, but did not always provide reasons for the origination of the rules in the first place. Thereby, the Roman Catholic Church often did not provide sufficient justification for why the faithful should remain obedient to them when confronted with private conflicts of conscience.[36] Secondly, moral theology became somewhat minimalistic, often telling the faithful to avoid certain behaviors, but not giving enough direction for the actualization of the Christian vocation, that is, outside of not committing Mortal Sin or fulfilling the basic religious obligations prescribed through the Church.[37] Thirdly, if specific actions were not explicitly forbidden, the laity would feel, sometimes, no particular religious obligation to avoid the behavior, essentially ignoring an individual call for sanctity in particular cir-

---

[34] Charles Taylor, *A Secular Age* (Cambridge, MA: Harvard University Press, 2007), 62-66.

[35] *See* Norman Tanner, S.J., ed. *Vatican II: The Essential Texts* (New York: Image Books, 2012).

[36] Germain Grisez, *The Way of the Lord Jesus Vol. 1: Christian Moral Principles* (Quincy, IL: Franciscan Press, 1997), 13.

[37] Ibid.

cumstances, personal character, time and place.[38] Finally, moral theology, in many ways, came to resemble a mere worldly legal system, complete with higher and lower courts of authority, a written body of laws, and a methodical code of universal legal procedures.[39]

Moral theology since the time of Trent came to resemble, in practice, the study of Confessional and Canon law, instead of finding needed insight in the more truly Christian study of spirituality; nourished through Scripture and in relation to the cultivation of the individual's personal development of character virtue.[40] Taken together these drawbacks provided good reasons for moral theologians to call for the greater renewal of the discipline at the time of Vatican II.[41] According to Catholic moral theologian Richard Gula:

> The sense that sin involves a broken relationship with God got lost when the law itself became the absolute object of loyalty. Legalism replaced the religious foundations of sin with juridical ones. Then, when taken to the extreme, sin became a transgression of a legal code rather than a failure to respond to God. To speak of sin in legal terms is to miss the important aspect of sin as a religious, relational reality which expresses our refusal to respond appropriately to God's love and mercy.[42]

One important reform of "legalism" is in seeing sin not simply in terms of individual acts, but also in terms of the condition or *power* under which the sinner becomes corrupted over time. In other words, the sins of the individual become, in effect, the outward signs of the interior corruption of sin—in the singular. In the classical formulation, sin means, literally, "to miss the mark"

---

[38] Ibid.

[39] *See* Harold Berman, *Law and Revolution.* Also, H. J. Schroeder, O. P., *Canons and Decrees of the Council of Trent* (St. Louis, MO: B. Herder Book Co., 1941)

[40] *See* James A. Coriden, *An Introduction to Canon Law.*

[41] Germain Grisez, *The Way of the Lord Jesus Vol. 1: Christian Moral Principles.*

[42] Richard M Gula, S.S., *Reason Informed By Faith: Foundations of Catholic Morality* (New York: Paulist Press, 1989), 91-92.

("harmatia" in Greek/"peccatum" in Latin/"hattah" in Hebrew).[43]
Peccatum, in the common usage, can mean to miss a target technically, say, for instance, in archery. However, in the religious usage
peccatum means to "miss the mark" in attaining one of the many
goods of human nature.

Whereas sin, ultimately, is the failure to be reconciled with
God as the final good of the human person, the Christian idea of
sin does not necessarily entail a "legalistic" failure of obligation in
this regard. Rather, sin is, most essentially, the willful destruction
of a relation or relationships. When the moral agent freely responds to another person or God in an abusive way (commission
or omission) to the detriment of any, or all, vital relations (with or
without breaking a moral commandment), the person commits sin.

In contrast to sinful acts, the condition of the sinner, *outside of
and before* the specific acts of immorality, is often underappreciated
in Catholic moral theology. However, the idea of sin as the "condition" of the sinner is not without precedent. In the Bible, for instance, sin is not simply irrational behavior or disobedience to God,
but also the condition of spiritual corruption conceived in almost
personalistic terms. Contra the predominance of the classical "teleological end-driven" morality of the Catholic tradition (which has
been influenced by Greek philosophical categories) Thomistic
scholar Josef Pieper notes that:

> use of the word (sin) to describe a condition is
> not unknown. For example in the New Testa-
> ment, especially in John, we encounter such
> statements as this: 'If you were blind, you have no
> sin' (John 9:41). Here sin seems to resemble a dis-
> ease, something one 'has,' like leprosy. Or when
> Paul says, 'dead to sin but alive to God' (Romans
> 6:11), he seems to be speaking of sin as a power
> conceived in almost personal terms. In fact the
> earliest mention of the concept of 'sin' in the Bi-
> ble ('If you do not do what is right, sin is crouch-

---

[43] Other words for sin in Biblical Hebrew are *peshah* and *awon*. Hattah is
close to peccatum, but none of these words can provide an absolute clarity of direct translation from the native Hebrew tongue. Still, all the Biblical words for sin (Latin, Greek, or Hebrew) imply the violation of *Hesed*
[faithful love of covenant].

ing at your door,' Genesis 4:7) must be interpreted in just such a sense.[44]

Sin, as such, is not simply the breaking of a moral rule, in the
external sense, but also that which occurs to the person upon going through with any particular sinful transgression. Moreover, sin,
in the case of Original Sin [peccatum originale originatum], is also
the inherent deficiency of the human condition itself. In the New
Testament it is made entirely clear that sin is *not* just moral disobedience to an authority. The meaning of the word is more layered.
It includes (at least) Original Sin [peccatum originale originans *or*
peccatum originale originatum], Actual Sins, and varying shades of
personal sin. In addition, social sin is not foreign to the Scriptures,
particularly in the prophetic literature.[45]

Sins can be primarily acts, but there are different ways of
understanding sinful acts in relation to salvation. Sinful acts can
originate in the corruption of character, in an omission, or in the
basic freedom that encompasses a "fundamental option" toward
God. In order to understand the meaning of sin in contemporary
Catholic moral theology, the next section addresses the notion of
the "fundamental option" with respect to moral judgment. Then,
moral judgment, as such, is discussed as it appears in the Gospel
for the purpose of showing that the New Covenant in Christ
altered the ways in which sin was (and is) seen relative to the
Legalism of the Old Testament. The "fundamental option" and
returning to the Scriptures for moral understanding are both ways
in which the legalistic tendency in moral theology has been and is
being remedied.

3. *Legalism:*
The Fundamental Option and Vatican II

As to the inadequacy of the juridical approach when treating
the conception of sin, the concept of "fundamental option" is an

---

[44] Josef Pieper, *The Concept of Sin* (South Bend, Indiana: St. Augustine's
Press, 2001), 29.
[45] Mark O'Keefe, *What are they Saying about Social Sin?* (New York: Paulist
Press, 1990), 5-25.

important corrective. Being that it is a relatively new term, albeit an older concept (implicitly at least), there are various interpretations regarding how best to make the concept fit within the tradition of the Catholic Church. Moral theologians Bernard Häring and Josef Fuchs were two of the first writers to approach the subject.

In particular, Häring viewed the concept of fundamental option as a means of better understanding the way in which freedom works in the life of the moral agent. The human person, being thoroughly dependent on God, is:

> called to give his response to God by the whole orientation of his/her life towards God as the ultimate end. In Biblical terms this means: God calls us to himself. The basic decision is whether our life will be one of listening and responding to him in and through all our attitudes and decisions. In secular language it is a question of giving ultimate meaning to existence and expressing that meaning in every facet of our lives and throughout our entire lifetime.[46]

For Bernard Häring, although the exercise of human freedom in performing moral acts is an important part of the picture, it is not the entire picture. Human freedom involves a more basic freedom than the categorical choices of individual actions. In other words, human persons also choose to direct the fundamental direction of their lives for or against "the Good" (or "what is good") in the first place.

Judging individual actions (when taken out of context) is highly uncertain or misleading because the judgement does not reach the interior depths of the total human subject or does not fully account for the subtleties of intention or circumstance.[47] Often times the context of an action is ignored in favor of seeing the action abstracted from the overarching story and underlying direction of the person's life. The fundamental option is not simply the choice for or against one or another particular good, but instead

---

[46] Bernard Häring, *Free and Faithful in Christ: Vol. 1: General Moral Theology* (New York: The Seabury Press, 1978), 164-165.

[47] Richard M Gula, S.S., *Reason Informed By Faith: Foundations of Catholic Morality*, 109-114.

the choice between orienting one's life toward "the Good" in the first place, or, choosing to not do so.

In the encyclical letter *Veritatis Splendor* Pope John Paul II approaches the concept of fundamental option after a balanced fashion. John Paul here recognizes that there is a greater concern among theologians for a more significant understanding of human freedom in our present age. He writes: "It has rightly been pointed out that freedom is not only the choice for one or another particular action; it is also, within that choice, a decision about oneself and a setting of one's own life for or against the Good, for or against the Truth, and ultimately for or against God."[48]

For many, the primary strength of the notion of "fundamental option" is the needed emphasis on the totality of the human person. The concept can be used for the purpose of breaking-through the barrier between individual acts and the total narrative structure of a virtuous life well-lived. With regard to these purposes alone, the "fundamental option" is, when understood in the above sense, an important reform of traditional Catholic moral theology.

John Paul II, after the said admission regarding the concept of a fundamental option, warns that there are theologians who take the idea too far in claiming that individual acts alone cannot fundamentally alter the moral or religious course of one's life.[49] For John Paul II, the "fundamental option" is the very ground of the movement of the Holy Spirit in response to God's calling, embodying the command, "whoever would save his life will lose it; and whoever loses his life for my sake and the Gospel's will save it" (Mark 8:35).[50] However, it is only in the particular free acts of the individual that the moral life finds, ultimately, its true expression.[51] In practice there is simply no other way of knowing the individual's "fundamental option" outside of the manifestation of the whole person's deepest interiority in the particular actions he or she takes. Although singular actions do not tell the whole story,

---

[48] John Paul II, *Veritatis Splendor*, encyclical letter, Vatican translation (Boston: Pauline Books & Media, 2003), paragraph 65.

[49] William E. May, *An Introduction to Moral Theology* (Huntington, IN: Our Sunday Visitor, 2003), 199-203.

[50] "Verily, verily, I say unto you, except a corn of wheat fall into the ground and die, it abideth alone: but if it die, it bringeth forth much fruit" (John 12:24).

[51] John Paul II, *Veritatis Splendor*, paragraph 65.

they remain an indispensable part of the total picture; that is, as far as moral judgment is concerned.[52]

Theologians in some circles have begun to view the "fundamental option" as a means of blurring the distinction between Venial and Mortal Sin—citing the anachronistic and awkward nature of this difference (1 John 5:17).[53] In their viewpoint Mortal Sin is to be reinterpreted as meaning only the ultimate choice for or against God, or, in other words, the "fundamental option" itself.

In bridging this gap between the different "ideological camps" John Paul II was prudent in holding to the position that the concept of "fundamental option" *can* be incorporated within the Catholic tradition without compromising the theoretical framework protecting the Church's teaching on moral absolutes. It remains possible to uphold the distinction between mortal and venial sin, while admitting the need for the inclusion of "something more," namely, the "fundamental option" applied within the parameters of John Paul II's encyclical.

In a welcome development for many Catholic moral theologians John Paul II does in fact implicitly acknowledge the need for viewing the human person in the totality of his or her "integrity" (from the Latin word *integer*, or "*one*") and the necessity of contextualizing actions within a unified narrative. In *Veritatis Splendor*, for example, the "drive toward wholeness" is alluded to as to the very reasons for sustaining in the traditional manner the order and balance between the person's "fundamental option" and his or her particular actions.[54] The Pope writes:

> To separate the fundamental option from concrete kinds of behavior means to contradict the substantial integrity and personal unity of the moral agent in his body and in his soul. A fundamental option understood without explicit consideration of the potentialities which it puts into effect and the determinations which express it does not do justice to the rational finality imma-

---

[52] John Finnis, *Moral Absolutes: Tradition, Revision and Truth* (Washington, DC: CUA Press, 1991). This short work gives a fine explanation of moral absolutes within the framework of Church moral teaching.

[53] "All wrongdoing is sin, but there is sin that is not mortal" (1 John 5:17).

[54] John Paul II, *Veritatis Splendor*, paragraph 66.

nent in man's acting and in each of his deliberate decisions. In point of fact, the morality of human acts is not deduced only from one's intention, orientation or fundamental option, understood as an intention devoid of a clearly determined binding content or as an intention with no corresponding positive effort to fulfill obligations of the moral life. Judgments about morality cannot be made without taking into consideration whether or not the deliberate choice of a specific kind of behavior is in conformity with the dignity and integral vocation of the human person. Every choice always implies a reference by the deliberate will to the goods and evils indicated by the natural law as goods to be pursued and evils to be avoided.

In the case of the positive moral precepts, prudence always has the task of verifying that they apply in a specific situation, for example, in view of other duties which may be more important or urgent. But the negative moral precepts, those prohibiting certain concrete actions or kinds of behavior as intrinsically evil, do not allow for any legitimate exception. They do not leave room, in any morally acceptable way, for the "creativity" of any contrary determination whatsoever. [55]

For John Paul II, if the substantial integrity of the human person is fragmented by separating the whole person from the individual agent's moral acts, then the fundamental dignity of the human self (body and soul) and the moral understanding of a given life is compromised. Pope John Paul in *Veritatis Spledor* divides the idea of the moral life into the New Testament questions: *What is moral good and evil?* (Mttw 19:17) and *What must be done to have eternal life?* (Mttw 19:16). The former question is addressed to the positive and negative precepts of the moral law; the content of the moral life. The latter question is a question of how to fulfill the moral life and in what *spirit* it must be done. John Paul is uncom-

---

[55] Ibid., paragraph 67.

promising on the absolute nature of the content of the first question, e.g. "circumstances or intentions can never transform an act intrinsically evil by virtue of its object into an act 'subjectively' good or defensible as a choice."[56] The Catholic Church has well-defined moral rules, albeit *intrinsically* evil acts are rare in definition. However, John Paul II also understands that, like the rich young man in the Gospel (Mttw 19), that the second question is the more important to Christ's calling—"the question is not so much about rules to be followed, but *about the full meaning of life*."[57] And again, Richard Gula here:

> A choice which arises from such a personal depth that it can significantly reverse or reinforce the fundamental direction of our life is a fundamental option. To qualify as a fundamental option, a choice must be rooted in a deep knowledge of self and a freedom to commit oneself. Through a fundamental option we express our basic freedom of self-determination to commit ourselves profoundly toward a certain way of *being in the world*.[58]

To be sure, the acts of the moral agent are important, but judgment concerns the totality of the person's life, not simply actions taken out of context.[59] God can judge individual actions, but fellow human beings, whatever their moral standing, ought to be careful when making judgments about the final standing of the moral agent's soul before God.[60] Only God sees the real heart;

---

[56] Ibid., paragraph 81.

[57] Ibid., paragraph 7.

[58] Richard M Gula, S.S., *Reason Informed By Faith: Foundations of Catholic Morality*, 80.

[59] In traditional Catholic moral theology "Mortal Sin" qualifies as a fundamental option insofar as the mortal sin radically breaks the relationship with God. However, the Catholic tradition also holds that for sin to be mortal there must be no impediments to "deep knowledge and the freedom of commitment." If impediments are present the sin is not mortal from the subjective stance, although the matter is still grave.

[60] Our inclination to do this is in part a result of the structure of our present day secular legal systems. Every crime or trial is an individual instance that narrows a legal case at hand to nothing but the most immediately relevant facts. As far as a system of judgment, the judgement of an

humans can and do err. In the Pastoral Epistle—"But who are you that you judge your neighbor?" (James 4:12) "Only God can answer the question about what is good, because he is the Good itself."[61]

The Church's understanding of mortal sin continues to suit the structure of the sacrament of penance. It works for the purpose of reconciling the sinner with the Body of Christ. However, since only God sees the heart, only those very close to the moral agent can have any kind of sufficient understanding of the person to even begin to approximate what God *can see* and does see.

In the next section another corrective of the legalistic tendency is addressed. The return to a more Scripture-based moral theology is a methodological shift that re-focuses moral theology on Biblical understandings of the moral life.[62] In particular, the transition from the external legalistic notions of sin in the Old Testament to the understandings of inner life of faith in the New Testament are explained for the purpose of seeing the ways in which the message of Jesus can sometimes become distorted for legalistic purposes. Returning to a Scriptural emphasis in moral theology is, like the fundamental option, another wanted remedy for the overemphasis on acts and law. The whole person's relationship to God's grace is integral to the Gospel message. Using the Scriptures to improve the practice of moral theology is a common theme among contemporary moral theologians for good reason.[63] As to moral judgment, the Scriptures offer a wealth of wisdom concerning God's justice and acts of the law. These themes are addressed

---

American court could not be any farther from the truth of God's judgment than it is now. And this is *despite* the fact that the courts originated in the canon law of the Catholic Church! *See* Harold Berman, *Law and Revolution*, for the convergences and divergences in history.

[61] John Paul II, *Veritatis Splendor*, paragraph 12.

[62] Richard M Gula, S.S., *Reason Informed By Faith: Foundations of Catholic Morality*, 165-169.

[63] *See* for example: Lisa Sowle Cahill, "The Bible and Christian Moral Practices," in *Christian Ethics: Problems and Prospects*, ed. Lisa Cahill and James Childress (Cleveland, OH: Pilgrim Press, 1996), 1-17. *See* also: Richard Gula, *What Are They Saying about Scripture and Ethics*, Revised Edition. (Mahwah, NJ: Paulist Press, 1995); Charles Curran and Richard McCormick, eds., *Readings in Moral Theology No. 4: The Use of Scripture in Moral Theology*, (New York: Paulist Press, 1984).

in the context of the problems outlined above concerning the historical presence of act-based legalism in the Church's praxis.

4. *Legalism:*
God's Justice and Sacred Scripture

In Biblical terms, when sin is understood in the sense of missing the mark, the mark referred to is the human subject's response to God and others. In some cases, this responsiveness of the moral agent takes the form of obedience or disobedience to religious commandments. In other cases, there is an entire realm of responsibility that is not possible to prescribe universally. In the realm of individual relationships and of the individual subject in history, the discernment of the moral agent involved is what truly matters. In the words of Gula:

> Legalistic mentalities which equate moral good-
> ness with obeying the letter of the law are still
> with us. For example, confession of sins is often
> made in light of the disciplinary laws of the
> church rather than the gospel call to love, justice,
> and forgiveness. Legalism stifles creativity, initia-
> tive, and conversion . . .
>
> It (legalism) looks for a rule to define the scope of
> personal responsibility rather than exercising
> moral muscle to engage in moral discernment.[64]

It is not surprising that "hattah" in Hebrew means not only to *miss the mark*, but also to offend. For the Hebrews, to offend against God is an offense against the covenant. For Christians, the covenant is not simply external to the self in the form of a legal code to obey. God's covenant, in Christ, is also within. The new covenant is founded upon grace, wholly underserved yet plentifully given. *But*, "What then shall we say? That the law is sin? By no means!" (Romans 7:7).

---

[64] Richard M Gula, S.S., *Reason Informed By Faith: Foundations of Catholic Morality*, 91.

Often times the depth of the person's offense is relative to the composition of the person's circumstances and intention, i.e. relational commitments, historical situation, subjective state, and so forth.[65] However, morality is not therefore relative to the individual. For example, when a person is given much in the way of graces, much is then expected—"More will be asked of one to whom more has been entrusted" (Luke 12:48). Jesus views the characters in the Gospel as individuals and judges them, not only on the basis of universal moral prescription, but also on all three components of a moral act: object, intention *and* circumstance. Given the particularities of the situation, everyone in the same circumstances ought to obey God's graces in the same way. Nevertheless, it is *not* possible to catalogue every possible circumstance and intention and abstract a "one-size-fits-all" universal morality that does justice to the Scriptures. Persons are called to respond to God's graces in different ways at different times. The notion that God's grace surpasses the judgments of the law is one of the major themes of the Gospel. The New Testament attests to the mistakenness of the tendency toward legalism.[66]

For a good example, Saint Paul preached freedom from law and obedience to Christ. "All things are lawful, but not all things are helpful" (1 Corinth 10:23). He did not preach freedom to disobey the Ten Commandments, but freedom to follow Christ, without seeking justification through the moral codes of Israel (Romans 3:21-31). In the opening passage of the *Gospel of Saint John*, it is written: "And from his fullness have we all received, grace upon grace. For the law was given through Moses; grace and truth came through Jesus Christ" (John 1:16-17). Christ is the new commandment of divine love and God's grace.

Christ is also the means of transformation *through / in / and with* which the human person is provided with the heart of flesh, replacing the heart of stone (Ezekiel 36:26-28). God's grace corrects the intentional state of the moral agent. The New Covenant

---

[65] David Hollenbach. *The Global Face of Public Faith: Politics, Human Rights, and Christian Ethics* (Washington, DC: Georgetown University Press, 2003), 19-38.

[66] For the "moderate" contemporary defense of the Catholic Scriptural hermeneutic *see* Sandra M. Schneiders, *The Revelatory Text: Interpreting the New Testament as Sacred Scripture* (San Francisco: HarperSanFrancisco, 1991).

is the interiorizing of the Old by way of the Holy Ghost.[67] Moral virtue does not consist simply in doing an action that others judge to be good; but it also means doing an objectively good action with a virtuous heart. Good actions arise from a virtuous heart. Similarly, sinful actions are not simply acts disconnected from persons. Evil actions arise from a vicious heart. External acts of obedience that are divorced from a virtuous heart remain contrary to the Spirit of Christ in the Gospel. "If we say we have no sin, we deceive ourselves, and the truth is not in us" (1 John 1:8).

The purpose of Christian practice is transformation and virtue, *sans* hypocrisy, *sans* pretending.[68] None is good but God (Matthew 19:17). Christ is the way through which the human person becomes the true *imago Dei*; a child of the most High. It is not obedience alone which gives new life. Everyone falls short (Romans 3:23). It is not faith alone which justifies. Faith without works is dead (James 2:26). Nor is it works alone which constitute salvation. No one comes to the Father, but through Christ (John 14: 6-7). Rather, it is in following God's graces that the human person is saved. In following God's grace the human person is led to Christ and becomes a member of Christ's mystical body. And not every member of the corporate body of Christ assumes the same function. Each member is judged individually according to the function of the part. Sin and moral judgment are, in part, relative to circumstances, situation, commitments, history, talents. In the analogy of Saint Paul:

> For the body does not consist of one member but many. If the foot should say, "Because I am not a hand, I do not belong to the body," that would not make it any less a part of the body. And if the ear should say, "Because I am not an eye, I do not belong to the body," that would not make it less a part of the body. If the whole body where an eye,

---

[67] So, for example, Commandment 6—*Thou shalt not commit Adultery* is the external act, while Commandment 9—*Thou shalt not covet thy neighbor's wife* addresses the interior sin or intentional state of the heart. And in *the Sermon on the Mount* the internalizing is tightened further. *Anyone who looks lustfully at a woman has already committed adultery with her in his thoughts* (Matthew 5:28).

[68] Richard M Gula, S.S., *Reason Informed By Faith: Foundations of Catholic Morality*, 186-187.

> where would be the hearing? If the whole body
> were an ear, where would be the sense of smell?
> But as it is, God arranged the organs in the body,
> each one of them, as he chose (1 Corinthians
> 12:14-18).

When acts are judged individually in isolation from the context in the corporate whole many aspects of the person's moral life as a subject in history are then missed.[69] The Ten Commandments are universal, but they are far from exhaustive in terms of the totality of the person under God. "Do we then overthrow the law by this faith? By no means! On the contrary we uphold the law" (Romans 3:2).

The ear is not judged for not smelling and the nose is not judged for not hearing. But the ear is judged for not hearing and the nose for not smelling. There is one law for the entire body (the Ten Commandments) and there is a law for each individual part (Luke 12:48). The law of grace in Christ's body reaches the depth of the individual subject, encompassing both intention, circumstance, and the unknown-XYZ of the heart's faith.

For example, Catholic moral philosopher Alasdair MacIntyre (as for moral particularity) writes:

> We all approach our own circumstances as bearers of a particular social identity. I am someone's
> son or daughter, someone's cousin or uncle; I am
> a citizen of this or that city, a member of this or
> that guild or profession; I belong to this clan, that
> tribe, this nation. Hence what is good for me has
> to be good for one who inhabits these roles. As
> such, I inherit from the past my family, my city,
> my tribe, my nation, a variety of debts, inheritances, rightful expectations and obligations. These
> constitute the given of my life, *my moral starting*

---

[69] Michael J. Himes, "The Human Person in Contemporary Theology: From Human Nature to Authentic Subjectivity," in *Introduction to Christian Ethics*, eds. Ron Hamel and Kenneth Himes, OFM (New York: Paulist Press, 1989), 58-60.

point. This is in part what gives my own life its moral particularity.[70]

MacIntyre is reaffirming here the necessity of addressing the "moral starting point" of each member of a given society. Addressing what makes one an individual does not negate the universal law one is under. The shift in emphasis improves the moral direction of each individual relative to his or her historical circumstances and subjective intentions. There *are* moral decisions (that are morally significant) that cannot find appropriate direction in *general* moral prescriptions.

The classical emphasis on human nature in moral theology viewed the person largely in terms of universal humanity, mostly because of the influence of Greek philosophy. In practice ordinary moral instruction often remained within the boundaries of the Ten Commandments and certain aspects of Church law. The more recent emphasis on *the person* has now come to see the individual personality in the full depth of the human subject's diversity. The new approach appreciates more fully the many ways in which the individual is called to serve God.[71] The newer shift in emphasis is closer to the spirit of Christianity. Consulting the Scriptures it becomes apparent that the moral life is founded upon the individual's relationship to God and others and requires more than strict legal codes.[72] In fact, the legalistic attitude is opposed to the spirit of the Gospel, as the Scriptures testify.[73]

---

[70] Alasdair MacIntyre, *After Virtue: A Study in Moral Theory*, Second Edition (London: Duckworth, 1985), 220.

[71] James F. Keenan, *A History of Catholic Moral Theology in the Twentieth Century: From Confessing Sins to Liberating Consciences* (New York: Continuum, 2010), 174-175.

[72] Richard Gula, S.S., *Reason Informed By Faith: Foundations of Catholic Morality*, 250-253.

[73] Marciano Vidal identifies five key marks about sin in the New Testament. First, sin arises from the heart of the person. Second, sin is measured, as far as content is concerned, in terms of offense to a human being. Third, sin touches on the core of the person and radical choices that he or she makes. Fourth, sin is lived, expressed and overcome in community. And fifth, *sin is manifest in non-Gospel like attitudes.* The fifth notion about sin, in particular, affirms the necessity of using the Scriptures to shed light on the spirit of the Christian moral life. Without the Scriptures the spirit is sometimes lost in favor of the letter, leading to non-Gospel like attitudes. *See* Marciano Vidal, *Moral Fundamental: Moral de Actitudes*, Seventh

For one key example, when Jesus sees a poor widow donating copper coins (a penny's worth) when the rich are haughtily giving their gifts to the treasury he remarks, "Truly I tell you, this poor widow has put in more than all of them; for they all contributed out of their abundance, but she out of her poverty put in all the living that she had" (Luke 21:1-4). In other words, had the rich donors shared the same station as the widow they would have given less and without the same spirit of caritas.

Robert Karris notes in the *New Jerome Biblical Commentary*, "Jesus decries the religious teaching which has caused a widow to give up all she has to preserve a decaying religious institution. Jesus lauds the generosity of the widow, who prepares the reader to note the generosity of Jesus, the self-effacing servant."[74] Having more, the rich believe they give more, and pride themselves on it. But they do not see that it is not only *how much* they give, it is also what they can give and in what spirit they give it. Moral judgment in this case is based more on the relative circumstances and intentions of the agents. The outward appearance of the act in the eyes of others is often deceiving and likely to be misjudged.

> A gluttonous man may succeed in concealing his gluttony, but if I could watch him all the time, I should catch him out. But I could watch a man all his life, and I should never know for certain whether or not he was proud, for the actions which we call proud or humble may have quite other causes. Pride is rightly called the root of all sin, because it is invisible to the one who is guilty of it and he can only infer it from results.[75]

For another example, the Beatitudes are the most exhaustive treatment of the interior state of holiness in the New Testament, although the Beatitudes are not laws to obey. The interior state of

---

Edition (Madrid: Editorial Perpetuo Socorro, 1990), 596-97; as found in Fr. Kevin O'Neil, C.Ss.R. "Personal Sin," WTU class outline, 2011.

[74] Robert J. Karris, "The Gospel According to Luke," in *The New Jerome Biblical Commentary*, eds. Raymond E. Brown, Joseph A. Fitzmyer and Roland E. Murphy (Upper Saddle River, NJ: Prentice Hall, 1990), 713.

[75] W. H. Auden, "Introduction," in Søren Kierkegaard, *The Living Thoughts of Søren Kierkegaard*, ed. W. H. Auden (New York: The New York Review of Books, 1952), xiii.

beatitudo is freely given by God, based not on earned merit, but on God's grace.[76] It is possible to resist the grace of beatitude once given or to try to mimic beatitude without truly having it. To understand here the meaning of moral behaviour, obedience and true *blessedness*, one need look no further than the Gospel's moral message. Christ did not proclaim, "I know the way." He did not proclaim, "I obey the way." He told his disciples, "*I am* the way, follow me" (John 14:6). In other words, the truth is within the heart of the believer and delivered by God's grace in Christ. The way of Christ is the fullness of Truth. Or, according to Saint Paul, "Be imitators of me as I am of Christ" (1 Corinthians 11:1).

The real measure of moral goodness is seen when the truth within the follower approximates the Truth of Christ.[77] Often, when the person follows he or she becomes (or can become) *The* Truth. Obedience to law is one means of appropriating the divine life, but it is ultimately insufficient. The rich man went away unhappy when Jesus told him what more was expected of him than obedience to moral commandments (Mttw 19:16-30). The rich man felt something missing even after keeping the moral law. He sought Christ and was challenged with personal discipleship. A tempting snare in the Christian moral life is to believe that keeping the law for the sake of the law, and not for love of God, is the way of God's call. It is not law or actions alone which constitute the Christian moral life, but the discernment of the person's relationship with God and others.[78]

When the individual encounters a challenging relationship faith is truly tested. The Good Samaritan who accepts the challenge of helping the beaten man on the side of the road responds to the suffering of another and proves the depth of his charity (Luke 10: 25-37). Often unnoticed is that, in the story, the Samaritan was not looking for a good work *for the sake of a good work* or for some other reason than to do what the situation commanded of him and God's grace allowed him to do in that instance. He responded charitably when appropriate, but not with self-righteous zeal, seeking his own reward or honor.[79]

---

[76] William May, *An Introduction to Moral Theology*, 231-233.

[77] Richard Gula, S.S., *Reason Informed By Faith: Foundations of Catholic Morality*, 197.

[78] Ibid., 314-328.

[79] Robert J. Karris, O.F.M., "The Gospel According to Luke," in *The New Jerome Biblical Commentary*, 701-702.

By contrast, Judas, before the Last Supper, believes that he is right in chastising Mary of Bethany for anointing Jesus with expensive ointment (Mark 14:3-9). His charity is false because he does not see that he is fixating on the idea of helping the poor for the purpose of taking the moral high ground while really acting out of resentment at another's favor [hanan].[80] At heart, even though his indignation appears noble in sentiment outwardly, Judas' charity is dishonest, or at best misguided and shallow. Or, as the old aphorism goes, "the road to hell is paved with good intentions," e.g. well-meaning intentions can dishonestly act as a cover or mask of sublimated reasons and/or serve as a self-righteous means to an actual lie in thought, word, and deed, etc. Or, as Saint Thomas Aquinas says,

> it often happens that man acts with a good intention, but without spiritual gain, because he lacks a good will. Let us say that someone robs in order to feed the poor: in this case, even though the intention is good, the uprightness of the will is lacking. Consequently, no evil done with a good intention can be excused. 'There are those who say: And why not do evil that good may come? Their condemnation is just' (Romans 3:8).[81]

The above examples from Scripture show how the Gospel can become distorted if treated like a law book and not like a tapestry of meaning. The focus on acts and law to the exclusion of enduring relationships of a personal nature leads to an emphasis on works without regard for intention or circumstance. [82] The Pharisee "is self-satisfied, finding some excuse for each of his failings." [83] In fact, the Pharisee "represents a 'self-satisfied' conscience, under the illusion that it is able to observe the law without the help of grace and convinced that it does not need mercy."[84] Acts are seen by others, whereas circumstances and intention are less visible. Those seeking rewards, or avoiding punishments, often

---

[80] Ibid., 625.

[81] As quoted in John Paul II, *Veritatis Splendor*, paragraph 78, footnote 128.

[82] James F. Keenan, *A History of Catholic Moral Theology in the Twentieth Century: From Confessing Sins to Liberating Consciences*, 183-188.

[83] John Paul II, *Veritatis Splendor*, paragraph 104.

[84] Ibid.

see little reward for right interior states. Circumstances are rarely seen by others in their fullness. The act itself (whether "good work" or sin) is the surest means to reward or punishment in the eyes of others, although not in the eyes of God. The tendency to emphasize acts and works to the point of hypocrisy is a natural tendency of the human person. When not vigilantly resisted it often becomes the default tendency of human nature. We have it on the authority of St. Alphonsus Maria De Ligouri, the patron saint of moral theologians, that: "It is not enough to do good works; they need to be done well. For our works to be good and perfect, they must be done for the sole purpose of pleasing God."[85]

It is clear that Christ preached charity to the poor and the blessedness of the poor, but he was not a mere social reformer. His message is far more subtle and powerful. Many of the religious zealots who wanted the messiah to liberate the Jewish people from Roman oppression were, naturally, among those most disappointed in the way of Jesus. Jesus circumvented many of their questions regarding the expectation of an earthly paradise. He tells his followers to render unto Cæsar that which is Cæsar's. It is Cæsar's likeness on the coin (Matthew 22:15-22). He tells Pontius Pilate "my Kingdom is not of this world" (John 18:36-38). Some even today continue to believe that Jesus was more like a philanthropist, doing good works for the public—that is, than being the Son of God or the foreseen prophet of the Kingdom of Heaven. Their disappointment continues whenever the World proves that Heaven is not possible here.

The parable of the laborers in the vineyard relates a similar lesson regarding God's justice in relation to works of the law. The laborers who spent all day working become resentful when those who came late, being idle most of the day, receive the same wages. They complain, "These last worked only one hour, and you have made them equal to us who have borne the burden of the day and the scorching heat." In response the householder replies, "Friend, I am doing you no wrong; did you not agree with me for a denarius? Take what belongs to you, and go; I choose to give to this last as I give to you. Am I not allowed to do what I choose with what belongs to me? Or do you begrudge me my generosity?" (Matthew 20:1-16). The laborers believe that their acts are not being reward-

---

[85] Saint Alphonsus Maria De Ligouri, *Practica di amar Gesú Cristo*, "VII, 3," as quoted in John Paul II, *Veritatis Splendor*, paragraph 78, footnote 129.

ed as they should. It seems to be "common sense" that those who do more work should receive more pay. Otherwise the law of reward appears unjust. In this parable the contrast between man's expectation of God's justice and God's justice is made clear. God's justice is not of this world. God's justice does not follow the practical rules of men. God's mercy is gratuitous, *not* retributive.[86]

Those who scrupulously keep the Commandments, but "throw stones" at those who do not, because they themselves keep the Commandments for the sake of obedience, not because the desire for virtue or truth is within them, are themselves missing the commanding theme of the Gospel. Moral virtue does not consist simply in doing an action that others judge to be good. It means doing an objectively good action with a virtuous heart. So that, "Whoever knows what is right and fails to do it, *for him* [emphasis added] it is sin (James 4:17). Virtuous actions arise from a virtuous heart. And a virtuous heart arises from virtuous actions. Similarly, sinful actions are not simply deeds disconnected from persons. Genuinely evil actions arise from a vicious heart, one that is or has been marked by vice. *But* those on the outside cannot see this, only God.

The great Christian saints never boasted of saintliness because they could see their own sin clearer than most and understood the nature of human weaknesses.[87] Even after keeping the Law, they realized that loving and obeying the Law is itself a grace God provides them with. Those genuinely called to sainthood realize that the function of a saintly vocation *in* and of the Body of Christ demands heroic sanctity of each individual. The saints of history have always known that there is much more to loving God than simple legal or moral obedience.[88]

The development of moral theology in the Catholic Church has progressed from the question of readmitting public sinners after grave sins in Patristic times to the penitential literature of

---

[86] Gustavo Gutierrez, *On Job: God-Talk and the Suffering of the Innocent* (Maryknoll, NY: Orbis Books, 1999), 11-17.

[87] William James, "LECTURES XI, XII AND XIII: Saintliness" and "LECTURES XIV AND XV: The Value of Saintliness," in William James, *The Varieties of Religious Experience: A Study in Human Nature Being the Gifford Lectures on Natural Religion Delivered At Edinburgh in 1901-1902* (New York: Signet Classic, 1983), 225-317.

[88] Saint Augustine, *Confessions*, trans. F. J. Sheed (Cambridge: Hackett Publishing, 2006), Book Eight: VIII-IX.

early monasticism. From there, the practice of confessing privately to a priest developed into mandatory private (auricular) confession for the entire Church. At times, Catholic moral theology became somewhat weighed down with legalistic understandings of sin and the discipline itself became somewhat isolated in practice from the relevant insights of spiritual and systematic theology.[89] Focusing strictly on the acts of the individual in isolation and seeing sin and forgiveness in legalistic terms led to problems that were addressed at the Second Vatican Council. Theological correctives such as the fundamental option and the re-emphasis on Scripture were, in turn, brought forth to meet the challenge.[90]

The person who places all hope in pleasing God through the extent of his or her works and obedience to law is often made prone to personal mistakes of a sinful nature. In many instances moral choices are between differing goods, where the chooser ignores one good in favor of another. Often missed here in choosing which good is seeing the commitments that God commands for him or her in particular.[91] The universal law does not aid decision making in such circumstances. All members of the Body of Christ are called to the highest holiness that the grace of God provides for. It is true that everyone who *disobeys* the Commandments of God places the relationship to God, the fountain of all holiness, in danger. However, those who scrupulously keep the Commandments, and continue to throw stones at those who do not, because they themselves keep the Commandments for the sake of obedience or reward and not because the desire for virtue or truth is in them, are themselves missing the more important thematic concern of the Gospel.

God gives his graces as He pleases. Imitating what sanctity ought to look like in order to assure you yourself that *you* deserve

---

[89] John Mahoney, *The Making of Moral Theology: A Study of the Roman Catholic Tradition*, 1-35.

[90] Richard Gula, S.S., *Reason Informed By Faith: Foundations of Catholic Morality*, 80-81 & 165-182.

[91] A good example of this is the verse on Martha and Mary. Martha does the servile work and Mary listens at the Lord's feet. Martha complains, as most perhaps would, "Lord, do you not care that my sister has left me to serve alone? Tell her to help me." Jesus replies, "Martha, Martha, you are anxious and troubled about many things; one thing is needful. Mary has chosen the good portion which shall not be taken away from her" (Luke 10:38-42).

Heaven and that others do not, does not suffice (it is actually the sin of hypocrisy). God's love is gratuitous. His justification is unmerited. God rewards the Love in Truth which resides in the heart, not the imitation of love from outside it. Love itself is not one particular work or another. Love is the *state of being* in an enduring relationship that transcends the individual acts of the relation.

In conclusion, the concept of the Fundamental Option is one means of correcting the legalistic tendency; a tendency that can sneak into the practice of moral theology as it is. The re-emphasis on Scripture is another necessary and important means of correction. The Gospel message is powerful, challenging and profound, yet subtle, and requires careful discernment in order to see the more hidden wisdom of the most challenging passages. Practicing moral theology without continual reference to the Scriptures is ultimately not enough. Focusing on acts and law alone, while ignoring the *spirit of the truth* in Christ, is also not enough . . . in the end. To be sure, there are numerous *lists* or litanies of sins (and virtues) in the Scriptures such as these:

> lovers of themselves, lovers of money, boasters, arrogant, abusive, disobedient to their parents, ungrateful, unholy, inhuman, implacable, slanderers, profligates, brutes, haters of good, treacherous, reckless, swollen with conceit, lovers of pleasure rather than lovers of God, holding to the outward form of godliness but denying its power. Avoid them! (2 Timothy 3:2-6)

> Do not be deceived: neither the immoral, nor idolaters, nor adulterers, nor sexual perverts, nor thieves, nor the greedy, nor drunkards, nor revilers, nor robbers will inherit the Kingdom of God (1 Corinth. 6:9-10).

Yet, how to make virtue incarnate or exorcise the spirit of sin is another matter altogether. As the Apostles teach us, the "letter kills, but the Spirit gives life" (2 Corinth. 3:6).

> You yourselves are our letter, written on our hearts, to be known and read by all; and you show that you are a letter of Christ, prepared by us,

> written not with ink but with the Spirit of the liv-
> ing God, not on tablets of stone but on tablets of
> human hearts (2 Corinthians 3:2-3).

Both the fundamental option and the methodological re-emphasis on Scripture succeed at counteracting legalism, that is, when contextualized within the authentic renewal of the Catholic moral tradition. *But*, even here there is still nothing enough sufficient to fulfill absolutely the Christian *moral life*.

Nevertheless, given recent developments in moral theology since Vatican II there is good hope that the Church's theology, in theory and practice, will continue the task of renewal (in thought, word, and deed) throughout the entire Church of God.

We now turn to a third corrective of the identified legalistic tendencies in the structures of traditional Catholic moral theology in examining the Virtue Ethics of moral philosopher Alasdair MacIntyre.

4. *Alasdair MacIntyre:*
Virtue Ethics, Narrative and Tradition

The incorporation of the discipline of *Virtue Ethics* into the Roman Catholic Church's juridical framework is yet another important corrective of the professed legalistic tendency in Catholic moral theology. Specifically, in "Virtue Ethics" there is an important shift away from an emphasis on "what a person is doing" to a greater emphasis on "*who* a person is" as well as "what a person is *becoming*." Of course, the question of "who a person *is*" is a more slippery one. The importance of the latter question often does not find adequate expression within the framework of the Catholic Church's traditional "rule-based" morality. The proper understanding of "Virtue Ethics" is an integral part of the ongoing reform of moral theology since Vatican II, perhaps for just this reason.

As we have seen, the "simple-minded" obedience to universal moral laws is no longer sufficient for Catholic moral practice in the modern world. Nowadays the traditional Catholic moral virtues are not surviving culturally in the absence of the historical bulwark that existed alongside the empowered civilization formerly known as *Christendom*. More subtle modes of moral and religious refinement are now needed, perhaps now more than ever. Otherwise, the Chrsitian moral life can or will remain bound to an empty conformity to law, which will often times come at an exclusion of the *living spirit of Christ* and the true religious vocations of Christianity. "Virtue Ethics" is an important refinement of morality. It possesses the meaningful subtlety wanted in order to salvage religion from contemporary moral chaos.

In the study of "Virtue Ethics" based on Aristotle and Thomas Aquinas, the fulfillment of good character requires a more refined inner sensitivity toward "good" and "evil," beyond the mere external conformity to rule. MacIntyre writes:

> Rule-following will often be involved in knowing how to respond rightly, but no rule or set of rules by itself ever determines how to respond rightly. This is because in the case of those rules that are always to be respected—'Never take an innocent life,' for example—they are never sufficient to determine how we ought to act, while with other rules what always has to be determined is whether in this particular case they are relevant and, if so, how they are to be applied. And there is no higher order rule by reference to which these questions can be universally answered.

> Knowing how to act virtuously involves more than rule-following.[92]

Ultimately, the state of being virtuous is the *state of being* whole-heartedly and habitually in pursuit of moral goods or "*The* Good" (in Platonic terms). The appropriate measure of virtue is the possession of the *habit* necessary (in potency as well as in act) for achieving desired moral ends. Understood this way, virtue is the *power* through which the moral agent is prepared to act virtuously. In other words, virtue remains latent in potentiality, even while there is no particular action under judgment.

---

[92] Alasdair MacIntyre, *Dependent Rational Animals: Why Human Beings Need the Virtues* (Chicago: Open Court, 2012 [1999]), 93.

In the case of Alasdair MacIntyre's interpretations of contemporary moral philosophy, rigorous aim is taken in many of his
writings at "The Enlightenment Project's" failure to establish moral norms on *purely rational* grounds.[93] In short, the so-called "Enlightenment Project" in moral philosophy left in its wake an inadequate and fragmented system of moral rules based on conflicting
and incommensurable moral theses.[94] MacIntyre attests that there
has been a fundamental change in moral science since the time of
the Enlightenment (in contrast to the classical ethical codes of
Rome, Greece, or the Roman Catholic Church). He states, at
length, in *Whose Justice, Which Rationality?*:

> It was a central aspiration of the Enlightenment,
> an aspiration the formulation of which was itself a
> great achievement, to provide for debate in the
> public realm standards and methods of rational
> justification by which alternative courses of action
> in every sphere of life could be adjudged just or
> unjust, rational or irrational, enlightened or unen-
> lightened. So, it was hoped, *reason would displace au-
> thority and tradition*. Rational justification was to
> appeal to principles *undeniable* by any rational per-
> son and therefore independent of all those social
> and cultural particularities which the Enlighten-
> ment thinkers took to be the mere accidental
> clothing of reason in particular times and places.
> And that rational justification could be nothing
> other than what the thinkers of the Enlighten-
> ment had said that it was came to be accepted, *at
> least by the vast majority of educated people*, in post-
> Enlightenment culture and social orders.
>
> Yet both the thinkers of the Enlightenment and
> their successors proved unable to agree as to what
> precisely those principles were which would be
> found undeniable by all rational persons. One

---

[93] Richard M. Gula, S.S., *What Are They Saying About Moral Norms?* (Mahwah, NJ: Paulist Press, 1982). See herein thoughts on recent developments of "normative ethics" in relation to Catholic Moral Theology.
[94] Alasdair MacIntyre, *After Virtue*, Chapter 2.

kind of answer was given by the authors of the *Encyclopédie*, a second by Rousseau, a third by Bentham, a fourth by Kant, a fifth by the Scottish philosophers of common sense and their French and American disciples. Nor has subsequent history diminished such disagreement. It has rather enlarged it. Consequently, the legacy of the Enlightenment has been the provision of an ideal of rational justification which *it has proved impossible to attain.*[95]

The pre-modern moral philosophy of Aristotle and Thomas Aquinas were nearly exclusively concerned with the description of virtues and vices within the context of a known and uncontested customary tradition. However, from "The Age of Enlightenment" onward moral philosophy has tended toward the use of Reason alone in determining "deontological" rules for moral behavior. MacIntyre, in a Herculean effort, has attempted to demonstrate that using the faculty of Reason by itself, detached from any or all traditions, necessarily ends in irreconcilable logical contradictions. He holds that conventional *moral norms* since the Enlightenment have *not* found the desired "missing link" of absolute unquestionable rational justification. Instead, all of the false rationalities of autonomous reason have ended in a mere *pretense* that a so-called "view from nowhere" is possible.[96]

For MacIntyre, morality is properly understood only within the framework of coherent moral traditions. Individual actions cannot be taken out of historical context without losing the full moral significance of the action understood. Given present polarized conflicts in moral opinion, returning to historical modes of moral enquiry is the novel solution MacIntyre offers. Otherwise, MacIntyre argues, the only remaining option for moral philosophy is to work from inside the disparate traditions of an ill-defined and contradictory de facto "Liberalism" or "Liberal individualism."

In Aristotle and Aquinas, virtue is understood within the context of an essential unity;—the unity of the individual virtues over

---

[95] Alasdair MacIntyre, *Whose Justice, Which Rationality?* (Notre Dame, IN: University of Notre Dame Press, 2003), 6. [emphasis added]

[96] *See* Thomas Nagel, *The View From Nowhere* (London: Oxford University Press, 1986).

the duration of an entire lifetime. In reality, the possession of the *habit of virtue* is best understood to be categorically *one*; that is, irreducible in its aspects. Although virtue can be discernable in individual actions of character, the true measure of it cannot be reduced beyond the singularity of its unity. The most appropriate object for measuring virtue is the enduring inner potential which actualizes *The Good* in every context, e.g. not simply virtuous actions taken in isolation one to another.[97]

Virtuous character essentially "adheres" in the person as a habitual state of being. This is the classical definition. And so, the judgment of the total person's moral standing is in fact greater than any single action taken, or for that matter any singular virtue. The nature of virtue is such that the person's total character cannot be divided into a fragmented picture of the whole, while not inevitably missing the integral nature of the virtues in the process. An important stance of MacIntyre's Virtue Ethics is that virtuous character requires the full integration of each individual virtue, one with the other, over the duration of an entire lifetime.

Aristotle does in fact say much the same in the *Nicomachean Ethics* in that the virtues, unlike individual actions of moral worth (but similar to the fundamental option perhaps), are all of one piece. So, the proper measure of virtue, being the potency of the inner life, is closer to the judgment of the "fundamental option," e.g. than to the judgment of an individual moral action. The drive in both cases is toward *wholeness*, qualitatively as well as temporally. And so the conclusion here, like that in the above sections, is that the final moral judgment lies with God's knowledge or understanding of the inner virtue (heart) of the person, not the partial analysis of external behaviors.

While dealing with the essential unity of the virtues in *After Virtue* MacIntyre writes: "the interrelationship of the virtues explains why they do not provide us with a number of distinct criteria by which to judge the goodness of a particular individual, but rather with *one complex measure*."[98] If the person is perhaps coura-

---

[97] Alasdair MacIntyre, *After Virtue*, "Chapter 14: The Nature of the Virtues."

[98] Alasdair MacIntyre, *After Virtue*, 155. Also, for an explanation of some of the weaknesses with the "strong theory" *see* Stanley Hauerwas, *A Community of Character: Toward a Constructive Christian Social Ethic* (Notre Dame, IN: University of Notre Dame Press, 1981), 141-145. Section 2.5 "The Unity of the Virtues" addresses this.

geous (a virtue), but not prudent, then he or she will likely be foolhardy in taking risks (a vice). Or if the person has faith (a theological virtue), but does not have hope, he or she will most likely despair once tested (a sin).

Partial virtue is a flaw of character, or in some cases outright sin. Deficiency of virtue is technically a failure of omission of sorts, but it nonetheless falls under the category of moral fault (or a sin in many instances). To cite Thomas Aquinas for authority, responding to the question *Whether Every Sin Involves An Act?*, he writes in *De Malo*, "Since then virtue, wisdom, and goodness are habits, it seems that sins are habits. But a habit can be present without an act. Therefore sin can be present without an act."[99] In other words, sin (vice) is understood by Aquinas as a habit of character—just as virtue (goodness) is by Aristotle; even though Aristotle does not explicitly acknowledge the religious category of "sin."

A delict of virtue will ultimately and eventually find expression in sinful actions when the relevant situation of temptation arises. Virtuous actions are inseparable from an appropriate and necessary narrative contextualization over time—in order to fully understand the moral quality of a person. If one performs virtuous actions in a single instance, say, and not in another, then the person's character is not virtuous in its totality. So the ancient Greeks were very right in their oft-recited maxim: "call no man happy until he is dead."[100] Or, in *The Book of Sirach*—"call no man happy before his death; by how he ends, a person becomes known" (Sirach 11:28).

In other words, only when the story of a given life led is actually finished can a personal narrative be understood in its moral entirety. In the wisdom of the Ancient World, the possibility was always admitted that the final act of life (the *finale*), or any given event during it, can either ruin or redeem the moral "caliber" of the overarching story and/or that which provides the essential narrative framework—in addition to the overall context.

On theological grounds one can say that at the deepest level virtue actually originates in neither action nor habit, but in a gratui-

---

99 *See* Thomas Aquinas, *On Evil* (Notre Dame, IN: University of Notre Dame Press, 1995), 40-47.
100 Aristotle, *Nicomachean Ethics,* trans. Martin Oswald (Upper Saddle River, NJ: Prentice Hall, 1999), Book I:10.

tous act of God's grace (*prevenient* grace or gratia illuminans). And that sin is also possibly an omission of character in this vein too, insofar as the person fails to respond to God's graces.[101] "Vocational callings" are at least partially dependent on life-circumstance and not just the narrower frame of an individual's isolated "free-will" [liberum arbitrium] choices.

The moral life of Christianity involves a singularity untouchable by human judgment and not adequately expressed through universal moral codes. The personal and traditional setting in which the individual agent's actions will eventually come to fruition determines, at least in part, *who* the person is called to become as well as *what* the person is called to do.

So, moral codes alone never fully reach the individual in his or her unfathomable particularity. For theologians seeking insight from contemporary moral philosophy, MacIntyre's ideas ought to be supplemented with practices of spiritual discernment and prayer for the purpose of informing the individual's sense of relation to his or her relevant cultural context. God's *will* is more than obedience to commandments, in the end, after all.

If a discerning person believes God is calling him or her to help the "wretched of the earth," say, as well as become an astronaut, instead of, say, finding the cure for cancer by running in a marathon, *then* the person doing the discernment of personal calling is operating outside of any specific moral rule that can help. A person who is in this instance who "sticks" to the rules *too much* (and therefore "misses" what God tells him or her to do individually in response to a calling) is acting (and existing) immorally under the *presumption* of being morally "good" (or at least of doing nothing wrong). Responding to God through prayer and discernment is an integral part of the morality of any act. More important, this cannot be done without the discernment of the narrative framework or in light of a traditional or historical context of meaning(s). Only when the individual's authentic character and personality are determined "under God" *in this way* does the individual

---

[101] For the circularity in the argument over the origination of virtue in action or habit *See* Stanley Hauerwas, *A Community of Character: Toward a Constructive Christian Social Ethic*, 138-139. In Section 2.2 "The Circularity Involved in the Acquisition of Virtue," from Chapter 7: Character, Narrative, and Growth in the Christian Life, (citing Aristotle) "I cannot be virtuous except as I act as a virtuous man would act, but the only way I can become a virtuous man is by acting virtuously."

fully understand the virtues necessary for his or her station in life. This is, as it is often believed, one of MacIntyre's key points as it applies to moral theology.[102]

In summing up this section; the only way to fully grasp the virtues is to contextualize virtue from within (inside) the sustained narratives of both a personal history and the history of traditional communities. The individual's "narrative quest," as MacIntyre calls it, can only occur, transpire or unravel, in the context of the historical (religious) life of a given society. The individual's character is not meaningful without this personal or community narrative structure. Lacking traditional context, virtuous actions are not fully understood or understandable.[103]

In his book *After Virtue* MacIntyre shows at length that the human person is *naturally* a "story-telling animal" who is best seen as such, e.g. man is a language-using creature who tells stories about himself. He draws from this that moral actions only become intelligible in the broader Gestalt of a meaningful (moral) story.[104] In *After Virtue* MacIntyre famously writes: "I can only answer the question 'What am I to do?' If I can answer the prior question 'Of what story or stories do I find myself a part?'"[105]

Given the veracity of this question, there can be seen a certain kind of "boorishness" as regards to the traditional modes of Catholic moral theology, where the breaking of universal moral codes alone qualifies as a recognizable sin(s). Disobeying the universal moral code of human nature or revelatory religion is not the only kind of sin. The failure to finely cultivate moral sensitivities to particular cultural meanings of moral worth also constitutes a kind of sin, nevertheless often overlooked. There is a personal realm of relation with God and religious culture that is impossible to fully universalize, as we have shown. Again, for MacIntyre, in response to the Kantian proponents of autonomous reason in modern philosophy:

---

[102] MacIntyre in places denies some interpretations of this. He states that *After Virtue* was often misconstrued as a "morality of virtues" *opposed* to a "morality of rules." *See* Alasdair MacIntyre, *Whose Justice? Which Rationality?*, Preface.

[103] Alasdair MacIntyre, *After Virtue*, "Chapter 15: The Virtues, the Unity of Human Life and the Concept of Tradition."

[104] Ibid, 216.

[105] Ibid.

> virtues are dispositions not only to act in
> particular ways, but also to *feel* in particular ways.
> To act virtuously is not . . . to act against
> inclination; it is to act from inclination formed by
> the cultivation of virtues. Moral education is an
> '*education sentimentale*'."[106]

As noted in the previous section, sin means before anything else to "miss the mark" in attaining universal human goods or sustaining the moral fidelity of relationships. However, sin can also mean in the deeper sense to "miss the mark" in performing or maintaining a character response with regard to an individual's lived personal and historic narrative or tradition. The relation of the individual to other characters and settings is not necessarily defined through universally binding moral codes alone. This, sometimes neglected, sphere of existence in traditional moral theology (where individuals form appropriate moral responses to the cultural milieux in which they find themselves) ought to be more carefully considered in seeking the continued development of the discipline.

A good concrete example of the above is BD. John Henry Cardinal Newman's (an Anglican-divine convert) description of a gentleman in his famous work *The Idea of a University*. Although it has never been thought religiously commanded that one *must* be a gentleman of Newman's type, the virtues Newman describes here are nonetheless morally desirable for some individuals in many (but by no means all) cultural or social contexts. Newman's ideal gentleman is an example of "universal" virtues for one *particular* type of person. Whereas, on the other hand, say, heavy-weight boxers, or dock-workers, or brick-layers, are not to be expected to embody the virtues of the ideal English Gentleman.[107] In other words, every ideal character type *should* embody the virtues that are

---

[106] Ibid., 149.

[107] Alasdair MacIntyre gives other examples of this kind of specified ideal of virtue in Benjamin Franklin, Jane Austen, and others. Franklin's famous list of character virtues in Enlightenment America: "Temperance, Silence, Order, Resolution, Frugality, Industry, Sincerity, Justice, Moderation, Cleanliness, Tranquility, Chastity, Humility." Benjamin Franklin, *The Autobiography of Benjamin Franklin* (Mineola, NY: Dover Publications, 1996), 64-72. *See* Alasdair MacIntyre, *After Virtue*, "Chapter 14: The Nature of the Virtues."

fitting to it, but an ideal is an excellence of virtue that cannot be universally prescribed in the same manner as religious ethical codes normally are. The virtues of Newman's ideal-type gentleman remain, in fact, *moral* virtues, even if those who do not possess them are not necessarily *immoral*.

To be sure, it would be impossible for any but an elite few to perfectly embody the following traits in Newman's description:

> it is almost a definition of a gentleman to say he is one who never inflicts pain. This description is both refined and, as far as it goes, accurate. He is mainly occupied in merely removing the obstacles which hinder the free and unembarrassed action of those about him; and he concurs with their movements rather than takes the initiative himself. His benefits may be considered as parallel to what are called comforts or conveniences in arrangements of a personal nature: like an easy chair or a good fire, which do their part in dispelling cold and fatigue, though nature provides both means of rest and animal heat without them. The true gentleman in like manner carefully avoids whatever may cause a jar or a jolt in the minds of those with whom he is cast;—all clashing of opinion, or collision of feeling, all restraint, or suspicion, or gloom, or resentment; his great concern being to make everyone at their ease and at home. He has his eyes on all his company; he is tender towards the bashful, gentle towards the distant, and merciful towards the absurd; he can recollect to whom he is speaking; he guards against unseasonable allusions, or topics which may irritate; he is seldom prominent in conversation, and never wearisome. He makes light of favours while he does them, and seems to be receiving when he is conferring. He never speaks of himself except when compelled, never defends himself by a mere retort, he has no ears for slander or gossip, is scrupulous in imputing motives to those who interfere with him, and interprets everything for the best. He is never mean or little in his disputes,

never takes unfair advantage, never mistakes personalities or sharp sayings for arguments, or in-
sinuates evil which he dare not say out. From a
long-sighted prudence, he observes the maxim of
the ancient sage, that we should ever conduct
ourselves towards our enemy as if he were one
day to be our friend. He has too much good sense
to be affronted at insults, he is too well employed
to remember injuries, and too indolent to bear
malice. He is patient, forbearing, and resigned, on
philosophical principles; he submits to pain, because it is inevitable, to bereavement, because it is
irreparable, and to death, because it is his destiny.
If he engages in controversy of any kind, his dis-
ciplined intellect preserves him from the blunder-
ing discourtesy of better, perhaps, but less educated minds; who, like blunt weapons, tear and
hack instead of cutting clean, who mistake the
point in argument, waste their strength on trifles,
misconceive their adversary, and leave the question more involved than they find it. He may be
right or wrong in his opinion, but he is too clear-
headed to be unjust; he is as simple as he is forci-
ble, and as brief as he is decisive. Nowhere shall
we find greater candour, consideration, indulgence: he throws himself into the minds of his
opponents, he accounts for their mistakes. He
knows the weakness of human reason as well as
its strength, its province and its limits. If he be an
unbeliever, he will be too profound and large-
minded to ridicule religion or to act against it; he
is too wise to be a dogmatist or fanatic in his infi-
delity. He respects piety and devotion; he even
supports institutions as venerable, beautiful, or
useful, to which he does not assent; he honours
the ministers of religion, and it contents him to
decline its mysteries without assailing or denounc-
ing them. He is a friend of religious toleration,
and that, not only because his philosophy has
taught him to look on all forms of faith with an
impartial eye, but also from the gentleness and ef-

feminacy of feeling, which is the attendant on civilization.

Not that he may not hold a religion too, in his own way, even when he is not a Christian. In that case his religion is one of imagination and sentiment; it is the embodiment of those ideas of the sublime, majestic, and beautiful, without which there can be no large philosophy. Sometimes he acknowledges the being of God, sometimes he invests an unknown principle or quality with the attributes of perfection. And this deduction of his reason, or creation of his fancy, he makes the occasion of such excellent thoughts, and the starting-point of so varied and systematic a teaching, that he even seems like a disciple of Christianity itself. From the very accuracy and steadiness of his logical powers, he is able to see what sentiments are consistent in those who hold any religious doctrine at all, and he appears to others to feel and to hold a whole circle of theological truths, which exist in his mind no otherwise than as a number of deductions.

Such are some of the lineaments of the ethical character, which the cultivated intellect will form, apart from religious principle. They are seen within the pale of the Church and without it, in holy men, and in profligate; they form the *beau-ideal* of the world; they partly assist and partly distort the development of the Catholic.[108]

In many instances the virtues of a given station of character are more important to the moral life than the moral goods universal to human nature. That being said, the ultimate question of moral theory is not then, categorically, "what are the laws of the universal moral code that everyone everywhere needs to obey?" Rather, the more relevant question is "what ought *I* to do, as an

---

[108] John Henry Cardinal Newman, *The Idea of a University*, ed. Daniel M. O'Connell, S.J. (New York: The American Press, 1941), 227-229.

individual, in response to all that goes into the historical composition of my personal character?" Similarly, according to Aristotle's oft-cited view of the moral life:

> to be affected when one should, towards the things one should, in relation to the people one should, for the reasons one should, and in the way one should, is both intermediate and best, which is what belongs to excellence.[109]

Every person is essentially an individual ontologically. In fact, the "dignity of the individual" is foundational to Catholic theology writ large. In religious terms, "God knows *you* by name."(Rev 21:27) Therefore, the treatment of an individual only in the context of fully universal moral categories is essentially a truncated view of ethics. To reiterate a quote from MacIntyre in the previous section (*Secton 4*):

> We all approach our own circumstances as bearers of a particular social identity. I am someone's son or daughter, someone's cousin or uncle; I am a citizen of this of that city, a member of this or that guild or profession; I belong to this clan, that tribe, this nation. Hence what is good for me has to be good for one who inhabits these roles. As such, I inherit from the past my family, my city, my tribe, my nation, a variety of debts, inheritances, rightful expectations and obligations. These constitute the given of my life, my moral starting point. This is in part what gives my own life its moral particularity.[110]

The moral sensitivity toward nuance of character is more possessed virtue, not just taught prescription. Many moral virtues are not universal. They are impossible for *everyone* to embody in any significant way. There *are* appropriate moral virtues (and inappropriate moral virtues) largely dependent on an individual's personal story or historical context. And so neglecting the virtues of charac-

---

[109] Aristotle, *Nichomacean Ethics*, Book II:6.

[110] Alasdair MacIntyre, *After Virtue*, 220.

ter does then in fact neglect the integrity of the Christian moral life in its *totality*. "But if God alone is the Good, no human effort, not even the most rigorous observance of the commandments, succeeds in "fulfilling" the Law, that is, acknowledging the Lord as God and rendering him the worship due to him alone (cf. Mt 4:10)."[111]

To review, in CHAPTER I: IMPORTANT THEMES IN CATHOLIC MORAL THEOLOGY we have established part of the historical context of Catholic Moral Theology, in addition to the past difficulties with the implicit rigid Legalism of Catholic praxis, as well as some of the strengths and weaknesses of the uses of the Fundamental Option (in order to address the difficulties of isolating human acts from the moral standing of the entire person) and of Sacred Scripture (in order to address the relation of Old Testament Legalism and hypocrisy to the teachings of the New Testament). And lastly, the relevance of Alasdair MacIntyre's "Virtue Ethics" has been shown to be instructive toward the ongoing reform of Post-Vatican II Catholic Moral Theology. In dissolving the pretentions of Enlightenment rationalism and seeing right actions in terms of the unity of character virtue or individual specificity, Virtue Ethics has likewise made a valuable contribution here.

We now turn to the ideas of Søren Aabye Kierkegaard in CHAPTER II: DESPAIR AND THE VIRTUE OF FAITH. The philosophical ideas of Kierkegaard (like in that of all of the above) can further contribute significantly to the discipline of Catholic Moral Theology. The theoretical framework of Kierkegaard's "theology" presents yet another potential *corrective* for the acknowledged blindspots of traditional act-based Legalism. The neglected interdisciplinary bridge between Moral Theology and *Christian Spirituality* is well founded upon Kierkegaard's notions of faith and despair, especially in seeing that the significance of despair—as such—to moral theology has not been as yet completely elaborated in many classical accounts of the Catholic tradition. This next chapter explores the virtue of faith in relation to the sin of despair in depth.

---

[111] John Paul II, *Veritatis Splendor*, Paragraph 11.

CHAPTER II

DESPAIR AND THE VIRTUE OF FAITH

Now there was, not far from where they lay, a castle called Doubting Castle, the owner whereof was Giant Despair; and it was his grounds they now were sleeping: wherefore he, getting up in the morning early, and walking up and down his fields, caught Christian and Hopeful asleep in his grounds. Then, with a grim surly voice, he bid them awake; and asked them whence they were, and what they did in his grounds. They told him they were pilgrims, and that they had lost their way. Then said the Giant, You have this night trespassed me, by trampling in, and lying on my grounds, and therefore you must go along with me. So they were forced to go, because he was stronger.

John Bunyan, THE PILGRIM'S PROGRESS

The dubiousness of abstraction manifests itself precisely in connection with all existential questions, from which abstraction removes the difficulty by omitting it and then boasts of having explained everything.

an abstract thinker is a double creature, a fantastic creature who lives in the pure being of abstraction, and an at times pitiful professional figure which that abstract creature sets down just as one sets down a cane. When reading the biography of such a thinker (for his books may very well be excellent), one sometimes shudders at the thought of what it means to be a human being. Even if a lacemaker made lace ever so lovely, it is still sad to think of this poor stunted creature, and thus it is comic to see a thinker who, despite all his bravura, *personally exists as a fussbudget, who personally did marry but was scarcely acquainted with or moved by the power of love, whose marriage therefore was presumably as impersonal as his thinking, whose personal life was without pathos and without passionate struggles and was philistinely concerned only about which university provided the best job.*

Johannes Climacus, CONCLUDING UNSCIENTIFIC
POSTSCRIPT TO PHILOSOPHICAL FRAGMENTS

Let a person apply this to himself, he who, although he feels the energy and the urge to venture into glorious battles, must be content with the sorriest of all, struggling with the cares about the necessities of life.

Money is and remains the absolute condition for living.

"Most men," you say, "live in order to make a living, when they have that, they live in order to make a good living; when they have that, they die."

those husbands who, as you once said of them, sit like lunatics, each in his marital cubicle, slave away in chains, and fantasize about the sweetness of engagement and the bitterness of marriage; those husbands who, according to your own correct observation, are among those who with a certain malicious glee congratulate anyone who becomes engaged.

Were it not for the juice of the red, red grapes
Who would here the longer tarry?
For nothing the eye of wisdom escapes
And all that it sees is misery.
Loud sounds the voice of the oppressed
The voice of the betrayed, from north to south.
Up brothers, let us drink instead
And forget this whole dismal earth.

Søren Kierkegaard, EITHER/OR II

A cattleman who (if this were possible) is a self before his cattle is a very low self,

Anti-Climacus, THE SICKNESS UNTO DEATH

1. *Kierkegaard's Relevance to Moral Theology*

This Chapter [CHAPTER II] is divided into two distinct parts. *Sections 2 & 3* thoroughly examine Alasdair MacIntyre (once more) in his critique of Søren Kierkegaard's ethical thought in *Either/Or: A Fragment of Life I & II* (1843). The central ethical act of fundamentally "affirming/negating" the categories of moral conscience is explained in great detail.

Sections 5-8 explore Kierkegaard's peculiar approach to the "concept" of sin in his philosophical treatise *The Sickness unto Death.* We will show that Kierkegaard's religious understanding of Despair in relation to Faith (or what is called the Religious Sphere of Existence) provides an important angle/perspective (often neglected) in the moral theology of the Catholic Church.

The work of the Danish philosopher Søren Kierkegaard describes an important, albeit distinctive, kind of sin.[112] For Kierke-

---

[112] The long story of Kierkegaard's life is filled with too many important marks to add significant biographical information sufficiently here. A philosopher first of all, Kierkegaard was a Magister (7 years of university) of his subject, in league with the intellectual giants of his time (Hamann, Schopenhauer, Hegel, Kant, Schiller, Lessing). He was also a man of some high status in Copenhagen having inherited a considerable fortune from his father. He was one of the wealthiest men in the country and known by the King of Denmark himself. Walter Lowrie relates an episode with the King in this regard: "During the trying years of 1846 and 1847 S.K. made several visits to King Christian VIII which he did not record in his journal until 1849. The favour of the king was clearly a relief from the scorn of the vulgar and the 'treachery' of the aristocrats who were thus furnished with 'a little difficulty to bite on.' Nevertheless he was reluctant to make these visits, and he did not go so often as the king wished. He held himself a little aloof because he knew that the king was inclined to offer him a sinecure, as a token of appreciation of him as a writer, and as a writer who steadily supported the monarchy. To S.K.'s surprise he found that King Christian knew about the bold part he had taken as a student in dissolving a meeting which threatened to end in a liberal demonstration. S.K. adroitly hinted that he could be serviceable only so long as he was independent; and he added characteristically, 'I have the honour to serve a higher Power, to the service of which my life is devoted.' Except on this delicate subject he was very frank and easy in his talks with the king. It goes without saying that he was humorous." Walter Lowrie, *Kierkegaard* (London: Oxford University Press, 1938), 359. Kierkegaard was also a close friend of and corresponded with Hans

gaard, there is the possibility of being *in sin*—untruth—without necessarily committing a sinful act; a kind of omission of the *Spirit*.[113] Kierkegaard names this sort of sin DESPAIR. In this case of despair, the inner self's "state of being" exists in a sinful manner, so that the despair of the self is that corruption in the spiritual aspect of the human person. Essentially, Kierkegaard believed that despair is the result of a fundamentally dishonest *relation* with God [Gud], moral conscience and/or Divine Revelation. Although actual moral culpability understood within the traditional framework of "full knowledge/full consent/grave matter" is not always apparent, despair is nevertheless an oft overlooked "mode of existence" where sin *is* (can be) nevertheless insidiously present.[114]

The state of despair amounts to a deficiency of virtue; in particular, the virtue of faith. When faith is absent, or lacking, (according to Kierkegaard) despair is the consequent condition. In other words, the human person is morally deficient if existing without the *virtue* of faith (the religious character's potency to act with faithful responses in relation). Kierkegaard scholar C. Stephen Evans comments:

> It should not be surprising that Kierkegaard, citing Romans 14:23, draws the corollary that 'the opposite of sin is not virtue but faith.' This statement is often misunderstood as a rejection of virtue theory on the part of Kierkegaard, a reading that puts Kierkegaard in tension with such contemporary thinkers as Alasdair MacIntyre . . . who argue that ethical thinking should focus on the virtues rather than simply on duties to act in particular ways. However, it is clear in the context

Christian Anderson (his contemporary). Famously, Kierkegaard tragically died shortly after withdrawing the last of his sizable inheritance (which he had spent liberally on carriage rides in the country and to publish his books). His funeral was purported to be a somewhat dreary affair. See footnote #207 at end of this chapter.

[113] Søren Kierkegaard, *Concluding Unscientific Postscript to Philosophical Fragments*, trans. Howard V. Hong and Edna H. Hong (Princeton, NJ: Princeton University Press, 1992), 208.

[114] The word in Latin is *deperatio*. It does not mean what Catholics mean as *despairing of God's mercy* being one of 6 "Sins Against the Holy Ghost." *See* APPENDIX A.

that this Kierkegaardian claim is not opposed to an ethics of virtue at all . . . The claim being made is that faith as genuine selfhood cannot be achieved simply through autonomous moral striving. Contemporary virtue theory does not use the term 'virtue' in this way, but rather to refer to those states of character in a person that are excellent and desirable, however they are achieved. In this sense, it makes sense to think of Kierkegaardian faith itself as a virtue, an excellence that makes a self genuinely human.[115]

Kierkegaard did not think of faith as an intellectual assent to propositions. Instead, faith is for him an all-encompassing virtue, or *power*, through which and by which the individual enters the "religious" mode of *existence* [tilværelse]. Catholic theologian Henri de Lubac explains Kierkegaard's position this way:

to believe is neither to know nor to understand, still less, of course, is it simply to profess a doctrine. Mystery is not a rational system; faith is not 'a starting-point for thought'; belief is not speculative; the real individual is face to face with a real God: that is the quite simple truth Kierkegaard is never weary of repeating.[116]

It is important to note that Kierkegaard's opponent and nemesis in philosophy was Georg Wilhelm Friedrich Hegel; a philosopher who tried to sift *all* of "world-history" into an exhaustive philosophical "system." To his credit, Kierkegaard disdained professors who spent their lives working on "world-history" while

---

[115] C. Stephen Evans, *Kierkegaard: An Introduction* (Cambridge, UK: Cambridge University Press, 2009), 181-182. *See* Romans 14:23, "But those who have doubts are condemned if they eat, because they do not act from faith; for whatever does not proceed from faith is sin."

[116] Henri de Lubac, S.J., *The Drama of Atheist Humanism* (San Francisco, CA: Ignatius Press, 1995), 103. Also, *see* the rest of Section 3. "Deeper Immersion in Existence" in Chapter 2: Nietzsche and Kierkegaard, of *The Drama of Atheist Humanism.*

forgetting to truly live their lives in the meantime.[117] He targeted with his greatest contempt those who became so abstracted from the reality of concrete existence that their very selves were lost in the pursuit of their science. The truth of existence is not an ideological system, known directly, but a life project that must be lived with *passion*.

Nevertheless, Kierkegaard was not an "irrationalist" existentialist as is often supposed. He was a brilliant logical dialectician in his own right. Here it is worth quoting Catholic philosopher Jacques Maritain at length. Maritain states that:

> in the eyes of Kierkegaard (Hegel's) ideological discourse *is of no importance*. Not that it is false, it is true on its level—but not on the level that matters, on the level of the absolute, of the truth that grips my vitals and on which I risk my life, my eternal destiny. In other words, the ideological discourse, with all its truths, is relativized, in the sense that while it is valid in general it is unconditionally valid only in general, but for no one in particular. But when it comes, contrariwise, to the real movement of thought, by which I go to the absolute and am saved in it, this movement, for Kierkegaard, requires first of all a rupture with the world of ideological discourse; it leaves this world behind it, in order to immerse itself in the subjective singularity, in whose depths the existential adhesion to the true is accomplished, in the blood as well as the mind.[118]

Kierkegaard believed that faith is essentially defined through existence, not cognition. For him, faith is, in reality, the most truthful immersion in existence. More precisely, faith is the *deepest* possible relationship with the divinity of Christ in Revelation. Kierkegaard understood life in this way, not just as speculative philosophy, but as the progression of life-stages through which

---

[117] Søren Kierkegaard, *Concluding Unscientific Postscript to Philosophical Fragments*, 144-188.

[118] Jacques Maritain, *Moral Philosophy: An Historical and Critical Survey of the Great Systems* (New York: Charles Scribner's Sons, 1964), 359-360.

faith becomes ever more authentic. He (like MacIntyre) believed that life is ultimately a religious "quest" constituted by the desire to overcome the despair of sin. However, in Kierkegaard's terminology, the despair of sin is not an action *per se*, but rather a persistent mode of existence; a sinful presence of character, if you will.[119]

To understand why this is so, first we must understand the meaning of the word for "despair" in the original Danish. The meaning of the word is sometimes mistaken by the translation. The word in Danish is *fortvivlelse*. In English, the word "despair," derivative of both French and Latin [desperatio], means quite literally "without hope." The word *fortvivlelse* is more closely related, etymologically, with the word for "doubt." Similarly, the root of the word, *tvivl* [doubt], is from the German word *zweifel*, also meaning "doubt." To clarify, *fortvivlelse* literally means "intensified doubt." Whereas in English the word "doubt" is cognitive, *fortvivlelse* is primarily existential. To doubt with the total person in relation to experience is an existential act akin to being without the virtue of hope [spes] (or faith [fides] in the broader sense of the word). However, to doubt with the intellect alone, in relation to statements of truth, is only cognitive. The cognitive act lacks the full "intensity" of Kierkegaard's meaning.[120]

For Kierkegaard, both sin and faith are actualized through an intensification of the awareness of being in despair; understood in the sense of an existential state, *not* a mere passion [in Latin passio] of sadness [in Danish tristitia]. Paradoxically, in order to be "cured" from despair, the person must first pass through a greater awareness of being in sin. The individual person, seeking salvation, will eventually come to the precipice of absolute choice, between either a real and confident faith humbly conceived, or become entrenched in sin more fully actualized in what Kierkegaard identifies as the lacunaes of weakness (personal doubt) and/or defiance (presumption/pride). The state of *being in faith* is that in which "the self in being itself and in willing to be itself is transparently grounded in God."[121]

---

[119] Søren Kierkegaard, *The Sickness Unto Death* (Princeton, NJ: Princeton University Press, 1985).

[120] Gregory R. Beabout, *Freedom and Its Misuses: Kierkegaard on Anxiety and Despair* (Milwaukee, WI: Marquette University Press, 2009), 83-84.

[121] Søren Kierkegaard, *The Sickness Unto Death*, 16-17.

To understand the relevance of Kierkegaard's theoretical framework to Roman Catholic moral theology let us now turn toward his understanding of the "stages along life's way." For Kierkegaard, there are three essential stages of existence. The *Æsthetic* stage is categorically qualified by "pleasure and pain," the *Ethical* by "good and evil" (or "good and bad") and the *Religious* by "faith and sin." To move from one stage to the next requires a *leap* into a new existential commitment of the self.

The driving spiritual force propelling this leap from one stage to the next is the conscious realization of the inadequacy of the previous stage, which is known essentially through the making conscious of despair. These two next sections approach Kierkegaard's ethical thought from the perspective of MacIntyre's critique of *Either/Or* so that the transition from the first stage (the æsthetic sphere) to the second stage (the ethical sphere) can be better understood.

However, not stopping at ethics, the final sections of this chapter [CHAPTER II] will explore the peculiarly *Religious* sphere in *The Sickness unto Death* (1849). It will be shown that Kierkegaard's theoretical framework, like the Fundamental Option, Virtue Ethics, or Sacred Scripture, is another excellent corrective of the acknowledged "blindspots" in Catholic moral theology, namely, the problematic noted in CHAPTER I regarding act-based "legalism." CHAPTER II concludes with an evaluation of Kierkegaard's contribution to moral theology from the perspective of a living religious faith.

2. *The Ethical Sphere:*
MacIntyre's Critique of Kierkegaard's Ethics in Either/Or

As we saw in CHAPTER I, the work of Alasdair MacIntyre evokes a pessimistic picture of ethical thinking in the modern world. In his book *After Virtue* MacIntyre delves into the "Enlightenment Project's" failure to establish moral norms on purely rational grounds as well as the necessity of virtue, narrative and tradition, in understanding moral acts or reasoning.

Toward the beginning of *After Virtue* MacIntyre dismisses Kierkegaard as both an irrationalist and pivotal forerunner of the contemporary moral crisis he sees. Kierkegaard's placement in *Af-*

ter Virtue suggests importance in both establishing the identity of the "modern self" and for anticipating much of what would come after Kierkegaard's time in moral theory; especially with respect to Friedrich Nietzsche's *genealogical* rejection of all traditional modes of moral enquiry as such.[122] MacIntyre writes:

> What I earlier picked out as the distinctively modern standpoint was of course that which envisages moral debate in terms of a confrontation between incompatible and incommensurable moral premises and moral commitment as the expression of a criterion-less choice between such premises, a type of choice for which no rational justification can be given.[123]

MacIntyre gives credit to Kierkegaard for the above discovery (or recognition) and then proceeds to critique him for ushering in the notion of "criterion-less" choice in ethics; or rather, for implicitly recognizing the underlying rational fallaciousness of philosophical debates concerning ethical epistemology.

According to MacIntyre, in the writings of Kierkegaard: "this element of arbitrariness in our moral culture was presented as a philosophical discovery—indeed as a discovery of a disconcerting, even shocking, kind—long before it became a commonplace of everyday discourse."[124]

This is, of course, the distinctively Sartean reading of Kierkegaard as a proponent of radical-choice. And so, Scottish Kierkegaard expert Alastair Hannay thinks that MacIntyre is off the mark here by reading back into Kierkegaard the later developments of Existentialism proper, e.g. Heidegger, Sarte, de Beauvoir, Camus, et cetera. Hannay explains that:

---

[122] *See* Alasdair MacIntyre, *Three Rival Versions of Moral Enquiry: Encyclopaedia, Genealogy, and Tradition* (Notre Dame, IN: University of Notre Dame Press, 1991). Macintyre provides a profound interpretation of "encyclopedia" and "genealogy" as the two modes of moral enquiry that reject the valid scientific application of any Tradition(s) in moral reasoning. *See* Friedrich Nietzsche, *The Birth of Tragedy and The Genealogy of Morals*, trans. Francis Golffing (Garden City, NY: Doubleday Anchor Books, 1956), for explanation of this rejection.

[123] Alasdair MacIntyre, *After Virtue*, 39.

[124] Ibid., 39.

Acute and perceptive as these and other thumb-
nail attributions often are, they invite us to read
Kierkegaard from somewhere quite far from his
elbow. The nearer we approach his elbow and
catch glimpses of what steered it both to and on
the page, the less easy it is to be convinced by the
picture sometimes conveyed of an astute manipu-
lator of world-culture working from a self-
imposed exile in his own land.[125]

That being duly noted, and notwithstanding MacIntyre's critique, Kierkegaard's account of morality *does* both bear the marks
of rationality, while, at the same time inadvertently (or posthumously) reflects much of MacIntyre's own subtle reasoning as to
moral norms, personal identity, and the formation of character.[126]
MacIntyre and Kierkegaard have an implicit agreement in that the
only way to actualize authentic human virtue is through the whole-
hearted engagement of the entire person in meaningful virtuous
relationships. An academic cohort of Kierkegaard scholars was in
fact commissioned to sort out these misunderstandings. The outcome is compiled in the volume *Kierkegaard After MacIntyre*, (with
MacIntyre's response to it included).[127]

In recent Catholic Teaching there is the Fundamental Option
made in freedom for or against The Good.[128] However, for Kierkegaard, there is an added nuance along these lines. Kierkegaard
saw that not only is there a choice between "good" and "evil," but
there is also a choice about choice itself. In other words, the individual can, in fact, "choose" to think and act in ethical terms, or
choose not to. The choice of "willfully ignoring" the ethical cate-

---

[125] Alastair Hannay, *Kierkegaard: A Biography* (Cambridge, UK: Cambridge
University Press, 2001), 439.

[126] John J. Davenport and Anthony Rudd, eds., *Kierkegaard After MacIntyre*
(Chicago: Open Court, 2001), 131-148.

[127] Ibid., 136.

[128] Bernard Häring, *Free & Faithful in Christ: Vol. 1: General Moral Theology*,
178. Häring uses contributions from the behavioral sciences and philosophy to support his case regarding the fundamental option. His citations
include Erikson, Spranger, Maslow, Frankl and Kierkegaard. Häring
writes that "His [Kierkegaard's] contribution can broaden our vision of
the fundamental option."

gories of moral conscience does not (in every case) involve one in
actions against The Good *per se*. Nevertheless, choosing to choose
to desire to exist in such a way is in itself sinful.[129]

In *Either/Or Part I* Kierkegaard's character of The Æsthete
sees no moral signification in choices. His attitude is described well
by Judge William here: "you say: I can either do this or that, but
whichever I do is equally absurd—*ergo*, I do nothing at all."[130] The
pure æsthete does not choose from inside the framework of "good
vs. evil."[131] Rather, The Æsethete sees life in a nihilistic vacuum
where the standard categories of ethical conscience do not carry
weight in the decision making process. Decisions are largely arbitrary because they are made in a void of moral *meaning*. The
Æsthete lacks ethical reasons for choices and is deprived of the
narrative meaning pursuant on long-term ethical commitments.[132]
In the *Diapsalmata* at the beginning of *Either/Or I* The Æsthete
betrays the nature of his character in these aphorisms about himself:

> What portends? What will the future bring? I do
> not know, I have no presentiment. When a spider
> hurls itself down from some fixed point, consist-
> ently with its nature it always sees before it only
> an empty space wherein it can find no foothold
> however much it sprawls. And so it is with me:
> always before me an empty space; what drives me
> forward is a consistency which lies behind me.
> This life is topsy-turvy and terrible, not to be en-
> dured.[133]

> Of all ridiculous things, it seems to me the most
> ridiculous is to be a busy man of affairs, prompt
> to meals, and prompt to work. Hence when I see
> a fly settle down in a crucial moment on the nose
> of a business man, or see him bespattered by a

---

[129] Søren Kierkegaard, *Either/Or II*, 169.

[130] Ibid., 170.

[131] *See* Friedrich Nietzsche, *Beyond Good and Evil: Prelude to a Philosophy of the
Future* (Mineola, NY: Dover Publications, 1997).

[132] C. Stephen Evans, *Kierkegaard: An Introduction*, 70-72. This is an excellent basic explanation of The Æsthete's character in context.

[133] Søren Kierkegaard, *Either/Or I*, 24.

carriage which passes by him in even greater haste, or a drawbridge opens before him, or a tile from the roof falls down and strikes him dead, then I laugh heartily. And who could help laughing? What do they accomplish, these hustlers? Are they not like the housewife, when her house was on fire, who in her excitement saved the fire-tongs? What more do they save from the great fire of life?[134]

It is quite remarkable that one gets a conception of eternity from two of the most appalling contrasts in life. If I think of that unhappy bookkeeper who lost his reason from despair at having involved his firm in bankruptcy by adding 7 and 6 to make 14; if I think of him day after day, oblivious to everything else, repeating to himself: 7 and 6 are 14, then I have an image of eternity.—If I imagine a voluptuous feminine beauty in a harem, reclining on a couch in all charming grace, without concern for anything in all the world, then I have a symbol for eternity.[135]

What is the power that binds me? How was the chain made with which the Fenris wolf was bound? It was wrought from the sound of a cat's paws walking over the ground, from women's beards, from the roots of rocks, from the nerves of bears, from the breath of fishes, and the spittle of birds. And thus I, too, am bound in a chain formed of dark imaginings, of unquiet dreams, of restless thoughts, of dread presentiments, of inexplicable anxieties. This chain is "very supple, soft as silk, elastic under the highest tension, and cannot be broken in two."[136]

---

[134] Ibid., 25.
[135] Ibid., 32.
[136] Ibid., 34.

My life is absolutely meaningless. When I consider the different periods into which it falls, it seems like the word *Schnur* in the dictionary, which means in the first place a string, in the second, a daughter-in-law. The only thing lacking is that the word *Schnur* should mean in the third place a camel, in the fourth, a dust-brush.[137]

The result of my life is simply nothing, a mood, a single color. My result is like the painting of the artist who was to paint a picture of the Israelites crossing the Red Sea. To this end, he painted the whole wall red, explaining that the Israelites had already crossed over, and that the Egyptians were drowned.[138]

I am like the Luneburger pig. My thinking is a passion. I can root up truffles excellently for other people, even if I get no pleasure out of them myself. I dig the problems out with my nose, but the only thing I can do with them is to throw them back over my head.[139]

And so, instead of moral criterion, The Æsthete chooses "æsthetically," that is to say, in accordance with the categories of "pleasure vs. pain." The Æsthete's life is a fleeting series of moments with no rational or moral signification. The last enemy of The Æsthete's cold cynicism is boredom. For example, (again in the *Diapsalmata*) The Æsthete writes in this well-known passage:

Marry, and you will regret it; do not marry, and you will also regret it. Marry or do not marry, you will regret it either way . . . Laugh at the world's stupidities, and you will regret it; weep over them, and you will also regret it. Laugh at the stupidities of the world or weep over them, you will regret it either way . . . Hang yourself, and you will regret

---

137 Ibid., 36.
138 Ibid., 28.
139 Ibid., 36.

> it; do not hang yourself, and you will also regret it. Hang yourself or do not hang yourself, you will regret it either way. This, gentlemen, is the sum and substance of all philosophy.

> Never have I been happy; and yet it has always seemed as if happiness were in my train, as if glad *genii* danced about me, invisible to others but not to me, whose eyes gleamed with joy. And when I go among men, as happy and glad as a god, and they envy me my happiness, then I laugh; for I despise men, and avenge myself upon them . . . When I see myself cursed, abominated, hated, for my coldness and heartlessness: then I laugh, then my wrath is satiated. If these good people really put me in the wrong, if they could actually make me do wrong—well, then I should have lost.[140]

The Æsthete's choices are essentially arbitrary, but for Judge William in *Either/Or II* the true fulfillment of the human person is only consummated through an absolute volitional choice fundamentally directed toward long-term ethical commitments—that is, in actualizing the conventional moral norms of a given society.

Judge William shouts at The Æsthete *'either/or!'* (Aut/Aut!) and advices him to "choose *yourself*."[141] In other words, make your choices demanded of you, *and* take them seriously! To Judge William, despite The Æsthete's blindness to moral value, in every choice there is an unavoidable ethical implication of enduring moral significance. Ethical commitment, the Judge sees here, necessarily draws the individual's character *deeper and deeper* into a life of consistent moral development; that is, through the exercise of moral freedom, properly understood.

Kierkegaard believed that the desire for moral meaning is, in fact, essential to the human condition. The rational verification of his ethical position is "loosely-premised" upon the presence of despair in the emptiness of the purely æsthetic existence. His "argument" runs thus: since beyond the aesthetic lies the ethical, and to resist the ethical is to despair of living in the absence of mean-

---

[140] Ibid., 40.

[141] Søren Kierkegaard, *Either/Or II*, 167.

ing, ethical commitments which acknowledge virtues and pursue human goods are, therefore, "natural" to the human person-hood.[142] In using the words of C. Stephen Evans:

> The aesthete's despair is a state he finds himself in; what he must do is take responsibility for the person he has become, to choose to be the per-son he is. In choosing his despair the aesthete transforms himself from immediacy to a task, for if I am responsible for who I am, then I am also responsible for who I will become. Despair is not to be chosen as an inevitable state to wallow in, but something the aesthete has freely chosen, and which he can therefore begin to change.[143]

The main difference between the ethical sphere and the æsthetic sphere is the interior response of the subjectivity to the phenomenon of despair. The Æsthete can deny despair, wallow in it, or redirect it as an occasion for improving himself. Often, "The sow is washed only to wallow in the mud" (2 Peter 2:22). *But*, des-pair, instead of dragging life downwards, can also propel life on-wards or upwards into an ethical existence of absolute respect for an individual's moral conscience.

The "trick" behind Kierkegaard's opus *Either/Or* is to inveigle an æsthetic reader, through the use of pseudonymous authorship, into confronting ethical choice seriously.[144] Although *Either/Or* is not "rational" discourse itself, in the sense of a logical argument spelled-out, it is nonetheless rationally received to the extent that it dispels an illusion and inveigles the reader into a new existential framework by way of "Godly Satire."[145]

---

[142] Ibid.

[143] C. Stephen Evans, *Kierkegaard: An Introduction*, 100.

[144] *See* Søren Kierkegaard, *The Point of View On My Work As An Author*, eds. and trans. Howard V. Hong and Edna H. Hong (Princeton, NJ: Princeton University Press, 1998).

[145] Walker Percy deployed this very same "trick" in most of his writing, e.g. allowing the reader to see differently through the use of narrative voice and fictional characters what would remain unconvincing using logical or "rational" argumentation alone. *See* our next Chapter here, CHAPTER III: Walker Percy and the Moral Imagination.

3. *The Ethical Sphere:*
Despair in Either/Or

After trying to discredit Kierkegaard's position toward the beginning of *After Virtue*, MacIntyre again invokes Kierkegaard, tellingly, before the heart of *After Virtue's* thesis on the "narrative unity of life" in Chapter 15. He writes: . . . "there is at least one virtue recognized by tradition which cannot be specified at all except with reference to the wholeness of human life—the virtue of integrity or constancy. 'Purity of the heart,' said Kierkegaard, 'is to will one thing'."[146]

There is an important contradiction in MacIntyre's reading of *Either/Or* here. First, he is accusing Kierkegaard of advocating fundamentally irrational choice, and then, he acknowledges Kierkegaard's absolute ethical *telos*. In fact Kierkegaard names his *telos* explicitly, something MacIntyre does not seem to do. "Purity of heart is to *will one thing*."[147] According to Kierkegaard, the "one thing necessary" (Luke 10:42)—in the ethical life—is the desire to choose in terms of "good and evil," that is, with the authenticity of a seeker after truth. The integrity of ethical commitment is, in fact, the one true constant in the ethical life.[148]

Toward the conclusion of *After Virtue*, MacIntyre makes a similar admission regarding the ultimate Good of the Good Life. He writes that "the good life for man is the life spent seeking the good life for man, and the virtues necessary for the seeking are those which will enable us to understand what more the good life for man is."[149] In the end, Kierkegaard and MacIntyre share this insight in common perhaps.[150] However, *despite* this agreement, in

---

[146] Alasdair MacIntyre, *After Virtue*, 203.

[147] Søren Kierkegaard, *Purity of Heart Is To Will One Thing: Spiritual Preparation for the Office of Confession.* trans. Douglas V. Steere (New York: Harper & Row, Publishers, 1948).

[148] *See* "The Balance Between the Esthetic and the Ethical in the Development of the Personality," in Søren Kierkegaard, *Either/Or II*, 156-333.

[149] Alasdair MacIntyre, *After Virtue*, 219.

[150] MacIntyre continues to deny the congruence. *See* John J. Davenport and Anthony Rudd, eds., *Kierkegaard After MacIntyre*, 339-355. This collection is based on MacIntrye's response to a symposium of Kierkegaard scholars held for the purpose of criticizing MacIntyre's position on this matter.

methodology they remain fundamentally different in philosophical outlook.

MacIntyre focuses on cognitive "doubts" while Kierkegaard targets *fortvivlelse*.[151] Fortvivlelse (as mentioned before) is essentially the dissipation of virtue to the point of being amoral or immoral, e.g. the life of The Æsthete.[152] MacIntyre's intellectual doubt seeks the objectification of traditional accounts of the right virtues (like The Judge), but Kierkegaard's "despair" is more akin to personal resistance that arises in response to the ethical demands of moral conscience. So, Kierkegaard explains that "doubt is thought's despair, despair is personality's doubt."[153]

The willed aggravation of moral choice is that of ethical despair. *Fortvivlelse* aggravates the moral agent's ability to choose once faced with important ethical decisions. Divided between desires for differing immanent goods, the self cannot *let-go* of selfish objectives and will not limit choices in the future by making definitive ethical commitments in the present. The only way to avoid these commitments is to remain in the æsthetic sphere. In the æsthetic sphere forvivlelse is the persistent mode of existence; blocking the power of the will to choose ethical choices.

The human person does not have a morally meaningful moral identity or self without these ethical commitments. Judge William explains that "Rather than designating the choice between good and evil, my *Either/Or* designates the choice by which one chooses good and evil or rules them out."[154] And in this metaphor of Judge William:

---

[151] Gregory R. Beabout, *Freedom and Its Misuses: Kierkegaard on Anxiety and Despair*, 83-93.

[152] MacIntyre identifies the *æsthete* to be one of three paradigmatic "characters" of the modern world. The other two are Max Weber's *bureaucrat* and the modern *therapist*. Both share with the æsthete the lack of ethical judgments made in the traditional sense of virtues and vices. For example, for the character of the *bureaucrat see* Max Weber, *From Max Weber: Essays in Sociology*, trans. H. H. Gerth and C. Wright Mills (New York: Routledge, 1948), & C. Wright Mills, *White Collar: The American Middle Classes* (Oxford, UK: Oxford University Press, 1951). And for a description of the *therapist's* character, Philip Reiff, *The Triumph of the Therapeutic: Uses of Faith after Freud* (Chicago: University of Chicago Press, 1987). Reiff's respected work is an excellent description of the amoral nature of modern therapy.

[153] Søren Kierkegaard, *Either/Or II*, 211.

[154] Ibid., 188.

Can you think of anything more frightful than that it might end with your nature being resolved into a multiplicity, that you really might become many, become, like those unhappy demoniacs, a legion, and you thus would have lost the inmost and holiest thing of all in a man, the unifying power of personality? . . . Truly, you should not jest with that which is not only serious but dreadful. In every man there is something which to a certain degree prevents him from becoming perfectly transparent to himself; and this may be the case in so high a degree, he may be so inexplicably woven into the relationships of life which extend far beyond himself that he almost cannot reveal himself. But he who cannot reveal himself cannot love, and he who cannot love is the most unhappy man of all.[155]

In the ethical sphere the final good and crowning virtue of the integrated personality (and of a transparent conscience) is charitable concern for the other. However, concern for the other and respect for conscience, though important, do not eliminate despair altogether. Despair persists even after all ethical commitments have been fulfilled, albeit in a different way. In other words, lacking the transcendent ends of religion, immanent ethical commitments are ultimately still in vain. For the "moralist" this can be counterintuitive, *but* it is true!

The ethical life that leans too heavily on ethical rules alone (with the assurances that all is well because), to the exclusion of responsiveness to the discernment of God's *will*, is in fact detrimental to the salvation offered in Christianity. The ethical person will inevitably, at times, violate conscience, often hypocritically. The only real reparation of the despairing soul is the repentance of the penitent transparently "before God" in relation to Christ. Kierkegaard illumines this inner movement repentance and starts to allude to the Religious Sphere with this fanciful poetic image in *Either/Or II*:

---

155 Ibid., 104.

> We read in fairy tales about human beings whom
> mermaids and mermen enticed into their power
> by means of demoniac music. In order to break
> the enchantment it was necessary in the fairy tale
> for the person who was under the spell to play
> the same piece of music backwards without mak-
> ing a single mistake. This is very profound, but
> very difficult to perform, and yet so it is: the er-
> rors one has taken into oneself one must eradicate
> in this way, and every time one makes a mistake
> one must begin all over. Therefore it is important
> to choose and to choose in time.[156]

Just in being in this fallen world the human person unavoidably takes "sin" into the condition of the self. External conformity
to rule and ethical commitment alone do not expel it. Often, the
ethical life will aggravate the problem insofar as the person becomes complacent or self-righteous. Kierkegaard disdains this presumption. Instead, at that end of *Either/Or* he declares: "over
against God we are always in the wrong."[157]

We now turn to the next stage of Kierkegaard's Stages Along
Life's Way for the purpose of examining the specifically "religious"
sphere of existence" in Kierkegaard's *The Sickness unto Death.*

4. *The Religious Sphere:*
Despair in Kierkegaard's The Sickness unto Death

The Sickness unto Death presents Kierkgaard's understanding of
the specifically "religious" despair in relation to the "ethical" and
"æsthetic" modes of existence.[158]

---

[156] Ibid., 164-165.

[157] Ibid., 341-345.

[158] *Anti-Climacus* is Kierkegaard's pseudonym in *The Sickness unto Death.* It
is widely believed by scholars that the reflection of Kierkegaard's own
thinking here is fairly direct and Anti-Climacus is not too much in a fictional voice to be unable to attribute his ideas to Kierkegaard himself.
Louis Dupré, "The Sickness Unto Death: Critique of the Modern Age,"
in *The Existentialists: Critical Essays on Kierkegaard, Nietzsche, Heidegger, and*

The preface of this dense little book opens thus, with an introduction on Lazarus' resurrection in *The Gospel of Saint John* that "This sickness is not unto death" (John 11:4)—

> Herr! Gibe uns blöde Augen
> für Dinge, die nichts taugen,
> und Augen voller Klarheit
> in alle deine Wahrheit.
>
> [Lord, give me weak eyes
> for things of little worth,
> and eyes clear-sighted
> in all of your truth.]

As we have seen, in the ethical sphere fortvivlelse is the result of the failure to choose ethically, that is, in terms of conscience. However, in a more foundational sense the presence of fortvivlelse is essentially a failure to live religiously as a self "before God." *Religious* despair, contrasted with "ethical" despair, is the condition of lacking the Faith in relation to the divinity of Christ.

In a well-known passage at the beginning of *The Sickness unto Death* Kierkegaard describes this paradoxical human condition—of being an embodied self-consciousness itself in relation—in this manner:

> A human being is spirit. But what is spirit? Spirit is the self. But what is the self? The self is a relation that relates itself to itself or is the relation's relating itself to itself in the relation; the self is not the relation but is the relation's relating itself to itself. A human being is a synthesis of the infinite and the finite, of the temporal and the eternal, of freedom and necessity, in short, a synthesis.
>
> . . . The human self is such a derived, established relation, a relation that relates itself to itself and in relating itself to itself relates itself to another.

Sarte, ed. Charles Guignon (Lanham, MD: Rowman & Littlefield, 2004), 33-52.

> The formula that describes the state of the self
> when despair is completely rooted out is this: in
> relating itself to itself and in willing to be itself,
> the self rests transparently in the power that es-
> tablished it.[159]

Kierkegaard's meaning here is that the human person, being a
creature of God, is necessarily structured to relation with God (the
power that establishes the relation). Something in the composition
of human nature can disrupt this however. If the human person
tries to establish its self in something other than God, the state of
disparate elements constituting the self disintegrates. To rest deci-
sively in any *created* good, either for æsthetic pleasure, or, even out
of a presumably admirable ethical obligation of social commitment,
is to commit a grave religious *sin* (wrong) of idolatry. In the end,
being that all immanent goods are by nature transient, idolatry
necessarily leads to despair—whether recognized in the consciousness and conscience *or not.*

In like manner, there are 3 distinct forms of despair that cor-
respond to the 3 stages of life's elevation: "despair as immediacy"
(æsthetic), "despair as weakness" (ethical) and "despair as defiance"
(religious). The Catholic categories of "invincible ignorance," "supine ignorance" and "willful ignorance" can be loosely juxtaposed
here (CCC 1790-1794).

The order of description in what follows is arranged in such a
way that the 3 forms of despair proceed according to the degree in
which the condition of despair becomes *more and more* conscious to
the individual. In the final "religious stage" of despair the self
reaches a sort of breaking-point between an Absolute Faith in relation to The Eternal or the hardened despair of final defiance. For
Kierkegaard, despair is encountered on this passage to authentic
faith. Not to know it is to fail to actualize the self's relation in
God.[160]

---

[159] Søren Kierkegaard, *The Sickness unto Death*, 13-14.

[160] Through the Catholic *lens* it is not possible to commit Mortal Sin
without "full knowledge" and "full consent." Kierkegaard's understanding of despair is not always a "grave" sin in the traditional sense. Nevertheless, the argument does NOT follow that people ought to remain ignorant, spiritually weak, or deficient in virtue and faith. As an outsider
voice to the Catholic Tradition, Kierkegaard's perspective remains an
important contribution to Catholic Moral Theology. It is difficult to ac-

5. *The Religious Sphere:*
Despair as Immediacy

The despair of immediacy: Ignorant immediacy is the starting default "level" on the progression toward authentic faith. The state of immediacy corresponds to the æsthetic sphere of existence. The ignorant blindness of cultural immediacy is an unreflective despair that is unaware of being despair. In other words, those in immediate despair are those who, drowning in the flow of sensate life, do not stop to reflect and rarely rise to but a momentary consciousness of the true condition of their self in relation to itself or in relation to God. Kierkegaard writes:

> The man of immediacy . . . is an accompanying something within the dimensions of temporality and secularity, in immediate connection with 'the other', and has but an illusory appearance of having anything eternal in it. The self is bound up in immediacy with the other in desiring, craving, enjoying, etc., yet passively; in its craving, this self is a dative, like the 'me' of a child. Its dialectic is: the pleasant and the unpleasant; its concepts are: good luck, bad luck, fate.[161]

The outward appearance of despair is missing. The latent spirit of despair needs only a little unpleasant jarring to come to light. Kierkegaard believed that the default state of the human condition is despair. Therefore, for Kierkegaard despair can be considered universal to human nature. Temporarily, the immediate man sometimes becomes vaguely aware of his condition once tried. However, his ignorance remains invincible in these cases (CCC 1793). C. Stephen Evans writes:

---

cuse him of legalism (he is often the polar opposite). However, no doubt he did have his own personal and theoretical faults. *See* for example the oldest and perhaps best biography of Kierkegaard, Walter Lowrie, *Kierkegaard*. Lowrie, an Anglican clergyman, wrote during the *living-memory* of Kierkegaard in Denmark. He in fact interviewed Kierkegaard's immediate *blood* descendants in his researches there. Also very good is the more recent biography of Alastair Hannay, *Kierkegaard: A Biography*.

[161] Søren Kierkegaard, *The Sickness unto Death*, 51.

One might think that the idea of unconscious despair is impossible. Perhaps it would be if human beings were fully transparent to themselves, Cartesian egos fully defined by consciousness. However, Kierkegaard, like Nietzsche and Freud after him, is a depth psychologist who thinks that full transparency is an ideal for humans but not a reality. If we take despair, as he does, primarily as a state or condition of the self, then it is not surprising that humans may be in this state without noticing it.[162]

Despair is not the *experience* of despair—that is, in the psychological (clinical depression) sense alone; it is also to possess the potential for despair in the first place. Despair is often latent in the human condition, while nonetheless present. In reality despair is never the result of something outside of the self. Rather, despair is the desire to *get rid of the self* once something upsets the immediacy of life. So, despair is *in* the basic vanity of worldly idols, *not* in each of the idols as such. Evans writes:

The real cause of despair is not the man's loss of the job or the girlfriend . . . the error is deeper. The loss of a job or a girlfriend is something contingent, but it cannot be a contingent thing that a person is in despair. What the loss of job or girlfriend really reveals is that the person was in despair all along, that his identity was built on something too fragile to be the basis of selfhood. When this fragile basis for identity is shattered, the self's underlying emptiness is revealed.[163]

After a troubling experience, rather than continue a life tranquilized with the trivial, the immediate man may start to live in the ethical categories of "right and wrong," or even muster a pretense of faith, but only as a defensive reflex or reaction against the world. The defense is a shallow mimicry. The immediate man: "bereft of imagination, as the philistine-bourgeois always is, whether alehouse

---

[162] C. Stephen Evans, *Kierkegaard: An Introduction*, 174.
[163] Ibid., 174.

keeper or prime minister . . . lives within a certain trivial compendium of experiences as to how things go, what is possible, what
usually happens."[164]

The immediate man remains invincibly blind to his despair
unless somehow rudely awakened from his slumber by a harsh and
inescapable reality (i.e. either personal ordeal or social catastrophes,
and such). Even then, however, lacking God's *illumination* of grace
[gracia illuminans] he cannot see his fault. Ultimately, the dawning
realization of the awe-full splendor of God is necessary to begin
the progression toward faith.[165] Otherwise, the reality of despair
will continue to be, defensively, pushed to the background where it
cannot disturb consciousness. In these cases the world is narrowed
and therefore limited to the point where it is manageable for the
individual, *but* presents a fundamentally dishonest vision of
reality.[166]

> There is a story about a peasant who went bare-
> footed to town with enough money to buy him-
> self a pair of stockings and shoes and to get drunk,
> and in trying to find his way home in his drunken
> state, he fell asleep in the middle of the road. A
> carriage came along, and the driver shouted to
> him to move or he would drive over his legs. The
> drunken peasant woke up, looked at his legs and,
> not recognizing them because of the shoes and
> stockings, said: "Go ahead, they are not my legs."
> When the man of immediacy despairs, it is impos-

---

[164] Søren Kierkegaard, *The Sickness unto Death*, 41.

[165] Eric Voegelin sees this awe (as do many others) as being at the begin-
ning of all things religious in human history. *See* Eric Voegelin, *Order and
History, Volume One: Israel and Revelation* (Baton Rouge, LA: Louisiana State
University Press, 1956).

[166] Ernest Becker, *The Denial of Death* (New York: Free Press Paperbacks,
1973). In Becker's psychoanalytic philosophy, the human person structures his or her character largely in defense against the reality of death,
disease or nature "red in tooth and claw." For Becker, the inherent absurdity of a self-conscious animal (who knows it will die) is an essential
reality of the human condition. People, Becker thinks, are universally
provoked to neurotically limit the clear vision of reality, thus obstructing
an honest appraisal of the human condition (*á la* Freud's defense mecha-
nisms).

sible to give a true description of him outside of the comic;[167]

The man of immediacy does not know himself, he quite literally identifies himself only by the clothes he wears,[168]

6. *The Religious Sphere: Despair as Weakness*

There is also a second form of despair—"despair as weakness." Two kinds of weakness are possible: "despair *in* weakness" and "despair *over* weakness"; the latter being the heightened sense on the road to authentic faith.

Essentially, despair "in weakness" is the despair over something earthly, a lost idol, whereas despair "over weakness" is to despair over the human condition as such. In the former case the person turns inward and despairs, understanding briefly the nature of the sickness in relation to God. However, rather than look deeper into the self's reflection of its own interiority, the person often returns to worldly affairs having learned nothing permanent about the self. Kierkegaard describes this move thus:

> Little by little, he manages to forget it; in the course of time, he finds it almost ludicrous, especially when he is together with other competent and dynamic men who have a sense and aptitude for life. Charming! He has happily married now for several years, as it says in novels, is a dynamic and enterprising man; at home in his own house the servants call him 'He Himself'.[169]

He has settled in, so to speak, retaining only a hint of spiritual depth. Putting aside "naïve illusions," he no longer sees the extraordinary. Challenged with the sense of the unknown, he reflex-

---

[167] Søren Kierkegaard, *The Sickness unto Death*, 53.
[168] Ibid.
[169] Ibid., 56.

ively buries himself in the immediate rush, hustle and bustle, of life. He evades the difficult questions and experiences that trouble him. He continues to cling to the idols of this world, not knowing anything else. But his despair is an "infinite passion over something of this world."[170] It is "immediacy with the admixture of a little dash of reflection."[171]

By contrast, "despair over weakness" is over nothing in particular. The ultimate vanity of life is seen, but no solution is offered. Theologian Karl Rahner explains in *The Possibility of Evading the Experience of Transcendence*:

> There is *perhaps* despairing involvement in the categorical realm of human existence. One goes about his business, he reads, he gets angry, he does his work, he does research, he achieves something, he earns money. And in a final, perhaps unadmitted despair he says to himself that the whole as a whole makes no sense, and that one does well to suppress the question about the meaning of it all and to reject it as an unanswerable and hence meaningless question.[172]

"Despair *over* weakness" often takes the form of what Kierkegaard calls the "ethical cultural man." The "ethical cultural man" (existing in the immanent ethical sphere) takes responsibility for his moral duties with unassuming conformity. However, he secretly harbors an awareness of profound mystery that he cannot explain. In moments of solitude he reflects upon it, although he dares not reflect too deeply for fear of unsettling the "everydayness" (Martin Heidegger's term) of his existence. "He fears being led too far out."[173] He fears "standing-out" *too much* from the crowd. Yet he is unable to forget it. He "not infrequently longs for solitude."[174] His despair is perhaps quiet and reserved, yet, *it is* real and unsettling as well.

---

[170] Ibid., 60.

[171] Ibid. 58.

[172] Karl Rahner, *Foundation of the Christian Faith: An Introduction to the Idea of Christianity*, trans. William V. Dych (New York: The Seabury Press, 1978), 33.

[173] Søren Kierkegaard, *The Sickness unto Death*, 64

[174] Ibid.

'Utterly superficial nonpersons and group people'
feel such a meager need for solitude that, like
lovebirds, they promptly die the moment they
have to be alone. Just like a little child has to be
lulled to sleep, so these people need the soothing
lullaby of social life in order to be able to eat,
drink, sleep, fall in love, etc.[175]

His (the despairer *over* weakness) despair is decidedly not the
feeling of psychological depression. Rather, the despair is over the
knowledge of despair itself. The person's despair is rooted in the
awareness of an objective condition, not simply a felt mental pathology. It is not *melancholia* or *acedia*. Kierkegaard does use the
word "depression" in other contexts with much the same meaning
as he is using the word despair here. But he does not mean what is
meant today by depression in modern psychiatry. The modern
clinical language of psychiatry did not yet then exist of course.
However, Kierkegaard is in fact widely recognized as anticipating
the nature of many later insights. He sees the *condition* of "depression" [despair] at the very heart of the nature of sin, saying:

If a depressed person is asked what the reason is,
what it is that weighs [tynge] on him, he will answer: I do not know; I cannot explain it . . . But
depression is sin, is actually a sin *instar omnium*
[that stands for all], for it is the sin of not willing
deeply and inwardly, and this is the mother of all
sins.[176]

And so, unlike despair that is "in" weakness, despair "over"
weakness is not dependent on any relation to earthly goods, or
other people. Inevitably, the condition is lasting in that it persis-
tently haunts his conscious state from an unknown source.

our man in despair is sufficiently self-inclosed to
keep this matter of the self away from anyone
who has no business knowing about it—in other

---

[175] Ibid.
[176] *Either/Or II*, 189.

words, everyone—while outwardly he looks every bit 'a real man'. He is a university graduate, husband, father, even an exceptionally competent officeholder, a respectable father, pleasant company, very gentle to his wife, solicitude personified to his children. And Christian?—Well, yes, he is that, too, but prefers not to talk about it.[177]

Kierkegaard names this defense against conscious despair "inclosing reserve" or *indesluttehed* in Danish. He continues: "Aside from his natural good nature and sense of duty, what makes him such a kind husband and solicitous father is the confession about his weakness that he has made to himself in his inclosed innermost being."[178]

The person's dawning sense of the overwhelming mystery of creation relative to the limitations of the human animal provides him with the beginning first steps [initium fidei] of the humility that precedes authentic faith. However, he sees not what to do with himself in response to it. He "misses" the virtue of faith and remains in despair *over* his weakness—in response to the hidden transcendence he cannot define, know or understand.

Further, the person who despairs over weakness is not "weak" for inability to face hardship. Rather, the weakness is failure to actualize the higher calling he sees by "secret" [secretum] or wants to see. Being too dependent on others or sunken in the immanence of his worldliness, he cannot stand truly "before God." He sits defensively entrenched and alienated from the world he lives in, refusing to take action on God's inner promptings—whatever they are.[179] He accepts ethical standards and lives with the consequent obligatory commitments. He lives without passion or a sense of real meaningfulness.[180]

This particular individual slips through the cracks of any and all universal systems, moral codes, or philosophical abstractions. He does not find ultimate fulfillment in the earthly, but still despairs of his inability to *let it go*. Having the continued sense of despair even while all universal ethical obligations have been met,

---

[177] Søren Kierkegaard, *The Sickness unto Death*, 63-64.

[178] Ibid., 64-65.

[179] *See* Søren Kierkegaard, *Fear and Trembling*.

[180] *See* the parable of the rich young man (Matthew 19:16-26).

again, he suffers for not seeing what more is possible and/or the spiritual strength to actualize it (whatever it is). His existence is immanent and he desires something transcendent. His despair is "supine" to a degree (CCC 1791). He remains ignorant of the trajectory of religious significance. Kierkegaard puts it this way:

> Every human existence that is not conscious of itself as spirit or personally conscious of itself before God as spirit, every human existence that is not transparently grounded in God but vaguely rests in and merges in some abstract universal (state, nation, etc.) or, in darkness over his self regards his capacities merely as productive powers without becoming in the deepest sense consciously aware of their source, regards his self, if he tries to understand it at all, as an inexplicable something—every such existence, whatever it achieves, be it most amazing, whatever it explains, be it the whole of existence, however intensively it enjoys life aesthetically—every such existence is nevertheless despair.[181]

Or, in the words of the Book of Ecclesiastes: *vanitas vanitatum vanitas*—"Vanity of vanities, says the Preacher, vanities of vanities! All is vanity" (Eccles: 1:2). And then, again, Kierkegaard once more on life's mystery writes in his journals and papers: "Hear the mother's scream in the hour of birth—see the death struggle at the very last—and then say if what begins and ends in this way can be intended for enjoyment."[182]

> And when the hourglass has run out, the hourglass of temporality, when the noise of secular life has grown silent and its restless or ineffectual activism has come to an end, when everything around you is still, as in eternity, then—whether you were man or woman, rich or poor, dependent or independent, fortunate or unfortunate, wheth-

[181] Søren Kierkegaard, *The Sickness unto Death*, 46.
[182] Søren Kierkegaard, *Papers and Journals: A Selection*, trans. Alastair Hannay (New York: Penguin Books, 2009 [1962]), 631.

er you ranked with royalty and wore a glittering crown or in humble obscurity bore the toil and heat of day, whether your name will be remembered as long as the world stands and consequently as long as it stood or you are nameless and run nameless in the innumerable multitude, whether the magnificence encompassing you surpassed all human description or the most severe and ignominious human judgment befell you—eternity asks you and every individual in these millions and millions about only one thing: whether you have lived in despair or not, whether you have despaired in such a way that you did not realize that you were in despair, or in such a way that you covertly carried this sickness inside of you as your gnawing secret, as a fruit of sinful love under your heart, or in such a way that you, a terror to others, raged in despair. And if so, if you have lived in despair, then, regardless of whatever else you won or lost, everything is lost for you, eternity does not acknowledge you, it never knew you—or, still more terrible, it knows you as you are known and it binds you to yourself in despair.[183]

. . . This is what the ancient Church Fathers meant when they said that the virtues of pagans were glittering vices: they meant that the heart of paganism was despair, that paganism was not conscious before God as spirit.[184]

7. *The Religious Sphere:*
Despair as Defiance

Defiance is the breaking-point juncture of absolute faith [tro]. In despair as defiance rather than make a final "leap" into the life

---

[183] Søren Kierkegaard, *The Sickness unto Death*, 27-28.
[184] Ibid., 46.

sustaining faith pursuant on the disciple's calling in Christianity, the person who is in conscious despair might try to *break-free* with an act of defiance—that is, by taking on great creative undertakings, by becoming debauched with a sensual life of dissolution, or committing suicide [selvmord: self-murder].[185] *But*, "the person in despair cannot die; 'no more than the dagger can slaughter thoughts' can despair consume the eternal."

In this third form of despair the person desires *in defiance* to be the self that he or she would wish [ønske] to be. The spirit of defiance is "willfully ignorant" of dependence on God (CCC 1792). "It recognizes no power over itself."[186]

> Figuratively speaking, it is as if an error slipped into an author's writing and the error became conscious of itself as an error—perhaps it actually was not a mistake but in a much higher sense an essential part of the whole production—and now this error wants to mutiny against the author, out of hatred toward him, forbidding him to correct it and in maniacal defiance saying to him: No, I refuse to be erased; I will stand as a witness against you, a witness that you are a second-rate author.[187]

The defiant person takes a stand as an autonomous individual. He decides to "go it alone," the world, others, and God be damned. With defiant despair (what Kierkegaard calls "demonic" despair) the fundamental imbalances of the self in relation to the world often become too great. Lacking the blind immediacy of the unreflective, or the social supports of the weak, the instability becomes too intense psychically for most and the personality begins to slouch toward disintegration. In essence despair as *fortvivlelse* is the desire to get rid of the self as an eternal self "before God." This desire can take myriad forms.

In the clinical language of Pulitzer-winner psychoanalyst Prof. Ernest Becker, the endless expansiveness of "spiritual possibility"

---

[185] *See* Albert Camus, "L'Absurde et le Suicide," en *Le mythe de Sisyphe: Essai sur l'absurde* (Paris: Gallimard, 1942).
[186] Søren Kierkegaard, *The Sickness unto Death*, 68.
[187] Ibid., 74.

or the stifling limitation of "human necessity" can create all sorts of characters who possess differing degrees of "psychosis" (too much possibility), "neurosis" (too much limitation), or "normalcy" (simple immediacy).[188] Kierkegaard explains that: "The person who gets lost in possibility soars high with the boldness of despair; he for whom everything becomes necessity overstrains himself in life and is crushed in despair; but the philistine-bourgeois mentality spiritlessly triumphs."[189] And in the words of the Gospel, this polarity of *spirit* is imagined in the story of *The Moonstruck Boy*:[190]

> Teacher, I brought you my son; he has a spirit that makes him unable to speak; and whenever it seizes him, it dashes him down; and he foams and grinds his teeth and becomes rigid; and I asked your disciples to cast it out, but they could not do so. He answered them, 'You faithless generation, how much longer must I be among you? How much longer must I put up with you? Bring him to me.' And they brought the boy to him. When the spirit saw him, immediately it convulsed the boy, and he fell on the ground and rolled about, foaming at the mouth. Jesus asked the father, 'How long has this been happening to him?' And he said, 'From childhood. It has often cast him into the fire and into the water, to destroy him; but if you are able to do anything, have pity on us and help us.' Jesus said to him, 'If you are able!— All things can be done for the one who believes.' (Mark 9:17-23 NRSV)

What is missing in all of these types is a passionate and total commitment to the transcendent and absolute *beyond*. What is needful is the theological synthesis of Christianity or the "leap of

---

[188] Ernest Becker, *The Denial of Death*, 67-92. Also *see* Sigmund Freud, *Civilization and Its Discontents* (New York: W. W. Norton & Company, 1989), Chapter 2. Freud's later work gives a more sober and scientific explanation of why lasting happiness is finally unachievable in this life.

[189] Søren Kierkegaard, *The Sickness unto Death*, 42.

[190] Selēniazesthai, "to be struck by the moon," was an ancient way of describing epilepsy. Daniel J. Harrington, S.J., "The Gospel According to Mark," in *The New Jerome Biblical Commentary*, 615-616.

faith" (to use Kierkegaardian terms). Missing this "leap" or lacking the synthesis, Kierkegaard sees that only varying degrees of lived despair are. He uses the poetic image of breathing in order to illustrate the prayerful movement of a person of faith. He writes: "Personhood is a synthesis of possibility and necessity. Its continued existence is like breathing (*re*spiration), which is an inhaling and exhaling . . . To pray is also to breathe, and possibility is for the self what oxygen is for breathing."[191]

To hold the breath [ruah] [pneuma] is to die. The human person has to necessarily exhale and *let-go* of possibility in order to stay alive spiritually. For God all things are possible (Matthew 19:26, Mark 10:27, 14:36, Luke 1:37). Sadly, for the human person there is natural and spiritual limitation. The healthy moral imagination breathes the clean air of the Creator's possibility, and yet is rooted in the sacramental reality of earthly creation. The confrontation here is with the absolute and undeniable final either/or. The call of faith can only be delayed for so long. The Clock ticks away and defiance hardens or dissipates. The Judge chimes in:

> I shout it to you, just like that woman who offered to sell Tarquinius a collection of books, and when he would not pay the price she demanded, she burned a third of the books and asked the same price; and when he again refused to pay the price she demanded, she burned the second third of the collection and asked the same price, until finally he did pay the original price for the last third.

> Choose despair, then, because despair itself is a choice, because one can doubt [tvivle] without choosing it, but one cannot despair [fortvivle] without choosing it.[192]

---

[191] Søren Kierkegaard, *The Sickness unto Death*, 40.
[192] Søren Kierkegaard, *Either/Or II*, 209.

8. *The Christian Vocation:*
Transparency Before God

Once self realizes the inherent despair of the immediate æsthetic and merely ethical existence an inner longing will probably take hold. The self begins to seek and search for The Absolute, not out of weakness or in defiance, but in a state of profound humility. The "search" for God begins transparently even if God is not explicitly acknowledged as a category of thought. What the human person truly yearns for is God's *presence*—selbstmitteilung, or the healing of the wound [gratia sanans] at the very heart of the human self; the despair of the self itself.

Seeing the dead ends of either scientific "objectivity," mundane rationality, or the diversions of culture, the person then has to try to become a self *before God*; and, *wants* to be that self. Having had a vision (through a glass darkly—1 Corinth 12:13) of of existence brsitling on the precipice of a dense chasm of darkness, the human self, instead of taking willful action, will then renounce self and then waits on God to reveal. The person is then opening to God's favor [hanan] and love. Life is then becoming more and more the discerning response to God, not the egoistic assertion of the self in the world.

> it turns out that there is one thing humans can do
> or fail to do, and that is to accept the fact that
> they can do nothing to acquire faith on their own.
> The one thing human beings can do to achieve
> salvation is to recognize that they can do nothing
> to achieve salvation. This recognition is essentially
> a recognition of sinfulness, an acceptance of the
> fact that we do not possess the Truth or the con-
> dition for gaining the Truth. If faith is 'the condi-
> tion' for having the Truth, then we could call the
> consciousness of sin the condition for the condi-
> tion.[193]

And so it is in the wisdom of the Scriptures: "Truly, truly, I say to you, unless a grain of wheat falls into the earth and dies, it remains alone; but if it dies, it bears much fruit. He who loves his

---

[193] C. Stephen Evans, *Kierkegaard: An Introduction*, 162.

life loses it, and he who hates his life in this world will keep it for eternal life" (John 12:24). To die to self and live for God is the most foundational (perhaps most difficult) movement of the spirit as well as the antithesis of the putrefying stench of lived despair; death in life.

> What, then, is depression? It is hysteria of the spirit. There comes a moment in a person's life when immediacy is ripe, so to speak, and when the spirit requires a higher form, when it wants to lay hold of itself as spirit. As immediate spirit, a person is bound up with all earthly life, and now spirit wants to gather itself together out of this dispersion, so to speak, and to transfigure itself in itself; the personality wants to become conscious in its eternal validity. If this does not happen, if the movement is halted, if it is repressed, then depression sets in.[194]

It is no trivial matter here—to be sure—to believe or not to believe in Christ. Being a matter of eternal life or death faith must be appropriated with the "most passionate inwardness," even if one misses the secure ground for rational belief.[195] The existential condition of the self existing with the sickness of self is only transcended through a continuous movement of resignation and faith. Resignation without faith is mere weakness and faith without resignation is brutal defiance.[196]

It is a choosing of one's Eternal Validity *before God*. This movement has its "Teleology within itself" and cannot be injected from the outside in. Only in Christ's mode of existence with its mediation of *"possibility and necessity"/"eternity and temporality"/"infinity and finitude"* is the divided-self overcome.[197] Kierkegaard states the truth more explicitly when he writes that: "The opposite of being in despair is to have faith."[198]

---

[194] Søren Kierkegaard, *Either/Or II*, 188-189.

[195] Søren Kierkegaard, *Concluding Unscientific Postscript to Philosophical Fragments*, 203.

[196] Søren Kierkegaard, *Either/Or II*, 57-67.

[197] *See* R. D. Laing, *The Divided Self* (New York: Pantheon Books, 1969).

[198] Søren Kierkegaard, *The Sickness unto Death*, 82.

The existing self [existerende] *before God* in this way, the individual can then properly discern particular actions, individual commitments, and live with the passionate freedom of a true disciple of Christ—instead of the passionless detachment of theory or law. This is an essentially higher ethic than any universal code can provide however sophisticated or authoritative in status. Again, it is a "Teleology within itself" to do so. A universal code can only speak universally. What is most important (esp. in the fractured communities of the present world) is, "what am I to do, and how am I to be, as an *individual*?" . . . "what does it mean to be human, to be born, to live and to die?" Kierkegaard's many important contributions to moral theology lie with the above existential questions. No less of an authority than Pope John Paul II writes in the papal encyclical *Fides et Ratio*:

> Christian philosophy therefore has two aspects. The first is subjective, in the sense that faith purifies reason. As a theological virtue, faith liberates reason from presumption, the typical temptation of the philosopher. Saint Paul, the Fathers of the Church and, closer to our own time, philosophers such as Pascal and Kierkegaard reproached such presumption. The philosopher who learns humility will also find courage to tackle questions which are difficult to resolve if the data of Revelation are ignored—for example, the problem of evil and suffering, the personal nature of God and the question of the meaning of life or, more directly, the radical metaphysical question, 'Why is there something rather than nothing?'

> The second aspect of Christian philosophy is objective, in the sense that it concerns content. Revelation clearly proposes certain truths which might never have been discovered by reason unaided, although they are not of themselves inaccessible to reason. Among these truths is the notion of a free and personal God who is the Creator of the world, a truth which has been so crucial for the development of philosophical thinking, especially the philosophy of being.

> There is also the reality of sin, as it appears in the
> light of faith, which helps to shape an adequate
> philosophical formulation of the problem of
> evil.[199]

For Kierkegaard, the life of the follower of Jesus requires absolute commitment in the *personal* depths of the subjective consciousness; that is, in contrast to the disengagement of scientific and philosophical abstraction. Disengagement is a process that abstracts the self from the self and makes subjective commitment difficult in the face of a world that demands radical choice; a world where one is facing an abyss of doubt and uncertainties. Once God arrests the person's will God cannot remain a concept vaguely acknowledged, but in no way integral to the person's experiences. God is approached, somehow, in a concrete revelation, in something tangible, neither as an angel or beast (á la Pascal).[200] The object of Revelation for the disciple of Christ is *The Incarnation of Christ*. Kierkegaard called *The Incarnation* event the "absolute paradox" because it seemingly reconciles the irreconcilable.

Christ is the logos ensarkos ['enfleshed' Logos]. He appears to us in the Divine Icognito—"who, though he was in the form of God, did not regard equality with God as something to be exploited, but emptied himself, taking the form of a slave, being born in human likeness" (Phil. 2: 6-7). Human history is here given absolute affirmation in this singular, vital event at the "fullness of time."[201] God comes as the *self-emptying love* [kenosis] of a slave [servant] for all. There is a hiddenness [krypsis] to God's way on earth.[202]

---

[199] John Paul II, *Fides et Ratio*, Vatican Translation (Boston: Pauline Books & Media, 1998), paragraph 76. Also, *see* Jack Mulder, *Kierkegaard and the Catholic Tradition: Conflict and Dialogue* (Indianapolis: Indiana University Press, 2010).

[200] *See* Blaise Pascal, *Pensées*, ed. Roger Ariew (Indianapolis, IN: Hackett Publishing Company, Inc., 2004). And, Nicholas Hammond, *Playing with Truth: Language and the Human Condition in Pascal's Pensées* (Oxford, UK: Clarendon Press, 1994), for further scholarly interpretation.

[201] Søren Kierkegaard, *Philosophical Crumbs* (Princeton, New Jersey: Princeton University Press, 1985), 1-71.

[202] *See* David R. Law, *Kierkegaard's Kenotic Christology* (Oxford, UK: Ox-ford University Press, 2013).

God's salvific economy of redemption from sin, known in *The Incarnation* of Christ, is received by faith. The authentic virtue of faith is *contemporaneous* with the *living spirit of God*. Faith is not a Dead Letter. Faith is the total commitment of self in faith. Faith is abandonment to God for the right reason, not just for its own sake. There *is* an object here to the relation. The religious believer *lets go* in faith in fulfillment of God's calling him or her. The Christian subject exists in humility (resignation) and "passionate inwardness" (faith).[203] The true calling of the individual who exists *before God* and in relation to Christ *in this way* is the true calling of the disciple or adherent in the modern world.

So to reiterate, universal moral codes alone do not resolve the moral and spiritual tensions at the crux of the human condition.[204] American philosopher William Barrett, in describing Kierkegaard's notion of the "suspension of the ethical" in *Fear and Trembling*, writes in *Irrational Man: A Study of Existential Philosophy*:

> such is the concreteness of existence that a situation may come under several rules at once, forcing us to choose outside any rule, and from inside ourselves. The most exhaustive ethical blueprint ever drawn up is the system of moral theology of the Catholic Church; and yet the Church has to supplement this by casuistry and the confessional.[205]

So too, Commandments are not negated. "By no means!" (Romans 3:31) The Law is fulfilled by subjectively existing without despair in relation to Christ. This is *the* Truth message of Christianity.[206]

To sum up on Kierkegaard; the religious existence possesses all the real thrill of a life or death struggle of eternal import. By

---

[203] *See* Søren Kierkegaard, *Concluding Unscientific Postscript to Philosophical Fragments*.

[204] *See* Søren Kierkegaard, *Fear and Trembling* (New York: Penguin Books, 1985), for Kierkegaard's oft-misunderstood "teleological suspension of the ethical."

[205] William Barrett, *Irrational Man: A Study in Existential Philosophy* (New York: Anchor Books, 1958), 168.

[206] Anthony Rudd, *Kierkegaard and the Limits of the Ethical* (Oxford: Oxford University Press, 1997), 140-173.

contrast everything else is spiritual constriction. Only in the "be-yond" of the "metaphysical dream" of Christianity and the *incarna-tional* reality of the sacramental world does the Christian imagina-tion or Spirit find its real freedom.

Kierkegaard died at an early age. He had spent the vast sum of his inheritance (he was one of the richer men in Copenhagen) on carriage rides in the country, the finer luxuries of life, and pub-lishing his own books. On the very day he withdrew the last bal-ance of his bank account he reputedly collapsed on the walk home and died soon thereafter. His life-long friend Emil Boehsen was the last to talk with him in the hospital. Kierkegaard died when he was only forty-two, November 11, 1855. In a moving letter by Søren's other close friend Hans Christian Andersen, Andersen describes the day of his funeral.

> Søren Kierkegaard was buried last Sunday, fol-lowing a service at the Church of Our Lady, where the parties concerned had done very little. The church pews were closed and the aisles unu-sually crowded. Ladies in red and blue hats were coming and going; ditto dogs with muzzles. At the grave-site itself there was a scandal: when the whole ceremony *there* was over (that is, when Tryde had cast earth upon the coffin), a son of a sister of the deceased stepped forward and de-nounced the fact that he had been buried in this fashion. He declared—and this was his point more or less—that Søren Kierkegaard had re-signed from our society, and therefore we ought not to bury him in accordance with our customs! I was not out there, but it was said to have been unpleasant. The newspapers say little about it. In last Thursday's number of *Fædrelandet* this nephew has published his speech along with some after-thoughts. To me the entire affair is a distorted picture of Søren K.: I don't understand it![207]

WE now turn to the subject of narrative arts in theological method, in particular, through the work of Southern Catholic nov-

---

[207] As quoted in Alistair Hannay, *Kierkegaard: A Biography*, 420.

elist Walker Percy. Percy (like Kierkegaard) understood the despair of what he called "modern malaise" in the present age (long after Kierkegaard wrote it) much better than most of his contemporaries. Moreover, Percy perfected an ideal craft or method of treating this persistent "sickness unto death." Tellingly, he begins his most well-known novel *The Moviegoer* with a quote in the heart of Kierkegaard's *The Sickness Unto Death*: "the specific character of despair is precisely this: it is unaware of being despair."[208]

This theme about despair and faith is in everything Percy did. Many of Percy's novels are exercises in the dawning consciousness of this very state of despair. And not just did he make concrete many of Kierkegaard's notions, or merely bring them up-to-date in the 20th Century context, Percy also made them more highly appealing through the poetic *comedia* of his wit, charm, imagination, prose.[209]

Or, as his close friend Shelby Foote tried to "needle" Percy once in a private letter (on the occasion of the novel *Lancelot* not selling as expected), "Dear Walker, Good to hear from you. It sounded to me like you had just the amount of despair in your soul to make you truly happy. Keep up the good work . . .".[210]

---

[208] Søren Kierkegaard, *The Sickness Unto Death*, 45.

[209] *See* Ralph C. Wood, *The Comedy of Redemption* (Notre Dame, IN: University of Notre Dame Press, 1988), for Percy's use of humor. *See* Percy's sardonic play on the name Ralph in *Lost in the Cosmos*: "You are Ralph to me and I am Walker to you, but you are not Ralph to you and I am not Walker to me. (Have you ever wondered why the Ralphs you know look as if they ought to be called Ralph and not Robert?)" Walker Percy, *Lost in the Cosmos* (New York: Farrar, Straus and Giroux, 1983), 107.

[210] Shelby Foote and Walker Percy, *The Correspondence of Shelby Foote & Walker Percy*, ed. Jay Tolson (New York: W. W. Norton & Company, 1997), 233.

CHAPTER III

WALKER PERCY AND THE MORAL IMAGINATION

TODAY is my thirtieth birthday and I sit on the ocean wave in the schoolyard and wait for Kate and think of nothing. Now in the thirty-first year of my dark pilgrimage on this earth and knowing less than I ever knew before, having only to recognize merde when I see it, having inherited no more from my father than a good nose for merde, for every species of shit that flies—my only talent—smelling merde from every quarter, living in fact in the very century of merde, the great shithouse of scientific humanism where needs are satisfied, everyone becomes anyone, a warm and creative person, and prospers like a dung beetle . . . men are dead, dead, dead; and the malaise has settled like a fall-out and what people really fear is not that the bomb will fall but that the bomb will not fall – on this my thirtieth birthday, I know nothing and there is nothing to do but fall prey to desire. Nothing remains but desire, and desire comes howling down Elysian Fields like a mistral. My search has been abandoned;

Binx Bolling, THE MOVIEGOER

Beware of people who think that everything is okay.

Walker Percy,
NOVEL-WRITING IN AN APOCALYPTIC TIME

God and not-god, getting under women's dresses and blowing your brains out. Whereas in fact my problem is how to live from one ordinary minute to the next on a Wednesday afternoon.

Walker Percy, THE SECOND COMING

1. *Walker Percy:*
Diagnosing the Modern Malaise

That struggle to enter the religious sphere will often seem the most interesting part of any story—that is, of an individual's spiritual quest in the world. However, many often will stop at this defiance. Often these characters are the most interesting of all; cautionary tales or antiheros, if you will, for those who live on the spiritual cusp of what it is to be human and who (in the end) go down in defeat.

The perennial archetype of the modern defiant character perhaps is Ivan Karamazov from Dostoevsky's Russian epic *The Brothers Karamazov.* Ivan, repulsed by history's terrible crimes, collects news accounts concerning barbaric violence against innocents. As Ivan relates, of "cutting the unborn child from the mother's womb, and tossing babies up in the air and catching them on the points of their bayonets before their mother's eyes."[211] Ivan discloses this morbid hobby to his pious brother Alyosha (a novice monk) in order to explain why he cannot countenance the god who permits these atrocities to occur. By a clean deduction Ivan can see that if God does not exist . . . then "all is lawful," he says.[212] The belief in a benevolent God, he thinks, is the only true sanction of moral conscience or final restraint against the sinful nature of man. In defiance against God and His world Ivan explains to Aloysha, "it's not God that I don't accept; only I most respectfully return him the ticket."[213]

Ivan thinks life is a curse, not a blessing. He asks Alyosha in blasphemous mockery, "Am I my brother's keeper?"[214] Believing thus, he detaches himself from all moral responsibility and indirectly allows his father to be murdered and his brother Dmitri to be wrongly accused of the crime of patricide. While the moral demands of conscience inescapably bear in upon the autonomy of

---

[211] Fyodor Dostoevsky, *The Brothers Karamazov*, trans. Constance Garnett (New York: The Modern Library, 1950), 283.

[212] Ibid., 313.

[213] Ibid., 291.

[214] "You are always harping upon it! What have I to do with it? Am I my brother Dmitri's keeper?" Ivan snapped irritably, but then he suddenly smiled bitterly. "Cain's answer about his murdered brother, wasn't it?" Ibid., 275.

his existence he has a nervous breakdown and ends up being haunted by hallucinations of the devil; presumably an alter ego.[215]

In what follows we will explore the work of American novelist Walker Percy with the intention of understanding the role of narrative arts in Catholic moral reflection; in much the same way as Dostoevsky above. Percy's narrative is an excellent way of seeing the fullness of human characters in relation, over time, in the form of philosophical novel-writing.[216]

Percy, originally trained in pathology, believed that fiction is, in fact, "scientific." Story-telling, as he understood it, is an indispensable form of knowledge through which the scientist or philosopher can diagnose the human condition. For Percy, science and art convey truths about reality. The object of science is the kind of truth attainable through the scientific method, whereas the object of the novelist is the truth of individual existence. As Percy wrote in a well-known statement:

> The great gap in human knowledge to which science cannot address itself is, to paraphrase Kierkegaard, nothing less than this: What it is like to be an individual, to be born, live, and die in the twentieth century. If we assume, consciously or unconsciously, that science can answer such questions, we will never be able to ask the questions, let alone answer them.[217]

For Percy, "the naming of the predicament of the self by art is its reversal. Hence the salvific effect of art. Through art, the predicament of self becomes not only speakable, *but* laughable."[218] By the deployment of narrative it is possible to "redeem the time" with *naming*, and therefore reversing, the malaises of modernity;

---

[215] Ibid., Book XI: IX. The devil. Ivan's nightmare.

[216] The definitive treatment of æsthetics as to Catholic Theology is the 7 volume opus of Hans Urs Von Balthasar, *The Glory of the Lord: A Theological Aesthetics*, 7 vols., eds. Joseph Fessio S.J. and John Riches. trans. Erasmo Leiva-Merikakis (San Francisco: Ignatius Press, 1982-1991).

[217] Walker Percy, "The State of the Novel: Dying Art Or New Science?" in *Signposts in a Strange Land*, ed. Patrick Samway (New York: Farrar, Straus and Giroux, 1991), 151.

[218] Walker Percy, *Lost in the Cosmos: The Last Self-Help Book* (New York: Farrar, Straus and Giroux, 1983), 121.

that is, through the communication of philosophical novel-writing. Naming the predicament of the (post)-modern self in relation to the traditional narratives of religion, or the fictional narratives of the novelist, provides the reader with perspectives necessary for better spiritual and/or moral discernment.

Before proceeding to the literature of Walker Percy it is important to understand some of the context of the cultural shifts that have radically altered the foundations of human consciousness in Western culture—esp. during the latter half of the twentieth century. The following broad description contextualizes Percy's "Christocentric" anthropology and, in turn, his theological approach toward novel-writing, morality and religion, in the contemporary world.

According to numerous cultural historians the end of the modern world's hope for unlimited progress is arguably datable to the *First World War*, where man fell upon man with such savagery that entire civilizations were irreversibly destroyed in the process.[219] Inevitably, throughout the twentieth century the traditional thoughts and customs of the Old World dissolved into a new blend of ideas called now, for lack of a better word, "postmodernism."[220]

In the postmodern world the total rejection of God (and Christian moral prescriptions) is no longer taboo.[221] Rather, the erosion of religious belief is rapidly becoming the norm.[222] For example, every culture has words that define it, essentially placing the denizens of the culture in relation to their symbolic worlds of

---

[219] Romano Guardini, *The End of the Modern World* (Wilmington, DE: ISI Books, 2001); Robert Nisbet, *The Present Age: Progress and Anarchy in Modern American* (Indianapolis, IN: Liberty Fund, 1988); and Erik von Kuehnelt-Leddhihn, *Leftism Revisited: From de Sade and Marx to Hitler and Pol Pot* (Washington, DC: Regnery Gateway, 1990), for a description of the devastations wrought by the war.

[220] *See* Jean-François Lyotard, *The Postmodern Condition: A Report on Knowledge*, trans. Geoff Bennington and Brian Massumi (Minneapolis: University of Minneapolis Press, 1984).

[221] *See* Kenneth J. Gergen, *The Saturated Self: Dilemmas of Identity in Contemporary Life* (New York: Basic Books, 1991).

[222] David Campbell and Robert Putnam, *American Grace: How Religion Divides and Unites Us* (New York: Simon & Schuster, 2010). This contemporary work has many relevant statistics concerning the decline of religious belief in America.

meaning. In the nineteenth century the words "individual, change, progress, reason, and freedom" influenced thought in ways that informed the West's sense of self and identity.[223] In the contemporary world the most significant words now include: "anxiety, alienation and despair."[224] Social historian Robert Nisbet states it well in *The Quest for Community*:

> The historic triumph of secularism and individualism has presented a set of problems that loom large in contemporary thought. The modern release of the individual from traditional class, religion, and kinship has made him free; but, on the testimony of innumerable works of our age, this freedom is accompanied not by a sense of creative release but by a sense of disenchantment and alienation. The alienation of man from historic moral certitudes has been followed by the sense of man's alienation from fellow man . . . 'The natural state of twentieth-century man,' the protagonist of a recent novel declares, 'is anxiety'. At the very least, anxiety has become a major state in contemporary imaginative writing. Underlying many works is the conception of man as lost, baffled, and obsessed.[225]

---

[223] Robert Nisbet, *The Quest for Community: A Study in the Ethics of Order and Freedom* (Wilmington, DE: ISI Books, 2010), 1-2.

[224] Percy's immediate family had seen modern war as well as the Civil War. His brother had fought with Jack Kennedy in WWII. Percy explains in an interview: "I was always fascinated by the excitement of war. The worst thing that happened was that my two brothers went into the army. They went into the most dangerous branches of the service. One brother flew a bomber, the other brother was on the Pacific, on a torpedo boat. He was on the same squadron as Jack Kennedy, he was Kennedy's friend, he saw Kennedy's boat get shot. And there I was like Castorp in The Magic Mountain, sitting on a mountain up in New York state." Walker Percy, *More Conversations with Walker Percy*, eds. Lewis A. Lawson and Victor A Kramer (Jackson, Miss: University Press of Mississippi, 1993), 81. *See* Thomas Mann, *The Magic Mountain* [Der Zauberberg], trans. H. T. Lowe-Porter (New York: Alfred A. Knopf, 1967 [1924]).

[225] Robert Nisbet, *The Quest for Community*, 7-8.

Like Nisbet, Percy believed that for the deracinated secular self of modernity community and social relationships are normally considered contingent, relative to the individual, and non-essential to one's identity. Instead of being bound to the particularities of time and place, the self is characteristically dislocated and detached from traditional community, standing over and against all traditions and social relationships as self-defining judge.[226] The position of the detached and autonomous individual in a culture of weakening religious ties and constraints is, de facto, that of the moral relativist.

The pervasive culture of moral relativism is clearly demonstrated in the controversial "mystery passage" of the *Casey* decision written by Supreme Court Justice Anthony Kennedy and now enshrined in the American legal system. It states: "At the heart of liberty is the right to define one's own concept of existence, of meaning, of the universe, and of the mystery of human life."[227] The implicit idea of the above statement is that the self is independent of all social constraints, that is, outside of the legal code itself. In other words, truth is relative to the individual.

Moreover, in part due to the all-encompassing authority of the scientific method to determine what truth is, the present day self is often experienced as "Cartesian" ego; an objective consciousness independent of the world in which he or she is situated.[228] The empirical method is indispensable to the natural sciences, but it remains wholly inadequate in terms of moral qualifications. Religious traditions are necessary constituents of a healthy moral

---

[226] Alasdair MacIntyre, *After Virtue: A Study in Moral Theory*, for the now classic description of moral philosophy's epistemological failure once divorced from tradition and community.

[227] Quoted in Gerard V. Bradley, *A Student's Guide to the Study of Law* (Wilmington, DE: ISI Books, 2006), 32-33. And, Russell Hittinger, *The First Grace: Rediscovering the Natural Law in a Post-Christian World* (Wilmington, DE: ISI Books, 2003), xxx-xxxii.

[228] Percy satirized and rebuked the all-encompassing scientific pretension to explain away "everything," esp. in such deceptive popularizing accounts as Carl Sagan, *Cosmos* (New York: Ballantine Books, 1980). "Carl Sagan explains everything without God, from the most distant galaxies to our own individual nastiness, which is caused by our reptilian brains." Walker Percy, "Novel-Writing in an Apocalyptic Time," in *Signposts in a Strange Land*, 159.

culture.[229] Although the presumption of a "view from nowhere" allows for a pretense of objectivity, in reality, the self remains essentially "being-in-the-world," to use Martin Heidegger's conceptual term.[230] The individual is not, by nature, outside of the world, and therefore, must necessarily reason from within the moral traditions and historical religions of the world.[231]

When society is composed of atomized individuals aspiring to transcendence through objective scientific consciousness, the world becomes a place where, in the absence of God and Christianity, alienation and anxiety will most likely take root, creating a "malaise."[232] Catholic philosopher Charles Taylor describes the characteristics of the malaise thus: "**1)** the sense of fragility of meaning, the search for overarching significance; **2)** the felt flatness of our attempts to solemnize the crucial moments of passage in our lives; **3)** the utter flatness, emptiness of the ordinary."[233]

Like Percy, Taylor believes that the secular self is no longer "enchanted" with superstitious beliefs or constrained by traditional communities. However, "exclusive humanism" has failed to fill the void where religion and community once flourished.[234] The shift from the pre-modern to the modern, and then, from the modern to the postmodern world, profoundly impacted the consciousness of the human person. With the technological advances of the scientific age and the rapid uprooting of traditional community in the twentieth century, the post-"modern self" has fundamentally reimagined what it means to be human.[235]

---

[229] Russell Kirk, "Civilization without Religion?" in Russell Kirk, *Redeeming the Time*, ed. Jeffrey O. Nelson (Wilmington, DE: ISI Books, 2006), 3-16. The phrase "redeem the time" is in T. S. Eliot: ". . . the fountain sprang up and the bird sang down—Redeem the time, redeem the dream . . ."

[230] *See* Martin Heidegger, *Being and Time* (New York: Harper & Row Publishers, 1962), Division I.

[231] *See* Donald W. Livingston, *Philosophical Melancholy and Delirium: Hume's Pathology of Philosophy* (Chicago: University of Chicago Press, 1998), 23-35, for an excellent account of the resulting state of mind when the philosophical act is divorced from tradition and custom.

[232] *See* Charles Taylor, *A Secular Age* (Cambridge, MA: Harvard University Press, 2007), Chapter 8.

[233] Ibid., 309.

[234] Ibid., Part V, 539-728.

[235] For the rarified academic debate on the meaning of science vs. religion, *see* the influential classic work on "all-encompassing science"—Edward O.

By contrast, the pre-modern world was characterized by an essentially transcendent "frame" of unified religious meaning and the richness of cultural community. The vision of the great "chain of being" dominated the metaphysical imagination.[236] According to Taylor, for the pre-modern understanding the world was seen in terms of an all-encompassing *hierarchy*, that is, a total hierarchy encompassing everything, from the most insignificant speck of dust, to the invisible world of angelic spirits. Community, kinship and religion, were the indissoluble bulwarks of unbreakable ties and loyalties. For the most part, the pre-modern self did not experience its individuality as an isolated ego, but, rather, was immersed in a greater whole where everything and everyone seeks its proper place in creation. In fact, there was almost an over-abundance of cultural meaning as such, meaning rooted in the inescapable orderings of society, the pageantry of religious festival and the integral reality of a transcendent God.[237]

Given the above social changes, contemporary Catholic moral theology ought to further reassess the way in which, not only it addresses moral problems, but also the relevance of the discipline to the contemporary individual. Ultimately, the contemporary individual is the moral agent *who* will have to make the choices. If the Catholic Church does not continue to address the culture as it currently is, the moral message may no longer be heard by the majority of Catholics. It is common knowledge that many *churchgoers* continue to "go through the motions," but do not see the relevance of religion to their daily lives. In particular, when confronted with the plurality of angles and opinions in the current culture, many are at a loss.[238]

The contemporary individual, not seeing the relevance of religion, will not (and cannot) remain in possession of his or her self when tested in the secularizing atmosphere of the Western World—so that moral theologians . . .

Wilson, *Consilience: The Unity of Knowledge* (New York: Vintage Books, 1998), as well as the rebuttal to it in Wendell Berry, *Life is a Miracle: An Essay Against Modern Superstition* (Berkely, CA: Counterpoint, 2000).

[236] Arthur O. Lovejoy, *The Great Chain of Being: A Study of the History of an Idea* (New York: Harper and Brothers, 1960), for a description of the Classical and Mediæval cosmology.

[237] Charles Taylor, *A Secular Age*, "Chapter 1," 25-89.

[238] *See* David Campbell and Robert Putnam, *American Grace: How Religion Divides and Unites Us.*

must therefore exercise careful discernment in the context of today's prevalently scientific and technical culture, exposed as it is to the dangers of relativism, pragmatism and positivism. From a theological viewpoint, moral principles are not dependent upon the historical moment in which they are discovered.[239]

In essence, the present cultural climate is working more to dissolve the inherited historical beliefs of previous generations than to nurture them.[240] The work of Walker Percy *can* contribute to the moral theology of the Church, both in understanding the predicament of the current milieux, but also, through creatively embracing the defining marks of modern consciousness, and then, refashioning them in a way that *will* improve the moral discernment of the reader.

Concerning the narrative arts and the discernment of the reader, Catholic moral theologian Patricia Lamoureux writes:

art affects us indirectly through the imagination because God's grace slips into our lives obliquely, often without our knowledge. Thus, the arts inform the moral life, not by providing direct lessons about moral principles or values, but indirectly and gracefully by helping people discern, through a dress rehearsal, the moral quality of certain ways of living. A good story invites us into the lives of its characters through the common humanity they exhibit, pulling us beyond our range of possibilities, enabling us to imagine ourselves in their roles, emphatically bridging the gap to others, and sharpening our capacity to discern what it means to live the good life.[241]

---

[239] John Paul II, *Veritatis Splendor*, encyclical letter, Vatican Translation (Boston: Pauline Books & Media, 2003), paragraph 112.

[240] Russell Kirk, *Redeeming the Time*, 3-16.

[241] Patricia Lamoureux, "Introduction," in *Seeking Goodness and Beauty: The Use of the Arts in Theological Ethics*, ed. Patricia Lamoureux and Kevin J. O'Neil (Rowman & Littlefield Publishers, 2004), 7.

Percy's re-imaging of moral and religious problems in the form of narrative story-telling is *one* way of helping the reader who is stuck in the "modern malaise" discern important moral lessons and once again re-imagine his or her self in Christian terms. Although the mode of Percy's craft was (and is) more appropriate for some individuals than others, his method of novel-writing continues to hold merit for its place in "Catholic" arts and contemporary moral theology in general.

2. *Walker Percy:*
Philosophical Novel-Writing

Walker Percy was an American novelist and essayist who wrote during the latter half of the twentieth-century. Percy, alongside Flannery O'Connor, was arguably the most reputable American Catholic novelist of the time.[242] He was an innovator of American fiction based on religious themes. He was descended of a long-line of Southern literary figures and important statesmen.[243]

Percy thought of himself as the proverbial canary in a coal mine. The canary, being lowered down a mine shaft in a cage with rowdy miners, smells something noxious and begins to cough and wheeze. Meanwhile, the miners, joking and laughing, do not realize *the canary is sick*.[244] Percy believed he was onto something important that the rest of society was missing. Although the engine of material progress continues largely undeterred to this day, Percy

---

[242] Paul Giles, *American Catholic Arts and Fictions: Culture, Ideology, Aesthetics* (Cambridge, UK: Cambridge University Press, 1992), 353-393. O'Conner wrote only two full-length novels before her life was cut short by Lupus. *See* Flannery O'Conner, *Wise Blood* (New York: Farrar, Straus and Giroux, 1949) & Flannery O'Conner, *The Violent Bear It Away* (New York: Farrar. Straus and Giroux, 1960).

[243] *See* William Alexander Percy, *Lanterns on the Levee: Recollections of a Planter's Son* (Baton Rouge: Louisiana State University Press, 1941). Also, for more background on the history of the Percy clan *see* Bertram Wyatt-Brown, *The House of Percy: Honor, Melancholy, and Imagination in a Southern Family* (New York: Oxford University Press, 1994).

[244] Walker Percy, *Signposts in a Strange Land*, 153-167. This proverbial analogy was also used and thus popularized by Friedrich Nietzsche in the 19th century.

nevertheless sensed something spiritually *rotten* beneath the surface; something, in fact, fundamentally dangerous. [245] According to Percy, the culture of dizzying technological advance and the spirit of "scientism" triumphant are deeply deficient in moral terms.

Percy's novels, in terms of morality, are deadly serious. However, in terms of artistic intent, they are essentially humorous. He had a unique gift for releasing cultural tension through the naming of the absurdities of the present age, while at the same time driving home a message of moral and religious significance.[246] Novel writing, he believed, is an important opportunity to create a community between novelist and reader, that is, where no such community existed. In a recent study of Percy from John Desmond:

> In his novels he [Percy] explored and satirized
> what he saw as the debilitated state of modern
> American culture, trapped in its self-absorbed in-
> dividualism, consumerism, violence, racism, and a
> general spiritual anomie. With characteristic pro-
> bity, he saw this debilitated state as a sign of the
> death throes of the collapse of a Western culture
> dominated by scientific humanism.[247]

Percy was a practicing Catholic. He was an essentially religious writer. His novels are fundamentally theological. Percy's end in writing was both to lift the reader's experience of alienation and,

---

[245] Two strong critiques against the idolatry of *techné* and 'The Machine' *see* José Ortega y Gasset, *The Revolt of the Masses*, trans. anon (New York: W. W. Norton & Company, 1932). And, "29. The Dynamo and The Virgin," in Henry Adams, *The Education of Henry Adams*, eds., Edward Chalfant & Edick Wright (Boston, MA: Massachusetts Historical Society, 2007).

[246] Percy's novels (esp. the later ones) were also somewhat "explicit." Caution to readers who do not care for serious modern fiction and are looking rather solely for light entertainment or popular novels. He was writing at a time when highly explicit novels *á la* the vein of James Joyce were being written to wide acclaim. *See* for example Percy's contemporary, Thomas Pynchon, *Gravity's Rainbow* (New York: Penguin Books, 2006) *1974 National Book Award Winner. Pynchon here is over-the-top graphic in his explicit depictions of sadism in war. Also, James Joyce, *Ulysses* (New York: Vintage Classics, 1990), for the classic comparison.

[247] John F. Desmond, *Walker Percy's Search for Community* (Athens, GA: The University of Georgia Press, 2004), 6.

like a medical surgeon perhaps, to diagnose and treat his or her experiences of anxiety, despair, depression, fear, boredom, loneliness, ennui, *anomie* or malaise. His books provide occasions for existential renewal.

Percy spoke from his own experience. A convert to Catholicism, he had spent the first stage of his life believing in *scientific humanism* alone. "Struck-down" with tuberculosis while still in medical school, Percy, now confronted with the prospect of an early death, sensed the basic inadequacy of the scientific method. He was highly attracted to the elegance of science, but nevertheless realized that science alone cannot provide the answers to life's ultimate questions.[248] Bed-ridden with illness, he devoted most of his time to reading.[249] In desperation he turned to the works of the existentialists (widely read back then) seeking consolation and answers. Through digesting the work of Søren Kierkegaard, in particular, he came to see the human condition in a new way.[250]

Percy realized, with Kierkegaard, that although science can speak of universal truth, *sub specie æternitatis*, the individual, existing before God, is incommunicable in scientific terms.[251] Percy came to see that scientific humanism, when treated as religion, is bankrupt.[252] Many of Percy's most important insights are anthropologi-

---

[248] Paul Elie, *The Life You Save May Be Your Own: An American Pilgrimage* (New York: Farrar, Straus and Giroux, 2003), 156-161.

[249] Walker Percy, "From Facts to Fiction," in Walker Percy, *Signposts in a Strange Land*, 187.

[250] Percy read novels too. Some of his stated influences include: Albert Camus, *The Stranger* (New York: Vintage Books, 1946); Franz Kafka, *The Metamorphosis* (New York: Bantam Classic, 1912); Fyodor Dostoyevsky, *Notes from the Underground* (New York: Signet Classics,1961); James Joyce, *A Portrait of the Artist as a Young Man* (New York: Penguin Books, 2003); and Jean-Paul Sarte, *Nausea*, trans. Lloyd Alexander (New York: New Directions Publishing, 2007). Percy's family tradition was also very influenced by William Faulkner (who Walker's Uncle Will knew on a personal basis and who played tennis once on their tennis courts—drunk—when Walker was a kid) as well as the deep Southern Stoicism of Marcus Aurelius and the romances of Sir Walter Scott. *See* Marcus Aurelius, *Meditations*, trans. Martin Hammond (New York: Penguin Books, 2006).

[251] Søren Kierkegaard, *Concluding Unscientific Postscript to Philosophical Fragments*, trans. Howard V. Hong and Edna H. Hong (Princeton, NJ: Princeton University Press, 1992), 217.

[252] *See* Shelby Foote and Walker Percy, *The Correspondence of Shelby Foote & Walker Percy*, ed. Jay Tolson (New York: W. W. Norton & Company,

cal in nature or religious in character. Percy saw the human person in terms of a "sovereign wayfarer" [homo viator], seeking his or her true homeland.[253] However, many today have tragically lost their way, that is, as pilgrims in a world of gratuitous mystery. Instead, they have settled for lives of theory and consumption, disinheriting themselves from God in the process. For Percy, with so many people sunk in the malaises of modernity, humanity is losing its direction in an essential manner.[254]

The fundamental objective of Percy's writing was to diagnose and heal. Percy was trained as a pathologist and early on realized that the only way to address the individual, *qua individual,* is through narrative arts. So, whereas the scientist can speak of universal empirical facts, it remains the task of the artist to recover the singular self from disintegration. In the fragmented societies of the contemporary world, the artist possesses one of the few modes of creating communities where authentic religious communication is possible. It was Percy's belief that novels ought to be deployed as instruments for the purpose of overcoming the alienation of the "modern malaise"; that is, through an appeal to the moral imagination. Regarding his fundamental philosophy of novel-writing, Percy wrote:

> The wrong questions are being asked. The proper question is not whether God has died or been superseded by the urban-political complex. The question is not whether the Good News is no longer relevant, but rather whether it is possible that man is presently undergoing a tempestuous restructuring of his consciousness which does not presently allow him to take account of the Good News. For what has happened is not merely the technological transformation of the world but something psychologically even more portentous. It is the absorption by the layman not of the scientific method but rather of the magical aura of

---

1997). These letters are indispensable in grasping how Percy thought privately. Foote was his close friend and intellectual compatriot even while they had disagreed on many things.

[253] *See* Gabriel Marcel, *Homo Viator: Introduction to a Metaphysics of Hope,* trans. Emma Craufurd (New York: Harper Torchbook, 1962 [1951]).

[254] Walker Percy, *Signposts in a Strange Land,* 204-221.

science, whose credentials he accepts for all sectors of reality. Thus in the lay culture of scientific society nothing is easier than to fall prey to a kind of seduction which sunders one's very self from itself into an all-transcending "objective" consciousness and a consumer-self with a list of "needs" to be satisfied. It is this monstrous bifurcation of man into angelic and bestial components against which old theologies must be weighed before new theologies are erected. Such a man could not take account of God, the devil, and the angels if they were standing before him, because he has already peopled the universe with his own hierarchies. When the novelist writes of a man "coming to himself" through some such catalyst as catastrophe or ordeal, he may be offering obscure testimony to a gross disorder of consciousness and to the need of recovering oneself as neither angel nor organism but as wayfaring creature somewhere in between.

And so the ultimate question is what is the term or historical outcome of this ongoing schism of consciousness. Which will be more relevant to the "lost" man of tomorrow who knows he is lost: the new theology of politics or the renewed old theology of Good News?[255]

The narrative form permits the singular philosophical statement of existential truth in a way that the physical and human sciences cannot. Moreover, art, once inseparable from the religious cult, has now been elevated to one of two remaining means of successfully transcending the imminence of the world (the other being science proper). Percy writes: "art and science, one the study of secondary causes, the other the ornamental handmaiden of rite

---

[255] Walker Percy, "Notes For A Novel About The End of The World," in *The Message in the Bottle: How Queer Man Is, How Queer Language Is, And What One Has to Do with the Other* (New York: Farrar, Straus and Giroux, 1975), 113.

and religion, were seized upon and elevated to royal highroads of transcendence in their own right."[256]

What fascinated Percy most is the peculiar state of human consciousness, where the self transcends the world through symbolic means, but then, must re-enter the world that he or she transcended. He named the phenomenon a *psychic law of gravity* and believed it to be, in fact, one of the defining marks of the self's experience in the modern world.[257]

In *Lost in the Cosmos* Percy explains that the self, more or less successfully, enters a symbolic "orbit" of the empirical world, that is, through art or science, but then, falls prey to estrangement. Upon re-entry the destabilized self seeks to reestablish connections with the banality of "everydayness," often unsuccessfully through such maladies as "neurosis, psychosis, alcoholism, drug addiction, epilepsy, florid sexual behavior, solitariness, depression, violence, and suicide."[258] The degree of the malady is directly proportionate to the "height" and success of the orbit.

For example, Percy understood Kierkegaard's description of the polarities and imbalances of the self to be paradigmatic of contemporary consciousness. In much of his work, Percy deployed Kierkegaard's theoretical framework in order to understand the famous "burn-outs" of artistic temperaments who manically ascend with possibility in the realm of infinitude. Similarly, Percy used Kierkegaard's ideas in order to diagnose the immanent flatness of the modern malaise, where limitation becomes suffocating with the near impossibility of transcendence through religious community.[259]

---

[256] Walker Percy, *Lost in the Cosmos*, 141.

[257] Ibid., 142.

[258] Ibid., 142.

[259] *See* Søren Kierkegaard, *The Sickness unto Death* (Princeton, NJ: Princeton University Press, 1985).

3. *Walker Percy:*
The Philosophical Novel and Moral Discernment

Most of Percy's novels are explorations to some degree of the above social or psychological phenomena.[260] In the twilight of religious communion, the main character is left searching for meaning, and the self is left without an effective anchor. Many of Percy's protagonists grow unstable searching for meaning in the disintegrated malaise of modernity and often become *defiant.*

In his third novel *Love in the Ruins* (1971), Percy presents an apocalyptic future where the human spirit is torn asunder in the absence of God and religion. The protagonist, Dr. Thomas More, is an ambitious, while somewhat delusional, psychiatrist.[261] In the book More makes a scientific discovery that will, he thinks, allow him to diagnose and fix the spiritual ailments of the world. Furthermore, Dr. More is a lapsed Catholic. He repeatedly diagnoses himself (and everyone else for that matter) as suffering from what he calls "angelism-bestialism."[262] Dr. More believes that the center is not holding. The human polarity is not being held together

---

[260] For our purposes here only two of Percy's six novels are looked at in any great depth. *The Moviegoer* (1961) is representative of Percy's earlier fiction and *Love in the Ruins* (1971) is an exemplar of his later period shift in focus, style, form, content. Percy's other novels are indispensable too and must be read in order to understand the whole corpus of literature in its entirety. They are as follows: Walker Percy, *The Last Gentleman* (London: Eyre and Spottiswoode, 1967); Walker Percy, *Lancelot* (London: Secker and Warburg, 1977); Walker Percy, *The Second Coming* (London: Secker and Warburg, 1981); & Walker Percy, *The Thanatos Syndrome* (London: Andre Deutsch, 1987). A better recent critical study of Percy (among many other somewhat "fawning" uncritical ones) is Kieran Quinlan, *Walker Percy, The Last Catholic Novelist* (Baton Rouge, LA: Louisiana State University Press, 1996). Quinlan does further what is being done here in analyzing Percy's other novels.

[261] Dr. More is modeled after, in part, the Don in Mozart's *Don Giovanni.* *See* Wolfgang Amadeus Mozart, *Mozart's Don Giovanni*, trans. Ellen H. Bleiler (New York: Dover Publications, 1964).

[262] Walker Percy, *Love in the Ruins: The Adventures of a Bad Catholic at a Time Near the End of the World* (New York: Picador, 1971), 208-218. In 1972 *Love in the Ruins* was a finalist for the National Book Award. Flannery O'Conner won that year (1972) for *The Compete Stories. See* Flannery O'Conner, *The Complete Stories* (New York: Farrar, Straus and Giroux, 1971).

through the culture in which he lives. After a fit of delusional inspiration he declares:

> the world is broken, sundered, busted down the
> middle, self ripped from self and man pasted back
> together as mythical monster, half angel, half
> beast, but no man . . . Some day a man will walk
> into my office as a ghost or beast or ghost-beast
> and walk out as a man, which is to say sovereign
> wanderer, lordly exile, worker and waiter and
> watcher.

> . . . Knowing, not women, said Sir Thomas, is
> man's happiness.

> . . . Learning and wisdom are receding nowadays.
> The young, who already know everything, hate
> science, bomb laboratories, kill professors, burn
> libraries.

> Already the monks are beginning to collect books
> again.

> . . . Poor as I am, I feel like God's spoiled child. I
> am Robinson Crusoe set down on the best possi-
> ble island with a library, a laboratory, a lusty Pres-
> byterian wife, a cozy tree house, an idea, and all
> the time in the world.[263]

At another point in the novel, Dr. More describes a revealing
experience with the Roman Catholic Church. On vacation with his
wife in a nameless place of no distinction, Dr. More leaves his wife,
gets on the freeway and finds a lonely out of the way church. Percy
writes:

> Here off I-51 I touched the thread in the laby-
> rinth, and the priest announced the turkey raffle
> and Wednesday bingo and preached the Gospel
> and fed me Christ—back to the motel then, ex-

---

[263] Ibid., 382-383.

hilarated by—what? By eating Christ or by the secret discovery of the singular thread in this the
unlikeliest of places, this geometry of Holiday
Inns and interstates? Back to lie with Doris . . .
"My God, what is it you do in Church?" . . . What
she didn't understand, she being spiritual and seeing religion as spirit, was that it took religion to
save me from the spirit world, from orbiting the
earth like Lucifer and the angels, that it took
nothing less than touching off the misty interstates and eating Christ himself to make me mortal again and let me inhabit my own flesh and love
her in the morning.[264]

Dr. More needs the historical "coordinate" of Christ to locate
himself, and therefore, get-aholt-of-his-self. When he becomes a
lapsed Catholic in the novel, he falls, by his own admission, into a
"disorderly" life.[265] Percy viewed the modern self as the *ghost who
haunts the cosmos*, knowing everything about the material world, but
little to nothing about himself.[266] The modern self has transcended
everything with science, everything but the individual self, the very
center of the subject's universe. The self is unspeakable because,
although it is possible to call someone else by name, how do you
name the "namer"? In other words:

> the self of the sign-user can never be grasped, be-
> cause, once the self locates itself at the dead cen-
> ter of its world, there is no signified to which a
> signifier can be joined to make a sign. The self has
> no sign of itself. No signifier applies. All signifiers
> apply equally . . .

> For me, certain signifiers fit you, and not others.
> For me, all signifiers fit me, one as well as another.
> I am rascal, hero, craven, brave, treacherous, loyal,
> at once the secret hero and asshole of the Cos-
> mos. You are not a sign in your world. Unlike

---

[264] Ibid., 254.

[265] Ibid., 6-30.

[266] Walker Percy, *Lost in the Cosmos: The Last Self-Help Book*, 5-13.

other signifiers in your world which form more or
less stable units with the perceived world-things
they signify, the signifier of yourself is mobile,
freed up, and operating on a sliding semiotic scale
from - $\propto$ to - $\propto$.

The signified of the self is semiotically loose and
caroms around the Cosmos like an unguided mis-
sile.[267]

In Percy's most well-known novel *The Moviegoer* (1961) the
protagonist Jack "Binx" Bolling practices what he calls, after the
spirituality of Thérèse of Lisieux, *the Little Way*.[268] Throughout the
novel, Bolling tries to self-consciously create a life of mundane
simplicity for the purpose of detaching himself from the world.[269]

---

[267] Ibid., 107. Walker was deeply influenced by the semiotics of Charles
Saunders Peirce. *See* C. S. Peirce, *Philosophical Writings of Peirce*, ed. Justus
Buchler (New York: Dover Publications, 1955), & *See* Kenneth Laine
Ketner and Walker Percy, *A Thief of Peirce: The Letters of Kenneth Laine Ket-
ner and Walker Percy*, ed. Patrick H. Samway, S.J. (Jackson, Miss: University
Press of Mississippi, 1995), for Percy's thoughts about semiotics. A more
recent "reductionist" account, contradicting Percy's religious understand-
ing of language, is literary figure Tom Wolfe, *Kingdom of Speech* (New York:
Little, Brown and Company, 2016).

[268] *See* Thérèse of Lisieux, *The Autobiography of Thérèse of Lisieux: The Story of
a Soul*, trans. John Beevers (New York: Doubleday, 2001 [1957]).

[269] Walker Percy, *The Moviegoer* (New York: Vintage Books, 1998 [1961]),
135-136. *The Moviegoer won the 1962 *National Book Award* over such
larger-than-life novels published that same year—like J.D. Salinger, *Franny and Zooey* (New York: Little, Brown and Company, 1961); Joseph Heller, *Catch-22* (New York: Simon & Schuster, 1961); & Richard Yates, *Revolutionary Road* (New York: Vintage Books, 1961). Most of Percy's other
novels were finalists for the "much-coveted" *National Book Award*: *The
Last Gentleman* in 1967, *Love in the Ruins* in 1972, and *The Second Coming* in
1981/82. Percy served as a judge for many years. In 1967 *The Last Gentleman* lost to Bernard Malamud, *The Fixer* (New York: Farrar, Straus and
Giroux, 1966), and was a runner-up with other notable novels like Louis
Auchincloss, *The Embezzler* (Boston: Houghton Mifflin Company, 1966).
The award can be said to have established Percy's reputation as an author
as well as acting as a continuing influence on the type of audience he
sought to reach. The awards don't have nearly as much integrity anymore
by most intelligent critical standards. Paul Fussell writes that: "Further

He fears losing his sense of wonder; a wonder he thinks sets him apart. Having exhausted his search for ultimate answers, or *transcendence* through the "vertical" reading of scientific texts, he begins what he calls the "horizontal search." Bolling is searching, not for more factual knowledge, but rather, for a new type of existence. In the beginning of the novel Bolling is not entirely sure what he is looking for himself, finding consolation mostly in going to the movies, making money, and having fleeting romances with his secretaries.[270] He thinks to himself in quiet despair (in classic Sartean fashion),

> Beauty is a whore.
>
> Money is a better god than beauty.
>
> Money is a good counterpoise to beauty. Beauty, the quest of beauty alone, is a whoredom. Ten years ago I pursued beauty and gave no thought to money. I listened to the lovely tunes of Mahler and felt a sickness in my very soul Now I pursue money and on the whole feel better.[271]

---

evidence of prole-drift in the book world is the replacement of the National Book Awards by the American Book Awards, so cunningly similar in name, so totally different in import. Where the National Book Awards used to signal critical merit, being determined by disinterested and intellectually impressive judges, the American simulacra, determined now by publishers and editors, advertising and merchandising people and bookstore employees, recognize not a book's excellence but its popularity and sales potential." Paul Fussell, *Class*, 175. Or, Shelby Foote here, "The thing has come full circle from the days when the Book Award was a sort of protest against lousy choices by the Pulitzers." Shelby Foote and Walker Percy, *The Correspondence of Shelby Foote & Walker Percy*, 174.

[270] The movies mentioned in *The Moviegoer* are all Golden Age of Hollywood features or B-movies. Here is an exhaustive list of the movies in the novel: *All Quiet on the Western Front* (1930), *The Third Man* (1949), *Stagecoach* (1939), *Panic in the Streets* (1950), *It Happened One Night* (1934), *Red River* (1948), *Holiday* (1938, with Cary Grant not Joseph Cotton), *The Oxbow Incident* (1943), *Dark Waters* (1944), *The Young Philadelphians* (1959), *Fort Dobbs* (1958), & *The Killers* (1946).

[271] Walker Percy, *The Moviegoer*, 196.

Throughout the course of the novel most of Bolling's inner dialogue is composed of critical examinations of the people who come in and out of his life. He sees the signs of despair others do not and therefore he is all the more closer to breaking out of its spell himself.[272] Toward the beginning of *The Moviegoer* he declares the nature of his search:

> What is the nature of the search? you ask. The search is what anyone would undertake if he were not sunk in the everydayness of his own life. This morning, for example, I felt as if I had come to myself on a strange island. And what does a castaway do? Why, he pokes around the neighborhood and he doesn't miss a trick. To become aware of the possibility of the search is to be onto something. Not to be onto something is to be in despair.[273]

What sort of tricks are Binx after? First of all, he looks for signs. What kind of signs? Percy explains in an essay "Novel-writing in an Apocalyptic Time":

> A sign of what? A sign that things have gotten very queer without anyone seeming to notice it, that sane people seem to him crazy, and crazy people sometimes look knowledgeable—a little like the movie *The Body Snatchers*, where everybody looks and acts normal, except that they are not—but no one notices,[274]

---

[272] It rarely is, but *The Moviegoer* can be said to be written in the "spirit" of the more well-known *Catcher in the Rye*. *See* J. D. Salinger, *The Catcher in the Rye* (New York: Little, Brown and Company, 1945). Bolling's attitude is very similar to Holden Caulfield's calling everyone "phony," et cetera. There are also some similarities with Proust, although Percy didn't like him or read *In Search of Lost Time* until long after *The Moviegoer*. *See* Marcel Proust, *Swann's Way: Remembrance of Things Past* (New York: Vintage International, 1989).

[273] Walker Percy, *The Moviegoer*, 13.

[274] Walker Percy, "Novel-Writing in an Apocalyptic Time," in Walker Percy, *Signposts in a Strange Land*, 155-156.

A recurring theme in Percy's writing is that the Jewish people are a sign that cannot be subsumed in the present scientific age. Somehow, in some way, the Jews are of key import for our salvation. In other words, "salvation comes from the Jews" (John 4:19-22), or, "the Jews are entrusted with the oracles of God" (Romans 3:2). Percy liked to show that it is the Jews alone who have a unique place in history; e.g. that cannot be subsumed under general scientific categories. They are a particular people and have a particular story of unique importance. Percy remarks in an essay:

> Where are the Hittites? Why does no one find it remarkable that in most world cities today there are Jews but not one single Hittite even though the Hittites had a great flourishing civilization while the Jews nearby were a weak and obscure people? When one meets a Jew in New York or New Orleans or Paris or Melbourne, it is remarkable that no one considers the event remarkable. What are they doing here? But it is even more remarkable to wonder, if there are Jews here, why are there no Hittites here? Where are the Hittites? Show me one Hittite in New York City.[275]

In another short essay which he titled *Why are you a Catholic?* Percy replied to the question with another question—"what else is there?"[276] For Percy, in response to the grandeur of creation, if the ultimate meaning of the world amounts to "scientific humanism," the world is then nothing but a great disappointment *in the end*. Percy, in his struggle with God, demanded something more.[277]

Percy believed that there are, in fact, two *telltale* signs of unacknowledged meaning in the present age; one being the self itself and the other being the Jews or the religions that encompass

[275] Walker Percy, "The Delta Factor: How I Discovered the Delta Factor Sitting at My Desk One Summer Day in Louisiana in the 1950's Thinking about an Event in the Life of Helen Keller on Another Summer Day in Alabama in 1887," in Walker Percy, *The Message in the Bottle: How Queer Man Is, How Queer Language Is, And What One Has to Do with the Other*, 6.

[276] Walker Percy, "Why Are You Catholic?" in *Signposts in a Strange Land*, 307.

[277] Walker Percy, "An Interview With Zoltán Abádi-Nagy," in *Signposts in a Strange Land*, 376.

Jewish history. The individual self and the unique history of the Jews are in *no way* explicable with the scientific method. Both the self and Jewish history (in particular the Christ event) will remain inexplicable signs of contradiction in terms of universal scientific facts no matter how sophisticated science becomes. [278] Science conveys truths *sub specie æternitatis*, that is, statements of fact that can be confirmed by anyone, anywhere, given the right intelligence and methods; e.g. "1+1=2," "ducks can quack," or "Paris is in France."[279] The Gospel of Christ, however, provides something of an altogether different kind.[280]

The Gospel provides Good News about an individual person and event, which is more akin to a "message in a bottle" (*á la* the novel *Robinson Crusoe*), cast ashore with a "message" vital to survival (salvation), than the sort of information obtained with the scientific method. News does not come about as scientific discovery (i.e. how to build a raft). Vital news must be delivered by a news-bearer who is a *concrete* individual—so, "the genius is what he is by himself, that is, by what he is in himself; an apostle is what he is by his divine authority."[281] The news-bearer does not convince with the detached intelligence of reason alone. Rather, the authority to deliver news comes more from his or her moral character or trust in communicating the message truthfully.[282] Not being able to *see* the authority of the religious news bearers, the content of the revelatory religion will continue to be truncated beyond recognition given the present limits on scientific understanding.[283]

---

[278] Walker Percy, "Why Are You Catholic," in *Signposts in a Strange Land*, 312.

[279] Walker Percy, "6: The Message in the Bottle," in Walker Percy, *The Message in the Bottle*, 119-149.

[280] John Henry Newman, *An Essay in the Development of Christian Doctrine* (Notre Dame, IN: University of Notre Dame Press, 1989). Newman's theory is perhaps the best known account of a "science" of religious doctrine and how it differs from other kinds of knowledge.

[281] Søren Kierkegaard, *The Book on Adler*, trans. Howard V. Hong and Edna H. Hong (Princeton, NJ: Princeton University Press, 1998). Addendum II "The Difference between a Genius and an Apostle," 175.

[282] Walker Percy, "6: The Message in the Bottle," in Walker Percy, *The Message in the Bottle: How Queer Man Is, How Queer Language Is, And What One Has to Do with the Other*, 144-149.

[283] Avery Dulles, *Models of Revelation* (Maryknoll, New York: Orbis Books, 1992)—provides the "scientific" theological cataloguing of the various "modes of revelation."

The typical *theorist-consumer* self of the contemporary world who places all his or her hope in the theories of science and need-satisfaction rarely sees the "message in the bottle" for what it is. Namely, revelation, as a mode of delivery, is considered wholly defective by the standard of the scientific method.[284] How can *the* saving truth come to us by means of an ignorance of modern science? The *Revelation* of Christianity is not an "empirical" fact studied or tested in a laboratory. The origin is *otherworldly* by admission. [285] Nevertheless, given the ultimate questions Christianity claims to answer, salvation's mode of revelation is, in fact, existentially as well as historically more appropriate to the human condition than either modern science or psychology or humanism or whatever else.[286]

The communication of the Biblical religion is built upon the virtues of relational trust in addition to Apostolic tradition, instead of that of an individual genius or a personal intelligence who tries to stand apart from history, but never entirely can.[287] Like a good story in any lesser book, The Bible narrative speaks to the imagination and the heart of man. The message is moral and religious, not scientific. The Bible is clear in this: that knowledge is not the road to salvation (1 Corinthians 13).[288]

---

[284] A counterpart to this narrow scientism is the "illative sense" of John Henry Cardinal Newman. Religious assent is not based on a mere propositional train of logic, it is an accomplishment of certainty through "converging antecedent probabilities and intuitive judgment." *See* John Henry Newman. *An Essay in Aid of a Grammar of Assent* (London: Longmans, Green, and Co., 1903).

[285] Walker Percy, "Why Are You Catholic," in *Signposts in a Strange Land*, 313-315.

[286] Philip Reiff, *The Triumph of the Therapeautic: Uses of Faith After Freud*, for the therapeutic or humanistic use of religious psychology, but without the religion.

[287] *See* Henri de Lubac, *The Drama of Atheist Humanism*, for the devolution of exclusive humanism into practical atheism.

[288] Walker Percy, "6: The Message in the Bottle," in Walker Percy, *The Message in the Bottle*, 119-149.

4. *Walker Percy:*
Uses of Moral Imagination in Catholic Moral Theology

Religious community remains the most important place
where *meaning* is communicated, although it is ultimately creative
art (done in the religious mode) that prepares the way for the re-
ception of the Gospel today. [289] Art *can* hook the read-
er/viewer/listener self with insights into the very experience of the
individual (as an individual) in the present age. For example, in
novel-writing, Walker Percy believed that there is truly no "literature of alienation," because any successful "literature of alienation"
is in fact the occasion for the condition's reversal. In other words:

> In the re-presenting of alienation the category is
> reversed and becomes entirely different. There is
> a great deal of difference between an alienated
> commuter riding a train and this same commuter
> reading a book about an alienated commuter rid-
> ing a train . . . The non-reading commuter exists
> in a true alienation, which is unspeakable; the
> reading commuter rejoices in the speakability of
> his alienation and the new triple alliance of him-
> self, the alienated character, and the author. His
> mood is affirmatory and glad: Yes! That is how it
> is!—which is an aesthetic reversal of alienation. [290]

For Percy, the so-called "literature of alienation" provides in
actuality the soundest basis for authentic communication, spiritual
healing and/or moral discernment, in the modern world. [291] The
hypothetical commuter on the train in the above passage is likely

---

[289] Ibid.

[290] Walker Percy, "4: The Man on the Train," in Walker Percy, *The Message in the Bottle*, 83.

[291] Percy adhered to a somewhat "atypical" or eccentric breed of psychiatry. He could remember such eminent psychologists as Harry Stack Sullivan visiting his Uncle Will when he was a kid. He was also a close lifelong
friend of Harvard psychologist Robert Coles, to whom he dedicated his
last novel *The Thanatos Syndrome* to. *See* Harry Stack Sullivan, *Conceptions of
Modern Psychiatry* (New York: W. W. Norton & Company, 1940), & Harry
Stack Sullivan, *Schizophrenia as a Human Process* (New York: W. W. Norton
& Company, 1962).

to be alienated in direct proportion to the degree he stakes everything on the *objective-empirical* method, that is, in ignorance of the religio-artistic mode of delivery. To quote Percy again:

> it is just when the [scientific] Method tries to grasp and categorize the existential trait that it is itself reversed and becomes a powerful agent not of progress but of alienation. It is just when the alienated commuter reads books on mental hygiene which abstract immanent goals from existence that he comes closest to despair . . . Take these two sentences that I once read in a book about mental hygiene: 'The most profound of all human needs, the prime requisite for successful living, is to be emotionally inclusive. Socrates, Jesus, Buddha, St. Francis were emotionally inclusive.' These words tremble with anxiety and alienation, even though I would not deny that they are, in their own eerie way, true. The alienated commuter shook like a leaf when he read them.[292]

The portrayal of alienation in literature is, in fact, the occasion for its reversal, whereas the subsuming of the individual under general psychological categories often further distances the self from itself. Percy believed that artistic expression is the *wellspring* through which authentic communities will grow in the future.

Literature, with the creative uses of language, can reawaken the moral imagination of souls sunk in the modern malaise, in a disintegrated culture, better than either traditional moralizing or direct preaching.[293] Percy believed that the traditional ideas of reli-

---

[292] Walker Percy, "The Man on the Train," in Walker Percy, *The Message in the Bottle*, 85.

[293] The following recent British novels are good examples of approaching theology with narrative. David Lodge, *Therapy* (New York: Penguin Books, 1995) is filled with themes from Kierkegaard. James Wood, *The Book against God* (New York: Picador, 2003) portrays a postmodern Ivan Karamazov character who "comes to himself" in a Percyian fashion. Also of interest is John Kennedy Toole, *A Confederacy of Dunces* (New York: Grove Press, 1980), which Percy helped publish, then winning the Pultizer (after Toole's suicide). And, Walter M. Miller, Jr., *A Canticle for Leibowitz* (New York: HarperCollins, 1959), which was one of Percy's

gion (for instance, "God," "love" and "redemption") have largely been subsumed in the secular culture, "worn thin like poker-chips," and no longer communicate the intended meaning.

> The great poets and novelist always wrote about the nature of God and love, of man and woman. But how can even Dante write about the love of God, the love of a man and woman, if he lives in a society in which God is the cheapest word in the media, as profaned by radio preachers as by swearing. And "love?" Love is the way sit-com plots and soap operas get resolved a hundred times a week.

> A dirge, a lament, even a jeremiad, implies an intact society.

> . . . it is something else to live in a time of great good and evil which nobody understands, where there are many kinds of discourse, each of which makes a kind of sense to its own community, but where the communities don't make sense to each other, and none of them makes sense to the novelist, who feels more and more like a canary being taken down the mine shaft with a bunch of hearty joking sense-making miners.[294]

> When the canary gets unhappy, utters plaintive cries, and collapses, it may be time for the miners to surface and think things over.[295]

---

favorite contemporary novels, and, to which he wrote a preface. Also, of course, Thomas Merton, *The Seven Storey Mountain: An Autobiography of Faith* (New York: Harcourt, Inc., 1948). Percy had corresponded and met with Merton over the years. They were often compared in the press as Catholic writers.

[294] Walker Percy, "Novel-Writing in an Apocalyptic Time," in *Signposts in a Strange Land*, 161.

[295] Walker Percy, "5: Notes for a Novel about the End of the World," in Walker Percy, *The Message in the Bottle*, 101.

Percy believed that the novelist writer can still diagnose the spiritual dis-ease he sees by indirectly reflecting in words and images the subtleties of moral problems the contemporary individual faces. In placing the self in relation to itself through art, narrative can, when, say, direct preaching will not work, *spell-out* the direction to God by creatively naming "the signs of the times" (Mttw 16:3).[296]

While the world loses the communal sense of religious meanings, traditional religious language does not convert and, in fact, often repels. For many, the shared moral vision of the post-Christianity West is now defined through such vagaries as "the achievement of human potential" or the vacuous "progress for the sake of progress."[297] Progress in what? Recognized explicitly or not, in the technological *Brave New World* soon to come, absent the transcendent end of Christian belief, life inevitably loses its meaning or is flattened in significance.[298] Percy believed that, in the current cultural climate, before the Good News of Christ is preached, the "bad news" of *sin* must first be salvaged. Not only is authentic

---

[296] William Spohn, "The Formative Power of Story and the Grace of Indirection" *in Seeking Goodness and Beauty: The Use of the Arts in Theological Ethics*, ed. Patricia Lamoureux and Kevin J. O'Neil (Rowman & Littlefield Publishers, 2004), 13-32, for the uses of indirection in teaching moral lessons through narrative arts or fictional characters.

[297] *See* (in toto) Richard Weaver, *Ideas Have Consequences* (Chicago: University of Chicago Press, 1984). Weaver's is a pessimistic, but honest, thoughtful and accurate account of ideology in the modern era. It was praised by eminent theologians such as Paul Tillich and Reinhold Niebuhr. Weaver chronicled the South's literary tradition, which before then was sparse in the Antebellum period or immediately after the war. There were few post-war figures of note except perhaps marginal writers like James Henry Hammond or Jubal Anderson Early. *See* Richard Weaver, *The Southern Tradition at Bay: A History of Postbellum Thought*, eds. George Core and M.E. Bradford (New Rochelle, NY: Arlington House, 1968) & James Henry Hammond, *Secret and Sacred: The Diaries of James Henry Hammond, a Southern Slaveholder*, ed. Carol Bleser (Oxford, UK: Oxford University Press, 1988). Also, Jubal Anderson Early, *A Memoir of the Last Year of the War for Independence in the Confederate States of America* (Columbia, SC: University of South Carolina Press, 2001).

[298] *See* Aldous Huxley, *Brave New World* (New York: First Perennial Classics edition, 1998). "The Savage," an outsider, calls the deracinated world of *Our Ford* Shakespeare's *Brave New World* once shown the truth by the "World Controller" Mustapha Mond.

Christian faith disappearing at a rapid pace, but the idea of sin is disappearing with it.

For social historian (and Percy's fellow Southerner) Richard Weaver, the beginning of this abandonment of the idea of sin is traceable to the Enlightenment intelligentsia. Weaver writes:

> The expulsion of the element of unintelligibility in nature was followed by the abandonment of the doctrine of original sin. If physical nature is the totality and if man is of nature, it is impossible to think of him as suffering from constitutional evil; his defections must now be attributed to his simple ignorance or to some kind of social deprivation. One comes thus by clear deduction to the corollary of the natural goodness of man.
>
> religion begins to assume an ambiguous dignity, and the question of whether it can endure at all in a world of rationalism and science has to be faced.
>
> The darkling plain, swept by alarms, which threatens to be the world of our future, is an arena in which conflicting ideas, numerous after the accumulation of centuries, are freed from the discipline earlier imposed by ultimate conceptions. The decline is to confusion; we are agitated by sensation and look with wonder upon the serene somnambulistic creations of souls which had the metaphysical anchorage. Our ideas become convenient perceptions, and we accept contradiction because we no longer feel the necessity of relating thoughts to the metaphysical dream.[299]

The flattening of the human person's *Metaphysical Dream* in favor of a world without the felt notion of moral good and evil followed closely upon the abandonment of the "transcendent frame" of religion for the *immanent frame* of the naturalist or empirical scientist. The *reductio ad absurdum* of this development is working itself out at this very time. For the individual who is bound

---

[299] Richard Weaver, *Ideas Have Consequences*, 4-5 & 20-21.

within the secular culture the greatest hope for conversion is Weaver's notion of a "complete action," or the Kierkegaardian existential *leap* of faith.

> Simple approbation is the initial step only; a developed culture is a way of looking at the world through an aggregation of symbols, so that empirical facts take on significance and man feels that he is acting in a drama, in which the cruxes of decision sustain interest and maintain the tone of his being.[300]

> The most important goal for one to arrive at is this imaginative picture of what is otherwise a brute empirical fact, the *donné* of the world. His rationality will then be in the service of a vision which can preserve his sentiment from sentimentality. There is no significance to the sound and fury of his life, as of a stage tragedy, unless something is being affirmed by a complete action.[301]

This individual absurd "leap of faith" into the deeper metaphysics of history, now more than ever *perhaps*, is necessary, if the person desires to possess the Faith, *that is*, in the absence of authentic religious communities or culture.[302] By the creation of intelligent communities of artistic expression (limited though they may be) the individual seeking salvation in the (post)-modern world can revive the *Spirit* of Christianity where it is being oppressed or distorted.[303]

In conclusion, the immanence of human flourishing alone cannot raise the individual into the religious *mode of existence* commanded by Christ. Inside the malaises of modernity, the reality of sin often remains hidden or obscured by oppressive forces. Only

---

[300] Ibid., 19.

[301] Ibid., 20.

[302] Søren Kierkegaard, *Concluding Unscientific Postscript to Philosophical Fragments*, 210-212.

[303] *See* Twelve Southerners, *I'll Take My Stand* (Gloucester, MA: Peter Smith, 1976). *I'll Take My Stand* represents a community of writers which Percy can be said to have been loosely affiliated with, esp. his fellow Catholic Southerner Allen Tate.

when sin is brought to light will the sick seek an otherworldly physician. And only when the individual is "grounded transparently in the transcendence of God" will the most insidious forms of sin become uprooted.[304] Finally, when communities once again overflow with religious meaning and artistic talents, the moral imagination and metaphysical dream can thrive.[305]

One more important note is that in the religious story of the Gospel, Christ did not *rationalize* who He was or what He came to do. He was not a systematic theologian. Instead He told captivating stories and mysterious parables that captured the imaginations of His hearers. He was not a simple "moralist," but forgave sins and *cursed the darkness*; the moral blindness and ignorance of the Pharisees.[306] The Gospel is, first and foremost, not a theology, but a narrative story that unfolds. Christianity is, in essence, a *historical* religion, that is, in the root meaning of the word *story*. It is, first of all, the narrative of the Holy Bible (primarily) where Christians can find and understand their true selves in the context of history. The idea of a linear story (or meta-narrative) is the essential component to the telling of Christianity in many respects. Here, regarding the story of Christ, Gilbert Keith Chesterton eloquently states the case more directly in *The Everlasting Man*:

---

[304] Søren Kierkegaard, *The Sickness unto Death*, 13-14.

[305] Peter Kreeft, "5. Walker Percy's Lost in the Cosmos: The Abolition of Man in Late-Night Comedy Format," in Peter Kreeft, *C.S. Lewis for the Third Millennium: Six Essays on The Abolition of Man* (San Francisco: Ignatius Press, 1994),

[306] Percy often took aim at the effeminate "fagged-out" Christianity of contemporary consumer-driven churches in America, e.g. the type of church in which people are "sent" to great emotional heights by singing *On Eagle's Wings* or holding hands before eating Christ in the Eucharist. He understood the dangers in sentimentality; something he saw in the proto-Nazi Germans of the Weimer Republic, i.e. "the German doctor who loves Mozart best of all and plays in a quartet as a relaxation from his experiments in the death camps—or the decent middle-class Englishman who flies the lead Lancaster bomber which marks out an undefended Dresden for firestorm." Walker Percy, "Novel-Writing in an Apocalyptic Time," in *Signposts in a Strange Land*, 156. *See* Michael Joncas, "On Eagle's Wings," in *Chalice Hymnal* (St. Louis, MO: Chalice Press, 1995), 77. *And see*, Vincent J. Miller, *Consuming Religion: Christian Faith and Practice in a Consumer Culture* (New York: Bloomsbury Academic, 2003).

To sum up; The sanity of the world was restored and the soul of man offered salvation by something which did indeed satisfy the two warring tendencies of the past; which had never been satisfied in full and most certainly never satisfied together. It met the mythological search for romance by being a story and the philosophical search for truth by being a true story . . . The more deeply we think of the matter the more we shall conclude that, if there be indeed a God, his creation could hardly have reached any other culmination than this granting of a real romance to the world. Otherwise the two sides of the human mind could never have touched at all; and the brain of man would have remained cloven and double; one lobe of it dreaming impossible dreams and the other repeating invariable calculations. The picture-makers would have remained forever painting the portrait of nobody. The sages would have remained for ever adding up numerals that came to nothing. It was that abyss that nothing but the incarnation could cover; a divine embodiment of our dreams; and he stands above that chasm whose name is more than priest and older even than Christendom; Pontifex Maximus, the mightiest maker of a bridge.[307]

And so, *characteristic of Christ* is his appeal to the parabolic or metaphorical *imagination*, often circumventing the specious questions of the logical intellect; in particular, the *cold* intellect divorced from the *heart*.[308] Moreover, conversion, being an ongoing experience of the entire person, is not so easily *nailed down* with rationalistic argument. In many cases, the sickness of sin is best attended to with the artistic use of words—that is, instead of more straight-

---

[307] Gilbert Keith Chesterton, *The Everlasting Man* (San Francisco: Ignatius Press, 2008 [1925]), 248.

[308] William James, "Is Life Worth Living," in William James, *The Will To Believe and Other Essays in Popular Philosophy* (New York: Dover Publications, 1956 [1897]), 32-62.

forward moral prescriptions using dead-letter meanings that do not *grip* the reader in any effective way.

In *so-called* "Catholic" literature, the subjective experience of the individual is approached in the context of a story. The reflection ought to be honest and the moral point indirect or left for the reader to discern. The purpose should remain clear, in the manner of the Gospel: to attract hardened hearts, raise *spirits*, while ultimately dispelling the modern malaise that plagues so many now. Percy—

> At the end of the age, the denizens of the age still profess to believe that they can understand themselves by the theory of the age, yet they behave as if they did not believe it. The surest sign that an age is coming to an end is the paradoxical movement of the most sensitive souls of the age, the artists and writers first, then the youth, in a direction exactly opposite to the direction laid down by the theory of the age.

> It is not an accident that in the nineteenth and the early twentieth century, the high-water mark of the old modern age, when the world had been transformed by Western man and the scientific revolution to his own use and people lived peacefully in the ethical twilight of Christianity, man should begin to feel most homeless in the same world where he had expected to feel most at home.

> How can the Harvard behaviorist, living in the best of all scientific worlds, begin to understand the behavior of the Harvard undergraduate who comes from the best of all lay worlds, the affluent, informed, democratic, and ethical East (let the professor specify this world, make it as good as he chooses), who nevertheless turns his back on both worlds and prefers to live like Dostoevsky's underground man?

> How can the Unitarian minister, good man that
> he is, who believes in all the good things of the
> old modern age, the ethics, the democratic values,
> the tolerance, the individual freedom, and all the
> rest—how can he begin to understand his son,
> who wants nothing so much as *out*, out from un-
> der this good man and good home and the good
> things professed there? It is of no moment what
> the son chooses instead—Hare Krishna, Process,
> revolution, or Zen; to him anything, *anything*, is
> better than this fagged-out ethical deadweight of
> five thousand years of Judeo-Christianity.[309]

We end here this chapter with another instance of a Percy
passage from *Love in the Ruins*. In one of the more telling episodes
Dr. Thomas More makes his long "procrastinated" confession to
his priest Fr. Renaldo Smith (with the "hairy fútbol wrists") in the
Epilogue of the novel. The incident is funny and slips discreetly
into the *deeper* theme of sin and reconciliation, love and despair.

There is no overt moralizing at all. It comes at the very end of
the novel. It is a kind of complex repentance that is both serious,
while also meant to be tongue-in-cheek in the way that Percy was
best known for. In his essay *Novel-Writing in an Apocalyptic Time* he
had written that . . . "There may be times when the greatest service
a novelist can do his fellow man is to follow General Patton's in-
junction: attack, attack, attack. Attack the fake in the name of the
real."[310]

And so, since it is such a telling scene, layered with ironies of
depth as well as insights which address our main concern here, we
cite it in full to close CHAPTER III:

> *My* [Thomas More] turn comes at last. I kneel in
> the sour darkness of the box, which smells of
> sweat and Pullman curtain.

---

[309] Walker Percy, "The Delta Factor," in Walker Percy *The Message in the Bottle*, 22-23.

[310] Walker Percy, "Novel-Writing in an Apocalyptic Time," in *Signposts in a Strange Land*, 161.

The little door slides back. There is Father Smith, close as close, cheek propped on three fingers, trying to keep awake. He's cross-eyed from twelve hours of fire-watching. A hundred brushfires flicker across his retina. These days people, convinced of world-conspiracies against them, go out and set the woods afire to get even.

"Bless me, Father, for I have sinned," I say and fall silent, forgetting everything.

"When was your last confession?" asks the priest patiently.

"Eleven years ago."

Another groan escapes the priest. Again he peeps at his watch. Must he listen to an eleven-year catalogue of dreary fornications and such? Well, he'll do it.

"Father, I can make my confession in one sentence."

"Good," says the priest, cheering up.

"I do not recall the number of occasions, Father, but I accuse myself of drunkenness, lusts, envies, fornication, delight in the misfortunes of others, and loving myself better than God and other men."

"I see," says the priest, who surprises me by not looking surprised. Perhaps he's just sleepy. "Do you have contrition and a firm purpose of amendment?"

"I don't know."

"You don't know? You don't feel sorry for your sins?"

"I don't feel much of anything."

"Let me understand you."

"All right."

"You have not lost your faith?"

"No."

"You believe in the Catholic faith as the Church proposes it?"

"Yes."

"Yet you say you do not feel sorry."

"That is correct."

"You are aware of your sins, you confess them, but you are not sorry for them?"

"That is correct."

"Why?"

"I couldn't say."

"Pity."

"I'm sorry."

"You are?"

"Yes."

"For what?"

"For not being sorry."

The priest sighs. "Will you pray that God will give you a true knowledge of your sins and a true contrition?"

"Yes, I'll do that."

"You are a doctor and it is your business to help people, not harm them."

"That is true."

"You are also a husband and father and it is your duty to love and cherish your family."

"Yes, but that does not prevent me from desiring other women and even contriving plans to commit fornication and adultery."

"Yes," says the priest absently. "That's the nature of the beast."

Damn, why doesn't he wake up and pay attention?

"But you haven't recently," says the priest.

"Haven't what?"

"Actually committed adultery and fornication."

"No," I say irritably. "But—"

"Hm. You know, Tom, maybe it's not so much a question at our age of committing in the imagination these horrendous sins of the flesh as of worrying whether one still can. In the firetower on such occasions I find it useful to imagine the brushfires as the outer circle of hell, not too hot really, where these sad sins are punished, and my toes toasting in the flames. Along comes Our Lady who spies me and says: 'O, for heaven's sake, you here? This is ridiculous.'"

Damn, where does he come off patronizing me with his stock priestly tricks—I can tell they're his usual tricks because he reels 'em off without even listening. I can smell the seminary and whole libraries of books "for the layman" with little priest-jokes. How can he lump the two of us together, him a gray ghost of a cleric and me the spirit of the musical-erotic?

More tricks:

"For your drinking you might find it helpful, at least it is in my case, to cast your lot with other drunks. Then, knowing how much trouble you're going to put your friends to if you take a drink, you're less apt to—though it doesn't always work."

"Thank you," I say coldly.

"Now let's see." He's nodding again, drifting off into smoke and brushfires. "Very well. You're sorry for your sins."

"No."

"That's too bad. Ah me. Well—"

He steals a glance at his watch. "In any case, continue to pray for knowledge of your sins. God is good. He will give you what you ask. Ask for sorrow. Pray for me."

"All right."

"Meanwhile, forgive me but there are other things we must think about: like doing our jobs, you being a better doctor, I being a better priest, showing a bit of ordinary kindness to people, particularly our own families—unkindness to those close to us is such a pitiful thing—doing what we can for our poor unhappy country—things which, please forgive me, sometimes seem more important than dwelling on a few middle-aged daydreams."

"You're right. I'm sorry," I say instantly, scalded.

"You're sorry for your sins?"

"Yes. Ashamed rather."

"That will do. Now say the act of contrition and for your penance I'm going to give you this."

Through the little window he hands me two articles, an envelope containing ashes and a sackcloth, which is a kind of sleeveless sweater made of black burlap. John XXIV recently revived public penance, a practice of the early Church.

"Go in peace. I'll offer my mass for you tonight."

"Thank you," I say, dumping the ashes in my hair . . .

Father Smith says mass. I eat Christ, drink his blood.

At the end the people say aloud a prayer confessing the sins of the Church and asking for the reunion of Christians and of the United States.

Outside the children of some love couples and my own little Thomas More, a rowdy but likable lot, shoot off firecrackers.

"Hurrah for Jesus Christ!" they cry. "Hurrah for
the United States!"[311]

---

[311] Walker Percy, *Love in the Ruins*, 396-400. [emphasis mine] This is the
same as (or similar to) the ending to *The Moviegoer* where Binx's siblings
"Hurray" for his brother Lonnie's being able to water-ski again in
Heaven—

"You mean he'll be able to ski?" The children cock their heads and listen like old men.
"Yes."

"Hurray!" cry the twins,

See Walker Percy, *The Moviegoer*, Epilogue. And of course this line is taken
as a recognizable reference to the Epilogue of *The Brothers Karamazov*, e.g.
"Hurrah for Karamazov!" Presumably, Percy is here alluding to the same
moral theme as Dostoyevsky in an admittedly more minor key. Fyodor
Dostoyevsky, *The Brothers Karamazov*, pg. 940.

The witches spoke with the habitual equivocation of oracles . . .

A little sign appears, "a cloud no bigger than a man's hand,"

Richard Weaver, IDEAS HAVE CONSEQUENCES

Chicago is on the Hudson River or Chicago is not on the Hudson River.

. . . war, the end of the world, Superman, Birmingham, flying, slithy toves, General Grant, the 1984 Olympics, Lilliput, Mozart, Don Giovanni, The Grateful Dead, backing and filling, say it isn't so, dreaming . . .

Walker Percy, THE MESSAGE IN A BOTTLE
& LOST IN THE COSMOS

Solomon and Job have known and spoken best about man's wretchedness, one the happiest, the other the unhappiest of men; one knowing by experience the vanity of pleasure, and the other the reality of afflictions.

Ecclesiastes shows that man without God is totally ignorant and inescapably unhappy.

Blaise Pascal, PENSEÉS

I think I had crawfish. What distinguishes Louisianians is that they suck the heads.

Walker Percy,
AN INTERVIEW WITH ZOLTÁN ABÁDI-NAGY

"Bob, where is Hammond?"
"What?" says Bob quickly.
"You mentioned Hammond, Louisiana. Where is it?"
"Where is Hammond," Bob repeats, looking at me. His eyes stray toward Max. "Okay, I give up. What's the gag?"
"Nothing. Forget it."

Walker Percy, THE THANATOS SYNDROME

Always it was Park Avenue, Fifth Avenue, Sutton Place . . . Well, too bad! Now you're getting an eyeful of a jack-legged walkup on the West Side!

He put tears into his voice that would have embarrassed the worst hambone Pagliacci.

The young man appeared to swell like a frog.

Tom Wolfe, THE BONFIRE OF THE VANITIES

a would-be Kierkegaard scholar might not want to be a self that cannot master Danish.

Kierkegaard (literally "churchyard," but with "graveyard" the primary connotation)

—Alistair Hannay

. . . the castle of arrrroouuuggghhhh . . .

MONTY PYTHON, SEARCH FOR THE HOLY GRAIL

his heart produces good, (LUKE 6:45)

PART I
CONCLUSION:

, but even life in a condo on a golf course. At risk of running an "ibid, ibid, ibid," *ad infinitum*, or of arousing what the Spanish call *blah, blah, blah, blah, blah, blah*, (6x, no more), we will refrain from reiterating *too much* what has been said and said again.[312] A brilliant flash of "pop-ping" light in the late-night hours, a sudden rude awakening can in a moment's breath perhaps transcend every imaginative vision of a former self. There is more to us than our thoughts. Casting all into doubt, or raising everything in hope, there is no absolute certainty about *anything* unless the *grip* of faith is real, true, truth. A truth grows and sprouts leaves, blossoming, so that you can live in its branches (Mark 4:30-32). The Word of Life is a "property" [proprietas?] of what we do not know, or what we know we do not know. That is *why*, maybe, we often try to say *it* over and over different each time, not being able. I've learned in the writing of this thesis. I can't help seeing that it is representative of a number of different things at times long forgotten. I can leave it with a prayer and in the spirit of a prayer, no more.

Barring Jesus! . . . *no* better voice can there be to speak here than Kierkegaard, or Percy, who knew themselves better than me. In trying to *sell* Christianity by means of Percy I am sure I am wrong to commandeer novels as a means to evangelize. He himself was much more modest about his virtues as religionist. He confesses in a private letter to Shelby Foote that, in spite of his Catholic credentials and readership—"I think that culturally speaking I am still a gloomy Georgia Presbyterian. It's impossible to escape one's origins altogether. I believe in the One Holy Catholic and Apostolic Church etc but its intellectual and I often don't feel a part of the feast like merry Louisianians."[313] He had no real enthu-

---

[312] *See* Joshua Furnal, *Catholic Theology after Kierkegaard* (Oxford, UK: Oxford University Press, 2016). Written one year before (2016) this here my self-publish book—by a professor at Radboud University, Netherlands. Published with Oxford University. Brainstorming for *my* project was begun in 2010. Neat coinciding? Furnal complements my work in providing more of the parallels with Catholic Theology writ large, rather than specifically Moral Theology; as in mine here. Hardcover edition at OUP selling $110.00 American!

[313] Shelby Foote and Walker Percy, *The Correspondence of Shelby Foote & Walker Percy*, 180.

siasm either for high-minded or lofty academic spiel or the so-called authorities of the scholarly establishment. He has his protagonist *Lancelot Andrewes Lamar* remark as to the intellectuals of the money-grubbing North:

> The Northerner is at heart a pornographer. He is an abstract mind with a genital attached. His soul is at Harvard, a large abstract locked-in sterile university whose motto is truth but which has not discovered an important truth in a hundred years. His body lives on Forty-second Street. Do you think there is no relation between Harvard and Forty-second Street? One is the backside of the other.[314]

No starving artist, Percy was very modest about his accomplishments in life. Shelby Foote, after losing the Pulitzer in 1975 to Dumas Malone, conceded to Percy, "Let's face it; those pocket-sagging Capote sums aint for the likes of you and me."[315]

No doubt, Walker and Søren would both agree about the cheapening of religion to suit the present age's fickle demands of haughty consumption. Kierkegaard characterizes this plebian dumbing-down of religion in the comfort loving modern urban populace here, writing:

> But in our old age let us not change Christianity into a seedy saloon-keeper who must think of something to draw customers, or into a carpet-bagger who wants to be a big success in the world. Of course, Christianity can hardly be said to have been a big success when it originally entered the world, inasmuch as it began with crucifixion, flogging, and the like. But God knows whether it actually wants to be a big success in the world. I rather think it is ashamed of itself, like an old man who sees himself rigged out in the latest fashion. Or, more correctly, I think it focuses its wrath

---

[314] Walker Percy, *Lancelot* (New York: Picador, 1977), 219.
[315] Shelby Foote and Walker Percy, *The Correspondence of Shelby Foote & Walker Percy*, 234.

against people when it sees this distorted figure that is supposed to be Christianity, a perfume-saturated and systematically accommodated and soiree-participating scholarliness, whose whole secret is half measures and then truth to a certain degree—when it sees a radical cure (and only such is it what it is) transmogrified nowadays into a vaccination, and a person's relation to it equivalent to having a certificate of vaccination.[316]

Of course, Kierkegaard is an even slipperier fish to catch in retrospect than Percy. I don't know Danish. I can't imagine what Kierkegaard would think of the majority of what is published about him. He would turn his nose up I think. No snippet of quotes featuring occasional interjections of modest insight can ever approximate the reading of his writings itself. *But*, he succeeds where I fail in that this way of reading him is exactly his point in leaving a written record for us; to take what he wrote as a mirror to see yourself, to understand more, but never entirely. Over against God we are always in the wrong. *Over against God we are always in the wrong.*

Kierkegaard is right. There is nothing written that ever does a theology, a philosophy, justice. So it is better to ask for mercy after such things, in the end. With Saint John the Evangelist we can say that "if every one of them were written down, I suppose that the world itself could not contain the books that would be written" (John 21:25). Then, Kierkegaard once more reminds us as to how little we do know about Our God. In that:

> God is not like a king in a predicament, who says to the highly trusted Minister of Interior, 'You must do everything; you must create the atmosphere for our proposal and win public opinion to our side. You can do it. Use your sagacity. If I cannot depend upon you, I have no one.' But in relation to God, there are no secret instructions for a human being any more than there are any backstairs. Even the most eminent

---

[316] Søren Kierkegaard, *Concluding Unscientific Postscript to Philosophical Fragments*, 293-294.

genius who comes to give a report had best come in fear and trembling, for God it not hard-pressed for geniuses. He can, after all, create a few legions of them; and wanting to make oneself indispensable in the service of God means *eo ipso* dismissal. And every human being is created in the image of God. This is the absolute; the little he has to learn from Tom, Dick, and Harry is not of great value.[317]

Kierkegaard bore more than a slight resemblance to his character "A" in *Either/Or*. His confusion about his vocation in life—once having broken off his engagement to Regina Olsen—inspired this beautiful "fragment of life" perhaps more than his later works. In his short life he appropriated the repentance before God he preached. Held fast in the most passionate inwardness he could say, "I repent myself out of the whole of existence." For, ". . . my victory over the world, that any human being who has not tasted the bitterness of despair has fallen short of the meaning of life."[318]

I can see the drift of correctives in this thesis (or, theses) needing yet another corrective of its own. A corrective that is more than words on paper. This corrective *is God*. God's grace (graces)—*gratia sanans et operans et illuminans et excitans*. The propositions of theology cannot encompass it. At a certain juncture it is best to fall silent. There is nothing to do except see the faults, the sin, and make the corrections. God provides the good that is not our own. It is *gratuitous* gift that can be abused, not earned. There is no Pelagian (or even semi-Pelagian) technique at our disposal to be other than what we are. You are you. I am me. God is who God is. Everyone short of Jesus is made with (at least) a little taint of sin; our inheritance. Therein lies our despair. We can only acknowledge it in a way pleasing to God. And then we can by His mercy see His mercy and amend. His mercy is in our salvation through Christ who reveals it. Jesus is Lord.

There is undoubtedly a limit in our adjusting to the demands of our passing culture, habits, vices, and virtues. A lost sense of history or a radical dislocation of the self is now present by near universal admission of the reflective. Theology sets itself the task

---

[317] Ibid., 260-261.
[318] Ibid., 208.

of addressing this. *But,* there is bad theology done in the *Holy Spirit* as well as good theology done in false or irreligious consciousness. I hope for the former at least, though I strive for more. I am sure I am mistaken in some instances. This piece was written at different times and places thereby reflecting an intellectual growth of sorts. So, I can only say along with G. K. Chesterton, who, once asked *what is wrong* with The World [le monde], his reply: Dear Sir, *I am*.[319]

Percy was a sinner. Kierkegaard was a sinner. Mere mortals who knew themselves as such. God made use of them I believe. And so do I too. They favored the *Apostle* to the *Genius* as spiritual inspiration in matters of religion, which is no other better sign of an election—*id est,* to see to do this. The pen (quill) which can write of humanism's vanity that . . . "The humorous self-sufficiency of genius is the unity of a modest resignation in the world and proud elevation above the world: of being an unnecessary superfluity and a precious ornament" . . . sees *Christ Jesus'* Church in Truth I believe.[320] 'O to be such an ornament! Such vain conceit is there in artistic pretensions! Or, like Judge Wilhelm to THE ÆSTHETE, "do you believe that one can sneak away just before midnight in order to avoid it?"

And so, here I'll try to sneak away from this thesis, leaving the saving truth—the answers to all the questions, left unsaid/unwritten. . . . however, implicitly known by me myself, of course. A certain gnostic secret to mystify the reader.

Like Saint John of the Cross; *nada, nada, nada,* there's just nothing more to do. Will-He-NILL-HE, it is really more a matter to hear Percy's candid accounting that I am just plain . . . "Fresh out of malice, piss, the love of God, hatred of things as they are, or whatever it takes, which I don't have."[321] Full-stop. We'll end here.

---

[319] This story about Chesterton may be "apocryphal," as there is no record of it, but it seems likely true—as nearly every authority on Chesterton thinks so. *See* Ian Ker, *Chesterton: A Biography* (Oxford, UK: Oxford University Press, 2011), for the relevant biographical information.

[320] Søren Kierkegaard, *The Present Age and On the Difference Between A Genius and An Apostle.* 108.

[321] Shelby Foote and Walker Percy, *The Correspondence of Shelby Foote & Walker Percy,* 129.

Seek a career, throw yourself into the world of business; it takes your mind off yourself, and you will forget your depression; work—that is the best thing to do.[322]

the proud thought: I am the person I am? By no means![323]

I tell you, on the day of judgment men will render account for every careless word they utter; for by your words you will be justified, and by your words you will be condemned (MTTW 12:36-37).

---

[322] Søren Kierkegaard, *Either/Or II*, 207.
[323] Ibid., 231.

APPENDIX A

you desire truth in the inward being;
therefore teach me wisdom in my secret heart.
(PSALM 51:6)

A "typical" Catholic Examination of Conscience and Confession of Sins

6 STEPS FOR A GOOD CONFESSION

1) Examine your conscience—what sins have you committed since your last good confession?

2) Be sincerely sorry for your sins.

3) Confess your sins to the priest.

4) Make certain that you confess all your mortal sins and the number of them.

5) After your confession, do the penance the priest gives to you.

6) Pray daily for the strength to avoid the occasion of sin, especially for those sins you were just absolved from.

ACT OF CONTRITION

O my God, I am heartily sorry for all my sins. Because of them I deserve the eternal pains of hell, but most of all because I have offended Thee my God who art all-good and deserving of all my love. I firmly resolve with the help of Thy grace to confess my sins, to do penance, to avoid the proximate occasion of sins and never to sin anymore. Amen.

FIRST COMMANDMENT
"I am the Lord your God, who brought you out of the land of Egypt, out of the house of bondage. You shall have no other gods before me."
(Exodus 20: 2-3)

Did I doubt or deny that God exists?

Did I refuse to believe what God has revealed to us?

Did I believe in fortune telling, horoscopes, dreams, the occult, good-luck charms, tarot cards, palmistry, Ouija boards, séances, reincarnation?

Did I deny that I was Catholic?

Did I leave the Catholic Faith?

Did I give time to God each day in prayer?

Did I love God with my whole heart?

Did I despair of or presume on God's mercy?

Did I have false gods in my life that I gave greater attention to than God, like money, profession, drugs, TV, fame, pleasure, property, etc.?

SECOND COMMANDMENT

"You shall not take the Name of the Lord your God in vain; for the Lord will not hold him guiltless who takes his name in vain." (Exodus 20:7)

Did I blaspheme or insult God?

Did I take God's name carelessly or uselessly?

Did I curse, or break an oath or vow?

Did I get angry with God?

THIRD COMMANDMENT

"Remember the sabbath day, to keep it holy." (Exodus 20:8)

Did I miss Mass Sunday or a Holy Day of Obligation through my own fault?

Did I come to Mass on time? Leave early?

Did I do work on Sunday that was not necessary?

Did I set aside Sunday as a day of rest and a family day?

Did I show reverence in the presence of Jesus in the Most Blessed Sacrament?

FOURTH COMMANDMENT

"Honor your father and your mother, that your days may be long in the land which the Lord your God gives you." (Exodus 20:12)

Did I disobey or disrespect my parents or legitimate superiors?

Did I neglect my duties to my husband, wife, children or parents?

Did I neglect to give good religious example to my family?
Did I fail to actively take an interest in the religious education and formation of my children?
Did I fail to educate myself on the true teachings of the Church?
Did I give scandal by what I said or did, especially to the young?
Did I cause anyone to leave the faith?
Did I cause tensions and fights in my family?
Did I care for my aged and infirm relatives?
Did I give a full day's work for a full day's pay?
Did I give a fair wage to my employees?

FIFTH COMMANDMENT
"You shall not kill." (Exodus 20:13)

Did I kill or physically injure anyone?
Did I have an abortion, or advise someone else to have an abortion? (One who procures an abortion is automatically excommunicated, as is anyone who is involved in an abortion, Canon 1398. The excommunication will be lifted in the Sacrament of Reconciliation).
Did I use or cause my spouse to use birth control pills (whether or not realizing that birth control pills do abort the fetus if and when conceived)?
Did I attempt suicide?
Did I take part in or approve of "mercy killing" (euthanasia)?
Did I get angry, impatient, envious, unkind, proud, revengeful, jealous, hateful toward another, lazy?
Did I give bad example by drug abuse, drinking alcohol to excess, fighting, quarreling?
Did I abuse my children?

SIXTH COMMANDMENT
"You shall not commit adultery." (Exodus 20:14)
"You shall not covet your neighbor's wife." (Exodus 20:17)

Note: In the area of deliberate sexual sins listed below, all are mortal sins if there is sufficient reflection and full consent of the will. "No fornicators, idolaters, or adulterers, no sodomites, . . . will inherit the kingdom of God." (1 Corinth. 6:9-10) "Anyone who looks lustfully at a woman has already committed adultery with her in his thoughts." (Mttw 5:28)

Did I willfully entertain impure thoughts or desires?

Did I use impure or suggestive words? Tell impure stories? Listen to them?

Did I deliberately look at impure TV, videos, plays, pictures or movies? Or deliberately read impure materials?

Did I commit impure acts by myself (masturbation)?

Did I commit impure acts with another—fornication (premarital sex), adultery (sex with a married person)?

Did I practice artificial birth control (by pills, device, withdrawal)?

Did I marry or advise anyone to marry outside the Church?

Did I avoid the occasions of impurity?

Did I try to control my thoughts?

Did I engage in homosexual activity?

Did I respect all members of the opposite sex, or have I thought of other people as objects?

Did I or my spouse have sterilization done?

Did I abuse my marriage rights?

SEVENTH & TENTH COMMANDMENTS

"You shall not steal." (Exodus 20:15)

"You shall not covet your neighbor's goods." (Exodus 20:17)

Did I steal, cheat, help or encourage others to steal or keep stolen goods? Have I made restitution for stolen goods?

Did I fulfill my contracts; give or accept bribes; pay my bills; rashly gamble or speculate; deprive my family of the necessities of life?

Did I waste time at work, school or at home?

Did I envy other people's families or possessions?

Did I make material possessions the purpose of my life?

EIGHTH COMMANDMENT

"You shall not bear false witness against your neighbor." (Exodus 20:16)

Did I lie?

Did I deliberately deceive others, or injure others by lies?

Did I commit perjury?

Did I gossip or reveal others' faults or sins?

Did I fail to keep secret what should be confidential?

OTHER SINS

Did I fast on Ash Wednesday and Good Friday?
Did I eat meat on the Fridays of Lent or Ash Wednesday?
Did I fail to receive Holy Communion during Eastertime?
Did I go to Holy Communion in a state of mortal sin? Without fasting (water and medicine permitted) for one hour from food or drink?
Did I make a bad confession?

SINS AGAINST THE HOLY GHOST

Presumption of God's Mercy
Despair [324]
Impugning the known truth
Envy at another's spiritual good
Obstinacy in sin
Final impenitence

---

[324] This is not Kierkegaard's notion of fortvivlelse. In *Either/Or II* Kierkegaard's character Judge Wilhelm explains: "The Bible says: For what would it profit a person if he gained the whole world but damaged his own soul; what should he have in return? Scripture does not state the antithesis to this, but it is implicit in the sentence. The antithesis would read something like this: What damage would there be to a person if he lost the whole world and yet did not damage his soul; what would he need in return? There are expressions that in themselves seem simple and yet fill the soul with a strange anxiety, because they become more obscure the more one thinks about them. In the religious sphere, the phrase 'sin against the Holy Ghost' is such an expression. I do not know whether theologians are able to give a definite explanation of it; . . . it is despair to gain the whole world and in such a way that one damages one's soul, and yet it is my deep conviction that to despair is a person's true salvation. Here again the significance of willing one's despair is evident, of willing in an infinite sense, in an absolute sense, for a will such as that is identical with absolute self-giving. But if we despair in a finite sense, then I damage my soul, for then my innermost being does not attain the breakthrough in despair; it locks itself in. It becomes hardened, so that finite despair is a hardening, absolute despair an infinitizing." Søren Kierkegaard, *Either/Or II*, 220-221.

SINS CRYING TO HEAVEN FOR VENGEANCE

Willful murder
The sin of Sodom
Oppression of the poor
Defrauding laborers of their wages

NINE WAYS OF BEING ACCESSORY TO ANOTHER'S SIN

1) By counsel
2) By command
3) By consent
4) By provocation
5) By praise or flattery
6) By concealment
7) By partaking
8) By silence
9) By defense of the ill done

THE SEVEN DEADLY SINS

1) Pride
2) Covetousness
3) Lust
4) Anger
5) Gluttony
6) Envy
7) Sloth

FOUR LAST THINGS TO BE REMEMBERED

1) Death
2) Judgment
3) Hell
4) Heaven

Whoever, therefore, eats the bread or drinks the cup of the Lord in an unworthy manner will be guilty of profaning the body and blood of the Lord. Let a man examine himself, and so eat of the bread and drink of the cup. For any one who eats and drinks without discerning the body eats and drinks judgment upon himself (1 Corinth. 11:27-29).

So, to receive Holy Communion while in the state of mortal sin (having committed a mortal sin which has not been confessed and forgiven in the Sacrament of Confession) is itself a mortal sin—a mortal sin of sacrilege.

God, be merciful to me a sinner! (Luke 18:13)

If you forgive the sins of any, they are forgiven; if you retain the sins of any, they are retained. (John 20:23)

though your sins be like scarlet, they shall be as white as snow; though they are red like crimson, they shall become like wool. (Isaiah 1:18)

If we confess our sins, he is faithful and just, and will forgive our sins and cleanse us from all unrighteousness. If we say we have not sinned, we make him a liar, and his word is not in us. (1 John 1:9-10)

Father, forgive them; for they know not what they do. (Luke 23:34)

forgive us our sins, for we ourselves forgive everyone who is indebted to us; (Luke 11:4).

BIBLIOGRAPHY

Adams, Henry. The Education of Henry Adams: An Autobiography. Boston and New York: Houghton Mifflin Company, 1918.

Aligheri, Dante. The Divine Comedy. trans. John Ciardi. New York: New American Library, 2003.

Anderson, Hans Christian. The Stories of Hans Christian Andersen. trans. Diana Crone Frank and Jeffrey Frank. Durham and London: Duke University Press, 2005.

Aquinas, Thomas. On Evil. trans. John A. Oesteble and Jean T. Oesteble. Notre Dame, IN: University of Notre Dame Press, 1995.

Aquinas, Thomas. Summa Theologica. trans. The Fathers of the Dominican Province. New York: Benzinger Brothers, 1920.

Aristotle. Nicomachean Ethics. Upper Saddle River, NJ: Prentice Hall, 1999.

Auchincloss, Louis. The Embezzler. Boston: Houghton Mifflin Company, 1966.

Augustine. Confessions. trans. F. J. Sheed. Cambridge: Hackett Publishing, 2006.

Aurelius, Marcus. Meditations. trans. Martin Hammond. New York: Penguin Books, 2006.

Balthazar, Hans Urs Von. The Glory of the Lord: A Theological Aesthetics, 7 vols. eds. Joseph Fessio S.J. and John Riches. trans. Erasmo Leiva-Merikakis. San Francisco: Ignatius Press, 1982-1991.

Barrett, William. Irrational Man: A Study in Existential Philosophy. New York: Anchor Books, 1990.

Beabout, Gregory R. Freedom and Its Misuses: Kierkegaard on Anxiety and Despair. Milwaukee, WI: Marquette University Press, 1996.

Becker, Ernest. The Denial of Death. New York: Free Press Paperbacks, 1973.

Berman, Harold J. Law and Revolution: The Formation of the Western Legal Tradition. Cambridge, MA: Harvard University Press, 1983.

Berry, Wendell. Life is a Miracle: An Essay Against Modern Superstition. Berkely, CA: Counterpoint, 2000.

Black, C.Ss.R. Peter, and Kevin J. O'Neil, C.Ss.R. The Essential Moral Handbook: A Guide to Catholic Living, Revised Edition. Liguori, Missouri: Ligouri Publications, 2006 [2003].

Bradley, Gerard V. A Student's Guide to the Study of Law. Wilmington, DE: ISI Books, 2006.

Brown, Raymond E., Joseph A. Fitzmyer and Roland E. Murphy, eds. The New Jerome Biblical Commentary. Upper Saddle River, NJ: Prentice Hall, 1990.

Buben, Adam, and Patrick Stokes. Kierkegaard and Death. Bloomington, IN: Indiana University Press, 2011.

Bunyan, John. The Pilgrim's Progress: From this World to that Which is to Come. Chicago: Moody Classics, 2007.

Cahill, Lisa, and James Childress, eds. Christian Ethics: Problems and Prospects. Cleveland, OH: Pilgrim Press, 1996.

Cahill, Thomas. How the Irish Saved Civilization: The Untold Story of Ireland's Heroic Role from the Fall of Rome to the Rise of Medieval Europe. New York: Doubleday, 1995.

Campbell, David, and Robert Putnam. American Grace. New York: Simon & Schuster, 2010.

Camus, Albert. Le mythe de Sisyphe: Essai sur l'absurde. Paris: Gallimard, 1942.

Camus, Albert. The Plague. trans. Stuart Gilbert. New York: Vintage Books, 1991 [1948].

Camus, Albert. The Stranger. New York: Vintage Books, 1946.

Capote, Truman. "Miss Belle Rankin." December, 1941. The Green Witch. Beinecke Rare Book and Manuscript Library, Yale University.

Capote, Truman. "Swamp Terror." June, 1940. The Green Witch, Commencement Issue. Beinecke Rare Book and Manuscript Library, Yale University.

Chalice Press. Chalice Hymnal. St. Louis, MO: Chalice Press, 1995.

Chesterton, G. K. The Everlasting Man. San Francisco: Ignatius Press, 2008 [1925].

Coriden, James A. An Introduction to Canon Law. Mahwah, NJ: Paulist Press, 1991.

Cunningham, Lawrence S. ed. Intractable Disputes About the Natural Law: Alasdair MacIntyre and Critics. Notre Dame, IN: University of Notre Dame Press, 2009.

Curran, Charles, and Richard McCormick, eds. Readings in Moral Theology No. 4: The Use of Scripture in Moral Theology. New York: Paulist Press, 1984.

Davenport, John J. and Anthony Rudd, eds. Kierkegaard after MacIntyre. Chicago: Open Court, 2001.

Desmond, John F. Walker Percy's Search for Community. Athens, GA: The University of Georgia Press, 2004.

Dostoevsky, Fyodor. The Brothers Karamazov. trans. Constance Garnett. New York: The Modern Library, 1950.

Dostoyevsky, Fyodor. Notes from the Underground. New York: Signet Classics, 1961.

Doyle, Sir Arthur Conan. The Adventures of Sherlock Holmes. New York: Barnes & Noble Books, 2004.

Dreiser, Theodore. Sister Carrie. ed. Donald Pizer. New York: W. W. Norton & Company, 1970 [1900].

Dulles, Avery. Models of Revelation. Maryknoll, NY: Orbis Books, 1992.

Early, Jubal Anderson. A Memoir of the Last Year of the War for Independence in the Confederate States of America. Columbia, SC: University of South Carolina Press, 2001.

Elie, Paul. The Life You Save May Be Your Own: An American Pilgrimage. New York: Farrar, Straus and Giroux, 2003.

Eliot, T. S. Four Quartets. New York: Harcourt, 1943.

Evans, C. Stephen, ed. Exploring Kenotic Christology: The Self-Emptying of God. Oxford, UK: Oxford University Press, 2006.

Evans, C. Stephen. Kierkegaard: An Introduction. Cambridge, UK: Cambridge University Press, 2009.

Faulkner, William. Novels 1926-1929: Soldier's Pay, Mosquitoes, Flags in the Dust, The Sound and the Fury. New York: Literary Classics of the United States, 2006.

Finnis, John. Moral Absolutes: Tradition, Revision and Truth. Washington, DC: CUA Press, 1991.

Foote, Shelby, and Walker Percy. The Correspondence of Shelby Foote & Walker Percy. ed. Jay Tolson. New York: W. W. Norton & Company, 1997.

Franklin, Benjamin. The Autobiography of Benjamin Franklin. Mineola, NY: Dover Publications, 1996.

Freud, Sigmund. Civilization and Its Discontents. New York: W. W. Norton & Company, 1989.

Freud, Sigmund. The Interpretation of Dreams. trans. Joyce Crick. Oxford, UK: Oxford University Press, 1999.

Freud, Sigmund. Totem and Taboo: Some Points of Agreement be-tween the Mental Lives of Savages and Neurotics. trans. James Strachey. New York: W. W. Norton & Company, 1950.

Freud, Sigmund. New Introductory Lectures on Psychoanalysis. trans. and ed. James Strachey. New York: W. W. Norton & Company, 1965.

Furnal, Joshua. Catholic Theology after Kierkegaard. Oxford, UK: Oxford University Press, 2016.

Fussell, Paul. Class: A Guide Through the American Status System. New York: Summit Books, 1983.

Gergen, Kenneth J. The Saturated Self: Dilemmas of Identity in Contemporary Life. New York: Basic Books, 1991.

Gibrian, Kahlil. The Prophet. New York: Alfred A Knopf, 1998.

Giles, Paul, American Catholic Arts and Fictions: Culture, Ideology, Aesthetics. Cambridge, UK: Cambridge University Press, 1992.

Gilson, Etienne. The Arts of the Beautiful. Dublin: Dalkey Archive Press, 2000 [1965].

Gilson, Etienne. The Christian Philosophy of St. Thomas Aquinas. New York: Octogon Books, 1988.

Grisez, Germain. The Way of the Lord Jesus Vol. 1: Christian Moral Principles. Quincy, IL: Franciscan Press, 1997.

Grisez, Germain. The Way of the Lord Jesus, Vol. 3: Difficult Moral Questions. Quincy, IL: Franciscan Press, 1997.

Guardini, Romano. The End of the Modern World. Wilmington, DE: ISI Books, 2001.

Guignon, Charles, ed. The Existentialists: Critical Essays on Kierkegaard, Nietzsche, Heidegger, and Sarte. Lanham, MD: Rowman & Littlefield, 2004.

Gula, S.S., Richard M. The Good Life: Where Religion and Morality Converge. Mahwah, NJ: Paulist Press, 1999.

Gula, S.S., Richard M. Reason Informed By Faith: Foundations of Catholic Morality. New York: Paulist Press, 1989.

Gula, S.S., Richard M. What Are They Saying About Moral Norms? Mahwah, NJ: Paulist Press, 1982.

Gula, S.S., Richard. What Are They Saying about Scripture and Ethics. Revised Edition. Mahwah, NJ: Paulist Press, 1995.

Gutierrez, Gustavo. On Job: God-Talk and the Suffering of the Innocent. Maryknoll, NY: Orbis Books, 1999.

Hamel, Ron, and Kenneth Himes, OFM, eds. Introduction to Christian Ethics. New York: Paulist Press, 1989.

Hammond, James Henry. Secret and Sacred: The Diaries of James Henry Hammond, a Southern Slaveholder. ed. Carol Bleser. Oxford, UK: Oxford University Press, 1988.

Hammond, Nicholas. Playing with Truth: Language and the Human Condition in Pascal's Pensées. Oxford, UK: Clarendon Press, 1994.

Hampson, Daphne. Kierkegaard: Exposition and Critique. Oxford, UK: Oxford University Press, 2013.

Hannay, Alastair and Gordon Marino, eds. The Cambridge Companion to Kierkegaard. Cambridge, UK: Cambridge University Press, 1998.

Hannay, Alastair. Kierkegaard: A Biography. Cambridge, UK: Cambridge University Press, 2001.

Häring, Bernard. Free & Faithful in Christ: Vol. 1: General Moral Theology. New York: The Seabury Press, 1978.

Hauerwas, Stanley. A Community of Character: Toward a Constructive Christian Social Ethic. Notre Dame, IN: University of Notre Dame Press, 1981.

Heidegger, Martin. Being and Time. New York: Harper & Row Publishers, 1962.

Heller, Joseph. Catch-22. New York: Simon & Schuster, 1961.

Hildebrand, Dietrich von,and Alice von Hildebrand. Morality and Situation Ethics. Quincy, IL: Franciscan Press, 1982.

Hittinger, Russell. The First Grace: Rediscovering the Natural Law in a Post-Christian World. Wilmington, DE: ISI Books, 2003.

Hollenbach. David. The Global Face of Public Faith: Politics, Human Rights, and Christian Ethics. Washington, DC: Georgetown University Press, 2003.

Huxely, Aldous. Brave New World. New York: HarperPerennial, 1998.

Hyman, Arthur, and James J. Walsh. Philosophy in the Middle Ages: The Christian, Islamic, and Jewish Traditions, 2nd Edition. Indianapolis, IN: Hackett Publishing Company, 1973.

James, William. The Varieties of Religious Experience: A Study in Human Nature Being the Gifford Lectures on Natural Religion Delivered At Edinburgh in 1901-1902. New York: Signet Classic, 1983.

James, William. The Will to Believe and Other Essays in Popular Philosophy. New York: Dover Publications, 1956 [1897].

John Paul II. Fides et Ratio. Vatican Translation. Boston: Pauline Books & Media, 1998.

John Paul II. Veritatis Splendor. Vatican Translation. Boston: Pauline Books & Media, 2003.

Joyce, James. A Portrait of the Artist as a Young Man. New York: Penguin Books, 2003.

Joyce, James. Ulysses. New York: Vintage Classics, 1990.

Kafka, Franz. The Castle, Definitive Edition. New York: Alfred A Knopf, 1959.

Kafka, Franz. The Metamorphosis. Bantam Classic, 1912.

Kafka, Franz. The Trial. New York: Alfred A. Knopf, 1955.

Keenan, James F. A History of Catholic Moral Theology in the Twentieth Century: From Confessing Sins to Liberating Consciences. New York: Continuum, 2010.

Ker, Ian. Chesterton: A Biography. Oxford, UK: Oxford University Press, 2011.

Ketner, Kenneth Laine, and Walker Percy. A Thief of Peirce: The Letters of Kenneth Laine Ketner and Walker Percy. ed. Patrick H. Samway, S.J. Jackson, Miss: University Press of Mississippi, 1995.

Kierkegaard, Søren. The Book on Adler. trans. Howard V. Hong and Edna H. Hong. Princeton, NJ: Princeton University Press, 1998.

Kierkegaard, Søren. The Concept of Anxiety: A Simple Psychologically Orienting Deliberation on the Dogmatic Issue of Hereditary Sin. trans. Reider Thomte. Princeton, NJ: Princeton University Press, 1980.

Kierkegaard, Søren. Concluding Unscientific Postscript to Philosophical Fragments: A Mimical-Pathetical-Dialectical Compilation, An Existential Contribution. trans. Howard V. Hong and Edna H. Hong. Princeton, NJ: Princeton University Press, 1992.

Kierkegaard, Søren. Either/Or I. trans. Howard V. Hong and Edna H. Hong. Princeton, NJ: Princeton University Press, 1987.

Kierkegaard, Søren. Either/Or II. trans. Howard V. Hong and Edna H. Hong. Princeton, NJ: Princeton University Press, 1987.

Kierkegaard, Søren. Fear and Trembling. trans. Alistair Hannay. New York: Penguin Books, 1985.

Kierkegaard, Søren. The Living Thoughts of Søren Kierkegaard. ed. W. H. Auden. New York: The New York Review of Books, 1952.

Kierkegaard, Søren. The Moment and Later Writings. trans. Howard V. Hong and Edna H. Hong. Princeton, NJ: Princeton University Press, 1998.

Kierkegaard, Søren. On My Work As An Author, The Point of View For My Work As An Author, and Armed Neutrality. eds. and trans. Howard V. Hong and Edna H. Hong. Princeton, NJ: Princeton University Press, 1998.

Kierkegaard, Søren. Papers and Journals: A Selection. trans. Alastair Hannay. New York: Penguin Books, 1996.

Kierkegaard, Søren. Philosophical Crumbs. trans. Howard V. Hong and Edna H. Hong. Princeton, NJ: Princeton University Press, 1985.

Kierkegaard, Søren. Practice in Christianity. trans. Howard V. Hong and Edna H. Hong. Princeton, NJ: Princeton University Press, 1987.

Kierkegaard, Søren. The Present Age and Of The Difference Between a Genius and an Apostle. trans. Alexander Dru. New York: Harper Torchbook, 1962.

Kierkegaard, Søren. Purity of Heart Is To Will One Thing: Spiritual Preparation for the Office of Confession. trans. Douglas V. Steere. New York: Harper & Row, Publishers, 1948.

Kierkegaard, Søren. Repetition: An Essay in Experimental Psychology. trans. Walter Lowrie. New York: Harper & Row, 1964 [1941].

Kierkegaard, Søren. The Sickness unto Death. trans. Howard V. Hong and Edna H. Hong. Princeton, NJ: Princeton University Press, 1985.

Kierkegaard, Søren. Stages on Life's Way. trans. Walter Lowrie, D.D. Princeton, NJ: Princeton University Press, 1940.

Kierkegaard, Søren. Works of Love. trans. Howard and Edna Hong. New York: HarperPerennial, 2009 [1962].

Kinkead, Rev. Thomas L. Baltimore Catechism Four. Charlotte, NC: Saint Benedict Press, 2010 [1891].

Kirk, Russell. Redeeming the Time. ed. Jeffrey O. Nelson. Wilmington, DE: ISI Books, 2006.

Kreeft, Peter J. Catholic Christianity: A Complete Catechism of Beliefs based on the Catechism of the Catholic Church. San Francisco: Ignatius Press, 2001.

Kreeft, Peter J. C.S. Lewis for the Third Millennium: Six Essays on The Abolition of Man. San Francisco: Ignatius Press, 1994.

Kreeft, Peter J. Socrates Meets Kierkegaard: The Father of Philosophy Meets the Father of Christian Existentialism. South Bend, IN: St. Augustine's, 2014.

Kuehnelt-Leddhihn, Erik von. Leftism Revisited: From de Sade and Marx to Hitler and Pol Pot. Washington, DC: Regnery Gateway, 1990.

Laing, R. D. The Divided Self. New York: Pantheon Books, 1969.

Lamoureux, Patricia, and Kevin J. O'Neil. Seeking Goodness and Beauty: The Use of the Arts in Theological Ethics. Lanham, MD: Rowman & Littlefield Publishers, 2004.

Langer, Susanne K. Philosophy in a New Key: A Study in the Symbolism of Reason, Rite, and Art. Cambridge, MA: Harvard University Press, 1957.

Lauder, Robert E. Walker Percy: Prophetic, Existentialist, Catholic Storyteller. New York: Peter Lang, 1996.

Law, David R. Kierkegaard's Kenotic Christology. Oxford, UK: Oxford University Press, 2013.

Lawson, Lewis A. and Victor A. Kramer, eds. Conversations with Walker Percy. Jackson, MS: University of Mississippi Press, 1985.

Lawson, Lewis A. and Victor A. Kramer, eds. More Conversations with Walker Percy. Jackson, MS: University of Mississippi Press, 1993.

Levasseur, Jennifer, and Mary A. McCay. eds. The Moviegoer at Fifty: New Takes on an Iconic American Novel. Baton Rouge, LA: Louisiana State University Press, 2016.

Livingston, Donald W. Philosophical Melancholy and Delirium: Hume's Pathology of Philosophy. Chicago: University of Chicago Press, 1998.

Lodge, David. Therapy. New York: Penguin Books, 1995.

Lovejoy, Arthur O. The Great Chain of Being: A Study of the History of an Idea. New York: Harper and Brothers, 1960.

Lowrie, Walter. Johann Georg Hamann: an Existentialist. Princeton, NJ: Princeton Theological Seminary, 1950.

Lowrie, Walter. Kierkegaard. London: Oxford University Press, 1938.

Lowrie, Walter. A Short Life of Kierkegaard. Princeton, NJ: Princeton University Press, 2013 [1942].

Lubac, S.J., Henri de. The Drama of Atheist Humanism. New York: Meridian Books, 1950.

Lyotard, Jean-François. The Postmodern Condition: A Report on Knowledge. trans. Geoff Bennington and Brian Massumi. Minneapolis: University of Minneapolis Press, 1984.

MacIntyre, Alasdair. After Virtue.: A Study in Moral Theory, Second Edition. London, Duckworth, 1985.

MacIntyre, Alasdair. Dependent Rational Animals: Why Human Beings Need the Virtues. Chicago: Open Court, 2012 [1999].

MacIntyre, Alasdair. God, philosophy, universities: A Selective History of the Catholic Philosophical Tradition. Lanham, MD: Rowman & Littlefield Publishers, 2009.

MacIntyre, Alasdair. The Tasks of Philosophy: Selected Essays Vol. 1. Cambridge, UK: Cambridge University Press, 2006.

MacIntyre, Alasdair. Three Rival Versions of Moral Enquiry: Encyclopaedia, Genealogy and Tradition. Notre Dame, IN: University of Notre Dame Press, 1991.

MacIntyre, Alasdair. Whose Justice? Which Rationality? Notre Dame, IN: University of Notre Dame Press, 1988.

Mackey, Louis. Kierkegaard: A Kind of Poet. Philadelphia: University of Pennsylvania Press, 1971.

Mahoney, John. The Making of Moral Theology: A Study of the Roman Catholic Tradition. Oxford: Clarendon Press, 1987.

Malamud, Bernard. The Fixer. New York: Farrar, Straus and Giroux, 1966.

Mann, Thomas. The Magic Mountain [Der Zauberberg]. trans. H. T. Low-Porter. New York: Alfred A. Knopf, 1967 [1924].

Marcel, Gabriel. Homo Viator: Introduction to a Metaphysic of Hope. trans. Emma Craufurd. New York: Harper Torchbook, 1962 [1951].

Maritain, Jacques. Art and Scholasticism and The Frontiers of Poetry. trans. Joseph W. Evans. New York: Charles Scribner's Sons, 1962.

Maritain, Jacques. Moral Philosophy: An Historical and Critical Survey of the Great Systems. New York: Charles Scribner's Sons, 1964.

Mauriac, François. Woman of the Pharisees (La Pharisienne) trans. Gerard Hopkins. New York: Henry Holt and Company, 1946.

May, William E. An Introduction to Moral Theology. Huntington, IN: Our Sunday Visitor, 2003.

Merton, Thomas. The Seven Storey Mountain: An Autobiography of Faith. New York: Harcourt, Inc., 1948.

Miller, Vincent J. Consuming Religion: Christian Faith and Practice in a Consumer Culture. New York: Bloomsbury Academic, 2003.

Miller, Jr., Walter M. A Canticle for Leibowitz. New York: HarperCollins, 1959.

Mills, C. Wright. Power, Politics & People: The Collected Essays of C. Wright Mills. ed. Irving Louis Horowitz. Oxford, UK: Oxford University Press, 1963.

Mills, C. Wright. White Collar: The American Middle Classes. Oxford, UK: Oxford University Press, 1951.

Mozart, Wolfgang Amadeus. Mozart's Don Giovanni. trans. Ellen H. Bleiler. New York: Dover Publications, 1964.

Mulder, Jr., Jack. Kierkegaard and the Catholic Tradition: Conflict and Dialogue. Bloomington, IN: Indiana University Press, 2010.

Nagel, Thomas. "Sin and Significance," review of The Message in the Bottle, by Walker Percy. The New York Review of Books, (September 18, 1975).

Nagel, Thomas. The View From Nowhere. London: Oxford University Press, 1986.

Newman, John Henry. An Essay in Aid of a Grammar of Assent. London: Longmans, Green, and Co., 1903.

Newman, John Henry. An Essay in the Development of Christian Doctrine. Notre Dame, IN: University of Notre Dame Press, 1989.

Newman, John Henry. The Idea of a University. Notre Dame, IN: University of Notre Dame Press, 1990.

Nietzsche, Friedrich. Beyond Good and Evil: Prelude to a Philosophy of the Future. Mineola, NY: Dover Publications, 1997.

Nietzsche, Friedrich. The Birth of Tragedy and The Genealogy of Morals. trans. Francis Golffing. Garden City, NY: Doubleday Anchor Books, 1956.

Nisbet, Robert. The Present Age: Progress and Anarchy in Modern American. Indianapolis, IN: Liberty Fund, 1988.

Nisbet, Robert. The Quest for Community: A Study in the Ethics of Order and Freedom. Wilmington, DE: ISI Books, 2010.

O'Conner, Flannery. The Complete Stories. New York: Farrar, Straus and Giroux, 1971.

O'Conner, Flannery. The Violent Bear It Away. New York: Farrar. Straus and Giroux, 1960.

O'Conner, Flannery. Wise Blood. New York: Farrar, Straus and Giroux, 1949.

O'Keefe, Mark. What are they Saying about Social Sin? New York: Paulist Press, 1990.

Ortega y Gasset, José. The Revolt of the Masses. trans. anon. New York: W. W. Norton & Company, 1932.

Packard, Vance. The Hidden Persuaders. New York: David McKay Company, 1957.

Pascal, Blaise. Pensées. ed. Roger Ariew. Indianapolis, IN: Hackett Publishing Company, Inc., 2004.

Peirce, Charles Saunders. Philosophical Writings of Peirce. ed. Justus Buchler. New York: Dover Publications, 1955.

Percy, Walker. Lancelot. London: Secker and Warburg, 1977.

Percy, Walker. The Last Gentleman. London: Eyre and Spottiswoode, 1967.

Percy, Walker. Lost in the Cosmos: The Last Self-Help Book. New York: Farrar, Straus and Giroux, 1983.

Percy, Walker. Love in the Ruins: The Adventures of a Bad Catholic at a Time Near the End of the World. New York: Picador, 1971.

Percy, Walker. Signposts in a Strange Land. New York: Farrar, Straus and Giroux, 1991.

Percy, Walker. The Message in the Bottle: How Queer Man Is, How Queer Language Is, and What One Has to Do with the Other. New York: Farrar, Straus and Giroux, 1975.

Percy, Walker. The Moviegoer. New York: Vintage Books, 1998.

Percy, Walker. The Second Coming. London: Secker and Warburg, 1981.

Percy, Walker. The Thanatos Syndrome. London: Andre Deutsch, 1987.

Percy, William Alexander. Lanterns on the Levee: Recollections of a Planter's Son. Baton Rouge: Louisiana State University Press, 1941.

Pieper, Josef. The Concept of Sin. South Bend, Indiana: St. Augustine's Press, 2001.

Pinckaers, Servais. The Sources of Christian Ethics. trans. Sr. Mary Thomas Noble, O.P. Washington, DC: The Catholic University of America Press, 1995.

Proust, Marcel. Swann's Way: Remembrance of Things Past. New York: Vintage International, 1989.

Pynchon, Thomas. Gravity's Rainbow. New York: Penguin Books, 2006.

Quinlan, Kieran. Walker Percy, The Last Catholic Novelist. Baton Rouge, LA: Louisiana State University Press, 1996.

Rahner, Karl. Foundation of the Christian Faith: An Introduction to the Idea of Christianity. trans. William V. Dych. New York: The Seabury Press, 1978.

Ratzinger, Joseph Cardinal, with Vittorio Messori. The Ratzinger Report: An Exclusive Interview on the State of the Church. trans. Salvator Attanasio and Graham Harrison. San Francisco: Ignatius Press, 1985.

Reiff, Philip. The Triumph of the Therapeutic: Uses of Faith after Freud. Chicago: University of Chicago Press, 1987.

Rowland, Tracy. Ratzinger's Faith: The Theology of Pope Benedict XVI. Oxford, UK: Oxford University Press, 2008.

Rudd, Anthony. Kierkegaard and the Limits of the Ethical. Oxford: Oxford University Press, 1997.

Sagan, Carl. Cosmos. New York: Ballantine Books, 1980.

Salinger, J. D. The Catcher in the Rye. New York: Little, Brown and Company, 1945.

Salinger, J. D. Franny and Zooey. New York: Little, Brown and Company, 1961.

Salzman, Todd A., ed. Method and Catholic Moral Theology: The Ongoing Reconstruction. Omaha, NE: Creighton University Press, 1999.

Samway, S.J., Patrick. Walker Percy: A Life. New York: Farrar, Straus and Giroux, 1997.

Sarte, Jean-Paul. Nausea. trans. Lloyd Alexander. New York: New Directions Publishing, 2007.

Schneiders, Sandra M. The Revelatory Text: Interpreting the New Testament as Sacred Scripture. San Francisco: HarperSanFrancisco, 1991.

Schroeder, O.P., H. J. Canons and Decrees of the Council of Trent. St. Louis, MO: B. Herder Book Co., 1941.

Stone, Brad Lowell. Robert Nisbet. Wilmington, DE: ISI Books, 2002.

Sullivan, Harry Stack. Conceptions of Modern Psychiatry. New York: W. W. Norton & Company, 1940.

Sullivan, Harry Stack. Schizophrenia as a Human Process. New York: W. W. Norton & Company, 1962.

Tanner, S.J., Norman, ed. Decrees of the Ecumenical Councils. Washington, DC: Georgetown University Press, 1990.

Tanner, S.J., Norman, ed. Vatican II: The Essential Texts. New York: Image Books, 2012.

Taylor, Charles. A Secular Age. Cambridge, MA: Harvard University Press, 2007.

Taylor, Charles. Sources of Self. Cambridge: Harvard University Press, 1989.

Thérèse of Lisieux. The Autobiography of Thérèse of Lisieux: The Story of a Soul. trans. John Beevers. New York: Doubleday, 2001 [1957].

Toole, John Kennedy. A Confederacy of Dunces. New York: Grove Press, 1980.

Twelve Southerners. I'll Take My Stand. Gloucester, MA: Peter Smith, 1976.

United States Catholic Conference, ed. and trans. Catechism of the Catholic Church, Second Edition. New York: Doubleday, 1995.

Vidal, Marciano. Moral Fundamental: Moral de Actitudes, Seventh Edition. Madrid: Editorial Perpetuo Socorro, 1990.

Voegelin, Eric. The New Science of Politics: An Introduction. Chicago: The University of Chicago Press, 1952.

Voegelin, Eric. Order and History, Volume One: Israel and Revelation. Baton Rouge, LA: Louisiana State University Press, 1956.

Waugh, Evelyn. Brideshead Revisited: The Sacred and Profane Memories of Captain Charles Ryder. New York: Little, Brown and Company, 1945.

Weaver, Richard M. Ideas Have Consequences. Chicago: Chicago University Press, 1948.

Weaver, Richard. The Southern Tradition at Bay: A History of Postbellum Thought. eds. George Core and M.E. Bradford. New Rochelle, NY: Arlington House, 1968.

Weber, Max. From Max Weber: Essays in Sociology, trans. H. H. Gerth and C. Wright Mills. New York: Routledge, 1948.

Wilson, Edward O. Consilience: The Unity of Knowledge. New York: Vintage Books, 1998.

Wolfe, Tom. The Bonfire of Vanities. New York: Farrar, Straus, Giroux, 1987.

Wolfe, Tom. Kingdom of Speech. New York: Little, Brown and Company, 2016.

Wood, James. The Book against God. New York: Picador, 2004.

Wood, Ralph C. The Comedy of Redemption. Notre Dame, IN: University of Notre Dame Press, 1988.

Wyatt-Brown, Bertram. The House of Percy: Honor, Melancholy, and Imagination in a Southern Family. New York: Oxford University Press, 1994.

Yates, Richard. Revolutionary Road. New York: Vintage Books, 1961.

Zwingli, Huldreich. Commentary on True and False Religion. eds., Samuel Macauley Jackson and Clarence Nevin Heller. Durham, NC: The Labyrinth Press, 1981.

PART II:
& OTHER ESSAYS

INTRODUCTION

I. AUTHENTIC AESTHETIC ENCHANTMENTS:
Social Imagination in Charles Taylor's *A Secular Age*

II. DIFFERING DIVINITIES IN ANCIENT ROME:
The Roman Imperial Cult versus Christian Worship
from Acts through the Pope

III. THE ORIGEN(S) OF CONSTITUTIONAL LAW:
Theories of Legal Order in the Context of History

***IV. THE MORALITY OF AMERICAN NEUTRALITY
IN WORLD WAR I:***
The Just War Tradition *In Mundo Huius Temporis*

V. LAW, VIRTUE OR HEAVEN:
Immanent Instantiation or Ultimate Fulfillment
in Thomas Aquinas' Written *Corpus*

VI. FUN, LOVE & PASSION:
A Thomistic Interpretation of Augustine's Sin

***VII. THE DEVELOPMENT OF JOHN HENRY
NEWMAN'S MARIAN THEOLOGY:***
The Cult of the Saints in Victorian England

CONCLUSION

POSTSCRIPTUM

Once a bitch always a bitch, what I say. I says you're lucky if her playing out of school is all that worries you.

". . . And what for? So a bunch of damn eastern jews I'm not talking about men of the jewish religion," I says. "I've known some jews that were fine citizens. You might be one yourself," I says.

"No," he says. "I'm an American."

"No offense," I says. "I give every man his due, regardless of religion or anything else. I have nothing against jews as an individual," I says. "It's just the race. You'll admit that they produce nothing. They follow the pioneers into a new country and sell them clothes."

. . . What I'm talking about is the fellows that sit up there in New York and trim the sucker gamblers."

. . . I don't want a killing; only these small town gamblers are out for that, I just want my money back that these dam jews have gotten with all their guaranteed inside dope. Then I'm through; they can kiss my foot for every other red cent of mine they get.

. . . It always takes a man that never made much at any thing to tell you how to run your business, though. Like these college professors without a whole pair of socks to his name, telling you how to make a million in ten years, and a woman that couldn't get a husband can always tell you how to raise a family.

. . . Like I say once a bitch always a bitch. And just let me have twenty-four hours without any dam New York jew to advise me what it's going to do. I don't want to make a killing; save that to suck in the smart gamblers with. I just want an even chance to get my money back. And once I've done that they can bring all Beale street and all bedlam in here and two of them can sleep in my bed and another one can have my place at the table too.

William Faulkner, THE SOUND AND THE FURY

The poseur *who seems to only to be preoccupied with others is in reality entirely taken up with himself. Indeed, the person he is with only interests him in so far as he is likely to form a favourable picture of him which in turn he will receive back.*

At school or in barracks the poseur has practically no chance of success. A consensus of opinion is almost certain to be formed against him, his companions see through him at once,

It is not easy to formulate it exactly, but it is a distinct perception of the incompatibility between a certain reality in which each one participates and this play-acting which degrades and betrays it.

On the other hand, the more artificial, unreal and, in a certain sense, effeminate the environment, the less the incompatibility will be felt.

Now, posing is a form of flattery, a manner of paying court while seeming to obtrude oneself. Beneath it all we invariably find self-love and, I might add, pretension.

To pretend is not only to aspire or aim high, it is also to simulate, and actually there is simulation in all posing.

From the moment I become preoccupied about the effect I want to produce on the other person, my every act, word and attitude loses its authenticity; and we all know what even a studied or affected simplicity can be.

From the very fact that I treat the other person merely as a means of resonance or an amplifier, I tend to consider him a sort of apparatus which I can, or think I can, manipulate, or of which I can dispose at will.

the idolatry of self,

Gabriel Marcel,
THE EGO AND ITS RELATION TO OTHERS

PART II
INTRODUCTION:

C. Wright Mills once wrote that, "the true gentleman in the eastern cities, and increasingly across the nation is usually a banker or a lawyer, which is convenient, for those who possess a fortune are in need of trusted, wise, and sober men to preserve its integrity."[1]

Lowly scholarship is decidedly not a gentlemanly vocation, that is, except for the occasional laborers of love. Academics, especially in America, have been paid relatively little regard as to power to do things about what they know. The intelligentsia, if there is such a thing in the U.S., is quite degraded and typically subject to a rather low-order of society, save a few exceptions. So, Mills once more, "By the powerful we mean, of course, those who are able to realize their will, even if others resist it."[2]

The tools at the disposal of the scholar are little more than persuasion and prestige. Specialists in every field often write to themselves, but are little heard outside of other experts in their subject matter. I don't doubt that many important things have been said in a void, where the truth is banished to obscurity and never really reaches beyond a small group of people. As for money and power, the recent graduate of Yale or Harvard is best suited to a job as a banker or a lawyer and thus, truth be told, that is where the majority of them end up.[3] The title professor does have a certain *panache*, but nearly only for the revered scientists of the age; the "useful" scientists that is. The humanities is a tougher field in the scheme of things.

In fact, the predominance of proletarian scholarship is endemic. Many disgruntled teachers turn to Karl Marx or National media politics for consolation. I suppose this is better than "middle-class" scholarship, heaven-forbid. But, one need not worry here, for every semblance of bourgeois cliché has been officially stricken from the higher levels of academic discourse long before

---

[1] C. Wright Mills, *The Power Elite* (Oxford, UK: Oxford University Press, 1956), 60.

[2] Ibid., 9.

[3] C. Wright Mills, "6: Old Professions and New Skills," in C. Wright Mills, *White Collar: The American Middle Classes* (Oxford, UK: Oxford University Press, 1951), 3. Lawyers, 4. Professors, 5. Business and the Professions, 121-141.

now. Still, everyone who sits down to write something about what they think ought to carefully consider why.

It is all too common in our day that writing is done in ignorance of "one thing or another" and that what gets put down on paper as a novel idea is really somewhere else already. With humility, anyone wishing to uncover some small truth or repackage old truths had better get a sense of the virtue called by ancient Greeks aidōs, "the candid recognition that the other is more important than yourself."[4] Too often an intellectual aspirant can get a bit heady with ideology or become far too impressed with what he or she knows. I know this from experience.

Seeing the limit-of-knowledge takes someone who is much more than half-educated. These half-educated people can be dangerous, as are the proletariat scholars at times. It is a terrible curse to have to think truth with no "right" to. One can imagine "out-of-sight" powerful people, who, in a class bubble, ought to listen to the reader of books and eater of budgeted cheese and crackers. But, it seems unlikely. On the other hand, the well-informed scholar at the lower level of the totem-pole should remember that—"there are in fact tiers and ranges of wealth and power of which people in the middle and lower ranks know very little and may not even dream."[5] *Id est*, as much as you read about it (?), you'll never really know.

A good Marxist will remind us that very rarely does anyone rise more than a notch or two from their accident of birth (in either direction). The rich remain the rich. The rich "out-of-sight" stay there too. The middle-class success story can maybe get to be upper middle-class or upper class. But, just as likely the middle-class children will end up in the lower middle or working-class or, gasp, proletariat. It is sad, but "Horatio Alger dies hard."[6]

There is not too much new under the sun as far social-class goes, short of some new techie-stuff that might reel-in a quick billion for the ruthlessly ambitious MIT graduate. Even then, however, this poor nouveaux is just the very same parvenu he was, with all his old social habits and breeding, but a much larger bank account perhaps. He may just spend his fortune on the crassest junk

---

[4] Roger Scruton, *I Drink Therefore I Am: A Philosopher's Guide to Wine* (London: Continuum, 2009), 35.

[5] C. Wright Mills, *The Power Elite*, 12.

[6] Ibid., 91.

money can buy. It is hard to think that many of the self-made capitalists of yesteryear who made their millions off an empire of sausages or some such thing can ever have the mind or temperament of a philosopher. Therein lies the heart of the problem—Plato's philosopher king is a dead ideal of history.

The professional educator is rarely any better. The great intellectual can be really right about nearly everything, have read all the important books, but, for all his or her mastery of language and knowledge, is skewered with *a word* by someone out of his social class in an ordinary interaction.[7] Paul Fussell gives us an illustration of the phenomenon,

> Thus it's purely for social-class reasons that university professors object to being denominated *educators*, because the term fails to distinguish them from high-school superintendents, illiterate young teachers with temporary "credentials," and similar pedagogic riffraff. The next time you meet a distinguished university professor, especially one who fancies himself well known nationally for his ideas and writings, tell him it's an honor to meet such a famous educator, and watch: first he will look down for a while, then up, but not at you, then away. And very soon he will detach himself from your company. He will be smiling all the time, but inside he will be in torment.[8]

—Eyes avert? Even the word "philosopher" has a queer hippie-esque sound to it. The fact is that the world pays little respect to ideas. "Modern social and corporate organization makes independence an expensive thing; in fact, it may make common integrity a prohibitive luxury for ordinary men."[9] And, "the individual does not rest easy, for he knows that the Juggernaut

---

[7] *See* Michael Oakeshott, *Rationalism in politics and other essays* (Indianapolis: Liberty Fund, 1991).

[8] Paul Fussell, *Class: A Guide Through the American Status System* (New York: Summit Books, 1983), 166.

[9] Richard Weaver, *Ideas Have Consequences* (Chicago: Chicago University Press, 1948), 16.

technology may twist and destroy the pattern of life he has made for himself."[10]

There is a big size reading public out there. This seemingly hopeful prospect of power is soon disheartened by a light perusal of the bestsellers lists. It is a gruesome fact that the particularly specious "self-help" genre outsells nearly anything in the remote range of books propounding heavy intellectual thoughts. Serious history or serious literature is at an all-time low ebb, but production of such things is higher than ever. Richard Weaver reminds us,

> to echo Nietzsche's bitter observation: 'Everyone being allowed to learn to read, ruineth in the long wrong not only writing but also thinking.' It is not what people can read; it is what they do read, and what they can be made, by any imaginable means, to learn from what they read, that determine the issue of this noble experiment. We have given them a technique of acquisition; how much comfort can we take in the way they employ it? In a society where expression is free and popularity is rewarded they read mostly that which debauches them and they are continuously exposed to manipulation by controllers of the printing machine—[11]

The issue with self-help reading is somewhat paradigmatic of much else that is being consumed. It is scientism, "pop" psychology, pop-culture, and the pervasive spreading ignorance of history run amuck. It is often that "self-help" genres get muddled together with serious philosophy in the social imagination. This is too bad. So—

> The problem with self-help ideas is not that they are wrong, but that they are one-sided. That is why latching onto them as if they were the answer to your problems cuts you off from a sensitivity to other virtues and ideals that are not only

---

[10] Ibid.
[11] Ibid., 13-14.

equally good, but are absolutely essential to living
a meaningful and fulfilling life.[12]

The "power of positive thinker" I would think can take my
cultural pessimism for, well, too pessimistic. And, that anything
written in anger, angst, insecurity, rage, or self-pity, is dubious at
best. This is right. No less, I am *genuinely* pessimistic (negative)
about a number of things. God-fearing too. That the universe may
collude in order to align my thoughts with losing my car-keys more
often is a risk I am willing to take, Norman Vincent Peale aside.

On the politico-religious end of things it is not much better
either. We have on the one hand a hopelessly propagandized and
brain-washed media spectatorship. By all normal civilizational
standards the mass-media is simply morbid. And the world of religion unfortunately dove-tails with the political media most of the
time. The written word is still the best place to find what is true.
Even here, though, there is no way out of the dilemma of who is
reading what. There is a rare glut of communication because of an
over-abundance of print, where the right minds can't find the right
thoughts. And a whole lot of people get a lot of wrong-headed
thinking in the process.

The founding father of sociology Max Weber would like to
point out of course that this is a typically Protestant character—the
reliance on the written word for all things good.[13] The old adage
was that the Protestant learns in writing and music, Catholics learn
in pictures, art, and ritual. We get more on this in a masterful work
by the imposing title *The Menace of the Herd*:

> In the remote background there can clearly be
> seen Johann Gutenberg, father of mechanical
> writing, the innocent promoter of the "intellectu-
> al," or rather semieducated masses, grandfather of
> the press. The blind, awe-filled worship of the
> printed word was to be initiated a century after
> Gutenberg by Protestantism with its bibliolatry.
> The printed word is highly honored in all
> Protestant countries and the "Book of Books,"

---

[12] Charles Guignon, *On Being Authentic*, (London and New York:
Routledge, 2004), ix-x.

[13] *See* Max Weber, *The Protestant Work Ethic and the Spirit of Capitalism*.

the Bible, ranges there as a *primus inter pares* inspiring respect before its lesser cousins. It is therefore in the Protestant countries that we see the worship of the printed word which developed into the "science" of advertising and the religious veneration of the daily press by the masses. If we compare the South German with the North German, for instance, we will see all the difference; the former remained always skeptical toward anything printed and expresses his distrust in the current phrase: "He lies like print."

It is, of course, in a way more human to believe the wildest rumors as long as they go from mouth to mouth and are told "into the face" than to trust a printed, usually anonymous piece of information.

Needless to say it is only in print-believing Protestant countries that people fall under the spell of advertising campaigns; the manufacturer or seller who would spend a proportionally equal sum for advertising the same merchandise in France, Italy, or Poland as in England or America would simply waste his money. *This truly archochlocratic way of influencing and hypnotizing people,* who often fall victims to gigantic frauds, *does not only require print-believing beings for victims but also an ochlocratically inclined culture—a homogeneous sand heap—in which the necessarily uniform appeal reaches mentally uniform human beings.*[14]

Or, even better is Friedrich Nietzsche's caution-to-the-wind-worded aphoristic rendering. Our friend Nietzsche appraises the Protestant/Catholic difference for us here: "the whole of Protestantism lacks the southern 'delicatezza'. There is an Oriental exaltation of the mind in it, like that of an undeservedly favoured or ele-

---

[14] Erik Ritter von Kuehnelt-Leddihn, *The Menace of the Herd, Or Procrustes at Large* (Milwaukee, MN: The Bruce Publishing Company, 1943), 55-56.

vated slave, as in the case of St. Augustine, for instance, who lacks in an offensive manner, all nobility in bearing and desires."[15]

That I am an undeservedly elevated slave who writes, as a Protestant or Catholic, is an assurance. It takes some of the pressure off. I am in point of fact a Protestant who converted to the Catholic Church who then went back to Protestant. Then Catholic once more, and now . . . who knows? Much of my writing is a reflection of this (to clear up any confusion).

That I would (or anyone else) reach an "oligarch of the universe" in writing seems extraordinary. That I would deserve to, probably not, but maybe. In this Part II of our book here my better essays in graduate school are brought "up-to-snuff." They are polished. My voice alters essay to essay, but the variation is not too drastic. There *are* contradictions in thought since each was written at separate periods of development.

Essays 1, 2, 3, 5 and 6, were written during my M.A. degree program in Philosophy and Religious Studies at *University of South Florida* (2012-2013). Essays 4 and 7 were written for the Department of Theology and Religion at *The Catholic University of America* in 2010. They are all on specialized subject matter, hopefully readable for wider audiences barring all of the necessary contextual background.

Nowadays, academic form, as with most other written forms, is looser than it once was. I try not to take too much liberty however. I do stick to the standard blueprint of recognizable academic research. Sometimes my creative desire can overtake my dryer scholarly ambition, but I have learned to refrain of throwing the "kitchen-sink" at people too much.

I am the type of person who reads every word of *Finnegan's Wake* from start to finish each Saint Patrick's day.[16] So, I can only hope I am more understandable. Seriously though, all kidding aside, it should be rewarding reading in spite of my having written much of it as a personal portfolio of sorts. A modest accomplishment to be sure, in the scope of everything, but my labor of love, call it what you will.

---

[15] Friedrich Nietzsche, *Beyond Good and Evil: Prelude to a Philosophy of the Future* (Mineola, NY: Dover Publications, 1997), 37.

[16] *See* James Joyce, *Finnegan's Wake* (New York: Penguin Books, 1999 [1939]).

I.

AUTHENTIC AESTHETIC ENCHANTMENTS:

SOCIAL IMAGINATION IN CHARLES TAYLOR'S *A SECULAR AGE*

It did not, presumably, occur to the Chartes sculptor to sign his name on the toe of an apostle he had finished on the West Portal. (Or to the Lascaux Cave painter.)

The attraction between the noughted self and the fiesta (quite literally a feast for the starved vacuole of self) exists on a continuum of affinities: at one end, say, the serious yet finally hopeless nostalgia of Henry Adams at Mont-Saint-Michel, at the other the more commonplace delectation of, say, Oppenheimer or Lawrence at a Pueblo festival in New Mexico

Walker Percy, LOST IN THE COSMOS

In that respect. Why these pompous, pointless block phrases?

Tom Wolfe, THE BONFIRE OF THE VANITIES

Just as according to Gresham's Law, bad money drives out good money, so, too, does modern mass culture make it increasingly difficult for anything better to hold its own.

Wilhelm Röpke, A HUMANE ECONOMY

The existence of a parasitic economy and a predatory political system produced a typically Roman urban institution that embraced both aspects of its life and gave them dramatic setting: the old practice of the religious blood sacrifice was given a new secular form in the arena.

Roman life, for all its claims of peace, centered more and more on the imposing rituals of extermination. In the pursuit of sensations sufficiently sharp to cover momentarily the emptiness and meaninglessness of their parasitic existence, the Romans took to staging chariot races, spectacular naval battles set in an artificial lake, theatrical pantomimes in which the strip and tease and lewder sexual acts were performed in public. But sensations need constant whipping as people become inured to them: so the whole effort reached a pinnacle in the gladiatorial spectacles, where the agents of this regime applied a diabolic inventiveness to human torture and human extermination.

The inhabitants of modern metropolises are not psychologically too remote from Rome to be unable to appreciate this new form. We have our own equivalent daily doses of sadism that follow, like contaminated vitamin capsules, our deficient commonplace food: the newspaper accounts, the radio reports, the television programs, the novels, the dramas, all devoted to portraying as graphically as possible every variety of violence, perversion, bestiality, criminal delinquency, and nihilistic despair.

Lewis Mumford, THE CITY IN HISTORY

1. *The Contemporary Aesthetic Atmosphere*

A work of art is a powerful instrument. Today, the course that the artistic medium will take in the future is uncertain, indefinite. The so-called contemporary "art-world" is widely thought to be in a stage of *gross* fragmentation. There is an acceptance of the fact that there is no more (and perhaps never will be again) a means by which to freeze art forever in an eternal or universal mode of understanding.[1] Prior ages have believed in the immortality of the artifacts that arose from the culture of the community, whether religious, commercial, hereditary, or otherwise. That view has faded.[2] The *historical consciousness* of the present age is a development that is irreversible save for the occurrence of mass amnesia. The world is conscious of the relativity of the past to the present and of the present to the future in a way that is largely unprecedented in human civilization.

It can be said that the perceived value of art-work has become unhinged from any objective measure at the same time that a veritable explosion of new modes of artistic production has arrived.[3] The current mass-marketing of the products of an industrial civilization is beyond repair or remedy. For example, the symphony on cassette, the flat two-dimensional screen of the television-set, the instant gratification of cheap entertainment, have contributed to a milieux that rips the accomplishments of former epochs from context.[4] The consequent corruption or degradation of æsthetic

---

[1] Terry Eagleton, "Chapter 14: From the Polis to Postmodernism," in Terry Eagleton, *The Ideology of the Aesthetic* (Oxford, UK: Blackwell Publishing, 1990).

[2] The history of æsthetic philosophy starts with Lord Shaftsbury and Edmund Burke and becomes a major area of enquiry with Friedrich Schiller and German Romanticism. *See* Edmund Burke, *A Philosophical Enquiry into the Origin of our Ideas of the Sublime and Beautiful*, ed. James T. Boulton (Notre Dame, IN: University of Notre Dame Press, 1968). & Friedrich Schiller, *On the Aesthetic Education of Man*, trans. Reginald Snell (Mineola, NY: Dover Publications, 2004). The philosophy of æsthetics reaches its zenith in Kant.

[3] *See* Immanuel Kant, *Critique of the Power of Judgement*, ed Paul Guyer. trans. Paul Guyer and Eric Matthews (Cambridge, UK: Cambridge University Press, 2000).

[4] *See* Jean-François Lyotard, *The Postmodern Condition: A Report on Knowledge*, trans. Geoff Bennington and Brian Massumi (Minneapolis: University of Minneapolis Press, 1984). Of course, many feel or think that much of

appreciation is becoming more apparent in larger segments of the general public.[5]

However, one need not give into an attitude of one-sided pessimism or nostalgia in order to combat the more cancerous tendencies of invasive artistic significations; significations that impose on the individual imaginative poisons in the mental atmosphere. The increase in size and scope of the potential industrial bludgeoning that the populace endures is cause for alarm, but ultimately the frustrated anxiety of the alienated individual is a deficient remedy.

There is much to celebrate in the way that the artistic enterprise of our civilization has in fact flourished. The beautiful is often perceived as an object of perennial value.[6] The concrete object which inspires æsthetic joy is experienced in greater degree now than in much of human history. Even when the beautiful is what the repulsive was yesterday, the efflorescence of opportunities for creativity is indisputable. Individuals express themselves with immunity in a marketplace of artistic expression that feeds innovative activity at all levels. The art-world is free from restrictions in a way that would outrage more closed societies.[7]

"Elitists" are free to determine art however they so please. The "common-man" [hoi polloi] is granted ample occasion to find the resources and materials necessary to pursue his or her inclinations wherever he or she should choose. Middle-class burghers often remain what they always were, town-merchants overly concerned with aping and mimicking the class above them.[8] Of course,

---

"postmodernism" is merely a "fashion" and not a significant intellectual distinction.

[5] José Ortega y Gasset, *The Revolt of the Masses*, trans. anon (New York: W. W. Norton & Company, 1932). Ortega y Gasset was one of the first to recognize the "hype" of mere technique and the idolatry of the machine.

[6] *That some philosophers may object to this statement there is no doubt.

[7] Terry Eagleton, *The Ideology of the Aesthetic*, 369. Eagleton writes: "The aesthetic becomes the guerrilla tactics of secret subversion, of silent resistance, of stubborn refusal. Art will pulverize traditional form and meaning, because the laws of syntax and grammar are the laws of the police. It will dance on the grave of narrative semantics and representation, celebrate madness and delirium, speak like a woman, dissolve all social dialectics into the flow of desire."

[8] *See* Paul Fussell, *Class: A Guide Through the American Status System* (New York: Summit Books, 1983).

the creativity of this class is notoriously complacent and banal.[9] Nevertheless, women in large numbers are afforded the æsthetic pleasure of planting gardens to replicate the finest traditions of the Lord's Manor. Aspiring young professionals are provided with an over-abundance of options in the marketplace of gadgets, widgets, home furnishings, or personal accoutrements, meaning that the possibilities are potentially limitless for fashioning an authentic individual lifestyle. Even the impoverished or destitute college student can be saturated with relative æsthetic satisfaction when provided the benefits of a full-stocked collection of favorite movies, music, poster art, or whatever.[10] The sheer magnitude of creative energy, æsthetic criticism and artistic activity, is continued proof that the æsthetic spirit is an unquenchable fire of the human heart that can rarely be extinguished once set free.[11]

All that aside, there is still a darker aspect of artistic creation, expression, individuality or mass-production, that is undeniably and ineradicably gurgling in the under-belly of a civilization spinning ever more frantically on an axis of inescapable æsthetic decadence.[12] The future of the more objectionable developments in artistic expression can be considered predetermined in ill-conceived ways.[13]

The subject of this essay is on the denunciation of the ignorance pervading the more absurd or abusive elements that are infecting the collective æsthetic atmosphere. For example, the acceptance of children "strung-out" on excessively violent or pornographic "amusements," the mass narcotizing of huge swaths

---

[9] *See* "Catholicism and the Bourgeois Mind," in Christopher Dawson, *Dynamics of World History*, ed. John J. Mulloy (Wilmington, DE: ISI Books, 2007).

[10] An excellent fictional rendering of contemporary college life and culture is in Tom Wolfe, *I Am Charlotte Simmons* (New York: Picador, 2004).

[11] *See* Charles Taylor, *A Secular Age* (Cambridge, MA: The Belknap Press of Harvard University Press, 2007), "Chapter 13: The Age of Authenticity."

[12] *See* C. S. Lewis, *The Abolition of Man or Reflections on education with special reference to the teaching of English in the upper forms of schools* (New York: HarperCollins, 2001 [1944]). Lewis here is one of the staunchest critics of the backwardness of modern ethical thought.

[13] *See* Tom Wolfe, *Hooking Up* (New York: Farrar, Straus and Giroux, 2000). This is a relatively spot-on fictional account of the trajectory of youth culture and the "science-dominated" atheistic future.

of the population with psychotropic medications, or the complete absence of any moral-restraints on individual expression, is an indication that there is a sickness in the social body that is in need of serious diagnosis and healing.[14] In other words, the 20th century push "to force the acceptance of pornography as medical science, filth as artistic realism, and abnormality as a mere difference of opinion" has been an ongoing battle for some time now (lost in any meaningful sense by the opposition to be sure).[15] *But* the question is asked, when is self-expressive individualism simply egotism masquerading as creativity?[16] Is the artistic enterprise empty of any moral content whatsoever? The time is ripe to re-assess the arts that glorify vice once hedonism and selfishness become normative measures of social worth.[17]

What follows deals with three major themes in ÆSTHETICS: **1)** Disenchantment, **2)** Signification and **3)** Authenticity. In particular, the sweeping narrative in Charles Taylor's *A Secular Age* is discussed with added attention paid to his rendering of the notions of disenchantment and authenticity.[18] The "big" idea of this essay is that artwork (and æsthetic understanding in general) requires a collective moral or religious enthusiasm to inspire or critique the relative merit of artistic endeavor—beyond individual expressionism itself. Authenticity is a deeply flawed value that cannot replace the notion of virtue and more traditional moral-modes of æsthetic creation.[19]

---

[14] A counterpoint to this *see* the somewhat "hell-bent conservative" condemnation of the entire pop culture of the 1990s in Robert Bork, "Chapter 7: The Collapse of Popular Culture," in *Slouching Toward Gomorrah* (New York, New York: ReganBooks, 1996).

[15] Anthony Harrigan as quoted in George Nash, *The Conservative Intellectual Movement in America Since 1945*, Thirtieth-Anniversary Edition (Wilmington, DE: ISI Books, 2008), 68.

[16] *See* Chapter IV. "Egotism in Work and Art" in Richard Weaver, *Ideas Have Consequences* (Chicago: Chicago University Press, 1948), 70-91.

[17] Noel Carroll, "Moderate Moralism," in *The British Journal of Aesthetics*, Vol. 36, No. 3 (July 1996). And *see* Theodor Adorno, *Minima Moralia: Reflections from Damaged Life*, trans. E.F.N. Jephcott (New York:Verso, 2005)

[18] Max Weber, *From Max Weber: Essays in Sociology*, trans. H. H. Gerth and C. Wright Mills (New York: Routledge, 1948). Weber was the first to address "disenchantment" as a phenomenon and to name it as that.

[19] *See* Vigen Guroian, *Rallying the Really Human Things: The Moral Imagination in Politics, Literature, and Everyday Life* (Wilmington, DE: ISI Books, 2005).

The so-called ironic attitude often turns malicious when there is no artistic standard outside of authenticating expressive projects subjectively amongst individual-judging *peers*. That the world writ large is disenchanted of creed, cult and sacrament, there is no doubt. However, the power of signification armed with the motor of mass technological delivery means that the individual is left especially vulnerable to the corrosive aspects of post-industrial American culture in now unheard of ways.[20] After the moral fabric deteriorates irreparably, the ethical code of an ironical artistic posture rooted in nothing but shifting ideas about authenticity is primed to become the source of further social disintegration.[21]

The conclusion of this critical essay is that the enchanted sacred significations of pre-modern civilization are transposed but never fully eradicated in any meaningful sense. The illusion of the modern disenchanted "buffered" identity is hazardous to the survival of the moral imagination when *all* artistic value-signification is appropriated *equally* in the relative mental filter of the individual's conscience or consciousness.[22] What is needed most it is believed is the re-invigoration of an awareness of the kind of psychological enchantment that persists in the human psyche *in spite* of the modern superstition that the human mind is fully rational or autonomous.[23]

2. *Enchantment and Signification*

Charles Taylor in *A Secular Age* presents a magisterial narrative of secular development in the modern world. Of particular interest is his discussion of the shifts in the social imaginary from the enchanted world-view of the Mediæval mind to the "buffered" identity of the isolated individual ego in the contemporary world.

---

[20] Criticism of the use of drugs and technology on brain chemistry is in Martha J. Farah, ed. *Neuroethics: An Introduction with Readings* (Cambridge, MA: The MIT Press, 2010).

[21] *See* Richard Rorty, *Contingency, Irony, and Solidarity* (Cambridge, UK: Cambridge University Press, 1989).

[22] Charles Taylor, *A Secular Age*, 27

[23] *See* Ernest Becker, Chapter Seven: "The Spell Cast by Persons: The Nexus of Unfreedom," in *The Denial of Death* (New York, New York: Free Press Paperbacks, 1973).

The integral ties of religion that bound the social order together have been largely replaced in the collective consciousness by an ethic of individual expression and private judgment. According to Taylor, the bulwarks of civilization have undergone tremendous upheavals that amount to a "Nova Effect" or paradigm-shift from the previous ages in the West.[24] In Part IV of his *Gifford Lectures* (on which *A Secular Age* is based) Taylor is concerned with the narratives of secularization that have developed since changes in the nineteenth century in particular. In this section Taylor critiques the artistic view that is based on an expression of unencumbered individuality. Even when the gifted individual succeeds in artistic enterprise, the general atmosphere that this idea of art gives rise to is ultimately a dangerously corrupted social environment for the moral imagination.[25]

In order to contextualize the position that art emancipated from moral restraint and enveloped in an explosion of technological growth is not necessarily æsthetic progress, Taylor's account of the archaic belief in sacramental signification is worth noting in large part. Taylor opens his narrative with an enlightened description of the process of disintegration and dis-embedding at the dawn of modernity.[26] That a full dis-enchantment has actually transpired is not necessarily the case, however. Where religion provided artistic fodder for the magical interpretations of material things, now artistic expression mostly fills the void left in the mind (once dis-enchanted)—that is, with another kind of enchantment (but "enchantment" nonetheless).

The power of the material object over the mind of an individual subjectivity is an undeniable fact of mass psychology that is well-documented in social-science and psychology.[27] The individu-

---

[24] *See* Charles Taylor, *A Secular Age*, "Part III: The Nova Effect," 299-419. Also *see* Thomas Kuhn, *The Structure of Scientific Revolutions* (Chicago: The University of Chicago Press, 1962).

[25] *See* Russell Kirk's description of the *Diabolic* Imagination, *Idyllic* and *Moral* Imaginations. Russell Kirk, "The Moral Imagination," in *The Essential Russell Kirk: Selected Essays*, ed. George A. Panichas (Wilmington, DE: ISI Books, 2007), 206-218. Kirk notoriously disliked the technological boosters of the modern era. He once referred to automobiles as "mechanical Jacobins."

[26] "Chapter 1: The Bulwarks of Belief," in Charles Taylor, *A Secular Age*, 25-89.

[27] *See* Ernest Becker, *The Denial of Death*.

al is never fully protected from the mysterious forces of symbol-mongering human nature, *despite* the illusion that technological control leads to.[28] There is cause to argue that the significance of material artifacts is in fact intrinsic to the nature of the human person.

In the Middle Ages, for instance, material things were widely thought to be possessed of magical attributes that could be *aimed* or controlled by various ritualistic actions or beliefs.[29] There were sacred objects that were "charged" with magical energy that then were superstitiously held to possess power over the natural world.[30] Taylor calls this understanding the "porous" self in contrast to the "buffered" self of modern man. There was no clear distinction in the Mediæval outlook between the material object and the sense of self-hood. That the invisible world of spirits could in fact *invade* the person at any given moment for ill or for good meant that the individual was possessed of a felt vulnerability that is largely absent today. The assurance of divine protection was of critical importance to the Mediæval understanding of survival.[31] When the sky and earth are enchanted with "evil demons" and mysterious creatures with potentially malevolent inclinations, the solitary person is left with no recourse but to harness the opposing forces for protection.[32] The belief in the goodness of one Deity that reigns and controls the invisible enemies dwelling in "hidden" places is an integral consolation and reassurance.[33]

Furthermore, when the world is thought enchanted, the co-operation and integrity of the collective is of higher importance. For instance, an object, person, season, place, building, or action, can have magical effects that then can either benefit or jeopardize the lives or well-being of fellow members of the community.[34]

---

[28] *See* Peter Kreeft, *C.S. Lewis for the Third Millennium: Six Essays on The Abolition of Man (San Francisco: Ignatius Press, 1994).*

[29] *See* Keith Thomas, *Religion and the Decline of Magic* (New York: Charles Scribner's Sons, 1971).

[30] *See* Eamon Duffy, *The Stripping of the Alters: Traditional Religion in England 1400-1580* (New Haven: Yale University Press, 1992).

[31] *See* R.W. Southern, *The Making of the Middle Ages* (New Haven: Yale University Press, August 1953).

[32] *See* C.S. Lewis, *The Discarded Image: An Introduction to Medieval and Renaissance Literature* (Cambridge, UK: Cambridge University Press, 1964).

[33] Charles Taylor, *A Secular Age*, 29-41.

[34] *See* Aldous Huxely, *The Devils of Loudun* (London: Vintage Books, 2005).

When an object is enchanted or *charmed* the belief in supernatural powers can lead people to correlate sacred objects with seasonal harvests, inclement weather, famine, disease or plague.[35] The harm caused in these cases is offset by the use of sacred objects that can then be aimed or used to counter the effect, precipitating good omens, fertility, victory in battle, favor in the afterlife, and so on, instead. The *absence of belief* in God then becomes a grave disadvantage to the individual when confidence in divine protection is essential to the survival of the tribe or the clan or the kingdom.[36]

According to Taylor, when the probability of these occurrences became uprooted in the popular imagination, many residual effects lasted. This process of disenchantment with the objects of the material world has led to the belief in a "buffered" self that largely exists in an impenetrable defensive shield that is not susceptible to material harm except for direct physical attack. There are no spiritual causes to storms, illness, luck, coincidence, or material well-being.[37] Taylor charts the course that replaced the Feudal hierarchy of priests, kings, nobles, barons, soldiers, serfs, farmers and guilds, with merchants of an enlightened puritan Calvinist bent. Taylor finishes the end of modernity with The Deist, then scientific humanism, then practical atheism. Supposedly, the latter three religious types are progressively secular and therefore immune to the mystical enchantment of person, place or thing. However, even after centuries of disenchantment the mysterious magnetic *pull* of material artifacts over the subjective human consciousness remains.

The *power* of the sports car to attract and heel the envious herd, the prestige of political or social authority and institutions, the mystique of fashion, architecture, or locales, is perhaps eliminated in the minds of fully dis-enchanted individuals, yet the reverence paid to particular persons or things or places nevertheless remains present in human psychology.[38] Even when this sort of

---

[35] *See* Joseph and Frances Gies, *Life in a Medieval City* (New York: Harper-Perennial, 1969).

[36] Charles Taylor, *A Secular Age*, 41-54.

[37] The unapologetic skeptical account of Mediæval magic, witchcraft, astrology, superstition is in Keith Thomas, *Religion and the Decline of Magic*. This should be read in conjunction with Eamon Duffy, *The Stripping of the Alters: Traditional Religion in England 1400-1580*, which gives the reasoned Catholic view and is a good counterpoint to Thomas' deconstruction.

[38] *See* "15. The Psycho-Seduction of Children," in Vance Packard, *The Hidden Persuaders* (New York: David McKay Company, 1957), for a de-

phenomenon is nakedly laid out in the cold language of science, those who make use of the new terminology still often fall under the spell of material objects at one time or another.[39] Scientists are not immune. In fact they can be made vulnerable to exploitation psychologically *because* of their scientific paradigm, *exempla gratia*: "the general fatuity of scientists in political matters, their naïveté and credulity before tricksters. The magician Randi says that scientists are easier to fool—e.g., by Uri Geller—than are children."[40]

Subconscious attitudes and actions are explained away, but never fully accounted for. The illusion of enchantment is replaced with the illusion of disenchantment, which is an enchantment of a different kind. Advertising, or the symbols that promote the most sophisticated art forms, continue to have a real effect on the subjective vision of each individual who digests a material object's respective signification. When artificial signification *carries with it* the authority of values set by an elite in-group, the magnetic effect of particular communal modes of behaviour, ways of material expression, or material symbols of power or importance, often become irresistible forces to reckon with in the manner of the most sacerdotal Mediæval superstition.[41]

The avaricious desire to participate in the *closed-circles* of those who determine the relative value (power) of objects, events, places, or words, in the material world is prevalent. *Who* these closed groups are (e.g., the "high priests" or Mandarins of cultural enterprise) often will provide the portent for what the dominant system of justice or sense of collective and individual well-being will become, or, what it already is.

---

scription of psychological manipulation techniques via child advertising. For example, studies done on how to psychologically condition children from an early age using actual child test-subjects as "lab rats." This is yet another seemingly overt reprehensible thing that nobody has had the wherewithal to do anything about. So, it is ignored, explained away, or covered-over, like so many other collateral spill-offs of technological "progress."

[39] Sigmund Freud, *Civilization and Its Discontents: With a Biographical Introduction by Peter Gay*, trans. James Strachey (New York: W.W. Norton and Company, 1961), 37-52.

[40] Walker Percy, *Lost in the Cosmos: The Last Self-Help Book* (New York: Farrar, Straus and Giroux, 1983), 117.

[41] *See* Thomas Keith, *Religion and the Decline of Magic*.

Social historian Lewis Mumford explains the nature of this elitism in that "Just as a few hundred great corporations control about half the industrial capital in the United States, so do a relatively small group from the financial and managerial classes control the organs of culture."[42] A remarkable few, that is, given *their* (whoever they are) disproportionate influence over the manufacture of cultural artifacts; as closed-off in many ways as a Mediæval caste. C. S. Lewis cites this often misunderstood parallel of modern enchantment and the magic-technics of earlier ages here:

> There is something which unites magic and applied science, [i.e. technology] while separating both from the 'wisdom' of earlier ages. For the wise men of old, the cardinal problem had been how to conform the soul to reality, and the solution had been knowledge, self-discipline, and virtue. For magic and applied science alike the problem is how to subdue reality to the wishes of men: the solution is technique.[43]

The belief in being in full-possession of oneself as a "buffered" individual is a relatively new mode of consciousness. Closed in-groups often determine with the most serious *gravitas* who must be followed by whom, who shall lead, and how to set the overriding concerns of the social community in question. This borders on the "magical" when the decisions are made based more on the *charisma*, "cult of personality," or material ornament of individual leaders, than some proposed rational purpose.[44] In the end, the assumed scientific rationality of full disenchantment in these corporate bodies and organs of culture (or those they influence) is only true in a limited fashion.[45]

When the "buffered self" is overcome by the sense of being determined from without by other persons and things, this feeling

---

[42] Lewis Mumford. *The City in History: Its Origins, Its Transformations, and Its Prospects* (New York. Harcourt, Brace & World, 1962), 538.

[43] C. S. Lewis, *The Abolition of Man or Reflections on education with special reference to the teaching of English in the upper forms of schools*, 77.

[44] *See* Max Weber, *From Max Weber: Essays in Sociology*.

[45] C. Wright Mills, "Man in the Middle: The Designer," in *Power, Politics & People: The Collected Essays of C. Wright Mills*, ed. Irving Louis Horowitz (Oxford, UK: Oxford University Press, 1963), 374-386.

is ultimately akin to the experience of the Mediæval person who was piously dependent on the unknown for security. For the Mediæval, the invisible realm of mysterious spirits was largely controlled through the enchantment of candles, bread, herbs, incantations, rituals, sacred times, sacred places, or sacred persons. [46] However, one of the most powerful enchantments came from the appreciation of religious or sacred art.[47] That art for æsthetic purposes continues to cause awe in the gaze of those who consume, view, experience, appreciate, or covet the material objects in question, is reason enough to realize that the world is more *enchanted* by the material-realm of objects than is often thought.[48]

The conclusion of the above is that, although belief in magical forces has dramatically altered since the beginnings of modernity, the continued fixation on the material extension of human personality is a reality and a well-documented fact. Sigmund Freud:

> Primitive men and neurotics, as we have seen, attach a high valuation—in our eyes an *over*-valuation—to psychical acts. This attitude may plausibly be brought into relation with narcissism and regarded as an essential component of it.
>
> In only a single field of our civilization has the omnipotence of thoughts been retained, and that is in the field of art. Only in art does it still happen that a man who is consumed by desires performs something resembling the accomplishment of those desires and what he does in play produces emotional effects—thanks to artistic illusion—just as though it were something real. People speak with justice of the 'magic of art' and compare artists to magicians. But the comparison is perhaps more significant than it claims to be. There can be no doubt that art did not begin as

---

[46] *See* Eamon Duffy, *The Stripping of the Altars.*

[47] *See* Mircea Eliade, *The Sacred and the Profane: The Nature of Religion*, trans. Willard R. Trask (London, UK: A Harvest/HBJ Book, 1959).

[48] *See* Slavoj Zizek, "Pornography, Nostolgia, Montage: A Triad of the Gaze," in *The Continental Aesthetics Reader*, ed. Clive Cazeaux (London and New York: Routledge, 2011), for an "up-to-date" interpretation of "the gaze" as regards passive media-watchers or consumers of modern media.

art for art's sake. It worked originally in the service of impulses which are for the most part extinct to-day. And among them we may suspect the presence of many magical purposes.[49]

Verily, the occurrence is possibly reducible to the simple behavioral conditioning of individual habit or the personal development of the personality since birth, yet the fact remains that the human self is not an isolated ego set apart from the material embodiments which create worlds of signification for the subject.[50] When an individual subject is removed from the traditional culture in which he or she was raised, the subjectivity will inevitably shift accordingly. The magnetic *pull* of collective environments becomes irresistible, but not necessarily to the point of losing the inmost sense of self-integration.[51]

This mysterious force of collective environment can be mere mass peer-pressure, what Freud called transference, and/or something even more difficult to name, qualify or quantify. For an example, in this (in-part) satirical narrative of present-day college life, journalist Tom Wolfe illustrates what is at stake as to the seductive pull of collective environments in this amusing fashion—

The preface to *I Am Charlotte Simmons* sets the tone for his novel about what is the increasingly no-holds-bar sexuality on contemporary campus life emancipated by decades of upheaval in values. He uses the fictional case study of a Nobel Laureate biologist "Victor Ransome Starling" to demonstrate what affect this pervasiveness of "cultural para-stimuli" has on amygdalectomized cats—an experimental discovery that apparently has its parallels in *homo sapiens*. Here is Wolfe's fantastical Nobel Prize winning experiment:

---

[49] Sigmund Freud, *Totem and Taboo: Some Points of Agreement between the Mental Lives of Savages and Neurotics*, trans. James Strachey (New York: W. W. Norton & Company, 1950), 89-90.

[50] The phenomenon of lasting changes in behavior by subconscious conditioning is well-documented and explained in these studies of Clinical Hypnosis—Milton H. Erickson, *My Voice Will Go With You: The Teaching Tales of Milton H. Erickson, M.D.* ed. Sidney Rosen (New York: W. W. Norton & Company, 1982) & D. Corydon Hammond, *Handbook of Hypnotic Suggestions and Metaphors* (New York: W. W. Norton & Company, 1990).

[51] Tom Wolfe, *I am Charlotte Simmons*, 1-2.

[Victor Ransome] Starling conducted an experiment in 1983 in which he and an assistant surgically removed the amygdala, an almond-shaped mass of gray matter deep within the brain that controls emotions in the higher mammals, from thirty cats. It was well known that the procedure caused animals to veer helplessly from one inappropriate affect to another, boredom where there should be fear, cringing where there should be preening, sexual arousal where there was nothing that would stimulate an intact animal. But Starling's amygdalectomized cats had gone into a state of sexual arousal hypermanic in the extreme. Cats attempted copulation with such frenzy, a cat mounted on another cat would be in turn mounted by a third cat, and that one by yet another, and so on, creating tandems (colloq., "daisy chains") as long as ten feet.

Starling called in a colleague to observe. The thirty amygdalectomized cats and thirty normal cats used as controls were housed in cages in the same room, one cat per cage. Starling set about opening cages so that the amygdalectomized cats might congregate on the floor. The first cat thus released sprang from its cage onto the visitor, embracing his ankle with its forelegs and convulsively thrusting its pelvis upon his shoe. Starling conjectured that the cat had smelled the leather of the shoe and in its excitement had mistaken it for a compatible animal. Whereupon his assistant said, "But Professor Starling, that's one of the controls."

In that moment originated a discovery that has since radically altered the understanding of animal and human behaviour: the existence—indeed, pervasiveness—of "cultural para-stimuli." The control cats had been able to watch the amygdalectomized cats from their cages. Over a period of weeks they had become so thoroughly steeped in an environment of hypermanic sexual obsession that behaviour induced surgically in the amygdalectomized cats had been induced in the control without any intervention whatsoever. Starling had discovered that a strong social or "cultural" atmosphere, even as abnormal as this one, could in time overwhelm the genetically determined responses of perfectly normal, healthy animals.[52]

And so, "cultural para-stimuli" *can* override the better instincts of cats, humans and (apparently) college coeds. This is funny in a way, but it is also a real illustration that shows the power of environmental pressure—in a moral sense—perhaps even better than a dryer non-fictional study would?

Nonetheless, the central concern here is that this pervasive "cultural para-stimuli" is real, but often claimed to be immeasurable, intangible, or something that can have no bearing on a policy of appraising the overarching æsthetics of a culture. For sure, those who continue to attest to the irrelevance of advertising, art, media, images, and technological innovations (that are steeped in sex, violence, nihilism, or cultural deconstructions) should be more hard pressed to defend their doings.

Whether it is Wolfe's hypermanic sex-crazed cats, Taylor's *porous* Mediæval religious enchantments, Freud's subconscious transferences, the mad advertiser's manipulative behaviouristic conditionings, the hypnotic attraction of the pop music icon, the mindless ritual of the ten o'clock news, or even the ideological mystique of "high-art" itself, the underlying phenomenon persists; that is, *despite* the "detached" explanations that try to dismiss it as unreal, irrelevant, unprovable, et cetera.

The lived environment that we live in is very important. And so, the feeling of living in farm country is very different from the experiences of an urban dweller.[53] And music, for another example, that is sent out on the air-waves *can* have a lasting and real biological effect on the moods, emotions and attitudes of listeners to the

---

[52] Ibid.

[53] *See* John Howey, *The Sarasota School of Architecture: 1941-1966* (Boston: MIT Press, 1997), for an example of über modern architectural styles of the 20th century. Or, *see* Jane Jacobs, *The Death and Life of Great American Cities* (New York: Random House, 1961), for arguments about conservation and more prudent city planning.

point of increasing heart-rate or changes in brain chemistry.[54] Or, when music is mass-produced and received via satellite by millions, the lived environment of the individual who is repelled by the sound of the new artistic mediums is left to come to terms with those who receive the noise without reservation.[55] Allan Bloom in his countercultural book *The Closing of the American Mind* characterized the modern music pervading *le monde* (much to the chagrin of his critics) with this colorful description:

> Picture a thirteen-year-old sitting in the living room of his family home doing his math assignment while wearing his Walkman headphones or watching MTV. He enjoys the liberties hard won over centuries by the alliance of philosophic genius and political heroism, consecrated by the blood of martyrs; he is provided comfort and leisure by the most productive economy ever known to mankind; science has penetrated the secrets of nature in order to provide him with the marvelous, lifelike electronic sound and image reproduction he is enjoying. And in what does progress culminate? A pubescent child whose body throbs with

---

[54] For a popular description of the effects on the brain "chemistry" by music *see* Oliver Sacks, *Musicophilia: Tales of Music and the Brain* (New York: Vintage, 2008). Or, Robert Jourdain, *Music, the Brain, and Ecstasy: How Music Captures Our Imagination* (New York: HarperCollins, 2002 [1997]).

[55] Roger Scruton, *The Aesthetics of Music* (Oxford, UK: Clarendon Press, 1997). Scruton seems to think that the "titillation" of music is secondary in importance to the conceptual understanding of music as disinterested. There is no meaningful emotional component to music that signifies an independent meaning apart from the language/words providing a musical piece's context. Music often solicits emotion or thoughts or ideas, but there is no *necessary* causal connection here. And there is no necessary causal connection between a de facto experienced emotion (however common to listeners) to even approximate explanations of the meaning of it. Musical notations or performances have no intrinsic *meaning* apart from human language. This is contrary to what many believe about the essence of music nowadays, e.g. where it is thought that it is the mainly emotional response that music elicits which is of most appeal or importance. For the degradation of music in popular society *see* Allan Bloom, *The Closing of the American Mind* (New York: Simon and Schuster, 1987), 68-81.

> orgasmic rhythms; whose feelings are made artic-
> ulate in hymns to the joys of onanism or the kill-
> ing of parents; whose ambition is to win fame and
> wealth in imitating the drag-queen who makes the
> music. In short, life is made into a nonstop,
> commercially prepackaged masturbational fanta-
> sy.[56]

Is this an expression of authentic musical progress here? Or is this a sign of a deeper problem that has been treated too dismissively by the cultural elites who determine our mass æsthetic productions? When millions of listeners subscribe to the message of the lyrics promoted by the "artistic inspiration" of the pop singer, they may ritualistically celebrate, build permanent monuments, or create artifacts inspired by the singer and their new-found vision of the "good life," e.g. a life informed by rock-concert attendance.[57] Rarely taken into account is that the imagination of the person who sees the new cultural æsthetic in terms of mental pollution will have to suffer assaults to the imagination or seek refuge with others of like mind "out of ear-shot."

---

[56] Allan Bloom, *The Closing of the American Mind*, 74-75.

[57] Søren Kierkegaard identifies music with *sensuous* immediacy as the very embodiment of its essence. Language he thinks is a higher order art, which he identifies as a medium of reflection. *Don Giovanni* in theme and technique is the perfect ideality of the "musical" idea (which he explains is *the* peculiarly erotic art-form). In his famous criticism *The Immediate Erotic Stages Or The Musical-Erotic* Kierkegaard writes: "the point certainly cannot be that music is closer to perfection as a medium than language, unless it is assumed that saying 'Uh' is more valuable than a complete thought . . . In other words, where language leaves off, music begins; when, as it is said, everything is musical, one is not progressing but retrogressing. This is why—and perhaps the experts will agree with me on this—I have never had any sympathy for the sublimated music that thinks it does not need words. Ordinarily, it thinks itself superior to words, although it is inferior . . . Reflection is fatal to the immediate, and therefore it is impossible for language to express the musical, but this apparent poverty in language is precisely its wealth. In other words, the immediate is the indeterminate, and therefore language cannot grasp it; but its indeterminacy is not its perfection but rather a defect in it." Søren Kierkegaard, *Either/Or II*, ed. and trans. Howard V. Hong and Edna H. Hong (Princeton, NJ: Princeton University Press, 1987), 69-70.

Take these above examples and magnify the situation expo-
nentially across the entire æsthetic universe of *passive* mass-
viewership, listening, etc. The conclusion is that there is a material
effect with respect to material art no matter what some would like
to believe. The town in the shadow of *Chartes* cathedral is an undeniable community given to a well-defined reflection of itself
through an artistic vision that is almost impossible to ignore
there.[58] Those who wake-up and admire the magnificent arches,
and even practice the religion from which the cathedral sprang,
will find that what differentiates those who live there from others
elsewhere is not so much that which is intrinsic to their human
nature, but rather the artistic vision that informs *their* particular
community.[59] The way the lived environment will leave a deep im-
print on those who fall under the *spell* of the wholly unique monuments of the place is nothing less than a sense of the "magical
thinking" that was woven into the embedded communities of
more superstitious ages.[60]

The human world [welt] is lived in a world of signs which
signify specific meaning(s). These worlds of meaning used to signify become amplified once given material embodiment. This material embodiment is magnified even more so once accepted in influential networks of sizable numbers. There is a mental aspect and a
material aspect to the material power that "enchants" in the modern sense. The material aspect is not separable from the mental
aspect like the Mediæval mind believed. The "sacrament of art" is
not *ex opere operato* like the Eucharist in the Middle Ages. Nonetheless, neither is the mental aspect separable from the material aspect
like the modern mind mostly tries to pretend it to be.[61] The sacra-

---

[58] *See* Henry Adams, *Mont Saint Michel and Chartes* (New York: Penguin Books, 1986).

[59] Roger Scruton, *The Aesthetics of Architecture: Princeton Essays on the Arts* (Princeton, NJ: Princeton University Press, 1979). Russell Kirk, "The Architecture of Servitude and Boredom," in Russell Kirk, *Redeeming the Time*, ed. Jeffrey O. Nelson (Wilmington, DE: ISI Books, 2006), 87-99.

[60] Charles Taylor, *A Secular Age*, "Chapter 3: The Great Dis-embedding."

[61] To be sure, there are inexplicable occurrences that border on "old-religion demonic possession." An amusing "non-fictional" rendering is portrayed in vivid detail by Jesuit Priest Malachi Martin. That there can be really evil "spirits" out there beyond the psychological is certainly worth taking into consideration. *See* Malachi Martin, *Hostage to the Devil: The Possession and Exorcism of Five Contemporary Americans* (HarperSanFrancisco

mental effect of material things persists in the mind even when the "sacredness" of the thing is not necessarily independent from it.[62]

The material world of artifacts affects the individual subjectivity without the explicit acknowledgment by the subject that this is the case. The power is not in the material object itself, but the group of subjectivities who interpret and come to communicative convictions over the matter's value.[63]

For example, the BMW car is not an object of universal desire or power until a majority of people is convinced that this is so. However, when a dominant group is convinced that the BMW that drives from point "A" to point "B" is an object of universal great value, the lone individual in opposition is burdened when trying to resist the mass of consumers who support this belief.[64] There *was* a time in history when the respectable wealthy looked "down their nose" at internal combustion engines for blighting cities with noise and pollution.[65] It was seen as the infernal engine among the satanic mills of the industrial proletariat. Snobbishness aside, the case for the ugliness of motor sprawl, or of the auto in general, is intellectually convincing on its own. Urban Historian Lewis Mumford explains in great depth the scourge of cars infecting *Megapolis* and the suburban wasteland of the present era here:

Edition. New York: HarperOne 1992 [1976])—especially see the "weirdest" story in the book of "Richard-Rita."

[62] *See* Karl Adam, *The Spirit of Catholicism*, trans. Dom Justin McCann, O.S.B. (New York: The Macmillan Company, 1936), 27-31. And, Edward Schillebeeckx, *Christ the Sacrament of the Encounter with God* (Franklin, WI: Sheed & Ward, 1963).

[63] Charles Taylor, *A Secular Age*, "Chapter 15: The Immanent Frame," 539-593.

[64] Examples of the ethical experiences of marginalized voices in a hostile or ignorant culture *see* (for racism), Malcolm X. *The Autobiography of Malcolm X: As Told to Alex Haley* (New York: Ballantine, 1979 [1964]). And for feminist voices and perspectives *see* Maureen Dowd, *Are Men Necessary? When Sexes Collide* (New York: G. P. Putnam's Sons, 2005); or Peggy DesAutels and Joanne Waugh, eds. *Feminists Doing Ethics* (Lanham, MD: Rowman & Littlefield Publishers, 2001).

[65] "29. The Dynamo and The Virgin," in Henry Adams, *The Education of Henry Adams*, eds., Edward Chalfant & Edick Wright (Boston, MA: Massachusetts Historical Society, 2007). A classic case of pessimism about the mechanical age.

What has happened to the suburb is now a matter of historic record. As soon as the motor car became common, the pedestrian scale of the suburb disappeared, and with it, most of its individuality and charm. The suburb ceased to be a neighborhood unit: it became a diffused low-density mass, enveloped in the conurbation and further enveloping it. The suburb needed its smallness, as it needed its rural background, to achieve its own kind of semi-rural perfection. Once that limit was overpassed, the suburb ceased to be a refuge from the city and became part of the inescapable metropolis, 'la ville tentaculaire,' whose distant outlying open spaces and public parks were themselves further manifestations of the crowded city.[66]

. . . Whilst the suburb served only a favored minority it neither spoiled the countryside nor threatened the city. But now that the drift to the outer ring has become a mass movement, it tends to destroy the value of both environments without producing anything but a dreary substitute, devoid of form and even more devoid of the original suburban values. We are faced by a curious paradox: the new suburban form has now produced an anti-urban pattern. With the destruction of walking distances has gone the destruction of walking as a normal means of human circulation: the motor car has made it unsafe and the extension of the suburb has made it impossible.[67]

. . . Under the present suburban regime, every urban function follows the example of the motor road: it devours space and consumes time with increasing friction and frustration, while, under the plausible pretext of increasing the range and

[66] Lewis Mumford. *The City in History: Its Origins, Its Transformations, and Its Prospects,* 505.
[67] Ibid., 506.

> speed of communication, it actually obstructs it and denies the possibility of easy meetings and encounters by scattering the fragments of a city at random over a whole region.
>
> At the bottom of this miscarriage of modern technics lies a fallacy that goes to the very heart of the whole underlying ideology: the notion that power and speed are desirable for their own sake, and that the latest type of fast-moving vehicle must replace every other form of transportation.[68]

So, ours is "the paradise of a society whose idea of bliss is leisure, gadgets, and continuous fast displacement on concrete highways."[69] Nevertheless, when commercial after commercial bombards the beer-drinking football spectator with images that sell the æsthetic utility of BMW, BMW will have significant adherents in the mass of sports fans. The path of least resistance for the participant in the football watching public is likely to accept the nearly universal attitude that "yes I, like you, want and desire that car," lest the individual become scapegoated, cast-out, or stigmatized for his or her lack of piety and reverence to the holy automobile.[70]

---

[68] Ibid., 507.

[69] Wilhelm Röpke, *A Humane Economy: The Social Framework of the Free Market*, Third Edition (Wilmington, DE: ISI Books, 1998), 37.

[70] Professor Paul Fussell further notes, not just the inherent ugliness of cars, but also the relative un-classiness of the infernal engine by more civilized social standards: "the automobile, like the all-important domestic façade, is another mechanism for outdoor class display. Or class lack of display we'd have to say, if we focus on the usages of the upper class, who, on the principle of archaism, affect to regard the automobile as very *nouveau* and underplay it consistently. Class understatement describes the technique: if your money and freedom and carelessness of censure allow you to buy any kind of car, you provide yourself with the meanest and most common to indicate that you're not taking seriously so easily purchasable and thus vulgar a class totem . . . You may not have a Rolls, a Cadillac, or a Mercedes. Especially a Mercedes, a car . . . which the intelligent young in West Germany regard, quite correctly, as 'a sign of high vulgarity, a car of the kind owned by Beverly Hills dentists or African cabinet ministers.' The *worst* upper-middle-class types own Mercedes," Paul Fussell, *Class*, 84-85.

That the world is a place which sustains a plurality of value-systems means that the individual can choose the group he or she will then become pressured to conform to (unlike the Middle Ages, say, where the heretical dissenter from the accepted norm was often put to the stake for heresy).[71] Even the individual who joins the group that resists the dominant values of the community will still experience the same pressure that the community at large experiences, but in the more minor key of the subgroup or subculture.

In every sociologically identifiable group there are material embodiments of the significant things, persons, ideas, that shape the in-group. These material objects then affect the members in ways that can never truly be objectified in any finally scientific way. The scientists themselves are often susceptible to the very same lure at one point or another. In fact, sometimes more so. The material world of human artifice continues to exert a tremendous force on the collective consciousness. More often than not, the subtle form that this takes is beneath the surface in the recesses of the human subconscious, in the collective and in the individual.[72]

3. *Critique of Authenticity*

Taking the "gist" of the arguments in the above sections as true, now it must be admitted that the impact on the social imagination that material objects of æsthetic signification possess is just as real as the power that objects charged with sacred power had to the Mediæval consciousness, albeit in a different manner. And art is not a private morality, then or now.[73] Even the art that is understood and celebrated in so-called closed circles of elites often has a disproportionate political influence on the world relative to the prestige or authority of the fashion. More often than not, art is

---

[71] *See* Thomas Keith, *Religion and the Decline of Magic.*

[72] *See* Otto Rank, *Art and Artist: Creative Urge and Personality Development*, trans. Charles Francis Atkinson. (New York: Agathon Books, 1975 [1932]).

[73] For a postmodern critical interpretation of the relationship of æsthetics to politics *see* Jacques Rancier, "Aesthetics as Politics" in *The Continental Aesthetics Reader*, ed. Clive Cazeaux (London and New York: Routledge, 2011).

informed by weighty philosophical or ideological cross-currents, political agendas, class-war.[74] Most popular consumption disappears down the memory-hole leaving little permanent mark on civilization, yet one heavy intellectual movement can underwrite changes in society in ways that are not readily apparent to the general public until long after. The ideas that drive some contemporary art-forms are often instrumental to the end of exploiting the illusion underlying the distinctly modern kind of enchantment described above.[75]

One word that is over-worn with regard to æsthetics is authenticity [eigentlich].[76] In Taylor's narrative, for instance, the word is used to define the entire secular age.[77] In particular, the spirit of enthusiasm that informs amoral individual expressiveness is a defining mark of the mass-production of "low-brow," "middle-brow," or "high-brow" artistic pursuits.[78] More common still is the attitude that the artwork is not important in itself, rather what counts is that the person who creates the art is authentic.[79] What is guarded against is the "false-consciousness" which aspires to represent an ideal-type that the self of the artist is not. This is a well-known "trope" in art criticism, but ultimately the culture that this overarching value of authenticity gives rise to is one in which the social ambiance is swamped in an atonal "hodge-podge" of competing artistic visions that neither recommend nor condemn anything except perhaps intolerance or in-authenticity. That is why the social imaginary remains fragmented at best or simply æsthetically

---

[74] Terry Eagleton, *The Ideology of the Aesthetic*, "The Marxist Sublime."

[75] *See* Tom Wolfe, *The Painted Word* (New York, New York: Picador, 2009 [1975]). Wolfe deconstructs the whole movement of modern art and demonstrates that "the emperor has no clothes" behind the mystique of it. He makes a good case that (post)modernism is simply a fashion and not even an ideology of any great lasting substance or import. Also, *see* Tom Wolfe, *From Bauhaus to Our House* (New York: Bantam Books, 1999 [1981]).

[76] *See* Charles Taylor, *The Ethics of Authenticity* (Cambridge, MA: Harvard University Press, 1991). And, Lionel Trilling, *Sincerity and Authenticity*, The Works of Lionel Trilling Uniform Edition (New York and London: Harcourt Brace Jovanovich, 1972).

[77] Charles Taylor, *A Secular Age*, "Chapter 13: The Age of Authenticity," 473-504.

[78] *See* Allan Bloom, *The Closing of the American Mind*.

[79] *See* Chapter IV. "Egotism in Work and Art" in Richard Weaver, *Ideas Have Consequences*, 70-91.

intolerable when the aesthetic feeling of the entire picture is appraised.

In the marketplace of the material embodiment of æsthetic ideas the best idea and the most accomplished talent might actually win out. The most pleasing æsthetic, the noblest ideas, the greatest virtues, can very well come to dominate through good taste alone the sensitivities of the public. To use an apt analogy, the person who neglects attending health concerns may recover spontaneously without taking any remedial measures. However, that that is a bad plan of health few would doubt. The more appropriate action is to do what is good for health and avoid what is detrimental. The same can be said as to the social organism. That almost no one desires to live in a cesspool or on a dung hill is enough to adhere to a universal consensus that not every environment is equally desirable. A few contrarian rebels or "punks" might truly desire these conditions in the best spirit of disobedience—just to challenge the authority that discriminates against those who authentically desire to do so.[80] They might even be "right" insofar as they can freely without being disproven by the standard of authenticity or value-free social science.[81] Nevertheless, should the general public join the daring few who break with the conventional desire for home and hearth, the minority that registers a complaint is legitimated.

Of course, this line of argument is a little facetious, but the *reductio ad absurdum* drives home the point that the æsthetic atmosphere is not free of social consequence or moral implications, even if there can be no moral standard to defend. There is a legitimate right to desire the establishment of more objective æsthetic judgments than the code of authenticity allows for.

Charles Taylor, in describing the contemporary urban metropolis screaming with individual expression, writes that it in fact sounds analogously like an "atonal banshee of emerging

---

[80] Chuck Palahniuk, *Fight Club* (New York: W. W. Norton & Company, 1996). This is a good example of the countercultural æsthetic of contrarian "punks and rebels" who shun comfort and prefer to live in filth. Supposedly, this is an æsthetic of "cool" in the name of cultural nihilism and angst.

[81] *See* Robert Walser, *Running with the Devil: Power, Gender, and Madness in Heavy Metal Music* (Hanover, NH: University Press of New England, 1993).

egomania."[82] Citing A. N. Wilson's *God's Funeral,* Taylor explains that:

> the 'atonal banshee of emerging egomania' unavoidably impinges through the ubiquity of advertising and the entertainment media, insistently calling us each to our own satisfaction and fulfillment, linking the powerful forces of sexual desire and the craving for wholeness, constitutive elements of our humanity, to products promoted to the status of icons, and in the process obscuring, emptying, and trivializing these forces themselves.[83]

And here, urban planning historian Lewis Mumford adds by describing in acerbic language this futuristic urban sprawl of modern *Megalopolises* in his seminal *The City in History*:

> the new species of town, a blasted, de-natured man-heap adapted, not to the needs of life, but to the mythic 'struggle for existence'; an environment whose very deterioration bore witness to the ruthlessness and intensity of that struggle . . . erecting sterile, space-mangling high-rise slabs that now grimly parade, in both Europe and America, as the penultimate contribution of "modern" architecture.

> Under the present dispensation we have sold our urban birthright for a sorry mess of motor cars.

> The form of the metropolis, then, is its formlessness, even as its aim is its own aimless expansion.

> But where are the new gods? The nuclear reactor is the seat of their power: radio transmission and rocket flight their angelic means of communica-

---

[82] *See* A. N. Wilson, *God's Funeral* (New York: W. W. Norton & Company, 1999).

[83] Charles Taylor, *A Secular Age,* 551-552.

tion and transportation: but beyond these minor agents of divinity the Control Room itself, with its Cybernetic Deity, giving His lightning-like decisions and His infallible answers: omniscience and omnipotence, triumphantly mated by science. Faced with this electronic monopoly of man's highest powers, the human can come back only at the most primitive level. Sigmund Freud detected the beginnings of creative art in the infant's pride over his bowel movements. We can now detect its ultimate manifestation in paintings and sculpture whose contents betray a similar pride and a similar degree of autonomy—and a similar product.

One of the ancient prerogatives of the gods was to create a man out their flesh, like Atum, or in their own image, like Yahweh. When the accredited scientific priesthood go a little farther with their present activities, the new life-size homunculus will be processed, too: one can already see anticipatory models in our art galleries. He will look remarkably like a man accoutered in a 'spacesuit': outwardly a huge scaly insect. But the face inside will be incapable of expression, as incapable as that of a corpse. And who will know the difference?[84]

So, that giant red-mangled-metallic "statue," resembling a pile of stool, out in front of our highest skyscrapers is probably no accident. It is there for all to see.

Still, Taylor (or, Mumford) does not seem to offer any great solution to what is a major problem of æsthetic environments in modern life.[85] The narrative that is in *A Secular Age* paints the pic-

---

[84] Lewis Mumford, *The City in History*, Chap. 17: "The Myth of Megalopolis," 542-543.

[85] Bret Easton Ellis, *American Psycho* (New York: Vintage Books, 1991), provides the contemporary example of how dark and twisted the world is becoming, especially in the present urban metropolis of greed and nihilism. This is satire, but on-the-mark as to the current depravity. A not-so-

ture of secularization in full awareness that the vast social movements being explained are not fully in the strength of human will to conquer. It has been written about and written about, but little has been done to amend any significant changes. Social movement in the tide of history conquers the individual willpower more than the reverse.[86] The problem, as Taylor puts it, is more akin to an illness without a cure. In the end Taylor is neither wholly pessimistic nor entirely nostalgic. His reading of history is an enlightened view that comes with years of study and experience. His diagnosis of the relative insufficiency of contemporary modes of artistic expression and the means by which they are either judged or controlled is that the present social situation can be seen in part as insufferable by more objective standards of artistic judgment.[87]

That is not to criticize any single part of the æsthetic determinations of culture (which often "come down" to the masses of civilization from *on high*). *But*, the most significant difficulty concerns the viability of the overall social imaginary once set adrift on uncharted waters of value-free science, mass cultural engineering, and artistic creation devoid of meaningful anchors.[88] That there are finer shades to the picture that this essay here presents is understood.

---

well written work of literature to be sure, but nonetheless noteworthy for its "cult-classic" popularity

[86] Taylor is originally a Hegelian. Hegel (a great influencer on Marx), in brief, saw social history as a strong determination of the individual in history—that is, in contrast to it being the other way around. *See* Georg Wilhelm Friedrich Hegel, *Hegel's Aesthetics: Lecture on Fine Art*, Vol. I, trans. T.M. Knox (Oxford, UK: Clarendon Press, 1975).

[87] Charles Taylor, *A Secular Age*, "Part V: Conditions of Unbelief, in its entirety."

[88] An example of the nature of modern abstract art near its peak *see* the Pulitzer Prize winning story of Willem de Kooning in Mark Stevens and Annalyn Swan, *de Kooning: An American Master* (New York: Alfred A. Knopf, 2004). Or, an earlier modernist artist *see* Sue Prideaux, *Edvard Munch: Behind the Scream* (New Haven and London: Yale University Press, 2005).

4. *Conclusion*

The world [le monde] is always "enchanted" by means of an æsthetic signification which informs the individual subjectivity. That the self is not truly *buffered*, but *porous*, albeit in a different manner than the Mediæval person, is the important point to take into consideration—as to where to go from here.

The æsthetic ambiance or the artistic decor of commercial products in a specified culture provides for many subconscious directives that inevitably end in moving the psychology of the individuals who compose the social body. The global world driven in new ways by electronic and artificial "inter-connectedness" is drawing even the most stubborn or stodgy individuals into an unpredictable and unprecedented wave of irreversible change.[89] That this change is in significant measure an æsthetic remodeling of the social environment along artistic-technological lines is an important piece of the dynamic. Perhaps the upheaval will manifest irrefutable progress. No one knows for sure. However, the chances are just as great that the world will become even more wretched æsthetically and socially than some think that it already is.

At the turn of the century Henry Adams famously railed against the asexual amoral power of THE MACHINE and the loss of the sense of power that the Virgin Mary had personified to civilization in the Middle Ages. By way of a juxtaposition of the Virgin Mary and the Dynamo Engine on display at the World's Fair exhibition of 1900, in *The Education of Henry Adams* Adams nostalgically reflects on the changes wrought by the burgeoning industrial age:

> Here opened another totally new education, which promised to be by far the most hazardous of all. The knife-edge along which he must crawl, like Sir Lancelot in the twelfth century, divided two kingdoms of force which had nothing in common but attraction. They were as different as a magnet is from gravitation, supposing one knew what a magnet was, or gravitation, or love. The force of the Virgin was still felt at Lourdes, and

---

[89] For perhaps the classic instance of pessimism at the dawn of the "industrial age" *see*, once more, "29: The Dynamo and the Virgin," in Henry Adams, *The Education of Henry Adams.*

seemed to be as potent as X-rays; but in America neither Venus nor Virgin ever had value as force—at most as sentiment. No American had ever been truly afraid of either ... American art, like the American language and American education, was as far as possible sexless. Society regarded this victory over sex as its greatest triumph, and the historian readily admitted it, since the moral issue, for the moment, did not concern one who was studying the relations of unmoral force. He cared nothing for the sex of the dynamo [engine] until he could measure its energy ...

The symbol was FORCE, as a compass-needle or a triangle was force, as the mechanist might prove by losing it, and nothing could be gained by ignoring their value. Symbol or energy, the Virgin had acted as the greatest force the Western world ever felt, and had drawn man's activities to herself more strongly than any other power, natural or supernatural, had ever done; the historian's business was to follow the track of energy; its complex source and shifting channels; its values, equivalents, conversions.

Whatever the view on the subject matter of this criticism, there persists in significant numbers people who feel a continuing grave dis-ease with the current social imagination that they are being fed; and being fed often despite no explicit consent being given to it (one way or another).[90] Dr. Taylor identifies this problem well

---

[90] Paul Goldberger, *Why Architecture Matters* (New Haven: Yale University Press, 2009), for an examination of the importance of clear philosophical thinking on architecture and an æsthetics of culture. So, Goldberg notes things like that living in the lush back-country of Greenwich, CT is a very different experience from the homogenous suburban sprawl of Bayonne, New Jersey. Living in a Robert Moses Corbusier-inspired housing-project-scheme is very different from a mansion on Park Avenue or an old brownstone on the East Side, etc. And it's not always just money [filthy lucre] that is at matter here. A history of New York urban planning *see* Robert A. Caro, *The Power Broker: Robert Moses and the Fall of New York* (New York: Vintage Books, 1975).

in defining the sense of false-immunity to that which is outside the isolated ego to be fundamental to the nature of ill-defined unease this constituent social body still experiences today.

The haphazard way in which the world functions in the midst of freedoms won by "liberal individualism" is hard to deny. Understanding the importance of the *enchantments* in advertising, religion, politics, or art, that influence cultural or æsthetic development is one step toward *even being able* to see that this is a problem of collective environments in the first place. The realization that the social body is impossible to heal in an environment where liberal individualism denies the very existence of a meaningful psychological effect made by artistic-social-significations is another.

So, even accepting the validity of these above descriptions and themes, the most fundamental issues remain unresolved (and perhaps as a practical matter unresolvable). How can the social imaginary improve when there is no agreement on what constitutes the state of health? The general public could just as easily end up on the proverbial "dung hill" if control is taken by those who in the name of addressing the difficulties outlined here miss the broader issue of *what* æsthetic environment is actually desirable.

As to the mass-propagandizing of the public by social engineers, Vance Packard, a resident of New Canaan CT in the 1950s, writes in his classic study of advertising *The Hidden Persuaders* about the implicit immorality of the techniques used in shaping our culture:

> What is the morality of the practice of encouraging housewives to be nonrational and impulsive in buying the family food?

> What is the morality of playing upon hidden weaknesses and frailties—such as our anxieties, aggressive feelings, dread of nonconformity, and infantile hang-overs—to sell products? Specifically, what are the ethics of businesses that shape campaigns designed to thrive on these weaknesses they have diagnosed?

> What is the morality of manipulating small children even before they reach the age where they are legally responsible for their actions?

What is the morality of treating voters like customers, and child customers seeking father images at that?

What is the morality of exploiting our deepest sexual sensitivities and yearnings for commercial purposes?

What is the morality of appealing for our charity by playing upon our secret desires for self-enhancement?

What is the morality of developing in the public an attitude of wastefulness toward national resources by encouraging the "psychological obsolescence" of products already in use?

What is the morality of subordinating truth to cheerfulness in keeping the citizen posted on the state of his nation?

The persuaders themselves, in their soul-searching, are at times exceptionally articulate in expressing their apprehensions and in admitting some of their practices are a *'little cold-blooded.'* [91]

In despairing over solutions Packard then keys-in on an attitude which in fact creates an immovable barrier in the psychology of the cultural elites, e.g. his neighbors, "the corporation executives" living in the secluded, clean, and private back-country of Connecticut. He sees the prevailing amoral attitude of these "hidden persuaders" *the* barrier to finding a proper corrective to the present ages' dreary æsthetic, dominated as it is by Megapolis, motor sprawl, pop culture, artistic nihilism, decadent advertising, and value-neutral social science. To illustrate the rebuke of these cor-

[91] Vance Packard, *The Hidden Persuaders* (New York: David McKay Company, 1957), 221-222. *See* Wilson Bryan Key, *Media Sexploitation: You Are Being Sexually Manipulated At This Very Moment. Do You Know How?* (New York: Signet, 1976).

porate masters he cites Alfred North Whitehead in that "knowledge doesn't keep any better than fish" (to them).[92] Words are cheap.

A saying sad, to be sure, but also too true unfortunately. And so ethical chatter is soon cheaply discarded once the nefarious "bottom-line" is at stake for our social developers. No one doubts anymore that the overall current of commercial industrial post-modern civilization is not easy to fight against. History sees it out.

A Cambridge classics professor, C. S. Lewis, had a keen eye for this tragedy of technological de-evolution. In the seminal *Abolition of Man*, he identifies three "innovations" he sees as particularly dangerous, to which the world seems to have adjusted without much fanfare to the contrary: "the aeroplane, the wireless, and the contraceptive." For the unreflective mass-man of modern cultural enterprise these new techniques of travel, communication, and reproduction mark the very essence of civilization's progress itself. Nonetheless, Lewis has grave reservations about the widespread ignorance of what is really at stake. He warns us in plain words:

> what we call Man's power over Nature turns out to be a power exercised by some men over other men with Nature as its instrument.[93]

> Each generation exercises power over its successors: and each, in so far as it modifies the environment bequeathed to it and rebels against tradi-

---

[92] And Packard adds that "The minister of my own church, Loring Chase (Congregational in New Canaan, Conn.), devoted his Lenten sermon in 1956 to the problem of prosperity. The self-denial pattern of Lent, he said, 'stands in vivid contrast to the prevailing pattern of our society, which keeps itself going economically by saying to us, 'You really owe it to yourself to buy this or that.' He described the national picture provided by our economy of abundance and stated: 'Over against this . . . one feels a certain embarrassment over Jesus' reminder that 'a man's life does not consist of the abundance of his possessions . . .'" He concluded that 'the issue is not one of few or many possessions. The issue is whether we recognize that possessions were meant to serve life, and that life comes first.'" Vance Packard, *The Hidden Persuaders*, 226-227.

[93] C. S. Lewis, *The Abolition of Man*, 55.

tion, resists and limits the power of its predecessors.[94]

The last men, far from being the heirs of power, will be of all men most subject to the dead hand of the great planners and conditioners and will themselves exercise least power upon the future.[95]

Man's conquest of Nature, if the dreams of some scientific planners is realized, means the rule of a few hundreds of men over billions upon billions of men.

the man-moulders of the new age will be armed with powers of an omnicompetent state and an irresistible scientific technique[96]

So, in these prophetic words we have a dismal picture indeed. The collective environment seems hopelessly set on its course in ways that, despite all the "power" of our technology in the present, there is practically *no* power to do anything anymore now to alter course. The old naïve hope is that the technological power "we" set up for ourselves will then continue to be organized, planned and modified, by the "good guys," namely, us (?). *But*, this is a mirage and a false hope. History bears out the fact that: "Once we killed bad men: now we liquidate unsocial elements"—the ever-looming final solution of history.

The nihilism of our planners, designers, advertising, media moguls, artists, music, intelligentsia, scientists, must be brought into check, but it seems that it can't be done. The posture of a disenchanted cold "seeing-through" of everything can only reap destruction and annihilation. For, "when the consulting rooms of psychiatrists, neurologists, and heart specialists fill up with the wreckage of our civilization, no paeans extolling motorcars and concrete will help."[97] The lonely crowd of last men will be para-

---

[94] Ibid., 56.

[95] Ibid., 57-58.

[96] Ibid., 58.

[97] Wilhelm Röpke, *A Humane Economy*, 78.

lyzed and impotent. They will be blind. It is a truism that, "To 'see through' all things is at the same time as not to see."[98]

And still, these more sophisticated criticisms are barred and ignored by the very media that is the object of critique. And so, the only practicable solution perhaps (?) appears in the form of making our small contributions to the civilizational picture in ways aligning with others of similar intentions . . . to hopefully gain control of the finished product—that is, while minimizing flaws from those who threaten the integrity of *your* (our) project.[99] Admittedly, this is a pretty dreary, dismal or hopeless, prescription / forecast / prognosis and most of these decisions will be or have been made for us already.[100] *But*, for those, who, lost as ciphers in the great MACHINE of infernal-combustion, technocracy, scientism, pollution, and exploitation, this is really all we can be said to have left.

---

[98] C. S. Lewis, *The Abolition of Man*, 81. And, David Reisman with Nathan Glazer and Reuel Denney, *The Lonely Crowd: A Study of the Changing American Character*, abridged by the authors (Garden City, NY: Doubleday Anchor Books, 1953).

[99] One industry that must be "tapped" or altered to achieve this is industrial and commercial design. The context of this idea is approached by C. Wright Mills, "Man in the Middle: The Designer," in *Power, Politics & People: The Collected Essays of C. Wright Mills*, 374-386.

[100] One must be *Stoic*, apparently, about it—here it should be imagined. *See* Marcus Aurelius, *Meditations*, trans. Martin Hammond (New York: Penguin Books, 2006).

BIBLIOGRAPHY

Adam, Karl. The Spirit of Catholicism. trans. Dom Justin McCann, O.S.B. New York: The Macmillan Company, 1936.

Adams, Henry. The Education of Henry Adams. eds., Edward Chalfant & Edick Wright. Boston, MA: Massachusetts Historical Society, 2007.

Adams, Henry. Mont-Saint-Michel and Chartes. New York: Penguin Books, 1986.

Adorno, Theodor. Minima Moralia: Reflections from Damaged Life. trans. E. F. N. Jephcott. New York: Verso, 2005.

Aurelius, Marcus. Meditations. trans. Martin Hammond. New York: Penguin Books, 2006.

Becker, Ernest. The Denial of Death. New York: Free Press Paperbacks, 1973.

Bloom, Allen. The Closing of the American Mind. New York: Simon and Schuster, 1987.

Bork, Robert. Slouching Toward Gomorrah. New York: ReganBooks, 1996.

Burke, Edmund. A Philosophical Enquiry into the Origin of our Ideas of the Sublime and Beautiful. ed. James T. Boulton. Notre Dame, IN: University of Notre Dame Press, 1968.

Caro, Robert A. The Power Broker: Robert Moses and the Fall of New York. New York: Vintage Books, 1975.

Carroll, Noel. "Moderate Moralism" in The British Journal of Aesthetics, Vol. 36, No. 3 (July 1996).

Cazeaux, Clive, ed. The Continental Aesthetics Reader. London and New York: Routledge, 2011.

Dawson, Christopher. Dynamics of World History. ed. John J. Mulloy. Wilmington, DE: ISI Books, 2007.

DesAutels, Peggy and Joanne Waugh, eds. Feminists Doing Ethics. Lanham, MD: Rowman & Littlefield Publishers, 2001.

Dowd, Maureen. Are Men Necessary? When Sexes Collide. New York: G. P. Putnam's Sons, 2005.

Duffy, Eamon. The Stripping of the Alters: Traditional Religion in England 1400-1580. New Haven: Yale University Press, 1992.

Eagleton, Terry. The Ideology of the Aesthetic. Oxford, UK: Blackwell Publishing, 1990.

Eliade, Mircea. The Sacred and the Profane: The Nature of Religion, trans. Willard R. Trask. London, UK: A Harvest/HBJ Book, 1959.

Erickson, Milton H. My Voice Will Go With You: The Teaching Tales of Milton H. Erickson, M.D. ed. Sidney Rosen. New York: W. W. Norton & Company, 1982.

Farah, Martha J., ed. Neuroethics: An Introduction with Readings. Cambridge, MA: The MIT Press, 2010.

Freud, Sigmund Civilization and Its Discontents: With a Biographical Introduction by Peter Gay. trans. James Strachey. New York: W. W. Norton and Company, 1961.

Freud, Sigmund. Totem and Taboo: Some Points of Agreement between the Mental Lives of Savages and Neurotics. trans. James Strachey. New York: W. W. Norton & Company, 1950.

Fussell, Paul. Class: A Guide Through the American Status System. New York: Summit Books, 1983.

Gergen, Kenneth J. The Saturated Self: Dilemmas of Identity in Contemporary Life. New York: Basic Books, 1991.

Gies, Joseph and Frances. Life in a Medieval City. New York: HarperPerennial, 1969.

Goldberger, Paul. Why Architecture Matters. New Haven: Yale University Press, 2009.

Gombrich, E. H. The Story of Art. London: Phaidon Press, 2003 [1950].

Guignon, Charles. On Being Authentic. London and New York: Routledge, 2004.

Guroian, Vigen. Rallying the Really Human Things: The Moral Imagination in Politics, Literature, and Everyday Life. Wilmington, DE: ISI Books, 2005.

Hammond, D. Corydon. Handbook of Hypnotic Suggestions and Metaphors. New York: W. W. Norton & Company, 1990.

Hegel, Georg Wilhelm Friedrich. Hegel's Aesthetics: Lecture on Fine Art, Vol. I. trans. T.M. Knox. Oxford, UK: Clarendon Press, 1975.

Howey, John. The Sarasota School of Architecture: 1941-1966. Boston: MIT Press, 1997.

Herrmann, Robert F. and the Attorneys at Menaker & Herrmann LLP. Law for Architects: What You Need To Know. New York: W. W. Norton and Company, 2012.

Huxley, Aldous. The Devils of Loudun. London: Vintage Books, 2005.

Jacobs, Jane. The Death and Life of Great American Cities. New York: Random House, 1961.

Johnson, Paul. Art: A New History. New York: HarperCollins, 2003.

Jourdain, Robert. Music, the Brain and Ecstasy: How Music Captures Our Imagination. New York: HarperCollins, 2002 [1997].

Kant, Immanuel. Critique of the Power of Judgment. ed Paul Guyer. trans. Paul Guyer and Eric Matthews. Cambridge, UK: Cambridge University Press, 2000.

Key, Wilson Bryan. Media Sexploitation: You Are Being Sexually Manipulated At This Very Moment. Do You Know How? New York: Signet, 1976.

Kirk, Russell. The Essential Russell Kirk: Selected Essays. ed. George A. Panichas. Wilmington, DE: ISI Books, 2007.

Kirk, Russell. Redeeming the Time. ed. Jeffrey O. Nelson. Wilmington, DE: ISI Books, 2006.

Kreeft, Peter J. C. S. Lewis for the Third Millennium: Six Essays on The Abolition of Man. San Francisco: Ignatius Press, 1994.

Kuhn, Thomas. The Structure of Scientific Revolutions. Chicago: The University of Chicago Press, 1962.

Lewis, C. S. The Abolition of Man or Reflections on education with special reference to the teaching of English in the upper forms of schools. New York: HaperCollins, 2001 [1944].

Lewis, C. S. The Discarded Image: An Introduction to Medieval and Renaissance Literature. Cambridge, UK: Cambridge University Press, 1964.

Lyotard, Jean-François. The Postmodern Condition: A Report on Knowledge. trans. Geoff Bennington and Brian Massumi. Minneapolis: University of Minneapolis Press, 1984.

Malcolm X. The Autobiography of Malcolm X: As Told to Alex Haley. New York: Ballantine, 1979 [1964].

Martin, Malachi. Hostage to the Devil: The Possession and Exorcism of Five Contemporary Americans, HarperSanFrancisco Edition. New York: HarperOne, 1992 [1976].

Mills, C. Wright. Power, Politics & People: The Collected Essays of C. Wright Mills. ed. Irving Louis Horowitz. Oxford, UK: Oxford University Press, 1963.

Mumford, Lewis. The City in History: Its Origins, Its Transformations, and Its Prospects. New York. Harcourt, Brace & World, 1962.

Nagel, Thomas. The View From Nowhere. London: Oxford University Press, 1986.

Nash, George. The Conservative Intellectual Movement in America Since 1945. Thirtieth-Anniversary Edition. Wilmington, DE: IS 2008.

Ortega y Gasset, José. The Revolt of the Masses. trans. anon. New York: W. W. Norton & Company, 1932.

Packard, Vance. The Hidden Persuaders. New York: David McKay Company, 1957.

Palahniuk, Chuck. Fight Club. New York: W. W. Norton & Company, 1996.

Percy, Walker. Lost in the Cosmos: The Last Self-Help Book. New York: Farrar, Straus and Giroux, 1983.

Prideaux, Sue. Edvard Munch: Behind the Scream. New Haven and London: Yale University Press, 2005.

Rank, Otto. Art and Artist: Creative Urge and Personality Development. trans. Charles Francis Atkinson. New York: Agathon Books, 1975 [1932].

Reisman, David, with Nathan Glazer and Reuel Denney. The Lonely Crowd: A Study of the Changing American Character. abridged by the authors. Garden City, NY: Doubleday Anchor Books, 1953.

Röpke, Wilhelm. A Humane Economy: The Social Framework of the Free Market, Third Edition. Wilmington, DE: ISI Books, 1998.

Rorty, Richard. Contingency, Irony, and Solidarity. Cambridge, UK: Cambridge University Press, 1989.

Sacks, Oliver. Musicophilia: Tales of Music and the Brain. New York: Vintage, 2008.

Schillebeeckx, Edward. Christ the Sacrament of the Encounter with God. Franklin, WI: Sheed & Ward, 1963.

Schiller, Friedrich. On the Aesthetic Education of Man. trans. Reginald Snell. Mineola, NY: Dover Publications, 2004.

Scruton, Roger. The Aesthetics of Architecture: Princeton Essays on the Arts. Princeton, NJ: Princeton University Press, 1979.

Scruton, Roger. The Aesthetics of Music. Oxford, UK: Clarendon Press, 1997.

Southern, R. W. The Making of the Middle Ages. New Haven: Yale University Press, August 1953.

Stevens, Mark and Annalyn Swan. de Kooning: An American Master. New York: Alfred A. Knopf, 2004.

Taylor, Charles. The Ethics of Authenticity. Cambridge, MA: Harvard University Press, 1991.

Taylor, Charles. A Secular Age. Cambridge, MA: The Belknap Press of Harvard University Press, 2007.

Thomas, Keith. Religion and the Decline of Magic. New York: Charles Scribner's Sons, 1971.

Trilling, Lionel. Sincerity and Authenticity. The Works of Lionel Trilling Uniform Edition. New York and London: Harcourt Brace Jovanovich, 1972.

Walser, Robert. Running with the Devil: Power, Gender, and Madness in Heavy Metal Music. Hanover, NH: University Press of New England, 1993.

Weaver, Richard M. Ideas Have Consequences. Chicago, IL: Chicago University Press, 1948.

Weber, Max. From Max Weber: Essays in Sociology. trans. H. H. Gerth and C. Wright Mills. New York: Routledge, 1948.

Wilson, A. N. God's Funeral. New York: W. W. Norton & Company, 1999.

Wolfe, Tom. The Bonfire of Vanities. New York: Farrar, Straus, Giroux, 1987.

Wolfe, Tom. The Electric Kool-Aid Acid Test. New York: Picador, 1968.

Wolfe, Tom. From Bauhaus to Our House. New York: Bantam Books, 1999 [1981].

Wolfe, Tom. Hooking Up. New York: Farrar, Straus and Giroux, 2000.

Wolfe, Tom. The Painted Word. New York, New York: Picador, 1975.

II.

DIFFERING DIVINITIES IN ANCIENT ROME:

THE IMPERIAL CULT VERSUS CHRISTIAN WORHIP FROM ACTS THROUGH THE POPE

Just eight centuries ago, we took from him what Thou didst reject with scorn, that last gift he offered Thee, showing Thee all the kingdoms of earth. We took from him Rome and the sword of Caesar, and proclaimed ourselves sole rulers of the earth, though hitherto we have not been able to complete our work.

But whose fault is that? Oh, the work is only beginning, but it has begun. It has long to await completion and earth has yet much to suffer, but we shall triumph and shall be Caesars, and then we shall plan the universal happiness of man.

But thou mightiest have taken even then the sword of Caesar. Why didst Thou reject that last gift? Hadst Thou accepted that last counsel of the mighty spirit, Thou wouldst have accomplished all that man seeks on earth—that is, some one to worship, some one to keep his conscience, and some means of uniting all in one unanimous and harmonious ant-heap, for the craving for universal unity is the third and last anguish of man.

Fyodor Dostoevsky, THE GRAND INQUISITOR

my holy Satan,

Thy will has ever commanded me—evil but lawful. Would that I had always served God and Saint Peter as faithfully as I have served thee.

S. Peter Damien (1007-1072) to Pope Gregory VII

We are in a strange time. I have not a shadow of a misgiving that the Catholic Church and its doctrine are directly from God—but then I know well that there is in particular quarters a narrowness which is not of God.

John Henry Cardinal Newman—

1. *Introduction*

Divinity in the Ancient Roman world was an important phenomenon of religious civilization. Understandings of the Sacred that imbued the religious and political leadership with charismatic or numinous authority played the decisive role in social-political relations for much of human history. Mysterious powers rooted in ancient traditions from "time-immemorial" flourished abundantly throughout the consolidated Roman Empire.[1]

Roman culture tolerated wide-ranging religious beliefs of occult diversity from *soothsayers*, oracles, prophets, priests, wandering-mystics, wizards, ghosts, sorcerers, gods, goddesses, various magical creatures, nature spirits, wood-sprites, sacred objects, sacred incantations or sacred sacrifices, all the way to the pinnacle of the "sacred pyramid" where divine emperors in Rome were worshipped or even God Himself worshipped incarnate in the Jewish carpenter from Palestine Jesus.[2]

The Christian notion of divinity is now widely accepted by Western religious consciousness for providing the normative basis of visions or understandings portraying the religious relation that is transcendent deity in communication with immanently mortal mankind.[3] Amidst the culture of the ancient Romans, however, Christianity was (more or less) subsumed by the Hellenized religion of Greece or the practical religion of the Polis in Rome. Christian civilization, to this very day, is heavily influenced by modes of discourse originating from the Roman world of politics or social life.[4]

Moreover, when Christ was made the sole divine object of exclusive worship, natural tensions arose with other religious practices from the ancient milieux.[5] In particular, the worship of the

---

[1] Thomas Bulfinch, *Bulfinch's Mythology* (New York: The Modern Library, 1993), "The Age of Fable."

[2] "Chapter VII: The War of Gods and Demons," in Gilbert Keith Chesterton, *The Everlasting Man* (San Francisco: Ignatius Press, 1925).

[3] Ittai Gadel, *Emperor Worship and Roman Religion* (Oxford, UK: Oxford University Press, 2002), 4-8.

[4] "Chapter IV: Virtue & Power: The Roman Tension," in Russell Kirk, *The Roots of American Order* (Wilmington, DE: ISI Books, 2003). This provides a context for contemporary politics.

[5] *See* Ramsay MacMullen. *Christianizing the Roman Empire* (New Haven, CT: Yale University Press, 1984).

Emperor is in direct conflict with the bold affirmation that *Jesus is Lord*, the one true God of Abraham, Isaac and Jacob, incarnate in the remote province of Israel, where dwelled one of the few persecuted religious peoples under Roman authority (Philippians 2: 1-11).

What is the underlying difference between the divinities of Ancient Rome and the God of Christianity? For point of comparison, there is a tremendous amount of academic literature on the subject.[6] To narrow down this broad question into just one or two key themes is necessary for more appropriately defining the thesis here. Divinity comes in various shades of meaning throughout religious history. Christianity is distinct from many pagan cults by worshipping visible divinity in the historical person of Jesus Christ. The Imperial cult likewise worshipped the visible head of civilization in the person of the Emperor. More significantly, the two religions are irreparably entangled in history by controversial divergences as well as similarities that came about in part due to shared cultural influences during the period.[7]

The thesis examined in what follows is that divinity in the Christian religion is radically opposed to the divinity of the Imperial cult in spite of important cross-currents in the scope of history. *The Book of Acts* in addition to the *Epistles of St. Paul* spell-out this opposition more explicitly than other parts of the New Testament by conveying the budding religion of Christ in interaction with gentile converts in the first century. Traditionally, Paul is understood to be the "Apostle to the gentiles" in this regard.[8]

For demonstrating the proposed differences in divine Godhood, first the Roman religion is best described in brief in order to

---

[6] The best book on this idea of a political divinity cult is Ernst H. Kantorowicz, *The Kings's Two Bodies: A Study in Mediaeval Political Theology* (Princeton, NJ: Princeton University Press, 1957).

[7] John Henry Newman, *An Essay on the Development of Christian Doctrine* (Notre Dame, IN: University of Notre Dame Press, 1989). This classic work appraises developments during the Patristic era that increasingly incorporated Roman practices into Christian worship or ecclesiology.

[8] Raymond Brown S.S., *Introduction to the New Testament* (New York: The Anchor Bible Reference Library, 1997), provides the "moderate" academic hermeneutic assumed here, i.e. the New Testament is (at least) historically reliable enough to provide general arguments for scholarly ends. The same for the Old Testament, *see* K. A. Kitchen, *On the Reliability of the Old Testament* (Grand Rapids, MI: Wm. B Eerdmans Publishing, 2003).

provide relevant historical context (section 2). Then, the post-Resurrection understanding of Christ's divinity can be compared with the Roman cult of emperor worship to draw out the contrasts involved (Section 3).[9] Finally, incorporated elements from Roman "religion" are arguably not (in actuality) intrinsic to the Christian religion per se, but rather later accommodations that arose in order to suit secular political interests toward the close of the Roman epoch. In essence, the concluding position is that Christianity compromised or softened the deeper ways in which the divinity of Jesus is radically contrary to Roman paganism (Section 4).

Lingering toward the end of the decaying Empire, the remnant of emperor worship can be personified, for instance, in the elevation of the Pope to "divine-type" status prior to the Middle Ages. Notions of divine personhood have continued to persist in the political realm of the Roman Church as well as in purely secular spheres of influence along the course of the centuries. Pseudo-state cults that turn political battles into fodder for secular theologies often unintentionally practice echoes of the ancient rituals pagan Rome used to celebrate the rites of the divine Godhead.

2. *Divinizing the Roman Emperor*

Various words can be used to describe the heart of Roman religion. The Emperor's *genius* [a special guardian spirit], for example, is central to the imperial cult.[10] Ancient Romans practiced an "open-tent" religion which incorporated almost every god or ritual into the pantheon of deities.[11] One common understanding is that the Roman State cared less about the actual beliefs of religious celebrations or sacrifices, that is, than the practical affairs of State-

---

[9] *See* N.T. Wright, *The Resurrection of the Son of God* (Minneapolis: Fortress Press, 2003), esp. "Part I: Setting the Scene" provides extensive descriptions of the Resurrection in the context of Roman history. Also *see* Peter Kreeft and Ronald K. Tacelli, *Handbook of Christian Apologetics: Hundreds of Answers to Crucial Questions* (Downers Grove, IL: Intervarsity Press, 1994), esp. Part 4.8 "The Resurrection", 175-198.

[10] "7: The Emperor's Genius in State Cult," in Ittai Gradel, *Emperor Worship and Roman Religion*.

[11] Ken Dowden, *Religion and the Romans* (London: Gerald Duckworth & Co., 1997 [1992]), 28-30.

craft. For instance, when conquered peoples were brought under the dominion of Roman authority there was little incentive to religiously convert the newly sanctioned subjects so long that the subjects accepted political rule. In practice, coercing religious belief could in effect often jeopardize the rule of State.[12]

Most of the gods that Rome sacrificed to or religiously believed in were in fact inherited from the Hellenized Empire of Alexander the Great or the Greek polis that came before.[13] Greek philosophy, by contrast, remained the minority discipline of select rarified individuals apart from popular religion. The specifically Roman form of religion was concerned primarily with the *lares* [jovial spirits or household gods], the *genius* of the paterfamilias or the *juno* of the mater-familias.[14] Public sacrifice was celebrated in traditional temples to Jupiter (Zeus) or other subordinate gods from Neptune (Poseidon) or Hercules to Mercury (Hermes) or Apollo.[15] Still, the Roman cult never took the gods of Greece nearly so seriously as the *genius* of the family or the Imperial religions that bolstered the State or Emperor. No clear line was drawn to separate religion from politics in the way that religion is now delineated (post-Christianity) from public ruler-ship today.[16] According to Albert Greiner's book *The Roman Spirit in Religion, Thought & Art*, for example:

> St. Augustine has preserved for us a profound saying of Mucius Scaevola, the Pontifex Maximus, whom Cicero had known in his youth. "There are," this official representative of Roman religion declared, "three kinds of religion: the poet's, the philosopher's, and the statesman's. The two first are futile or superfluous or positively harmful; only the third can be accepted." Here we have a pre-

---

[12] *See* Edward Gibbon, *The History of Decline and Fall of the Roman Empire*, Abridged Edition, ed. David Womersley (London, UK: Penguin Books, 2000), which notoriously blamed Roman decline on the Christian religion.
[13] *See* Edith Hamilton, *Mythology* (New York: Grand Central Publishing, 1942).
[14] Ken Dowden, *Religion and the Romans*, 2. And, "8: 'In Every House?': The Emperor in the Roman Household," in Ittai Gradel, *Emperor Worship and Roman Religion*.
[15] "The Age of Fable," in Thomas Bulfinch, *Bulfinch's Mythology*.
[16] Ittai Gradel, *Emperor Worship and Roman Religion*, 6.

fect expression of the Roman political tradition in respect to religion. The gods were made to serve the State.[17]

The plebian class was largely illiterate or submissive with no means to distinguish one cult from another outside of instinctual reactions or cultural habits.[18] What George Santayana said of Christianity, namely, "Our religion is the poetry in which we believe," can likewise be applied to the practical citizens of the Roman republic.[19] Myth or reality need not have exact lines of demarcation for religious praxis.

State-sanctioned religious practices, however, were nevertheless integral to Roman imperialism. *Flamens* [temple priests], the *Arval Acta*, or especially the *genius* or divinity of the Emperor himself were the very bulwarks of stable political order that demanded an altogether different kind of piety from the ever increasing pagan deities or mystery cults celebrated by the masses.[20] The worship of the *divus* of the Emperor is an understandable culmination of the "spirit" of the Roman peoples.

Zeus is the king God above all others. That the Emperor came to use the mantle of Zeus to lay claim to absolute authority or immortal status relative to the challengers of his throne is perfectly rational.[21] In the pragmatic way of Roman thinking, having the Emperor worshipped for being Zeus is a triumphant political maneuver. That there is an entire existing apparatus of priests, Imperial officials, sacred traditions, temples, in addition to ready devotion from the mobs of religious adherents who satisfy the appetite for blood sacrifice while placating the fearful beyond, makes the temptation to divinize the Emperor more or less inevitable.[22]

---

[17] Albert Greiner, *The Roman Spirit in Religion, Culture & Art* (London: UK: Kegan Paul, Trench, Trabner & Co., 1926), 365.

[18] Ibid., 366.

[19] George Santayana, *Interpretations of Poetry and Religion*, eds. William G. Holzberger and Herman J. Saatkamp, Jr. (Cambridge, MA: MIT Press, 1989), 20.

[20] "2: Before the Caesars," in Ittai Gradel, *Emperor Worship and Roman Religion.*

[21] Suetonius, *The Lives of the Twelve Caesars.* trans. J.C. Rolfe. (New York: Barnes & Noble, 2004).

[22] Ken Dowden, *Religion and the Romans*, 2.

Still, there remain significant difficulties with the succession of Emperors each assuming the crown of Zeus. Zeus is the "sky god" who is supreme in power, albeit for the Romans Jupiter is possessed of personal traits common to humanity at large.[23] In other words, Emperors can fall short of the mark of divine perfection in the traditional Christian sense of moral rectitude when the king-god is king by will or power alone rather than via the Hebrew kind of justice involved with Yahweh or the Law. Jupiter consorts with women on earth or lies to rivals while being deceived by enemies. Jupiter is little different in myth than the expectations one might have of Jupiter divinized "in" the fickle temperaments of power-mad Emperors.[24]

In the end, the *apotheosis* of the Emperor is an altogether different matter from the God incarnate in Jesus of Nazareth.[25] Christianity introduced another type of divinity separate from political aspirations. The *numen* of the Emperor which resembles the *genius* of the paterfamilias is neither what is honored by the early Imperial cult nor what is meant by divinity in the later Christian period.[26] Hugo Rahner explains:

> the gods were regarded as demons, the works of a spirit contrary to God, against whom the empire of Christ was at war from the very beginning, and the genius of Caesar was a demon, a nonentity before the divine power of Christ, but a dangerous nonentity.[27]

So-called divine honors are just one aspect of high respect due to the cult of the Emperor. There is overlap, but the power of the "sacred" (divinity) is not simply another way of saying the

---

[23] Edith Hamilton, *Mythology*, 27-28.

[24] The idea of "Divine Madness" (or the berserker) in history can be found in the now classic study Michel Foucault, *Madness and Civilization: A History of Insanity in the Age of Reason*, trans. Richard Howard (New York: Random House, 1964).

[25] *See* Suetonius, *The Lives of the Twelve Caesars*.

[26] "10: Numen Augustum," in Ittai Gradel, *Emperor Worship and Roman Religion*.

[27] Hugo Rahner, *Church and State in Early Christianity*, trans. Leo Donald Davis, S.J. (San Francisco: Ignatius Press, 1992 [1961]), 9.

same thing across religious boundaries.[28] Rather, isolation of God into the Greek categories (omniscience, omnipotence, etc.) known by the attributes of Jewish religious prescriptions or prophetic revelations is wholly other than the polytheistic Greek deities who mix with capricious mankind or the mystical protections of the paterfamilias tied into ancestral rights of the Patrician class. The Patriarchal definition of political status (which is one of the most important underlying elements of Roman religion) in the Roman world played an essentially contrary role to the radical redefinitions of Christian revelation when contextualized within the framework of history.

3. *The Divinity of Jesus Christ*

Mystical powers that enchanted sacred persons with numinous qualities left undeniable impressions on certain followers from the tribe, the clan, the village, the polis or the Empire in antiquity. Mysterious cults akin to the *genius* of the Romans are not altogether unique to Roman patterns of divinity. Rather, the occurrence of divine charisma in the leader of spiritual communities is likewise present deep in the Hebrew tradition that the Christian churches inherited. Abraham, who is the patriarch of the Jewish race, is the exemplar representative of the paterfamilias. Swiss theologian Karl Barth draws the connection in *The Epistle to the Romans* thus:

> The impression made upon us by a man's works is the memory which they evoke in us of a strange and invisible occurrence. The stronger the impression, the clearer is the recollection. This means that the conspicuous righteousness of Abraham and of men like him, their religious *genius*, the importance of their character and behavior, may provide a ground of boasting before men and the bar of history—an ill-advised reading of history may lead to no more than a satisfied

---

[28] *See* Marcea Eliade, *The Sacred & the Profane: The Nature of Religion* (New York: Harecourt Brace Jovanovich, 1959).

boasting in the power of human personality,
&c.—but not *before God*.[29]

The qualitative distinction made by Barth is that the *genius* is often judged by the standard of human personality or charisma whereas the special quality of the religiously-inspired person is under the aspect of [sub specie] God.[30] The Emperor is assumed to be the highest god of the Greek pantheon, but Zeus is not omnipotent, nor is Zeus omniscient.[31] Rather, Zeus is paradigmatic of powerful mortals who impress with the force of personality alone. According to Ittai Gradel, the difference can be framed in terms of relative divinity in polytheism or the absolute divinity of Christianity.[32]

The presence of repentance, mercy, justice, morality, *caritas*, *vertitas*, or Abraham's solitary *fides* in the one true God who reveals, is in no way indicative of the immorality or the colorful personalities of ancient mythology or even the imaginative "divine rights" of an Emperor's virtuous fancy or political acclamation. Gradel states the difference in this manner:

> Our ingrained distinction between religion and politics is not relevant in the pagan Graeco-Roman context, and, correspondingly, pagan antiquity did not distinguish between 'worship' and 'honours'; divine worship was an honour which differed from 'secular' honours, such as, for example, the erection of a statue, only in degree, not in kind . . . The Christian God is divine and all-powerful in an absolute sense, as the creator and ruler of the whole universe, not only in relation to those asking for His assistance in worship; He is the God even of those who do not recognize Him or His existence.[33]

---

[29] Karl Barth, *The Epistle to the Romans*, trans. Edwyn C. Hoskyns (Oxford, UK: Oxford University Press, 1968) 119.

[30] *See* Søren Kierkegaard, *The Present Age and On the Difference Between A Genius and An Apostle*, trans. Alexander Dru (New York: Harper & Row, 1962).

[31] Edith Hamilton, *Mythology*, 27-28.

[32] Ittai Gradel, *Emperor Worship and Roman Religion*, 321-324.

[33] Ibid., 29.

Religion is not separable from the political sphere of Roman influence. Gradel makes the case that there is in a sense one way in which the Emperor cult represents an absolute divinity in the context of paganism.[34] However, the absolute cannot be absolute in the same way when contrasted with the Christian absolute. There is contention whether the Imperial cult actually impressed the notion that Cæsar is "actually" the top god of myth in the literal sense or just simply in terms of the desserts of divine honours paid in tribute for extraordinary contributions to the Polis.[35] No doubt, the practice of divinizing the Emperor became an important matter solely toward the instrumental affairs of the State once having reached critical mass of devotion or acceptance in the hearts of the populace. There is an essentially relevant distinction to be made in terms of the actual divinity of sacred persons versus the more muted notion of divine status.[36]

Jesus Christ cannot be recognized by the Roman State in like manner to the other deities that proliferate in dramatic fashion throughout Ancient history (with little fanfare from either philosopher or Statesman). Christianity is essentially contradictory of the State-cult by challenging the absolute divinity of the Emperor—however loosely held.[37] For the Romans, Jupiter was often seen in terms of a symbol of total power over the highest imaginable height of the world or the heavens. Incarnation for the Christian is not simply worshipping the symbol of Yahweh in the person of Jesus.[38] Rather, the "even more than Zeus" absolute divine of God Himself is absolutely the person who is the humble Jew named Jesus even more so than Jupiter is the *divus* of Cæsar.[39] Of course, the stress on the comparison is perhaps overwrought by the proximity of historical circumstance between the birth of the Emperor-cult alongside the birth of Christ and Christianity. Still, the foundational divergence is incredibly relevant when subtleties are magnified by assimilation or encounter through the following centuries,

---

[34] Ibid., 321-324.

[35] Ibid., 30-32.

[36] Ibid., 29.

[37] Ibid., 333.

[38] *See* Wolfhart Pannenberg, *Jesus—God and Man*, trans. Lewis L. Wilkins and Duane A Priebe (Philadelphia: The Westminster Press, 1968).

[39] Ittai Gradel, *Emperor Worship and Roman Religion*, 333.

ultimately culminating in the confrontation of Cæsar over Christ or Christ over Cæsar.[40]

The early Christian church felt the impending conflict so soon as the first "council" in Jerusalem was commenced, which sought to distinguish the importance of Jewish rites of circumcision when interacting with the gentile world outside of explicit Judaism (Acts 15: 1-21). Paul likewise directly relates pastoral difficulties with gentile converts in several epistles. For example, Paul forbids eating food sacrificed to pagan idols as well as warns that the gods of polytheism can possibly unleash "demons" (1 Corinthians 8: 1-13). He takes the more tolerant view when evangelizing Greek philosophers, especially after confronting the temple to the unknown god in Athens (Acts 17: 16-34). Moreover, Barnabas himself is mistaken for Zeus while Paul is thought to be Hermes by the peoples of Lystra—who then attempt to offer sacrifice to the distraught disciples. The following verses from *The Book of Acts* accentuate the differences of the two kinds of divinity:

> Paul, looking at him intently and seeing that he had faith to be healed, said in a loud voice, "Stand upright on your feet." And the man sprang up and began to walk. When the crowds saw what Paul had done, they shouted in the Lycaonian language, "The gods have come down to us in human form!" Barnabas they called Zeus, and Paul they called Hermes, because he was the chief speaker. The priest of Zeus, whose temple was just outside the city, brought oxen and garlands to the gates; he and the crowds wanted to offer sacrifice. When the apostles Barnabas and Paul heard of it, they tore their clothes and rushed out into the crowd shouting, "Friends, why are you doing this? We are mortals just like you, and we bring you good news, that you should turn from these worthless things to the living God, who made the heaven and the earth and the seas and all that is in them" (Acts 14: 9-15 NRSV).

---

[40] James Hitchcock, *History of the Catholic Church* (San Francisco: Ignatius Press, 2012), 60.

Exemplified in the above passage is the stark dichotomy that at first appears relatively unimportant, but instead explodes into an incredible misunderstanding. Christian cult worship and the notion of divine power are similar enough to create parallels that can be mistaken when crossing religious lines. Still, Paul who knows Christ personally is deeply offended by the comparisons with Zeus or Hermes or the sacrifice of oxen. There is "sacrifice" in the Christian religion, but of an altogether different meaning. There is honor or devotion toward the power of the divine in paganism, but the service of miracle is not regarded in at all in the same way.

Richard J. Dillon writes in *The New Jerome Biblical Commentary* that Paul's "little sermon contains an invitation to turn from benighted idolatry to nature's self-disclosing Creator, which early Christian preachers inherited from Hellenistic-Jewish counterparts (cf. 1 Thess 1:9), but there is no Christological conclusion here, perhaps because monotheistic conversion was still wanting among Lystrans. In any case, this passage is but a preview of the gentile *kerygma*."[41] In the end, the God who is Jesus' divinity is radically different from the immanent gods who do not actually transcend nature. Jupiter is most powerful, but Jupiter is one imperfect part of the universe, rather than the transcendent Creator of all that is. That that Creator is incarnate (fully God as well as fully Man) in the person of Jesus Christ (who by the standards of political power is no more important than any other person in the herd of subjects honoring the "divine" Emperor) is perhaps beyond "critical" importance insofar as the equivocation of the word divinity goes. The differing cults of pagan sacrifice or Christian churches warrant words with radically separate meanings in order to emphasize the differences rather than what is shared in common regarding the numinous or divine quality of "sacred persons," i.e. the divine Cæsar or Christ.

---

[41] Richard J. Dillon, "Acts of the Apostle," in *The New Jerome Biblical Commentary*, eds. Raymond E. Brown, Joseph A. Fitzmeyer, S.J. & Roland E. Murphy, O.Carm. eds. (Upper Saddle River, NJ: Prentice Hall, 1990), 750.

4. *Divinity in the Roman Church*

The notion of the divine person did not cease with the death and/or resurrection of Christ. Often in Christian theology the relative sanctity of each individual member is referred back to the mystical body of Christ that dispenses divine graces or gifts (1 Corinthians 12:12-31). In the Eastern churches of Byzantium divine "honors" or divinization amongst holy participants in the Christian religion were to be expected. The Apostles, for instance, were often seen as divine by special relation of their proximity to Christ or the way in which they continued the mission of "miraculous" powers without necessarily fully partaking in the actual incarnate reality of Jesus himself (Galatians 1:11-2:10).

The relative importance of charismatic leadership waned following the Apostolic Age, being replaced with more formalized modes of institutional religious practices. Divinity was typically detached from the particular qualities of sacred persons through being tied-in rather with the visible religious political structures that came to rival even the Imperial government itself. Soon, the Pope (the bishop of Rome) or various other Patriarchs (Alexandria, Antioch, Jerusalem, Constantinople, etc.), for example, ruled solely by right of religious office rather than with any special type of charismatic recognition.[42] Authority was kept intact primarily by adherence to traditions or the tradition-based developments of "doctors" of theology together with Greek philosophers.[43] Entangled in Roman politics, the Roman Church eventually reflected many of the same modes of understanding that the Imperial court used to mediate divine status in politics.[44]

Saints were set apart by the Roman Church for recognized holiness, but never in the same way that sacred persons were identified in Ancient paganism in terms of genius, *numen* or paterfamili-

---

[42] "The Grand Inquisitor," in Fyodor Dostoevsky, *The Brothers Karamazov*, trans. Constance Garnett (New York: The Modern Library, 1996), 273-294.

[43] John Henry Newman, *An Essay in the Development of Christian Doctrine*, Chapter II & V.

[44] "Book Fourth: Chapter 7: Of the Beginning and Rise of the Romish Papacy, till It Attained a Height by Which the Liberty of the Church Was Destroyed, and All True Rule Overthrow," in John Calvin, *Institutes of the Christian Religion*, trans. Henry Beveridge (Peabody, MA: Hendrickson Publishers, 2008).

as. Sainthood involved no *genius* or no *divus*, but rather reflected imitation of the one truly divine person Jesus. Sacred qualities were absolutely defined in communion with the standard set *before God* (to use the phrase of Barth) essentially measured by the Incarnation, life, death, Resurrection, and then Ascension into Heaven of Jesus Christ.[45] However, the "mystical body of Christ," i.e. the visible Roman Church, eventually became more or less universally deemed the final judge on religious matters when interpreting the ultimate significance of the above.[46]

"Christ the King" is an important High Mediæval notion of divine rule via the Christian religion.[47] The divine quality of the *Holy See* possessed by the Pope in the Middle Ages often reflected the desire to imitate the reputed magnificence of Ancient Rome.[48] Calling the lands of the Roman Catholic Church the "Holy Roman Empire" purposefully laid claim to the ancient rights and honors from the Ancient world, albeit sanctified by the Pope who spoke directly for God *ex cathedra*.[49] An important issue for consideration is that the lowly circumstances of Jesus can be over-emphasized or de-emphasized in contemporary or pre-modern interpretations of the "spirit" of Christianity—dependent on historical perspectives or political ideology. Sometimes Christ is identified with poverty, the meek or the humble, but more often than not the Roman Church, with the inheritance of Roman politics, made the case for the special divinity of royalty, noble lineage, or sacred ruler-ship.[50]

The spirit of the paterfamilias or the *genius* of the ruler never fully left Roman religion or the Western world. With an eye toward modern political interpretations, Austrian scholar Erik Ritter von Kuehnelt-Leddihn states the older Roman Catholic view of Christ in this way:

---

[45] Karl Barth, *The Epistle to the Romans*, 119.

[46] *See* Ernst H. Kantorowicz, *The Kings's Two Bodies*.

[47] *See* Hans Urs Von Balthasar, *The Office of Peter and the Structure of the Church* (San Francisco: Ignatius Press, 1986 [1974]).

[48] "Book Fourth: Chapter 6: Of the Primacy of the Romish See" in John Calvin, *Institutes of the Christian Religion*.

[49] *See* Ernst H. Kantorowicz, *The Kings's Two Bodies*.

[50] *See* Gustavo Gutiérrez, *A Theology of Liberation: History, Politics and Salvation*, eds. and trans. Sister Caridad Inda and John Eagleson (Maryknoll, NY: Orbis Books, 1973), for the Christ of the poor, that is, opposed to the Christ of the rich.

As for the "Son of the carpenter," tekton in Greek means carpenter but also house-builder, architect, contractor. Joseph, moreover, was not an "ordinary Jew," but as a descendent of David he was of royal blood and, therefore, in the eyes of his compatriots, a potential heir to the Throne of Judea. The angel characteristically addressed him as "son of David." (Christ too was addressed as "Son of David" . . . and had to flee to avoid being proclaimed king. He made his position clear: "My kingdom is not of this world." Yet when Pilate asked Him whether He was king, Christ answered in the affirmative). As for the Virgin Mary, she was the niece or grandniece of Zacharias and Elizabeth, both Aaronites and therefore of the priestly caste; thus she also belonged to the highest Jewish social layer, and like her spouse, was of Davidic descent.[51]

Noble birth or hereditary bloodlines continued to influence the discernment of divinity in much the same way that the *genius* of the paterfamilias in Rome influenced political leadership.[52] Familial

[51] Erik Ritter von Kuehnelt-Leddihn, *Leftism Revisited: From de Sade and Marx to Hitler and Pol Pot* (Washington, DC: Regnery Gateway, 1990), 95-96.

[52] A *Tekton* was *not* of the lower social strata in ancient Palestine. There is no fair comparison with the word *carpenter* today. Joseph was not a "blue-collar worker" or proletarian by today's standards. The status of *Tekton* as an educated owner of land practicing a lucrative trade was more akin to the standing of a respected "middle-class" lawyer, although even that comparison falls short as an analogy. The fact is that the "white collar" trades carrying high social status today didn't exist then at all. A *Tekton* as a town/city worker was of higher regard than, say, many of the agricultural workers in the countryside. Agriculture was the dominant "industry" at this time and for most of human history. It is true that Galilee was considered in some ways a "backwater" to the seat of power in Jerusalem, but Joseph was said to have descended from Bethlehem (which can perhaps "loosely" be seen in today's terms as a "respectable suburb" to the capital Jerusalem), *not* Nazareth where Jesus was in fact raised. Bethlehem is also where (according to Luke) Joseph and Mary were called for the census and where Jesus *of Nazareth* was born (in accordance with the prophecy of Isias). The Holy Land of Israel is a very small territory (the

descent played an important role in the Ancient world, while falling out of favor with the ethos of Christianity in contemporary political climates dominated by democratic reason alone. Still, the mystical enchantments or magnetism of the sacred individual in matters of religion have been traditionally tied-in more so with some kind of hereditary or social mark of distinction throughout pre-modern history. In terms of the Roman Church or the Mediæval Papacy, the notion of holy birth or succession remained integral to the entire system of ruler-ship.[53] Pope Pius XII in an *Allocution to the Roman Patriciate and Nobility* on January 5, 1941 states here that:

> The nature of this great and mysterious thing that is heredity—the passing through a bloodline, perpetuated generation to generation, of a rich ensemble of material and spiritual assets, the continuity of a single physical and moral type from *father to son*, the tradition that unites members of one same family across the centuries—the true nature of this heredity can undoubtedly be distorted by materialistic theories. But one can, and must also, consider this reality enormously important in the fullness of its human and supernatural truth.
>
> One certainly cannot deny the existence of a material substratum in the transmission of hereditary characteristics; to be surprised at this would have

---

size of New Jersey) and was not very densely populated around AD 1 (far less inhabitants than a small modern city). *To walk* from Nazareth to Jerusalem today (using GPS) is little more than a day's travel or roughly 120 km. Tekton is also akin to *tectum* [roof], as in, "DÓMINE, non sum dignus, ut intres sub *tectum* meum: sed tantum dic verbo, et sanábitur ánimam tuam in vitam ætérnam. Amen."

[53] *See* Plinio Correa de Oliviera, *Nobility and Analogous Traditional Elite in the Allocutions of Pius XII: A Theme Illuminating American Social History* (Lanham, MD: Hamilton Books, 1993). This outlines in a somewhat propagandistic form the old-line Roman Church political scheme that in the secular form borders on contemporary "right-wing" fascism, *á la* Franco's Spain. This is an example of the Christ who is more a Christ of the rich over the Christ whose primary concern is only with the poor.

to forget the intimate union of our soul with our body, and in what great measure our most spiritual activities are themselves dependent on our physical temperament.[54]

Or, in this allocution of Benedict XV the old-line right of noble lineage is made even more explicit. On January 5, 1917 the Pope in his address *Our Lord Jesus Christ Willed to Be Born Poor, but He Also Wanted to Have a Signal Relationship with the Aristocracy*:

> Before God there is no preference of person. Yet there is no doubt, writes Saint Bernard, that the virtue of nobles is more pleasing to Him, because it is more resplendent.

> Jesus Christ Himself was noble, as were Mary and Joseph, being descended of royal lineage, even though their virtue eclipsed their splendor in His humble birth, . . .[55]

For yet another example of this stance, in an earlier allocution of Pope Leo XIII on January 24, 1903, with clear language the Pope praises Jesus' royal birth in this manner:

> And Jesus Christ, although He chose to spend His private life in the obscurity of a lowly dwelling, passing for the son of a laborer, and although in public life He so loved to associate with the common people, helping them in every manner possible, still He chose to be born of royal stock, choosing Mary as a mother and Joseph as putative father, both of them scions of the Davidic line. And yesterday, the feast of their marriage, we were able to repeat with the Church the beautiful words, "*Regali ex progenie Maria exorta regulget*" [Mary shows herself to us all refulgent, born of royal stock].[56]

---

54 Ibid., 433. [emphasis added].

55 Ibid., 471.

56 Ibid., 470.

All this is downplayed now, of course, and these statements were made long-before the Liberation Theology of the latter 20th century. These arguments have also resurfaced in places like the popularization of an obscure Mediæval heresy by the poorly-written and historically ignorant (but New York Times bestseller) *Da Vinci Code*.[57] So, there *has been* an easily exploitable shift in emphasis as to the nature of Christ's estate, *but* the High conception of Christ the King is still the dominant image for the Roman clergy even till this very day. This is the case *despite* all the slanderous misconceptions to the contrary.

Apostolic Succession within (inside) the Roman Catholic Church has assumed an irrevocable importance based on the "laying on of hands." This ancient ritual co-notates some sort of unbreakable mystical chain transmitting the spiritual line of "holiness" from a divine origin—supposedly, with Peter at Pentecost. Once the divine rights of secular (this-worldly) rulers, from the Roman Cæsar himself to the Kings of Mediæval Christendom or the Emperors of later Cæsaro-Papism in Eastern Byzantium, were challenged by the "divine" right of the Roman Church's succession, investing the clergy (or specifically the Pope) with divine honors above every other claimant of sacred-rule rose in political importance.

The actualization of Papal supremacy in the sense of absolute divine Kingship is much later in development than the Patristic period, essentially beginning with the Gregorian Reforms or the Investiture controversy during the 11th century, then culminating with the Imperial clerisy of Innocent III or Boniface VIII. Thereafter, the Pope's authority was made effectively divine by status of an absolute decree over all temporal matters of dominion.[58]

Granted, the sole right of the Papal monarchy to rule the "spiritual" as well as the political realms is not without historical precedent. For instance, Anglican convert John Henry Newman made an eloquent case during the Victorian period in England for the implicit traditional development of the Papal office.[59] None-

---

[57] *See* Carl Olson and Sandra Miesel, *The Da Vinci Hoax: Exposing the Errors of the Da Vinci Code* (San Francisco, CA: Ignatius Press, 2004).

[58] "Chapter 2: The Origin of the Western Legal Tradition in the Papal Revolution," in Harold Berman, *Law and Revolution: The Formation of the Western Legal Tradition* (Cambridge, MA: Harvard University Press, 1993).

[59] "Chapter IV: Section III: Papal Supremacy" in John Henry Newman, *An Essay on the Development of Christian Doctrine.*

theless, the model for divine rights in the political sphere—inherited from Mediæval Christendom—is still directly inspired (even if not always consciously) by the emperor cult in Ancient Rome or other perennial types of ruler-cults throughout history, albeit in tempered form due to predominant Christian influences.[60]

5. *Conclusion*

In summing up; what began in terms of the radically different presence of divinity in the Christian religion (fundamentally opposed to the Imperial cult), inevitably assumed various practices or accoutrements of the old Roman religion through assimilation or encounter over the course of the centuries. In general, the Mediæval re-birth of Roman Imperialism, christened by the inheritance of Christ, re-presented the worship of divinity through ruler-cult in the form of Papal absolutism wedded to the secular princedoms of European territory, often via intentional imitation of the sometimes imaginary zenith of Ancient Roman civilization seen as the Divine Emperor Augustus.

---

[60] *See* Ernst H. Kantorowicz, *The Kings's Two Bodies: A Study in Mediaeval Political Theology.*

BIBLIOGRAPHY

Balthasar, Hans Urs Von. The Office of Peter and the Structure of the Church. San Francisco: Ignatius Press, 1986 [1974].

Barth, Karl. The Epistle to the Romans. trans. Edwyn C. Hoskyns. Oxford, UK: Oxford University Press, 1968.

Berman, Harold. Law and Revolution: The Formation of the Western Legal Tradition. Cambridge, MA: Harvard University Press, 1993.

Brown, Raymond E., Joseph A. Fitzmeyer, S.J. & Roland E. Murphy, O.Carm., eds. The New Jerome Biblical Commentary. Upper Saddle River, NJ: Prentice Hall, 1990.

Brown, Raymond E. Introduction to the New Testament. New York: The Anchor Bible Reference Library, 1997.

Bulfinch, Thomas. Bulfinch's Mythology. New York: The Modern Library, 1993.

Calvin, John. Institutes of the Christian Religion. trans. Henry Beveridge. Peabody, MA: Hendrickson Publishers, 2008.

Chesterton, Gilbert Keith. The Everlasting Man. San Francisco: Ignatius Press, 1925.

Correa de Oliviera, Plinio. Nobility and Analogous Traditional Elite in the Allocutions of Pius XII: A Theme Illuminating American Social History. Lanham, MD: Hamilton Press, 1993.

D'Aulaire, Ingri and Edgar Parin D'Aulaire. Book of Greek Myths. New York: Delacorte Press, 1962.

Dio, Cassius. The Augustan Settlement. Roman History 53-55.9. ed. and trans. J. W. Rich. Warminster, England: Aris & Phillips, 1990.

Dowden, Ken. Religion and the Romans. London: Gerald Duckworth & Co., 1997 [1992].

Eliade, Marcea. The Sacred & the Profane: The Nature of Religion. New York: Harecourt Brace Jovanovich, 1959.

Ephraim, Emerton. trans. The Correspondence of Pope Gregory VII: Selected Letters from the Registrum. New York: Columbia University Press, 1932.

Foucault, Michel. Madness and Civilization: A History of Insanity in the Age of Reason. trans. Richard Howard. New York: Random House, 1964.

Gibbon, Edward. The History of the Decline and Fall of the Roman Empire, Abridged Edition. ed. David Womersley. London, UK: Penguin Books, 2000.

Gradel, Ittai. Emperor Worship and Roman Religion. Oxford, UK: Oxford University Press, 2002.

Graves, Robert. I Claudius: From the Autobiography of Tiberius Claudius. New York: Vintage International, 1989.

Greiner, Albert. The Roman Spirit in Religion, Culture & Art. London: UK: Kegan Paul, Trench, Trabner & Co., 1926.

Gutiérrez, Gustavo. A Theology of Liberation: History, Politics and Salvation. eds. and trans. Sister Caridad Inda and John Eagleson. Maryknoll, NY: Orbis Books, 1973.

Hamilton, Edith. Mythology. New York: Grand Central Publishing, 1942.

Josephus, The Life and Works of Flavius Josephus. trans. William Whiston. Philadelphia, PA: The John C. Winston Company, 1957

Kantorowicz, Ernst H. The Kings's Two Bodies: A Study in Mediaeval Political Theology. Princeton, NJ: Princeton University Press, 1957.

Kirk, Russell. The Roots of American Order. Wilmington, DE: ISI Books, 2003.

Kitchen, Kenneth A. On the Reliability of the Old Testament. Grand Rapids, MI: Wm. B Eerdmans Publishing, 2003.

Kreeft, Peter and Ronald K. Tacelli. Handbook of Christian Apologetics: Hundreds of Answers to Crucial Questions. Downers Grove, IL: Intervarsity Press, 1994.

Kuehnelt-Leddihn, Erik von Ritter. Leftism Revisited: From de Sade and Marx to Hitler and Pol Pot. Washington, DC: Regnery Gateway, 1990.

Kuehnelt-Leddihn, Erik von Ritter. The Timeless Christian. trans. Ronald Walls. [?] 1969.

MacMullen, Ramsay. Christianizing the Roman Empire. New Haven, CT: Yale University Press, 1984.

Mommsen, Theodor. The History of Rome, 5 vols. Glencoe, IL: The Free Press, 1894.

Mumford, Lewis. The City in History: Its Origins, Its Transformations, and Its Prospects. New York. Harcourt, Brace & World, 1962.

Newman, John Henry. An Essay on the Development of Christian Doctrine. Notre Dame, IN: University of Notre Dame Press, 1989.

Olson, Carl, and Sandra Miesel. The Da Vinci Hoax: Exposing the Errors of the Da Vinci Code. San Francisco, CA: Ignatius Press, 2004.

Pannenberg, Wolfhart. Jesus—God and Man. trans. Lewis L. Wilkins and Duane A Priebe. Philadelphia: The Westminster Press, 1968.

Rahner, Hugo. Church and State in Early Christianity. trans. Leo Donald Davis, S.J. San Francisco: Ignatius Press, 1992 [1961].

Santayana, George. Interpretations of Poetry and Religion. eds. William G. Holzberger and Herman J. Saatkamp, Jr. Cambridge, MA: MIT Press, 1989.

Suetonius. The Lives of the Twelve Caesars. trans. J. C. Rolfe. New York: Barnes & Noble, 2004.

Wright, N. T. The Resurrection of the Son of God. Minneapolis. Fortress Press, 2003.

III.

THE ORIGEN(S) OF CONSTITUTIONAL LAW:

THEORIES OF LEGAL ORDER IN THE CONTEXT OF HISTORY

Just to the extent that the new powers were shadowy, impossible to pin down or come to grips with, etherialized, they were all the more effective.

One might breach a city wall or kill a king: but how could one assault an international cartel?

Lewis Mumford, THE CITY IN HISTORY

A. The pick, spade, and crow.
Q. What is the use of the crow?

Q. What were you then asked?
A. Whence came you?
Q. Your answer?
A. From Babylon.
Q. Of what were you then informed?

High Priest (to Scribe) : Have you any thing, worthy companion?
Scribe : Nothing, Most Excellent.
High Priest : I know of nothing, unless the workmen from the ruins have something for our inspection.

Jah-buh-lun, Je-ho-vah, G-o-d, at low breath, as described before.

Duncan's Ritual of Freemasonry,
ROYAL ARCH, OR SEVENTH DEGREE

"Grandpa!" I shouted. "Be careful! Oh, gee!

Who's going to drop it? Will you . . . ? Or will he . . . ?"

"Be patient," said Grandpa. "We'll see.

We will see . . ."

Dr. Seuss, THE BUTTER BATTLE BOOK

'Twas brillig and the slithy toves
Did gyre and gimble in the wabe;
All mimsy were the borogoves
And the mome raths outgrabe.

Lewis Carroll, JABBERWOCKY

POZZO. — Debout! Charogne! (Il tire sure la corde, Lucky glisse un peu.
A Estragon et Vladimir.) Aidez-moi.

VLADIMIR. — Mais comment faire?

POZZO. — Soulevez-le!

Estragon et Vladimir mettent Lucky debout, le soutiennent un moment, puis
le lâchent. Il retombe.

Samuel Beckett, EN ATTENDANT GODOT

1. *Introduction*

Constitutional order is a delicate accomplishment.[1] Practical government originating in constitutional theories of Law or Right cannot neglect the deep roots that undergird civilization without grave social consequence.[2] Ancient traditions that have acceptably defined moral order throughout history can be left aside only by ambushing with radical violence the natural orders of human society.[3] Re-defining the constitution of a given *terroir* improperly is incredibly hazardous to the gentle balance of common fellowship or diplomacy that peacefully binds together cohesive units of society in freedom.

Present history is not free from catastrophic world-events that have effectively routed traditional sensitivities toward communal integrity necessary for non-coerced cooperation; cooperation beyond violently enforced customs or conventions by the modern State.[4] In history, natural or traditional political orders develop prior to the formal Legal State, which is often originated to supplement perceived faults with societies free from absolute coercion.[5] Collapse of voluntary or customary order will inevitably

---

[1] *To see* an excellent as well as complex portrait of American Constitutional History, Dumas Malone wrote an excellent 6 vol. history of Thomas Jefferson that encompasses the full narrative of the Republic's founding. Dumas Malone, *Jefferson and His Time*, 6 vols. (Charlottesville, VA: University of Virginia Press, 1981).

[2] *See* Thomas Jefferson, *The Life and Selected Writings of Thomas Jefferson: including the Autobiography, The Declaration of Independence and His Public and Private Letters*, eds. Adrienne Koch and William Peden (New York: Random House, 2004). *See* Alexander Hamilton, John Jay, and James Madison, *The Federalist: A Commentary on the Constitution of the United States*, ed. Robert Scigliano (New York: Random House, 2000).

[3] Russell Kirk, *The Roots of American Order* (Wilmington, DE: ISI Books, 2003), provides a well-written textbook of the importance deep traditional roots have toward *integral* political and legal order.

[4] John V. Densen, ed., *The Costs of War: America's Pyrrhic Victories* (New Brunswick, NJ: Transaction Publishers, 1999), contains essays on the gradual loss of freedom in America—because of more than 200 years of State warfare.

[5] Robert Nozick, *Anarchy, State & Utopia* (New York: Basic Books, 1974), charts the course, from natural incentives in a "state of nature" of absolute individual freedom, to the process of State origination as an agent of protection.

lead to an incentive for fabricating legal theories or political ideologies of various radical stripes. Coercive measures of presumed positivist legal ideology, for example, are usually made practically expedient in order to fill the vacuum where customs fall prey to decaying legal conventions—often due to popular revolt or acts of war.[6]

Some modern legal theories meant to tame the void of disintegrating political frameworks since World War I or World War II have attempted to lay claim to exclusive rationalism grounded solely in indisputable "scientific" reason.[7] Majority rule, "positive law," Nation-State sovereignty, liberalism, socialism, "martial law," international treaty systems, World Government, etc., are often muddled together in the political realm by means of fruitless discussions without universally acceptable rational convictions aside from perennial political coercion or force.[8] Endless conversation with little means of agreement often ends abruptly with violent plunder or radical constraints on liberty, that is, after having usurped the aid of the de facto State apparatus (i.e. during war).[9] Still, each and every interventionist ideology can do no more in practice than assume the mantle of established rights from former civilizations by "cleverly" re-ordering a perennial justification for force or coercion.[10]

---

[6] Erik von Kuehnelt-Leddihn, *Leftism Revisited: From de Sade and Marx to Hitler and Pol Pot* (Washington, DC: Regnery Gateway, 1990), explains the death of "liberalism" by way of radical ideology, esp. throughout the Austrian Empire during the aftermath of two World Wars.

[7] Hans Kelsen, *General Theory of Law and State*, trans. Anders Wedberg. (Cambridge, MA: Harvard University Press, 1945), is used here to exemplify one of the more important attempts in the post-war period to fully rationalize the conceptual scheme of Positivist Legal Orders.

[8] Fredrick A. Hayek, *The Constitution of Liberty* (Chicago, IL: Chicago University Press, 1978), identifies the true nature of Statehood in coercion, while stopping far short of absolute freedom by endorsing the legitimacy of "liberal regimes."

[9] Danilo Zolo, *Victor's Justice: From Nurenberg to Baghdad* (New York: Verso, 2009), shows that newly established States or peace-treaties are inevitably determined by victorious pre-established orders.

[10] Stephen Turner, *Explaining the Normative* (Cambridge, UK: Polity Press, 2010), with great fluency and sociological expertise explains the entire spectrum of contemporary philosophical positions that address the idea of "the normative" in ethics.

Destruction of political orders by violent wars historically creates opportunities for ambitious innovators armed with an ideological persuasion to manufacture new authorities in order to rationally justify the use of violent coercion amongst naturally "free" individual peers in society.[11] None of the proposed rational justifications of modern legal theory have contributed any added "rational" substance to the pre-existent orders of irrational ruler-ship. Rule of force is rule of force whether the rationalization is "God wills it," enlightened despotism, or the so-called "pure theory of law."[12] There is no "rational" basis for the legitimacy of the modern State other than coercion and force practically accepted. Law or natural political order (custom or convention) exist prior to the attempted rationalization of the formal State, so the "burden of proof" is on thinkers who advocate replacing one irrational type of traditional rule with another equally irrational justification for monopolizing force—that is, by parasitically reaping through coercion the spoils of prior civilizations.

2. *Statist Legal Monopoly*

Legal or "non-legal" aggression is always an "act of war" by one set of individuals against another set of individuals.[13] An act of war forces the person attacked to respond by either retaliating or submitting. Every juridical or political rationalization provided for violent coercion is an "irrational" cover for attacking with force or threat of force in order to cause surrender or to bend the will of an opposition. When one individual is confronted by another individual who threatens coercion, the coercion is either accepted for whatever reason (religious, tribal, traditional, political, legal or ideological) or rejected.

---

[11] Robert Nisbet, *The Present Age: Progress and Anarchy in Modern America* (Indianapolis, IN: Liberty Fund, 2003), narrates this sort of development in modern American history.

[12] Hans Kelsen, *General Theory of Law and State*, 3-47.

[13] Robert Nozick, *Anarchy, State & Utopia*, for example, further explains war present in the absence of "legitimate" authority in terms of competition (violent or non-violent) among purely voluntary "mutual protection agencies", e.g. protection-rackets absent monopoly State coercion.

When legal directives are accepted for reasons other than co-ercion, coercion is then unnecessary.[14] Should one party reject the false legal validity of Law backed solely by threats of violence, in-terested parties can either **1)** attack each other **2)** submit to attack **3)** walk away from conflict.[15] A state that arrests an offender of the legal regime is in effect declaring war (violent force) on that indi-vidual temporarily, while the individual de facto remains "free" to resist, retaliate or submit, albeit with (more or less) predictable re-sults.[16] That every "offender" of the actual legal regime is practical-ly forced to submit simply hides the underlying anarchy that per-sists irrespective of effective enforcement by an absolute State bolstered by legal fictions.[17]

Even Hans Kelsen, who defended the absolute separate do-main of Law, admits in Part VII of the *General Theory of Law and State* (with regard to legal versus de facto authority) that:

> From the point of view of normative jurispru-
> dence, the order to pay taxes differs from the

---

[14] Murray Rothbard, *The Ethics of Liberty* (New York: NYU Press, 2003), 17-21, "Natural Law vs. Positive Law," defines one "natural law principle" fundamental for *successful* anarchy, i.e. "the law of non-aggression." For Rothbard, the State often "unethically" aggresses "worse" than individu-als—so that rationalized State monopolies can in theory violate every ethical principle, except State monopoly.

[15] Ludwig von Mises, *Human Action: A Treatise on Economics*, Vol. 1 (Indi-anapolis, IN: Liberty Fund, 2007), Parts 1 & 2, explains "methodological individualism" that is "de facto" accepted for the duration of this thesis, e.g. only an individual person can be an agent of action. Collectives have no actual "will" in reality.

[16] *See* Michael Oakeshott, *Rationalism in politics and other essays* (Indianapolis: Liberty Fund, 1991). In the end all else besides force amounts to mere "talk" and obscurantism in politics. Oakeshott quotes an ancient Chinese saying here as to the impotent moralist in politics: "Chaff from the win-nower's fan, said Lao Tzu, can so blear the eyes that we do not know if we are looking north, south, east or west; at heaven or at earth . . . All this talk of goodness and duty, these perpetual pin-pricks, unnerve and irritate the hearer; nothing, indeed, could be more destructive of inner tranquili-ty."

[17] Carl Schmitt, *Constitutional Theory*, trans. Jeffrey Seitzer (Durham, NC: Duke University Press, 2008), acknowledges that positive law is not justi-fied apart from some kind of "justice" prior to or outside of the positivist legal order.

gangster's threat and the request made by the
friend by the fact that only the tax order is issued
by an individual who is authorized by a legal order
assumed to be valid . . . From the standpoint of
Max Weber's sociological jurisprudence, the difference is that the individual who receives the notice to pay his tax interprets this notice in such a
way. He pays the tax considering the command to
pay it as an act issued by an individual authorized
by an order which the taxpayer considers valid.[18]

Weber is nearer the reality here than Kelsen's ultimate failure
to rationally justify universal legality.[19] Whether one party in society uses the words "state" or "law" to justify acts of aggression is
irrelevant. Interested parties in opposition have no necessary or
actual "legal" or political connection other than "enemy combatants" or "cooperative alliances" similar to the relations of international affairs.[20] Respect for the Law is de facto purely voluntary.
Therefore, modern statehood is legal fiction. Recognized states
remain simply one type of "private" interest association amongst
others wishing to violently impose universal recognition via predominant "customary" consent in the name of some illusory "public" good. The fact remains that threats of irresistible violent force
(an act of war by the State "domestically or abroad") is nothing
other than an arbitrary "victor's justice" or mere "legal peace" that

---

[18] Hans Kelsen, *General Theory of Law and State*, Part XII: L: C.
[19] Harold Berman, *Faith and Order: The Reconciliation of Law and Religion*
(Cambridge, UK: William B. Eerdman's Publishing, 1993), 239-250,
"Chapter 10: Some False Premises of Max Weber's Sociology of Law,"
provides an alternative critique (from the angle of traditionalism) of both
Weber and the de facto positivism that typically still results even after
Kelsen's *grundnorm* "premise" is left aside for Weber's "sociology of law."
[20] This is a different line of reasoning from the "legal realism" of Oliver
Wendell Holmes or the "legal positivism" of H. L. A. Hart—two of the
more influential legal theorists of the 20th century. *See* Robert P. George,
"What is Law: A Century of Arguments," in Robert. P. George, *The Clash
of Orthodoxies: Law, Religion, and Morality in Crisis* (Wilmington, DE: ISI
Books, 2001), 211-228.

is used to hammer out necessary practical truces during (or after) times of warfare.[21]

The only truly viable project for practical legal theory (substantiated by the above) is either **A)** the "organic" (natural) reduction of State monopolies of political coercion, which inevitably creates relative states of anarchy (social disorder in the absence of formal ruler-ship) or spontaneous order via customs, conventions or traditions, supported by voluntary associations of collective interest (church, guild, family, society, local community, economic ventures, militia, charitable organizations, cultural institutions, etc.),[22] or **B)** temporary rational acceptance in practice of irrational enforcement by the monopolies of "positive law," meaning (in effect) the practical surrender of individual interests as well as collective autonomy possessed by the intermediary (non-State) free-associations of social life.[23]

3. *Anarchy & Freedom*

Regarding "Option A," why is "organic reduction" more viable than say draconian or radical political measures to alter State functions so that no single authority possesses the sole "right" to irrational force or coercion? One important answer is that the "natural order" that replaces the irrational "positive law" order remains irrational.[24] Practical collective consequence (the determinations of history) is an issue for the individual as well as collec-

---

[21] Danilo Zolo, *Victor's Justice: From Nurenberg to Baghdad*, describes anarchic national-interest or self-interest functioning internationally absent prior re-cognition of formal trans-national legal structures.

[22] *See* Michael Oakeshott, *Rationalism in politics and other essays*, for how intermediary bodies remain more important than rational schemes held by those with no real political authority.

[23] Robert Nisbet, *The Quest for Community: A Study in the Ethics of Order and Freedom* (Wilmington, DE: ISI Books, 2010), eloquently emphasizes the role of voluntary intermediary institutions that have been eroded because of coerced State encroachments into private spheres of social life.

[24] Russell Kirk, *The Conservative Mind: From Burke to Eliot* (Washington, DC: Regnery, 2001), rhetorically exemplifies the case for non-radical political action, esp. after accepted social traditions have already been radically routed by wars or ideological revolutions.

tives in the long-run. Radical political action based on individual ideological preference is akin to starting a war to cause peace when there is already peace. Radical anarchic measures of State destruction are typically not viable.[25] Anarchy is contingently desirable in practice relative to the "positive" content of legal coercion, while order in addition to "universal" satisfaction of desire with absolute freedom is always theoretically ideal, but contingently possible in practice dependent on historical circumstances.[26]

---

[25] *See* Gore Vidal, *Perpetual War for Perpetual Peace: How We Got To Be So Hated* (New York: Thunder's Mouth Press/Nation Books, 2002). Vidal interprets an "inside account" of the Oklahoma City bombing as retaliation for the unconstitutional and grotesque killing of men, woman, and children by Federal agents under Janet Reno at Waco Texas. McViegh recanted after his trial—that is, before he was mechanically killed by the State in cold blood (on a live camera feed broadcast to public "spectators"), he cited H. L. Mencken in that, "Every normal man must be tempted at times to spit on his hands, hoist the black flag, and begin slitting throats." McVeigh also cited the numerous instances he had seen of violence perpetrated by U.S. Military authorities, much worse and in greater numbers, on innocents in his service to the wars in the Middle East. He, in the end, Vidal thinks, realized that outright war by an individual on a State (however tyrannical), such as our own, can never work even if in some ways justified.

[26] John Locke, *Second Treatise on Government* (Indianapolis, IN: Hackett Publishing Company, 1980), was inspired by the unrepeatable American experiment in terms of an ideal opportunity for successful liberty to constitute free-states that (in the end) remained only a partial reality in the primarily "unsettled" territory of America. Old World quarrels or customs typically rendered positive modern-State elimination or reduction either impractical or outright impossible in Europe. Of course, the American "original sin" was the exploiting of the weaknesses of indians and buying slaves from Africa. There could be no absolute break with the sinful history of humankind it seems. Slavery itself had nearly disappeared from the Western World due to the influence of Christianity. It came back unfortunately upon exploration and colonization of lands and peoples—unknown—who were weaker and had foreign religions, manners, culture, technology, race, history, etc., and were rich in natural resources. That it happens that Europeans did this first to other lands is somewhat arbitrary in retrospect. It is hard to believe that other cultures would not have done the same if it had happened in the reverse—given what we know. In fact, some of the colonies were truly savage in comparison. But, this (the hypocrisy of slavery) is also something that can be (sometimes righteously) used to argue for the negation of *all* governmental legal au-

Moreover, forcibly imposing absolute ideological preference is practically impossible, that is, without first usurping the State mechanism of absolute coercion on behalf of ideology, which rarely works anyhow. For example: an absolute State intervention to minimize or control State intervention, i.e. "liberal regimes" protected by an absolute "rule of law" or absolute Statist communism to eradicate the State.[27] When the "positive law" is reduced or eliminated the primitive state of freedom is the inevitable consequence. However, problems have arisen historically when attempts have been made to eliminate State intervention. Typically, nostalgia for State coercion naturally re-appears due to instinctual or primitive human desires for well-being (food, shelter, life, private or common property, private or collective interest, freedom from natural or artificial inequalities) or rampant capricious greed for power or dominion in the absence of monopolistic State coercion.[28]

Wants, needs or desires, can be lost barring Statehood, but not necessarily so provided satisfactory voluntary means of human cooperation.[29] There can be no guarantee for individual or collective well-being either way.[30] The presumed correlation of State-

---

thority (enacted before the modern era), and often is used this way by leftist ideologues especially.

[27] Carl Schmitt, *Constitutional Theory*, 167-249, outlines political conundrums involved with the *Rechsstaat* "liberal regime."

[28] Ludwig von Mises, *Human Action: A Treatise on Economics*, gives rigoristic "evidence" (argument) that non-coerced individual cooperation is able (in theory) to sustain material well-being just as well if not better than interventionist states (at least in theory). This is "in theory" of course and does not mean that there will be an overall more "happiness" of satisfaction guaranteed either way. Mises is not a utilitarian. He does show that many of the coerced benefits that the State claims as coming solely as its largesse or doing are often outright political lies attributable to mere redistribution of one group at the expense of another.

[29] Henry Hazlitt, *Economics in One Lesson* (New York: Three Rivers Press, 1979), sufficiently explains (in part) the "economic" fallacies involved as to scarcity of material well-being without State intervention. For the opposing side of ways the market can cause harm *see* Michael Sandal, *What Money Can't Buy: The Moral Limits of the Markets* (New York: Farrar, Straus and Giroux, 2012).

[30] Fredrick Bastiat, *The Law* (Auburn, AL: The Ludwig von Mises Institute, 2011), further argues that opposition to the State is not necessarily intentional opposition to collective well-being, peace or cooperation.

hood with the "common good" is an ideal-type fabrication. States can use coercion to the advantage of some, but never everyone and sometimes to the detriment of most. Absence of formal State measures (anarchy) can likewise benefit some, all, or none. Utility is no justification for coercion nor is utility an adequate rationalization for eliminating coercion. Expected utility is impossible to predict or impossible to universally satisfy or subjectively quantify and is beside the point.[31] Rather, elimination of State coercion is based on the refutation of every proposed rationalization for absolute rarified collective force beyond free individual control over acts of "private" judgment.

Still, practical surrender to positive regimes might be necessary in practice for the short-term even when theoretical opposition is kept intact (Option B). For instance, nothing exists outside of the positive law to rationally justify opposition to the positive law other than that positive law is "irrational" coercion. So there is really nothing to oppose positive law with other than the assertion of private judgment in respective realms of individual influence. Nonetheless, positive law is often an act of violent aggression potentially contrary to the interests of one individual or collective interest of groups of individuals. Noted already, an act of political coercion rationalized by positive law is an act of war on an individual who can then either retaliate or surrender.

Practical opposition that denies the rational pretense of positive law can be effectively "irrational" so long that political will or history inescapably or consistently thwart "non-legal" opposition (religious, ideological, private, or otherwise) by collectively imposing absolute positive legal orders with the immunity of popular consent (majority rule) or theoretical tyranny (ideology).[32] Practical surrender is sometimes justified when the enemy (the State) is deemed unavoidably more powerful in the rationally foreseeable future.[33]

---

[31] John Stuart Mill, *Utilitarianism* (Indianapolis, IN: Hackett Publishing Group, 2002). Mill's is an altogether different line of argument that arrives at some similar material conclusions, but is peripheral to the argument being made here.

[32] Carl Schmitt, *Legality & Legitimacy* (Durham, NC: Duke University Press, 2004), 3-27, critiques majority rule as well as Kelsen's "positivism."

[33] *See* Albert Jay Nock, *Our Enemy, the State* (Caldwell, Idaho: The Caldwell Printers, 1959).

4. *Human Nature*

Before examining critiques of the two most common modern rationalizations of State legal monopoly, namely, majority rule or "positive law ideology," one highly relevant fundamental philosophical issue deserves brief treatment. A common objection to leaving individuals free to determine justice however they see fit (within autonomous spheres of influence) is that human nature is so corrupted that anarchy can never be synonymous with rational order. Rather, order is only synonymous with coercive State legal domination.

The most famous proponent of this view is Thomas Hobbes who believed that an absolute Leviathan State is necessary to restrain man's violent appetites or maintain peaceful relations.[34] Contrary to Hobbes, there is no adequate reason to presume that states (typically at war with one another or perpetrating arbitrary tyrannies on subjects) have any sort of qualitative exemption from the corruptions in human nature that Hobbes so adamantly believes will conquer civilized behavior without the aid of Leviathan government.

Why is the State less corruptible than the individuals the State coerces?[35] Fallible individuals run the State too, so the State is an amplification of potential corruption (rather than a reduction) by seizing absolute or indisputable measures of force in ways that singular individuals cannot. Quoting *The Leviathan* in this regard, Hobbes states in *Part I: Chapter VIII: Of the Natural Condition of Mankind as Concerning their Felicity, and Misery*:

> Whatsoever therefore is consequent to a time of war, where every man is enemy to every man; the same is consequent to the time, wherein men live without other security, than what their own strength, and their own invention shall furnish them withal. In such condition, there is no place for industry; because the fruit thereof is uncertain:

---

[34] Thomas Hobbes, *Leviathan*, ed. J.C.A. Gaskin (Oxford, UK: Oxford University Press, 1996), 58-110.

[35] *See* John Chipman Gray, *The Nature and Sources of the Law*, Second Edition (Boston: Beacon Press, 1962 [1909]). A good compendium of classical Anglo-American legal theories.

and consequently no culture on earth; no navigation, nor use of commodities that may be imported by sea; no commodious building; no instruments of moving, and removing such things as require much force; no knowledge of the face of the earth; no account of time; no arts; no letters; no society; and which is of all, continual fear, and danger of violent death; and the life of man, solitary, poor, nasty, brutish, and short.[36]

Contrary to Hobbes' celebrated passage above, life is solitary, poor, nasty, brutish and short, even with the absolute Statist measures. Moreover, life is often that way by means of the State's fault (i.e. war or tyranny). Of course, states during the time of Hobbes were altogether different than modern nation-states. Nevertheless, the "commodious" living that Hobbes so ardently thinks arrives solely from the bequest of State beneficence, remains but an illusory order that is provided no real factual point of reference for comparison.

Life without State intervention or coercion is the fabrication of Hobbes' imagination filled with pre-modern historical speculations. Therefore, Hobbes' "states of nature" where everyman incessantly attacks every other man is simply the fancy of theory.[37] Hobbes' conclusion about human nature assumes that the State is an enormous instrument of well-being for the corruption of Leviathan's subjects. However, the State is likewise irreparably an instrument of the very same corrupt nature from which rulers apparently have some kind of exemption according to Hobbes. State action is potentially more corrupt than any free individual or group of individuals cooperating or settling differences in freedom. So, State or no State, the notion of Hobbes that overarching dominance by the Leviathan is the only absolute remedy for social ills is in reality instead just one more legal fiction or faulty rationalization used to justify Statist legal monopolies when placed in historical perspective.[38]

---

[36] Thomas Hobbes, *Leviathan*, 84.

[37] Ibid., 82-86.

[38] Stephen Turner, *Explaining the Normative*, explains "normative" conceptual schemes with comprehensive expertise showing the pragmatic side of most rule-making.

5. *Positive Law*

Conceptual schemes that emphasize the universal rule of positive law have been relatively recent developments when considered in terms of history.[39] An important aspect of the near universal dominance of positive law thinking over modern nation-states is that the necessity or desirability of positive law is often correlated with social disorder caused by the rout of traditional voluntary forms of government.[40] Government institutions useful to expedite improvement of the natural role of leadership in society are in fact wholly different from monopoly coercion by statute justified with illegitimate reasons apart from pre-established traditions of cooperation. Moreover, pre-established traditions of free-cooperation often suffer the institution of positive law by loss of autonomy or authority over individual conscience.[41]

Hans Kelsen is one of the foremost Continental thinkers of legal theory in the post-war era. Carl Schmitt, who deeply influenced the same type of legal theory, is an important critic of Kelsen's "pure" justification of legal norms. To demonstrate the inherent fallacy of "positive" legal monopoly, Schmitt's critique of Kelsen is worthy of note. Schmitt's magisterial work *Constitutional Theory*, for instance, addresses Kelsen's theory of "positive law" in this manner:

---

[39] Positive laws once had to have justification outside of the written legal code itself. That view is fading as every agent of legislation in history is divested of any authoritative right to have judged—that is, because of the racism, sexism, ignorance, and "wrong-headedness" of anyone before the latter half of the 20th century. This, of course, is probably how our more egregious present abuses of justice will be seen by our "betters" in the future in much the same way. For example, there can be no question about how we will be judged for decisions bearing on the value of human life. For the bizarre and morbid history of the nature of our present policies on cloning, stem-cells, abortions, genetic engineering, etc., see the disturbing account of social-scientific darwinism in Edwin Black, *War Against the Weak: Eugenics and America's Campaign to Create a Master Race* (New York: Four Walls Eight Windows, 2003).

[40] Robert Nisbet, *The Present Age: Progress and Anarchy in Modern America*, narrates the demise of every social authority other than the "bureaucratic State" directed by "majority will," "positive law" or monopolization of violent coercion.

[41] Ibid.

> [With Kelsen] only positive norms are valid, in
> other words, those which are actually valid.
> Norms are not valid because they should properly
> be valid. They are valid, rather, without regard to
> qualities like reasonableness, justice, etc., only,
> therefore, because they are positive norms. The
> imperative abruptly ends here, and the normative
> element breaks down. In its place appears the tau-
> tology of a raw factualness; something is valid
> when it is valid because it is valid. That is "posi-
> tivism."[42]

Incentives to justify legal norms apart from routed traditions or dead-letter natural law assertions precipitated during the post-war period various attempts by Kelsen or others to ground positive legal statues in an altogether different category from every other customary social prescription. "Positive laws" often tend to first reflect customs or conventions (basic laws) unenforced by universal coercion.[43] However, after the State endorses juridical norms alone, positive law is effectively detached from society so that one social institution (the State) comes to dominate every sector of society via supposedly rational legal monopoly. Kelsen's rationalism of positive law is nothing but the tautology of raw factualness Schmitt identifies above.

Similar to the *grundnorm*, the "pure theory of law" is either rationally absolute or one of the thinnest legal fictions in the history of mankind used to justify an enforced coercion of potentially every social relation. Carl Schmitt sees through Kelsen's faulty reasoning by pointing out the practical consequences of the "pure theory" of positive law.

Significantly, Kelsen's political allegiances no doubt influenced his legal theory. There is cause to suspect that Kelsen innovated with regard to whether objective rationalism is desirable in order to cover his other subjective interests. The effect of context of the post-war period on his thinking is probable. Schmitt's sys-

---

[42] Carl Schmitt, *Constitutional Theory*, 64.

[43] Orestes A. Brownson, *The American Republic: Its Constitution Tendencies & Destiny* (Wilmington, DE: ISI Books, 2003), holds a similar position to Schmitt that government originates in "natural" constitutions prior to the "formal" constitution.

tem is stronger than Kelsen's by admitting the necessity of locating legitimacy of Law somewhere outside of the fact-hood of coercive actual laws. Schmitt states:

> A norm can be valid because it is correct. The logical conclusion, reached systematically is natural law, not the positive constitution. The alternative is that a norm is valid because it is positively established, in other words, by virtue of an existing will. A norm never establishes itself (that is a fantastic way of speaking).[44]

Natural law, tradition, customs, conventions, moral codes, religion, ideology, "status relations," "basic laws" or organic political societies prior to the State, respectively pre-date purely rational legal norms in the succession of history.[45] Legal norms cannot justify legal norms. That is merely an incredibly abstruse or dense way of rationalizing one type of coercion or force over all others. Schmitt is no traditionalist nor is Schmitt an advocate of irrational modes of political discourse. Nevertheless, political authority other than Law is necessarily inseparable from jurisprudence after having rejected Kelsen's theory of autonomous positive legality. Schmitt offers an alternative view that law is one aspect of pre-existent political unity prior to the State.[46]

Once states do in fact originate in order to reflect an inherent legitimacy in pre-State political constitutions, the concrete legal order of the political State then presumes an added authority contingent on accepted sovereignty of substantially unified territories.[47] Contra Kelsen, Schmitt explains the reality of "positive law" with an eye toward history thus: "The concept of legality inherits the situation established by princely absolutism; specifically, the elimination of every right to resistance and the "grand right" to

---

[44] Carl Schmitt, *Constitutional Theory*, 64.

[45] John Finnis, *Natural Law and Natural Rights* (Oxford, UK: Clarendon Press, 1982), provides one of the more successful attempts to improve classical natural law doctrine (Aquinas) in order to defend against criticism from contemporary legal scholars such as H. L. A. Hart. *See* H. L. A. Hart, *The Concept of Law* (Oxford, UK: Clarendon Press, 1961).

[46] Carl Schmitt, *Constitutional Theory*, 97-124.

[47] Ibid., 97-124.

unconditional obedience."[48] Schmitt's theory is correct in seeing the lacuna in Kelsen's ultimately vain attempt to ground every act of political force or coercion in one basic rational premise of un-objectionable normative right. Still, Schmitt's foundational theory is likewise mistaken in thinking that sovereignty maintains an inherent authority, other than threat of violent force, after de facto political unity ceases apart from State coercion.[49]

6. *Majority Rule*

The "Majority will" is one of the most commonly recognized authorities in modern nation-states other than "positive law."[50] Peaceful elections in democratic societies where election results do not instigate riots or violent revolution from minorities is often de facto accepted by the majority who participate in the voting process. Elected officials then write laws possessing the gravitas of popular consent, but in fact no more "legitimacy" than any other act of force or coercion. Contrary to popular opinion, majority rule is no guarantor of universal mutual beneficence. Rather, majorities often plunder or oppress minorities or reign disaster on the entire nation.[51] More importantly, once absolute legal "right" is absolute-

---

[48] Carl Schmitt, *Legality and Legitimacy*, 10.

[49] Carl Schmitt, *Constitutional Theory*, 97- 24.

[50] For an example of the majority will's acceptance of overt constitutional violation *see* the example of an unquestionable misreading of Federal banking powers to "coin money" in Bray Hammond, *Banks and politics in America: From the Revolution to the Civil War* (Princeton, NJ: Princeton University Press, 1957), esp. "Chapter 4: Money, Banking, and the Federal-Constitution, 1787-1791," and "Chapter 5: The Bank of the United States, 1791-1811."

[51] Gregory A. Mark, "The Corporate Economy: Ideologies of Regulation and Antitrust, 1920-2000," in *The Cambridge History of Law in America*, Vol. III, eds. Michael Grossberg and Christopher Tomlins (Cambridge, UK: Cambridge University Press, 2008), 613-652. This provides a description of the history of corporation constitutionality in the 20th century. The idea of private-public corporations radically altered the principles of democracy at the hands of a complicit majority and in violation of the Constitution. For a deeper history of corporations as legal entities *see* Harold Berman, *Law and Revolution*—which traces these collective corporate "persons" back to the idea of the *Mystical Body of Christ* in the Catholic

ly tied to popular will, the de facto regime cannot then be legally or forcefully resisted in any manner so long that the political authority of the State creates the appearance of serving one segment of the public "legally." Rule by the mob or tyranny of the majority is less rare than is often thought.[52]

No intelligent individual consents to rule by preponderance of opinion when some critical aspect of life is at stake. 10 million scientifically illiterate individuals will never judge more adequately than one trained doctor who studies or practices medicine for a living when a patient is in need of medical assistance. Likewise, 20 million individuals lacking physical fitness will never outpace the one Olympic athlete who reaches the pinnacle of athletic excellence. No number of head-counting improves any type of activity beyond the talents of those who actually have the expertise of excellence, however few. "Majority will" is practically useful only insofar as peace is maintained or participants in the political process contented with an allotted share of the franchise. Still, majority rule is not an ultimate solution, but rather often the source of complacency, dissatisfaction, or minority oppression.[53]

> It is probable that "democracy" is the most original form of "organized" society. One could well imagine that if seven out of ten cavemen wanted to do a thing collectively in one way and the three others decided differently, the majority of these cavemen (assuming that they are of about equal bodily strength) could force the rest to accept their decision. The rule of majorities, in combina-

---

Church of the Middle Ages. Of course, in the present day it is more of a means of protectionism or loopholes for these artificial constructs of the state. It is often thought that corporations are "private" entities as opposed to the "public" government that needs to control them, while actually they are creations of the "public" State. In fact, the modern nation-state often parasitically thrives off of their existence. It is not easy to peirce the *corporate veil* to hold these state constructs to account.

[52] Plato, *The Republic*, trans. Desmond Lee (London, UK: Penguin Books, 2003), exemplifies the ancient distrust of mob-rule.

[53] Erik Ritter von Kuehnelt-Leddihn, *Liberty or Equality: The Challenge of Our Time* (Caldwell, Idaho: The Caxton Printers, Ltd., 1952), demonstrates the reasons why liberty is fundamentally incompatible with equality and vice versa why equality cannot tolerate liberty.

tion with the employment of brutal force, is likely
to be the most primitive form of government in
the development of mankind.[54]

A majority vote of 80% that rules a minority of 20% is no different in principle than 51% ruling 49%.[55] Nobody advocates poll-
ing popular opinion for matters of objective excellence with defin-
able measure. Simple head-counting guarantees perfection or
success in statecraft no more than one great leader who seizes de
facto power then rules the state in a way that popularly "satisfies"
more constituents even without prior popular consent.[56] Moreover,
democracies can constitutionally commit democratic suicide by
voting for absolute dictators who permanently eradicate democracy.

Distrust of mob-rule is deeply embedded in history. Often,
education plus democracy is proposed for solution. Nonetheless,
education is just as likely to either propagandize or coerce individuals, rather than producing effective "democratic" citizens. No
matter what the rationalization, a line is crossed when the State
monopolizes coercive force. Coercion rationalized by law or political rule necessarily harms some, while not necessarily benefitting
others. The inevitable result is the same whether the State is imperfectly participatory by popular or indirect elections or restricted by
"rule of law" to the "positive" legal order described in section (5).
To demonstrate this aspect of democratic futility, Carl Schmitt
writes:

> The old teaching of a right to resistance
> distinguishes among two types of "tyrants": he
> who arrives at the seat of power in a legal manner,
> but then exercises and abuses power badly or
> tyrannically, that is, the *tyrannus ab exercitio*; further,
> the *tyrannus ab sequetitulo*, who achieves power
> without legal title and is indifferent as to whether
> it exercises power well or badly . . . Only he who

---

[54] Erik Ritter von Kuehnelt-Leddihn, *The Menace of the Herd, Or Procrustes at Large* (Milwaukee, MN: The Bruce Publishing Company, 1943), 103.

[55] Carl Schmitt, *Constitutional Theory*, 303-307.

[56] Erik von Kuehnelt-Leddihn, *The Menace of the Herd, Or Procrustes at Large*, sustains an interesting historical attack against democratic dogma.

exercises state or state-like power without the 51%
majority on their side is illegal and a tyrant.[57]

Some might object to rejecting democratic legitimacy in that
democracies typically "function" better than other sorts of coercion. Still, even when tyranny is not manifest for the majority, violent oppression alone is the basis of State force for those who oppose the potentially limitless participatory government without
external prescriptions against abuses of force. More often than not
the individual sense of having one fair stake in the system is historically disproven by the fact that most democracies end in short
order through de facto control by self-interested minority participants who function outside of public knowledge.[58] Money, power,
threat of violence or private influence aside from voting, can never
be eliminated from formal Statehood.[59] Therefore, states remain
little other than material institutions of brute force accepted with
no more absolute rationalization than any other act of force. Democracy provides no intrinsic reason why one person can violently
aggress against another's natural freedom.

---

[57] Carl Schmitt, *Legality & Legitimacy*, 29.

[58] *See* Walter Isaacson & Thomas Evans, *The Wise Men: Six Friends and the
World They Made: Acheson, Bohlen, Harriman, Kennan, Lovett & McCloy* (New
York: Touchstone, 1986). This is "Court History" that shows that even at
the height of democratic success in America (contrary to popular perception) relatively few individuals actually ruled the State and in ways largely
unbeknownst to the general public—who were largely content not knowing having "authorized" those in office via elections. For an alternative
account of secret cabals overriding public authority *see* G. Edward Griffin,
The Creature from Jekyll Island: A Second Look at the Federal Reserve (Westlake
Village, CA: American Media, 2001), esp. "5. Nearer to the Heart's Desire"
85-106, "17. A Den of Vipers" 341-360, & "23. The Great Duck Dinner"
471-503. The fact was that at the very peak of Wall Street Capitalism in
the 1920s, 30s, 40s, "Half a dozen men at the top of the Big Five Banks
could upset the whole fabric of government finance by refraining from
renewing Treasury Bills." And this was not wholly secret either: "The
names of some of these banking families are familiar to all of us and
should be more so. They include Baring, Lazard, Erlanger, Warburg,
Schröder, Seligman, the Speyers, Mirabaud, Mallet, Fould, and above all
Rothschild and Rockefeller." Carroll Quigley, *Tragedy and Hope*, 52.

[59] *See* Vance Packard, *The Ultra Rich: How Much is Too Much?* (Boston: Little, Brown and Company, 1989).

7. *Conclusion*

To sum up; Statist legal monopoly is not necessary even when the development of absolutist legal regimes is often inevitable. Making "right" laws relative to positive laws that have absolute factual legality (meaning de facto accepted authority for coercing others) is not an adequate solution to the problem of what is the "right" law. Saying no law is right or wrong, but rather simply that the law is the law when the law commands obedience is ultimately defeatist. Individual agents act for reasons outside of the de facto laws that tell you to "act in this way or not in that way."

Moral norms remain moral norms for those who act for moral reasons.[60] Moral laws remain moral laws for those who write laws to enforce norms for moral reasons. That will never change. Absent moral prescriptions, legality as such is then just a matter of an individual's interpretation of the world of force or coercion that confronts action or inaction in the person's private sphere of influence. Some individuals will privately influence the "public" sphere one way or another, but that in no way alters the fact that the "public" State is not qualitatively different from individual prerogatives when defined by Statehood rather than voluntary cooperation, tradition, violent force, or whatever. People are too often in awe of the power or prestige of the State and are then left impotent to face it down. C. Wright Mills notes the sad truth that, "Most men are encouraged to assume that, in general, the most powerful and the wealthiest are also the most knowledgeable or, as they might say, 'the smartest'." Unfortunately, this is simply not true however much "the sheep" would like it so.

The Law is either "right," or the law is nothing. When there is no conceptual scheme to defend the pretenses of law, there is anarchy or there is simply customary law that is enforced with the means appropriate to the individuals who are in a position to enforce what is desirable (individually or collectively). There is only semantic difference when Statist formal law is really just another body of customary laws seeking to rationalize violence or "jus-

---

[60] *See* Thomas Aquinas, *Treatise on Law*, trans. Richard J. Regan (Indianapolis, IN: Hackett Publishing Company, Inc., 2000).

tice"—that is, in order to eliminate some kinds of violence, coercion, and "justice" from the realm of politics, but not others.[61]

Often it is thought that State law is absolutely necessary to the institution of private property for those who defend private ownership in certain terms. But the State is actually the gravest threat to property for those who favor it. In fact, the democratic state of *Corporate Statism* is more opposed to the real spirit of what it means to own than *Communsim* in its pure ideological form—which actually takes the metaphysical aspect of property more seriously than democratic capitalism. Richard Weaver (who was once sympathetic to Socialist agrarianism in America) explains the much

---

[61] Customary laws persist regardless of *how much* the State monopolizes all aspects of life. Corporations, businesses, churches, et cetera, often have distinctive rules which enforce *moral* precepts (often without calling them that) by coercive measures of punishment or reward. So, the ancient Biblical rule in the Davidic psalms: "*Him who slanders his neighbor secretly I will destroy. The man of haughty looks and arrogant heart I will not endure*" (Psalm 101 NRSV) is close akin to the corporate compliance culture of say (for example) a large modern hedge fund like Bridgewater Capital. Bwater's *Principle 5A*—in one of the more complex corporate business codes (drawn-up personally by the owner)—is as follows:—"Never say anything about a person you wouldn't say to them directly, and don't try people without accusing them to their face. Badmouthing people behind their backs shows a serious lack of integrity and is counterproductive. It doesn't yield any beneficial change, and it subverts both the people you are badmouthing and the environment as a whole. *Next to being dishonest, it is the worst thing you can do at Bridgewater* (emphasis added). Criticism is both welcomed and encouraged at Bridgewater, so there is no good reason to talk behind people's backs. You need to follow this policy to an extreme degree. For example, managers should not talk about people who work for them without those people being in the room. If you talk behind people's backs at Bridgewater, you are called a *scummy weasel*." So, this is a kind of "moral justice" enforced based on an understanding of *moral right* and wrong, which in turn is a kind of formal/informal custom to accept or not-accept by those under the private authority of the company. No one thinks that a state law should coerce this (or can), but, despite this, what is the essence of the difference really in moral terms? *See* Ray Dalio, "Principles," accessed January 1, 2017, https://www.principles.com. Or, *see* another more traditional private citizen's "code of ethics" in, say, *The Boy Scout Handbook's* classic mottos of "scout's honour," BE PREPARED, & DO A GOOD TURN DAILY. Again, these are "private virtues" not "State-virtues." Robert C. Birkby, *The Boy Scout Handbook*, Tenth Edition (Irving, TX: Boy Scouts of America, 1990).

deeper side of the metaphysical right to own property. He writes in Chapter VII: "The Last Metaphysical Right" in *Ideas Have Consequences*:

> I would make it abundantly clear that the last metaphysical right [to property] offers nothing in defense of that kind of property brought into being by *Finance Capitalism*. Such property is, on the contrary, a violation of the very notion of *proprietas*. This amendment of the institution to suit the uses of commerce and technology has done more to threaten property than anything else yet conceived. For the abstract property of stocks and bonds, the legal ownership of enterprises never seen, actually destroy the connection between man and his substance without which metaphysical right becomes meaningless. Property in this sense becomes a *fiction* useful for exploitation and makes impossible the sanctification of work. The property which we defend as an anchorage keeps its identity with the individual.[62]

> Under present conditions money becomes the anonymous cloak for wealth, telling us how much a man has no longer tells us what he has.[63]

> Big business and the rationalization of industry thus abet the evils we seek to overcome. *Ownership through stock* makes property an autonomous unit, devoted to abstract ends, and the stockholder's area of responsibility is narrowed in the same way as is that of the specialized worker. *Respecters of private property are really obligated to oppose much that is done today in the name of private enterprise*, for corporate organization and monopoly are the very

---

[62] Richard M. Weaver, *Ideas Have Consequences* (Chicago: Chicago University Press, 1984 [1948]), 132-133. [emphasis mine]
[63] Ibid., 141. [emphasis mine]

means whereby property is casting aside its privacy.[64]

Private property cannot without considerable perversion of present laws be taken from the dissenter, and here lies a barrier to *Gleichschaltung*. Nothing is more certain than that whatever has to court public favor for its support will sooner or later be prostituted to utilitarian ends.[65]

The moral situation is the distributive ownership of small properties. These take the form of independent farms, of local businesses, of homes owned by the occupants, where individual responsibility gives significance to prerogative over property. Such ownership provides a range of volition through which one can be a complete person, and it is the abridgment of this volition for which monopoly capitalism must be condemned along with communism.[66]

Aside from property, WAR is often cited as the unquestionable reason to necessitate Statist monopoly of legal control. Yes, war is. That will not change either. From Biblical times the nature of man could be seen as it is, in that—"You desire and do not have; so you kill. And you covet and cannot obtain; so you fight and wage war" (James 4:2). There is (and always will be) an element of "mimetic rivalry" in all human activity. No amount of absolute enlightened scientism can ever eradicate the desires to *have* and to *take* from others. Resentments are too deep.

And so, Randolph Bourne once wrote during the progressive era in America: "war is the health of the State."[67] He is correct in that the inevitable incentive to centralize coercive violence in one monopoly corporate body is more often than not due to the threat of violence from others. An individual who lives peacefully with

---

[64] Ibid., 133. [emphasis mine]

[65] Ibid., 136.

[66] Ibid., 133-134.

[67] Randolph Bourne, "the State," in *We Who Dared to Say No to War: American Anti-War Writing From 1812 to Now*, eds. Murray Polner and Thomas Woods (New York: Basic Books, 2008), 132-140.

other individuals sharing customs, traditions, institutions or "constitutional" practices in common, will often necessitate mobilization through means of internal coercion, that is, in order to counteract external coercion.

In the epigraph at the beginning of this essay, the fundamental simplicity of politics is drawn from the moral of a children's story. In Dr. Suess' *The Butter Battle Book*, an arbitrary difference of custom leads to an escalating war over how to butter bread.[68] Every time one side invents an instrument of war to force the other side to submit, the opponent counters in like kind. Finally, the cold escalation ends with both sides in a stalemate of mutually assured destruction. Neither side wins, but both sides are the loser. The peaceful cooperation or internal harmony of the two opposing civilizations ends with everyone living in fear. Everyone is worse off (less satisfied) than when the war started. The reason for the war was trivial and arbitrary, but the lesson remains the same with respect to the reality of politics the world over.

Some believe the vast majority of mankind is too stupid to manage their own affairs.[69] Therefore, an elitist in-group of enlightened despots or benevolent dictators is often thought necessary to manage the world (legally) by "social engineering" with

---

[68] To be sure, the "weirdness" of cultural differences is perennial. David Brooks in his discussion of cultural differences provides the reader with this example of just how strange outside customs can seem: "Some Asian cultures have very low back-pain rates, but many people there do suffer from *koro*, a condition in which men become afflicted by the feeling that their penises are retracting into their bodies. The treatment involves asking a trusted family member to hold the penis twenty-four hours a day until the anxiety goes away." David Brooks, *The Social Animal: The Hidden Sources of Love, Character, and Achievement* (New York: Random House, 2011), 151.

[69] This may be a half truth in certain cases, but it is worth noting that an important distinction is made between *authentic cultural elites* vs. TOADS— or those with power, but no traditional authority. *See* Plinio Corrêa de Oliveira, *Nobility and Analogous Traditional Elites in the Allocutions of Pius XII: A Theme Illuminating American Social History* (York, PA: Hamilton Press, 1993), "Appendix I: Chapter II 2a. & 2d." describes where "the Toads" and "the Jet-Set" fit-in to the traditional caste of elites in American history.

threats of violent force or simple rational pleading.[70] There is an important difference when custom is enforced by an elite cabal of BIG BROTHER social engineers who know best in terms of what the Statist legal monopoly ought to do.[71] One group of scientific political "theorists" who determine the lives of billions irrespective of consent (World Government), or the elected sovereigns who determine the lives of millions in one pre-established territory relative to others (the State), or the simple village chieftain who influences what his neighbors do, each possess entirely separate magnitudes in terms of desirable political reality.

At least when the "chieftain" starts acting intolerably the tribe can depose him quite effectively. However, when the State is allowed coercive measures altogether out of proportion to the means individual subjects have available for control or retaliation (legal or illegal) in turn, the size or constitution of the government relative to the reach of the government is very significant. Nevertheless, when the "big" neighbor next door, or the neighboring state with bigger guns, wants to tell you what to do unprovoked, the significance of size matters as well, albeit in the opposite direction. In other words, there is pressure toward anarchy and there is pressure toward monopolizing Statist coercion, for the most part dependent on threat from an external or internal invader.

Peaceful cooperation will never survive without some mechanism of violent coercion. The agent of violent coercion often necessitates maximization in terms of the scale of enforcement. When the world is at war, Statist legal monopolies often remain not just practically expedient, but rather in critical need of totalitarian control in order to defend against aggression. For instance, in the event of World War III, the impossibility of establishing World

---

[70] *See* Abbott Gleason, Jack Goldsmith, and Martha C. Nussbaum, eds. *On Nineteen Eighty-Four: Orwell and Our Future* (Princeton, NJ: Princeton University Press, 2005).

[71] *See* Ross Clark, *The Road to Big Big Big Brother: One Man's Struggle Against the Surveillance Society* (New York: Encounter Books, 2009). Richard Weaver notes that in our near future (by way of a simple deduction in the 1950's)—"in the monolithic police state which is the invention of our age, assisted as it is by technology, surveillance becomes complete." In other words, totalitarian surveillance is unquestionably becoming not just possible, but also desirable *and* necessary. We are fast approaching the absolute PANOPTICON state of Jeremy Bentham's utopian nightmare. Richard Weaver, *Ideas Have Consequences*, 135.

Statehood will probably become (all of a sudden) practical necessity, meaning an actual possibility.[72] Barring such conflicts, most individual states remain more or less content with the status quo of highly de-centralized (meaning non-coerced) World Law. The same can be said of individuals who exist peacefully without formal law insofar as the condition remains desirable until threatened.

Why? Without war present the inclination of human nature typically desires freedom to determine one's own right or to live peacefully with those who live at peace with that determination. Some neighbors will typically want to tell other neighbors what to do, but that rarely causes violence in societies that have customs or traditions to arbitrate differences or bind the political unity together apart from coercive measures.[73] This fact remains whether for-

---

[72] We never know (or can see) the "paradigm shift" until it is already upon us. We have no idea what it will be until it is here. *See* Thomas Kuhn, *The Structure of Scientific Revolutions* (Chicago: The University of Chicago Press, 1962), & Giorgio Agamben, *Homo Sacer: Sovereign Power and Bare Life*, trans. Daniel Heller-Roazen (Stanford, CA: Stanford University Press, 1995).

[73] One of the more blatant examples of the push to *New World Order* was George Herbert Walker Bush's unconstitutional intervention in Kuwait. Conservative intellectual Russell Kirk denounced Bush at the time for what he knew to be an overt act on behalf of the globalist agenda and international interests. Kirk writes: "A war for Kuwait? A war for an oil-can! The rest is vanity; the rest is crime. A Republican administration in Washington contrived entry into the Spanish-American War. Since then, until 1991, it was Democratic governments of the United States that propelled the United States to war, if sometimes through the back door: the First World War, the second World War, the Korean War, the Indo-Chinese wars. But an unimaginative, "democratic capitalist" Republican regime, early in 1991, committed the United States, very possibly, to a new imperialism. For Mr. Bush's "New World Order" may make the United States detested—beginning with the Arab peoples—more than even the Soviet empire was. Mr. Bush's people hinted at their intention of stationing an American army "presence" permanently on the Persian Gulf, to insure the steady flow of petroleum to the consumers of the United States. Increasingly, the states of Europe and the Levant may suspect that in rejecting Russian domination, they exchanged King Log for King Stork. President Bush's assembling of half a million men in the deserts of Arabia, and then bullying and enticing Congress into authorizing him to make war, sufficiently suggests that conservative views are not identical with the measures of the Republican party. We learn from the saturation-bombing in Iraq that genuine conservatives—as distinguished

mal states have been constituted of not. Voting, or "positive law," or customary tradition, each seek the same end, namely, the defense of integrity within groups of individuals who desire to peacefully act in common. However, in the end there is no Law outside of the *right* of the individual to determine for his or her self.[74]

Even a Vatican globalist like then Joseph Cardinal Ratzinger admits that ultimately there is no universally agreeable law to bind all nations with. He writes as to the pre-political nature of international law that, "there is no single rational or ethical or religious 'world formula' that could win acceptance by everyone and could then provide support for the whole."[75] So, even for the then future Pope, there is *no* secular-world-order rationality (based on Immanuel Kant's reason or anyone else's) that can in fact function as a universal basis for government or World Statehood. No doubt, this is a disappointing conclusion for any monolithic world power who would like to lay claim to control everything; e.g. Communism, United Nations, Democratic Capitalism, Catholic Church, or otherwise. There IS an important distinction of moral law and civil law—*non videtur esse lex, quae iusta non fuerit.*[76]

---

from arrogant nationalists—have a hard row to hoe when they endeavor to teach the American democracy prudence in foreign relations;" Russell Kirk, "Toward a Prudent Foreign Policy," in *The Politics of Prudence*, 2nd Edition (Wilmington, DE: ISI Books, 2004 [1993]), 221-222.

[74] Here is Oakeshott's "shot" at the politics of the armchair soapbox Rationalist: "when he is not arrogant or sanctimonious, the Rationalist can appear a not unsympathetic character. He wants *so much* to be right. Like a foreigner or a man out of his social class, he is bewildered by a tradition and a habit of behaviour of which he knows only the surface; a butler or an observant house-maid has the advantage over him. And by some strange self-deception, he attributes to tradition (which, of course, is pre-eminently fluid) the rigidity and fixity of character which in fact belongs to ideological politics. His cast of mind is gnostic." Michael Oakeshott, *Rationalism in politics and other essays*, 36.

[75] Joseph Cardinal Ratzinger, "2. What Keeps the World Together: The Prepolitical Moral Foundations of a Free State," in Joseph Cardinal Ratzinger, *Values in a Time of Upheaval*, trans. Brian McNeil (New York: The Crossroad Publishing Company, 2006), 31-44.

[76] Augustine of Hippo, as quoted in John Paul II, *Evangelium Vitae*: Encyclical Letter, Vatican translation (Boston: Pauline Books & Media, 1995), 118.

So finally, in conclusion, to quote a poem by W. H. Auden on this fundamental ambiguity underlying our legal fictions, Auden in *Law Like Love* tells us in prose:

> Law, say the gardeners, is the sun,
> Law is the one
> All gardeners obey
> To-morrow, yesterday, to-day.
>
> Law is the wisdom of the old,
> The important grandfathers feebly scold;
> The grandchildren put out a treble tongue,
> Law is the sense of the young.
>
> Law, says the priest with a priestly look,
> Expounding to an un priestly people,
> Law is the words in my priestly book,
> Law is my pulpit and my steeple.
>
> Law, says the judge as he looks down his nose,
> Speaking clearly and most severely,
> Law is as I've told you before,
> Law is as you know I suppose,
> Law is but let me explain it once more,
> Law is The Law.
>
> Yet law-abiding scholars write:
> Law is neither wrong nor right,
> Law is only crimes
> Punished by places and by times,
> Law is the clothes men wear
> Anytime, anywhere,
> Law is Good-morning and Good-night.
>
> Others say, Law is our Fate;
> Others say, Law is our State;
> Others say, others say
> Law is no more,
> Law has gone away.

And always the loud angry crowd,
Very angry and very loud,
Law is We,
And always the soft idiot softly Me.

If we, dear, know we know no more
Than they about the Law,
If I no more than you
Know what we should and should not do
Except that all agree
Gladly or miserably
That the Law is
And that all know this,

If therefore thinking it absurd
To identify Law with some other word,
Unlike so many men
I cannot say Law is again,
No more than they can we suppress
The universal wish to guess
Or slip out of our own position
Into an unconcerned condition.

Although I can at least confine
Your vanity and mine
To stating timidly
A timid similarity,
We shall boast anyway:
Like love I say.

Like love we don't know where or why,
Like love we can't compel or fly,
Like love we often weep,
Like love we seldom keep.[77]

To sum up; the right to act against the will of others, or the necessity to submit to the will of others, is contingent on the strength of the will of others, the means of violence others will use,

---

[77] W. H. Auden, *Collected Poems, ed. Edward Mendelson* (New York: The Modern Library, 2007), 260-262.

the means of defending against another's will, or the notion of having the Right to defend against another's will. Outside of this, the modern age's "rule of law" is merely an illusion propped up by the legal *sycophants* of power, ignorant of everything else but the de facto norm, in the National State—*lex iniusta non est lex.*[78]

That some choose to live thinking this way is not arbitrary but an important subjective fact-hood of practicing legal theory. Other ways of thinking simply entitle the coercion of others to violently force submission for reasons of illusory authority, nothing more.

Others say, others say

---

[78] See "XII. UNJUST LAWS," in John Finnis, *Natural Law and Natural Rights,* 351-366.

BIBLIOGRAPHY

Agamben, Giorgio. Homo Sacer: Sovereign Power and Bare Life. trans. Daniel Heller-Roazen. Stanford, CA: Stanford University Press, 1995.

Auden, W. H. Collected Poems. ed. Edward Mendelson. New York: The Modern Library, 2007.

Aquinas, Thomas. Treatise on Law. trans. Richard J. Regan. Indianapolis, IN: Hackett Publishing Company, Inc., 2000.

Bastiat, Fredrick. The Law. Auburn, AL: The Ludwig von Mises Institute, 2011.

Beckett, Samuel. En attendant Godot. Paris: Les Editions De Minuit, 1952.

Berman, Harold. Faith and Order: The Reconciliation of Law and Religion. Cambridge, UK: William B. Eerdmans Publishing Company, 2000.

Berman, Harold J. Law and Revolution: The Formation of the Western Legal Tradition. Cambridge, MA: Harvard University Press, 1983.

Birkby, Robert C. The Boy Scout Handbook, Tenth Edition. Irving, TX: Boy Scouts of America, 1990.

Black, Edwin. War Against the Weak: Eugenics and America's Campaign to Create a Master Race. New York: Four Walls Eight Windows, 2003.

Brooks, David. The Social Animal: The Hidden Sources of Love, Character, and Achievement. New York: Random House, 2011.

Brownson, Orestes A. The American Republic: Its Constitution Tendencies & Destiny. Wilmington, DE: ISI Books, 2003.

Carroll, Lewis. The Complete Works of Lewis Carroll. London: The Nonesuch Press, 1989 [1939].

Carozza, Paulo, Mary Ann Glendon, and Colin Picker. Comparative Legal Traditions in a Nutshell. 4th Edition. St. Paul, MN: West Publishing Co., 2016 [1982].

Clark, Ross. The Road to Big Brother: One Man's Struggle Against the Surveillance Society. New York: Encounter Books, 2009.

Densen, John V., ed. The Costs of War: America's Pyrrhic Victories. New Brunswick, NJ: Transaction Publishers, 1999.

Dr. Suess. The Butter Battle Book. New York: Random House, 1984.

Duncan, Malcolm C. Duncan's Masonic Ritual and Monitor or Guide to The Three Symbolic Degrees of the Ancient York Rite and To the Degrees of Mark Master, Past Master, Most Excellent Master, and the Royal Arch. New York: Crown Publishers, [?].

Factor, Regis A., and Stephen P. Turner. Max Weber: The Lawyer as Social Thinker. London and New York: Routledge, 2004.

Finnis, John. Natural Law and Natural Rights. Oxford, UK: Clarendon Press, 1982.

Garner, Bryan A. Black's Law Dictionary. St. Paul, MN: West Publishing, 1996.

George, Robert. P. The Clash of Orthodoxies: Law, Religion, and Morality in Crisis. Wilmington, DE: ISI Books, 2001.

Gleason, Abbott, Jack Goldsmith, and Martha C. Nussbaum, eds. On Nineteen Eighty-Four: Orwell and Our Future. Princeton, NJ: Princeton University Press, 2005.

Glendon, Mary Ann. A Nation Under Lawyers: How the Crisis in the Legal Profession is Transforming Society. Cambridge, MA: Harvard University Press, 1996.

Gray, John Chipman. The Nature and Sources of the Law, Second Edition. Boston: Beacon Press, 1962 [1909].

Griffin, G. Edward. The Creature from Jekyll Island: A Second Look at the Federal Reserve. Westlake, CA: American Media, 2001.

Grossberg, Michael and Christopher Tomlins. The Cambridge History of Law in America, Vol. III. Cambridge, UK: Cambridge University Press, 2008.

Hamilton, Alexander, John Jay, and James Madison. The Federalist: A Commentary on the Constitution of the United States. ed. Robert Scigliano. New York: Random House, 2000.

Hammond, Bray. Banks and Politics in America: From the Revolution to the Civil War. Princeton, NJ: Princeton University Press, 1957.

Hand, Learned. The Spirit of Liberty: Papers and Addresses of Learned Hand. New York: Alfred A. Knopf, 1952.

Hart, H. L. A. The Concept of Law. Oxford, UK: Clarendon Press, 1961.

Hatch, JD, Scott, and Lisa Zimmer Hatch, MA. Paralegal Careers for DUMMIES. Hoboken, NJ: John Wiley & Sons, 2006.

Hayek, Fredrick. The Constitution of Liberty. Chicago, IL: Chicago University Press, 1978.

Hobbes, Thomas. Leviathan. ed. J. C. A. Gaskin. Oxford, UK: Oxford University Press, 1996.

Holmes, Jr. Oliver Wendell. The Common Law. New York: Dover Publications, Inc., 1991 [1881].

Isaacson, Walter & Evan Thomas. The Wise Men: Six Friends and the World They Made: Acheson, Bohlen, Harriman, Kennan, Lovett & McCloy. New York: Touchstone, 1986.

Jefferson, Thomas. The Life and Selected Writings of Thomas Jefferson: including the Autobiography, The Declaration of Independence and His Public and Private Letters. eds. Adrienne Koch and William Peden. New York: Random House, 2004.

John Paul II. Evangelium Vitae: The Gospel of Life. Boston: Paulist Books & Media, 1995.

Kantorowicz, Ernst H. The King's Two Bodies: A Study in Mediaeval Political Theology. Princeton, NJ: Princeton University Press, 1957.

Kelsen, Hans. General Theory of Law and State. trans. Anders Wedberg. Cambridge, MA: Harvard University Press, 1945.

Kelsen, Hans. What is Justice? Justice, Law, and Politics in the Mirror of Science: Collected Essays by Hans Kelsen. Berkeley and Los Angeles: University of California Press, 1957.

Kirk, Russell. The Conservative Mind: From Burke to Eliot. Washington, DC: Regnery, 2001.

Kirk, Russell. The Roots of American Order. Wilmington, DE: ISI Books, 2003.

Kirk, Russell, The Politics of Prudence, 2nd Edition. Wilmington, DE: ISI Books, 2004 [1993].

Korsgaard, Christine M. Creating the Kingdom of Ends. Cambridge, UK: Cambridge University Press, 1996.

Koskenniemi, Martti. The Gentle Civilizer of Nations: The Rise and Fall of European Law 1870-1960. Cambridge, UK: Cambridge University Press.

Kuhn, Thomas. The Structure of Scientific Revolutions. Chicago: The University of Chicago Press, 1962.

Kuehnelt-Leddihn, Erik Ritter von. Liberty or Equality: The Challenge of Our Time. Caldwell, Idaho: The Caxton Printers, Ltd., 1952.

Kuehnelt-Leddihn, Erik von. The Menace of the Herd, Or Procrustes at Large. Milwaukee, MN: The Bruce Publishing Company, 1943.

Kuehnelt-Leddihn, Erik von. Leftism Revisited: From de Sade and Marx to Hitler and Pol Pot. Washington, DC: Regnery Gateway, 1990.

Locke, John. Second Treatise on Government. Indianapolis, IN: Hackett Publishing Company, 1980.

Mill, John Stuart. Utilitarianism. Indianapolis, IN: Hackett Publishing Company, 2002.

Mises, Ludwig von. Human Action: A Treatise on Economics. Vols. 1-4. Indianapolis, IN: Liberty Fund, 2007.

Nisbet, Robert. Prejudices: A Philosophical Dictionary. Cambridge, MA: Harvard University Press, 1982.

Nisbet, Robert. The Present Age: Progress and Anarchy in Modern America. Indianapolis, IN: Liberty Fund, 2003.

Nisbet, Robert. The Quest for Community: A Study in the Ethics of Order and Freedom. Wilmington, DE: ISI Books, 2010.

Nozick, Robert. Anarchy, State and Utopia. New York: Basic Books, 1974.

Oakeshott, Michael. Rationalism in politics and other essays. Indianapolis: Liberty Fund, 1991.

Ortega y Gasset, José. The Revolt of the Masses. trans. anon. New York: W. W. Norton & Company, 1932.

Packard, Vance. The Ultra Rich: How Much is Too Much? Boston: Little, Brown and Company, 1989.

Parfit, Derek. Reasons and Persons. Oxford, UK: Clarendon Press, 1984.

Plato, The Republic. trans. Desmond Lee. London, UK: Penguin Books, 2003.

Polner, Murray and Thomas Woods, eds. We Who Dared to Say No to War: American Anti-War Writing From 1812 to Now. New York: Basic Books, 2008.

Ratzinger, Joseph Cardinal. Values in a Time of Upheaval. trans. Brian McNeil. New York: The Crossroad Publishing Company, 2006.

Rawls, John. A Theory of Justice. Cambridge, MA: The Belknap Press of Harvard University Press, 1971.

Rothbard, Murray. The Ethics of Liberty. New York: NYU Press, 2003.

Sandal, Michael. What Money Can't Buy: The Moral Limits of the Markets. New York: Farrar, Straus and Giroux, 2012.

Schmitt, Carl. Legality and Legitimacy. Durham, NC: Duke University Press, 2004.

Schmitt, Carl. Constitutional Theory. trans. Jeffrey Seitzer. Durham, NC: Duke University Press, 2008.

Turner, Stephen. Explaining the Normative. Cambridge, UK: Polity Press, 2010.

Vidal, Gore. Perpetual War for Perpetual Peace: How We Got To Be So Hated. New York: Thunder's Mouth Press/Nation Books, 2002.

Zolo, Danilo. Victor's Justice: From Nurenberg to Baghdad. New York: Verso, 2009.

The cold queen of England is looking in the glass;
The shadow of the Valois is yawning at the Mass;
. . .
Mahound is in his paradise above the evening star,
(Don John of Austria is going to the war.)
He moves a mighty turban on the timeless houri's
knees,
His turban that is woven of the sunset and the seas.
He shakes the peacock gardens as he rises from his
ease,
. . .
St. Michael's on his Mountain in the sea-roads of the
north
(Don John of Austria is girt and going forth.)
. . .
King Philip's in his closet with the Fleece about his
neck
(Don John of Austria is armed upon the deck.)
. . .
The Pope was in his chapel before day or battle broke,
(Don John of Austria is hidden in the smoke.)
. . .
And he finds his God forgotten, and he seeks no more
a sign—
(But Don John of Austria has burst the battle-line!)
. . .
Cervantes on his galley sets the sword back in the
sheath
(Don John of Austria rides homeward with a wreath.)
. . .
And he smiles, but not as Sultans smile, and settles
back the blade . . .
(But Don John of Austria rides home from the Crusade.)

Gilbert Keith Chesterton, LEPANTO

IV.

THE MORALITY OF AMERICAN NEUTRALITY IN WORLD WAR I:

THE JUST WAR TRADITION *IN MUNDO HUIUS TEMPORIS*

Sméagol won't grub for roots and carrotses and—taters. What's taters, precious, eh, what's taters?

'Po-ta-toes,' said Samwise Gamgee

J. R. R. Tolkein, THE TWO TOWERS

Vienna, as we saw, was almost taken and only saved by the Christian army under the command of the King of Poland on a date that ought to be among the most famous in history: September 11, 1683.

Hilaire Belloc, THE GREAT HERESIES

Blessed are the peacemakers, for they shall be called the sons of God.
(MTTW 5:9)

There isn't a minute despair.
We're Michael Hammond?
He'll chael Hamman
#$^&*@! Michael Hammond
Get up, a get get down … nine-one-one is joke in yo town
… They don't care 'cause they stay paid anyway
… they can t be betray
Aaaaieooow …
Aaaieoow!
Aaieow …

Public Enemy, FEAR OF A BLACK PLANET

The Horror! [Kurtz]

Joseph Conrad, HEART OF DARKNESS

1. *International War*

It is the explicit intention of this essay to examine the idea of international law (as to wars of intervention) using the particular historical case study of American involvement in World War I. The primary concern of this essay is with the implications of WWI for the discipline of Catholic Moral Theology. There is no pretense of rigoristic historical scholarship, although historical facts are dealt with in moderate detail for the purpose of mounting the case. Special attention is paid at the end of the essay to the homegrown American antiwar movements—esp. that of William Jennings Bryan—during the time of the conflict, how they sued for peace, and whether their arguments square with Biblical principles and Catholic Tradition.

Also looked at in some depth are the parallels of World War I and present day warfare; in particular, Joseph Ratzinger's Regensburg Address and the religious history of September 11th, 2001.

And finally, Pope Benedict XV, himself neutral during WWI, is looked to as the Catholic exemplar of a true diplomatic mediator and Christian peacemaker during a war of muddied origins. If his sage advice had been heeded many future ills could have been avoided.

There are two levels here to the thesis in question. The first is that international neutrality before and during war, as a political position, is in full accord with the traditional Just War Doctrine as Catholics have more or less universally understood it.[1] This is especially true of the work of the Spanish Dominican Francisco de Vitoria, who was the first to fully come to grips with the issue of international law during the birth of a new era of imperial nation-states in the late 16th and early 17th centuries.

The second layer, which follows closely upon the first, is that American involvement leading up to and after 1917 was highly detrimental to the cause of peace and prolonged the European Civil War into a second round of conflict, even more deadly than the first, namely the Second World War.

Taken together these two positions present a powerful case for a "conservative" and scrupulously prudential foreign policy,

---

[1] Lisa Sowle Cahill, *Love Your Enemies: Discipleship, Pacifism, and Just War Theory* (Minneapolis: Augsburg Fortress, 1994), for a good textbook outline of the traditional understanding of Just War.

both in terms of the *jus ad bellum* and *jus in bello*, which can then be used as a prescription for staying out of future foreign entanglements.

2. *What Is Meant By CONSERVATIVE*

The origin of the word "conservative" in modern political discourse can be found most definitively in the work of 18th century Scotch-Irish statesman Edmund Burke.[2] Russell Kirk, an American-born Burke scholar, once loosely defined conservatism as the "negation of ideology." To quote Kirk:

> In essence, the conservative person is simply one who finds the permanent things more pleasing than Chaos and Old Night. (Yet conservatives know, with Burke, that healthy 'change is the means of our preservation.') A people's historic continuity of experience . . . offers a guide to policy far better than the abstract designs of coffee-house philosophers. But of course there is more to the conservative persuasion than this general attitude.[3]

This more was drawn up in various writings by Kirk in the postwar aftermath to counteract the fatigue of a defeated West and to reground civilization in Western traditions. In sum, conservatives believe in an enduring and transcendent moral order, adherence to "custom, convention and continuity," while at the same time guiding change by the governing virtue of prudence.

They are chastened by the principle of the imperfectability of man and hold that freedom and property are closely allied. Furthermore, a conservative celebrates variety and *voluntary* community, while fearing both centralized power and the loosening of re-

---

[2] George H. Nash, *The Conservative Intellectual Movement in America Since 1945*, Thirtieth-Anniversary Edition (Wilmington, DE: ISI Books, 2008), provides intellectual history of the Anglo-American conservative tradition in the Post-War period.

[3] Russell Kirk, "Ten Conservative Principles," in Russell Kirk, *The Politics of Prudence*, 2nd Edition (Wilmington, DE: ISI Books, 2004 [1993]), 16.

straints on man's passions. Kirk once quipped that conservatives "prefer the devil they know to the devil they don't know."[4] Without say, he was no fan of the new-fangled "Porsche conservatives."

Now having defined "conservative" somewhat outside of the narrower partisan sense of it, it is not difficult to see how these principles sprang warmly out of the bosom of the Catholic Church in history, yet remain universal in their flexibility to individual circumstances. It can be safe to say that the Catholic Church is conservative in orientation and has filled the role of cultural "custodian" or steward of Western civilization better than any other institution (on the whole).[5]

As we will show, war is highly destructive of each the above tenets. The foreign policy of Woodrow Wilson in particular was antithetical to the noble vision that conservatives have traditionally embraced. Austrian noble, diplomat and scholar, Erik von Kuehnelt-Leddihn asserts about Wilson, in his history of the modern era *Leftism Revisited*, that:

> Wilson was a genuine ideologue in the narrow sense of the term; his plan, unfortunately, was not to make democracy safe for the world, but rather to make the world safe for democracy. He conducted a jihad, a holy war to extend the American form of government.[6]

It is with this in mind that we now turn to the tradition of international law and the history of the U.S.'s foreign interventions.

---

[4] Russell Kirk, *The Conservative Mind: From Burke to Eliot* (Washington, DC: Regnery Publishing, 1985) 8-10. Kirk is paraphrasing Ambrose Bierce. *See* Ambrose Bierce, *The Unabridged Devil's Dictionary*, eds. David S. Schultz and S.T. Joshi (Athens & London: The University of Georgia Press, 2000).

[5] George H. Nash, *The Conservative Intellectual Movement in America*, notes the Roman Catholic leanings of the "traditionalist conservatives" in the United States during the Post-War/Cold War period.

[6] Erik von Kuehnelt-Leddihn, *Leftism Revisited: From de Sade and Marx to Hitler and Pol Pot* (Washington, DC: Regnery Gateway, 1990), 203.

3. *International Law and Foreign Conflicts*

Not digging too deeply into the tangled debates over international law, it is of note that the very idea itself has its origin in the teachings of the Roman Catholic Church. International law arose mainly out of the writings of the Spanish Scholastics in the late 16th century in response to the "age of discovery" and the Spanish state's confrontation with pagan natives in the New World. It quickly became necessary to define a moral code of conduct for dealing with foreign peoples who were not organically descended from a common civilization. It was largely through the efforts of two Spanish churchmen that this welcome development in international law came about.

Francisco de Vitoria and Francisco Suarez ushered in the modern era of political thought with their writings on a broad range of topics—from the nature of state authority to the rudiments of economic theory.[7] As noted, the impetus of their work in the field of international law was the abuse of indigenous peoples in the Americas by the Conquistadors. The outcome of their deliberations came out solidly on the side of a "human rights" ethic. In short, they asserted the dignity of pagan peoples by nature of a shared humanity.[8] The rights of primitive peoples, afforded by the natural law, were to be honored in spite of foreign beliefs and alien governance. The international prospect of foreign enterprise led to a needed reassessment of the classical Just War Doctrine and many valuable insights evolved from Suarez's and de Vitoria's studies. Their work can be critically mined for insights that are still applicable to today.[9]

Classical international law took a sharp turn in 1914 at the onset of the First World War. The nature of this regression de-

---

[7] Also of high importance in history is Hugo Grotius. *See* Hugo Grotius, *The Rights of War and Peace: Including the Law of Nature and of Nations*. trans. A. C. Campbell, A.M. (New York and London: M. Walter Dunne, Publisher, 1901).

[8] A classic example of the "spirit" of this paternalistic attitude of the colonists *see* Rudyard Kipling, "The White Man's Burden (1899)," in Rudyard Kipling, *A Choice of Kipling's Verse*, ed. T. S. Eliot (London: Faber and Faber, 1941), 136-137.

[9] Thomas E. Woods, Jr., *How the Catholic Church Built Western Civilization* (Washington, DC: Regnery Publishing, 2005), 133-151.

serves a preliminary treatment here. [10] Speaking from a classical liberal perspective, historian and economist Murray Rothbard puts forth the view that:

> the classical international lawyers from the 16th through the 19th centuries were trying to cope with the implications of the rise and dominance of the modern nation-state. They did not seek to "abolish war," the very notion of which they would have considered absurd and Utopian . . . *the desideratum* . . . was to curb and limit the impact of existing wars as much as possible. Not to try to "abolish war," but to constrain war with limitations imposed by civilization. [11]

Rothbard in this essay *America's Two Just Wars: 1775 and 1861* then goes on to establish two key ideas that were developed by the classical international lawyers. The first was not to target civilians. Direct participants were to be identified as the only combatants and those innocent of the conflict were to be spared within reason. After the advent of mass democracy, *all* citizens would eventually come to be identified with the modern state and the government's power of conscription in particular would eventually broaden the scope of modern war to its current proportions. In Rothbard's opinion this "whittled away this excellent tenet of international law." [12]

More to the point is the second idea of the international lawyers, which is of grave importance in modern times and central to the thesis under consideration. The idea is that it is the responsibil-

---

[10] Austrian economist Murray Rothbard would be considered a doctrinaire "libertarian" in modern America. Individual liberty and property rights are central to his position. Although this is not the political position of the essay, Rothbard's stance is descended from a prestigious line of American political philosophy, e.g. Jeffersonian and Jacksonian democracy to the "Old Right" or New Left that strongly opposed both World Wars. The concern here is with the liberty of sovereign nations and not with individual liberty per se.

[11] Murray Rothbard, "America's Two Just Wars: 1775 and 1861," in *The Costs of War: America's Pyrrhic Victories*, ed. John Denson (Edison, NJ: Transaction Publishers, 1999), 120.

[12] Ibid., 120.

ity of all civilized nations to "preserve the rights of neutral states and nations." Rothbard says here that:

> in the modern corruption of international law that has prevailed since 1914, "neutrality" has been treated as somehow deeply immoral. Nowadays, if countries A and B get into a fight, it becomes every nation's moral obligation to figure out, quickly, which country is the "bad guy," and then if, say, A is condemned as the bad guy, to rush in and pummel A in defense of the alleged good guy B.[13]

The danger of this approach is that it lends itself to unnecessary escalation and/or black and white thinking. On the other hand, the classical understanding was that neutrality was actually the *more noble* option and was considered "a mark of high statesmanship." One can say that this is easy enough to see. There is higher probability that conflicts will "get out of hand" and that massive casualties will result when the idea of "collective security against aggression" takes shape. This idea was so vital to the escalation of the two World Wars and continued as a strategic blunder during the aftermath.[14]

That a coalition should police-the-world is a deceptively dangerous one. This notion can first be attributed to Woodrow Wilson who harbored dreams of effective World Government. However, the problem with international police action writ large is that of jurisdiction and authority. Police and judges, acting within borders, have the legal right to enforce the laws of their sovereignty. But once this kind of action is extended to other nations, any act of *unprovoked* aggression, be that of violence or coercion, can be considered an act of war. Therein lies the danger. If countries band together in a conflict, there will be polarization, escalation and then mass destruction, *id est*, if peace efforts fail. Furthermore, the "aggressor" and "victim" in any given war are, as most historians will likely point out, not so easily identified.

---

[13] Ibid., 120.
[14] Ibid., 121.

> In real life . . . causes become tangled, and history
> intervenes. Above all, a nation's current border
> cannot be considered as evidently just as a per-
> son's life and property. Therein lies the problem.
> How about the very different borders ten years,
> twenty years, or even centuries ago? How about
> wars where claims on all sides are plausible?[15]

There is no impartial judge among enemy combatants. From
a moral standpoint, only the neutral state, disentangled from the
webs of interest, can play the role of peacemaker. Any other position taken by a nation, unprovoked, is, de facto, that of an aggressor.

Wilson had another idea that proved equally disastrous. The
idea was that the United States has a moral obligation to impose its
form of government on the rest of the world in the name of a
"human rights" agenda. Most of the world for most of history has
not known "democracy" and has no native desire or capacity for it.
It is foolish to pretend that foreign peoples can be "given" what
you possess culturally through force of arms. This was essentially
Wilson's gravest mistake. Kuehnelt-Leddihn puts it succinctly:

> Wilson suffered from the Great American Malady,
> the belief that people the world over are "more
> alike than unlike"; in other words, that non-
> Americans are nothing more than inhibited, un-
> derdeveloped could-be Americans with the mis-
> fortune of speaking a different language.[16]

The following section will deal with this supposed "humanitarian" justification so widely used to violate strict neutrality. Unfortunately, the cry for "human rights" became the rallying point
of American intervention during the build-up to war. American
journalist Bill Kauffman, with a note of irony, writes:

> Americans entered the First World War largely
> because, in Herbert Agar's phrase, Woodrow Wil-

---

[15] Ibid., 121.
[16] Erik von Kuehnelt-Leddihn, *Leftism Revisited: From de Sade and Marx to Hitler and Pol Pot*, 204.

son "and his countrymen were destined to teach the whole world how to govern itself." Prussian militarism was run amok. Heretofore the United States, in obedience to the injunctions of its founders, had ignored the periodic wars of the Old World. But we were now a World Power, and no self-regarding World Power could stay out of the fray.

This was "Our War for Human Rights," as one of the numerous propaganda books of 1917 put it. The Germans, a warlike race "obsessed with the spirit of militarism," must be crushed by a militarized America so that "the principles of liberty for which [America] has ever stood may be perpetuated throughout the world."[17]

4. *"Humanitarian" Wars of Intervention*

Very few wars have ever been fought for genuinely humanitarian ends.[18] Starting with Wilson perhaps, international wars for "human rights" have largely been shams meant to cover self-interest. Before going into the history of World War I in greater depth, it is first necessary to deal with this leading justification for American intervention as a case *in abstracto*. First of all, what is meant by "human rights"? For the sake of clarity, it is important to have a proper understanding of this popular catch-all-watch-word. "Human rights" language can (and does) become unintentionally (or intentionally) destructive to international stability, domestic order, and the true freedom to do what is right and good. This kind of talk is often misused by ambitious politicians toward subversive ends, as will be shown in the case of Wilson.

---

[17] Bill Kauffman, *Ain't My America: The Long, Noble History of Antiwar Conservatism and Middle-American Anti-Imperialism* (New York: Metropolitan Books, 2008), 66-67.

[18] Russell Kirk, "Toward a Prudent Foreign Policy," in *The Politics of Prudence*, 206-222.

There must be a distinction made between rights based on a Natural Law, which tend to be broad and inclusive (such as a right to life) and civil rights which are particular to a given political territory or point in time. The term "human rights" has a tendency to blur this distinction and is inclusive of many civil rights that may be desirable to some, but are by no means universal.

For instance, it is unwise to export American civil liberties and the "rights" Americans enjoy, and cannot imagine life without, to a country that does not have the necessary cultural institutions, customs and/or desire for such things. In most instances to do so is disastrous. Utopian visions usually destroy rather than fulfill and sober politics is the "art of the possible." American civilization did not spring out of the mind of an ideologue like Pallas Athena from Zeus, but took centuries of slow and painful growth, not to mention historical and cultural continuity with the much older traditions of her ancient mother European civilization.[19] Wars often lead to the death of civilizations, rarely to "human rights." Wars for "human rights" are like a perpetual war for perpetual peace, a contradiction in terms.[20]

So what should a list of rights look like? For the purposes of an easy illustration, the conservative position held by Edmund Burke is more to the point than something akin to a universal Bill of Rights—ready for export and imposition on the rest of the world. A call for uniformity based on American cultural mores, or any other set of abstracted principles for that matter, is always a dangerous endeavor. Burke stated a more sensible understanding of "rights" in response to the ideology of the French Revolution; a revolution that sought to impose a radical vision of life on a people rooted in the ancient traditions of Christendom. He sought a more minimalist approach that allows for the organic variety of culture rather than an abstracted ideology based on secular Reason alone.

> if civil society be made for the advantage of man, all the advantages for which it is made become his right. It is an institution of beneficence; and law

---

[19] For an account of these converging traditions *see* Russell Kirk, *The Roots of American Order* (Wilmington, DE: ISI Books, 2003).

[20] *See* Gore Vidal, *Perpetual War for Perpetual Peace: How We Got To Be So Hated* (New York: Thunder's Mouth Press/Nation Books, 2002).

itself is only beneficence acting by rule. Men have a right to live by that rule; they have a right to do justice, as between their fellows, whether their fellows are in public function or in ordinary occupation. They have a right to the fruits of their industry, and to the means of making their industry fruitful. They have a right to the acquisitions of their parents; to the nourishment and improvement of their offspring; to instruction in life, and to consolation in death. Whatever each man can separately do, without trespassing upon others, he has a right to do for himself; and he has a right to all which society, with all its combinations of skill and force, can do in his favor. In this partnership all men have equal rights; but not to equal things.[21]

So, men have a right to *their* civilization by Burke's lights. Bandying about ideas like equality and liberty will lead nowhere unless these ideas are incarnate in real institutions and people. It is all too easy to destroy freedom in the name of equality or to destroy life in the name of peace. The more modest task is to maintain order while preserving (and slowly expanding) what liberties people are fortunate enough to have been afforded by their given time and place. Most wars have been fought in the name of justice [dike], but justice is a hard-fought virtue in a fallen world. There will be no justice unless it is governed by prudential judgment before everything else. After all, who is to say when it is necessary to sacrifice one civilization to try to save another?

In contrast to Burke's more level-headed understanding of "rights," it is worth quoting Russell Kirk at length to drive home the absurdity of the Wilsonian idealism of World War I:

Has anyone troubled to inquire of the zealots for "human rights" as to precisely what political and social conditions may be regarded as a satisfactory fulfillment of the "human rights" ideal? We may suppose that, as a minimum, all the articles of

---

[21] Edmund Burke, *Reflections on the Revolution in France* (New York: Penguin Books, 2004), 149-150.

America's Bill of Rights would have to be observed and enforced most scrupulously; that governments would be carried on by "moderate" or
"middle of the road" parties of a social-
democratic cast (parties of a kind almost nonex-
istent in most of the world); that perfect freedom
of expression, including street demonstrations by
militant factions, would be not merely guaranteed,
but encouraged; that a country's armed forces
would be reduced to a minimum, if not abolished
altogether; that of course secret police forces
would be forbidden, and ordinary police directed
by citizens' committees; that universal suffrage
would prevail, with frequent elections; that a welfare state would provide a large proportion of cit-
izenry with generous entitlements; that every demand for more abundant rights would be
promptly satisfied. In effect, the "human rights"
vision for the world is a latter-day version of the
more advanced sentimental liberalism of Victorian England, plus a very considerable dose of socialism . . .

A principle difficulty of this utopian notion of
"human rights" triumphant is that such a society,
in most of the world, would be overthrown in
very short order by one ideological gang or another—even if it did not collapse of its own
weight. The liberal dream began to turn into a
nightmare a century ago. The bent world in which
we find ourselves will not tolerate such coffee-
house political philosophy. Things will be as they
will be;[22]

The nightmare Kirk refers to can be said to have begun with
World War I, which then led to the rise of the great tyrants of the
20th century. If America had remained with strict neutrality on

---

[22] Russell Kirk, "XVII: The Illusion of 'Human Rights'," in Russell Kirk, *Redeeming the Time*, ed. Jeffrey O. Nelson (Wilmington, DE: ISI Books, 1999), 237.

moral grounds, the history of the century may have been written very differently. It is to this history that we now turn.

5. *The History of the Conflict*

Historian and diplomat George F. Kennan once famously remarked that "all lines of inquiry, it seems to me, lead back to it [World War I]."[23] In a controversial book called *Churchill, Hitler and the Unnecessary War*, American politician and writer Patrick J. Buchanan makes the arguable case that the United States could have sat out World War II without grave consequences to Western civilization or the National interest.[24] His case for neutrality in World War II rests on the shaky attempt at historical revisionism; always a foggy endeavor. However, the primary value of the book is not in this conclusion, but in the description of the bridge between the two wars and the highlighting of easily avoided political blunders made along the way. His historical critique of the leadership of Britain and America is also important for the empirical (scientific) and factual defense of neutrality as a position in theory. He writes that:

> historians will look back on 1914-1918 and 1939-1945 as two phases of the Great Civil War of the West, where the once-Christian nations of Europe fell upon one another with such savage abandon they brought down all their empires, brought an end to centuries of Western rule, and advanced *the death of* (our) *civilization.*[25]

The facts of history are difficult to deny. In World War I alone eight million soldiers were killed and twenty million more

---

[23] George Kennan, *American Diplomacy, 1990-1950* (Chicago: The University of Chicago Press, 1951), 56.

[24] Buchanan is quoted here not for his political positions at large, but for his more recent efforts to bring antiwar conservatism back into the mainstream.

[25] Patrick J. Buchanan, *Churchill, Hitler, and the Unnecessary War: How Britain Lost Its Empire and the West Lost the World* (New York: Three Rivers Press, 2008), xvii.

were wounded. And it is the horror of war statistics that in "1916 one million Frenchmen and Germans were killed in a single battle."[26] Moreover, twenty-two million civilians were killed or injured in the First World War, while countless others suffered intangibly for generations from the war. Furthermore, if World War I was indeed the cause of the Second World War, then it is necessary to place that conflict on the scales as well. In numbers and consequences World War II was even worse.[27]

Most non-partisan historians would agree that there is no single culpable party in the First World War. However, history attests that:

> had Britain not declared war on Germany in 1914, Canada, Australia, South Africa, New Zealand and India would not have followed the Mother Country in. Nor would Britain's ally Japan. Nor would Italy, which London lured with secret bribes of territory from the Habsburg and Ottoman empires. Nor would America have gone to war had Britain stayed out. Germany would have been victorious, perhaps in months.[28]

This is not to demonize Great Britain of course, only to point out that at this critical juncture, when the war was escalated to a truly global level, there were still other viable options on the table. Containment of Germany, an admittedly third rate imperial power,

---

[26] Walker Percy, "The Delta Factor: How I Discovered the Delta Factor Sitting at My Desk One Summer Day in Louisiana in the 1950's Thinking about an Event in the Life of Helen Keller on Another Summer Day in Alabama in 1887," in Walker Percy, *The Message in the Bottle: How Queer Man Is, How Queer Language Is, And What One Has to Do with the Other* (New York: Picador, 1975), 27.

[27] The classical moral principles of the Just War Doctrine do not see consequences as having any bearing on decisions of war. Proportionality (or consequentialism) is a predictive measure that is similar to utilitarian calculation, e.g. believing in the ability to control results or predict outcomes with near objective certainty. Catholic moral teaching is much stricter than proportionalism or utilitarianism, in that the consequences of an action do not determine *in any way* the morality of an action.

[28] Patrick J. Buchanan, *Churchill, Hitler, and the Unnecessary War: How Britain Lost Its Empire and the West Lost the World*, xvii.

was always a possibility. When all the dust settles after it becomes apparent that no European nation benefited from the war. This is especially true of Great Britain, as they had the most to lose and did. Buchanan holds that it was actually in Britain's best interest (not to mention the rest of the world's) to remain neutral after the annexation of Belgium. He states the case thus:

> Consider: When Winston Churchill entered the cabinet of the Admiralty in 1911, every nation recognized Britain's primacy. None could match her in the strategic weapons of the new century: the great battle fleets and dreadnoughts of the Royal Navy . . . Yet by Churchill's death in 1965, little remained . . . What happened to Great Britain? What happened to the empire? What happened to the West and our world?[29]

The answer to these questions is made apparent in retrospect: the hubris of an avoidable war occurred. The moral case for British neutrality in World War I will not be consistently argued here, let alone the more controversial case of World War II. However, the thesis in question is concerned with the involvement of the United States; a thoroughly independent party at the outset. It is the position here that the second critical juncture, after the British Empire's declaration of war, was the decision of America to intervene. Kuehnelt-Leddihn goes further to state that:

> certainly 1917 was the most fateful year of our century. Woodrow Wilson decided to throw the American sword on the scales without realizing that he lacked the knowledge to win peace and the power to make it last. And in fact, World War I and its seemingly permanent aftermath still haunts us.[30]

If America had stayed out of the war it is very likely that there would have been a "peace without victory" made possible. There

---

[29] Ibid., xvi.

[30] Erik von Kuehnelt-Leddihn, *Leftism Revisited: From de Sade and Marx to Hitler and Pol Pot*, 202.

would have been no Versailles Treaty and no power vacuum on the Continent. Without the destruction of the Austro-Hungarian Empire, and the fall of the Czar in Russia, it is likely that a second world war could have been averted. The relative peace of the previous century was a direct result of a delicate balance between the major Continental powers and Russia. The *heavy-handed* aftermath of the war undid what took centuries to build up and could only be replaced by coercion and force.

During the War and after it, Wilson was blind to see this, mostly due to his strong prejudice against European monarchy. Unfortunately, he lacked the foresight to see that out of the rubble of crushed civilizations would arise monsters like Hitler and Stalin. Kuenhelt-Leddihn calls Wilson's distaste for monarchy "folkloric." This despite, and perhaps because of, Woodrow's Princeton education. So that, "the ignorance of the former president of Princeton in matters of history and geography was simply prodigious."[31] . . .

> although the Austro-Hungarian monarchy figured hardly at all in the popular imagination of Americans, it was utmost on the minds of leftist intellectuals . . . No wonder, then, that the upshot of it all, the most tangible result of World War I, was the dismemberment of Austria-Hungary. It transformed the geopolitical position that gave Hitler an ideal start for his military and nonmilitary conquests. With the fall of the monarchy in Russia, Germany was bordered in the East by a power vacuum.[32]

Wilson stubbornly refused to cooperate with peace efforts, mainly because it was Austria-Hungary and the Pope who were alone in suing for peace and neither was a democracy or a democrat. Perhaps if the conservative inclination to save rather than destroy had prevailed there would have been no second war. Many historians take this for granted to the point that it has "almost" become cliché to blame the actions of the Allies after the war for the rise of Hitler and World War II.

---

31 Ibid., 205.

32 Ibid., 203.

after the solid bloc of the Austro-Hungarian monarchy had been smothered into unrecognizable fragments, Germany was put in the most advantageous geopolitical situation. It was now only a question of time when a rejuvenated and reinforced Germany would enter into a receivership for the liquidated estates of the dual monarchy. The imaginary "road to Bagdad" was now a reality.

To illustrate the situation better one might visualize a cage (Central Europe) containing a lion and a tiger, Austria and Germany. The Allies killed the lion, carved him up, broiled its slices, and left these on a platter. Then they humiliated the tiger beyond words, clipped his tail and ears, cut his claws, wounded his back, starved him, and locked the cage. Our "democratic" simpletons were highly astonished when the tiger started to eat the remains of his former cage mate once he had finished the job of licking his wounds.

It must be realized that the Habsburgs in exile meant the green light for Prussianized Germany. When William II arrived in Amerongen the way for Adolf Hitler was open, when Charles I debarked from a British cruiser on the shore of an African island to die a bitter death in exile, the war was lost for the Allies. That it took them twenty years to become aware of this truth has no bearing on the matter.[33]

---

[33] Erik Ritter von Kuehnelt-Leddihn, *The Menace of the Herd, Or Procrustes at Large* (Milwaukee, MN: The Bruce Publishing Company, 1943), 155-156.

6. *Was American Involvement a Just Cause?*

Before proceeding to the moral analysis of American involvement in World War I, it is necessary to dispel some of the illusions about the reasons given for the intervention. The most common arguments given attempt to demonstrate the fact of direct German aggression against the United States. The Zimmerman telegram and the sinking of the *Lusitania* are often cited as examples of this kind of aggression. It was only after the attack on the *Lusitania* that the leadership of the nation was given the green light to intercede from Congress and the approval of an otherwise noncommittal populace.[34] Right up until the eve of the war there was still a strong grassroots antiwar resistance in the United States, born of a deeply engrained American tradition of staying out of foreign wars, especially in Europe. At the time, the words of George Washington's farewell address to "beware of foreign entanglements" were not far from the popular imagination. However, once war was declared the government cranked up the propaganda machine and soon a "crusade for democracy" had widespread appeal for the proverbial "man on the street."[35]

George Creel, the official *Minister of Propaganda* in the United States, *did* in fact perpetrate unprecedented manipulations of the American populace to get the *hoi polloi* to enter into or continue to support the War. Many have now long-forgotten everything but the "success" of it all in retrospect. *But,* the abuses of the Creel Commission, and its masterminds in people like Freudian mass-psychoanalyst Edward Bernays, were not so far in outlook or temperament from Germany's great intellectual of "mass-man" Joseph Goebbels himself, though some would have it otherwise.[36] Or even men like Erich Ludendorff—"young, abrasive, brilliant—and

---

[34] The *Lusitania* which was "carrying 1,257 passengers, including 440 women and 129 children, and a crew of 702, sank in the North Atlantic with a loss of 1,198 lives, including 120 Americans." Warren H. Carroll and Anne W. Carroll, *The Crisis of Christendom: A History of Christendom*, Vol. 6 (Front Royal, VA: Christendom Press, 2013), 266.

[35] Noam Chomsky, *Media Control: The Spectacular Achievements of Propaganda* CD-ROM (New York: Seven Stories Press, 2004).

[36] *See* Edwin Black, *War Against the Weak: Eugenics and America's Campaign to Create a Master Race* (New York: Four Walls Eight Windows, 2003), for the sordid history of the origins of Nazi initiatives by means of the American Eugenics movement.

pitiless, a man who always believed that the ends justify the means."[37]

Still, despite the onslaught of propaganda and unconstitutional travesties like the Espionage and Sedition Act, there were many in power who hesitated to enter or support it. Tracing the attack on the *Lusitania* to the dual declarations of war zones on the high seas by both Great Britain and Germany, Senator George W. Norris (R-NE) delivered a speech to the Senate on April 4, 1917, shortly before the declaration of war on Good Friday, April 6 of that same year. Despairing of the imminent conflict, he makes a last ditch effort to point out that:

> it is unnecessary to cite authority to show that both of these orders declaring military zones were illegal and contrary to international law. It is sufficient to say that our government has officially declared both of them to be illegal and has officially protested against both of them. The only difference is that in the case of Germany we have persisted in our protest, while in the case of England we have submitted.[38]

Norris then outlines the three courses of action that could have been taken. **1)** The United States could have gone to war with both nations for violating international law and interfering with the right to neutrality. **2)** The United States could have taken sides and hypocritically defied one and submitted to the other, which the leadership finally did. And **3)** the third course would have been to remain neutral with regard to both. Senator Norris opted for the latter of these—which was in fact the moral choice—but it was already a foregone conclusion. The United States had already been involved in the war, almost from the start.[39]

---

[37] Warren H. Carroll and Anne W. Carroll, *The Crisis of Christendom*, 264.
[38] George W. Norris, "Wealth's Terrible Mandate," in *We Who Dared To Say No To War: American Antiwar Writing From 1812 To Now*, eds. Thomas E. Woods and Murray Polner (Philadelphia: Basic Books, 2008), 119-120.
[39] Ibid., 120-123

7. *The Underlying Motive for American Intervention*

Woodrow Wilson came into office on the campaign slogan "he kept us out of war," but this was never actually Wilson's intention. The fact of the matter is that England and France were financially drained from the war and very early on had to resort to loans from the United States. Their banker of choice was the New York financial giant J. P. Morgan. By 1917, there had been an enormous amount of money tied-up with England and France, as well as a profitable trade in contraband. However, there were also legitimate fears that Germany could possibly win the war with the strategic use of of U-boats. Should this happen, Morgan and the other industrial interests would have been devastated by financial losses. The trade in armaments and war bonds was big business and needed to be protected. American historian Thomas Fleming puts it this way:

> Wilson talked and—talked and talked—about neutrality and apparently convinced himself that he was neutral. But the United States he was supposedly running was not neutral, in thought, word or deed, thanks to Wellington House in London—and the international banking firm of J.P. Morgan in New York. The storied founder of the firm had died in 1913; it was now headed by his son, "Jack" Pierpont Morgan, who spent six months out of the each year on his English estate and was a totally committed Anglophile. Morgan and his fellow bankers were the key players in the shift from genuine to sham neutrality. The war was barely two days old when the French government, through Morgan's Paris branch, requested a loan of $100 million.[40]

The strongest opponent of the War, within Wilson's own cabinet, was the "Great Orator" and "Great Commoner" Secretary

---

[40] Thomas Fleming, *The Illusion of Victory: America in World War I* (New York: Basic Books, 2003), 68-69.

of State William Jennings Bryan. [41] Bryan was a populist who commanded a politically significant amount of votes and thus was tolerated by the administration. He early on pointed out that "money is the worst of all contrabands because it commands everything else."[42] This is especially true of politicians and the press. The most telling episode of the pre-war ordeal came after the sinking of the *Lusitania*. As Fleming reports the story:

> When the Lusitania was sunk, William Jennings Bryan was one of the few Americans who resisted the hysteria whipped up by Wellington House and its American mouthpieces. Citing the Lusitania's cargo manifest, which listed the ammunition as well as material for uniforms and leather belts in its cargo, he told Woodrow Wilson: 'A ship carrying contraband should not rely on passengers to protect her from attack—it would be like putting women and children in front of an Army.'[43]

Bryan was promptly dismissed and the better of the two men stepped down soon afterward.[44] In contrast to the brave witness of William Jennings Bryan, there is only rare evidence to contradict the suspicion that the official declaration of war was premeditated. Needless to say, there is a certain irony in a war fought to "spread

---

[41] *See* William Jennings Bryan and Mary Baird Bryan, *The Memoirs of William Jennings Bryan* (Chicago, Philadelphia, and Toronto: The John C. Winston Company, 1925). Bryan's memoirs (compiled and edited by his wife Mary Baird) give an intimate portrayal of the events of his life.

[42] For more on the money mechanizations of the hidden elites in America's financial-political history *see* G. Edward Griffith, *The Creature from Jekyll Island: A Second Look at the Federal Reserve* (Westlake Village: CA: American Media, 2001); & Bray Hammond, *Banks and Politics in America: From the Revolution to the Civil War* (Princeton, NJ: Princeton University Press, 1957). Hammond's is a more sympathetic and scholarly account. While the admission is made that centralized banking is unconstitutional by all fair historico-legal standards, Hammond understands and approves of its use as a practical matter.

[43] Thomas Fleming, *The Illusion of Victory: America in World War I*, 70.

[44] William Jennings Bryan and Mary Baird Bryan, *The Memoirs of William Jennings Bryan*, 406-411.

democracy" by the "power elitists" of London and New York.[45]
As C. Wright Mills reminds us: "there are in fact tiers and ranges
of wealth and power which people in the middle and lower ranks
know very little and may not even dream."[46] ". . . People are either
accepted into this class or they are not"[47] . . . "By powerful we
mean, of course, those who are able to realize their will, even if
others resist it."[48]

8. *Neutrality and the Catholic Just War Doctrine in Theory and Practice*

The Just War Doctrine as it has classically been formulated
was meant to restrain war and to limit conflicts, *not* to eliminate the
possibility of war altogether. The traditional doctrine holds that
certain conditions must be met before a war is justified. According
to the older version of the doctrine, **1)** a war must be declared by a
sovereign authority, **2)** in defense against an injustice, and **3)** un-
dertaken as a last resort with a good chance for success. Furthermore, there must be **4)** a *right intention* and not a lust to dominate
[libido dominandi]. Finally, **5)** there must be *proportionality* between
the damage done and the means of correcting it.[49] It is on this last
point that the contemporary debate on war often turns.[50]

How can a modern war be justified when the potential for
mass destruction is a "clear and present danger" in almost all conflicts using modern weapons technology?[51] The Just War Doctrine
was developed in the context of a very different world, but Human
Nature is constant—that is, as to violence and the desire for

---

[45] *See* C. Wright Mills, *The Power Elite* (Oxford, UK: Oxford University
Press, 1956).

[46] Ibid., 12.

[47] Ibid., 11.

[48] Ibid., 9.

[49] *See* Oliver O'Donovan, *The Just War Revisited* (Cambridge, UK: Cambridge University Press, 2003).

[50] A classic example of how a stalemate works as deterrence in conflicts is
"The Hatfields and the Coys." *See* Paul Ramsay, *The Just War* (New York:
Charles Scribner's Sons, 1968), Chapter 8: "The Hatfields and the Coys,"
168-177.

[51] Carroll Quigley, *Tragedy and Hope: A History of the World in Our Time*
(New York: The Macmillan Company, 1966), 255.

vengeance or retaliation. "Man's inhumanity to man" must be reckoned with then as now.

de Vitoria and Suarez, building on the work of St. Augustine and St. Thomas, were the first to theorize about the meaning of war in the context of international law. In those days the Western world was, supposedly, still ruled by chivalric values and for the most part limited wars, both in scope and by the nature of the weapons used.[52] "During the Middle Ages nationalism was extremely weak."[53] One knight slaying another knight on the battlefield in loyalty to the king, baron, lord, vassal, tribal chieftain, or whatever—or even two armies of men standing across from one another on an open field firing single-shot muskets until the Colonel yells "stop"—does not compare to the Western Front or Hiroshima, where men are mowed down by machine guns or entire populations incinerated *en masse* to the very last woman and child. Where, for example, is the proportionality between the murder of Archduke Ferdinand and 23 million dead?

> The First World War was a catastrophe of such magnitude that, even today, the imagination has some difficulty grasping it. In the year 1916, in two battles (Verdun and the Somme) casualties of over 1,700,000 were suffered by both sides. In an artillery barrage which opened the French attack on Chemin des Dames in April 1917, 11,000,000 shells were fired on a 30-mile front in 10 days.[54]

And this is not to paint a simplistic picture of either modern or ancient warfare, only to be wary of the change in history between the periods when the doctrine was formulated and this previous [20th] century. The principles remain sound, but the application *must* now be different in several important ways at least. Wars should be declared less often, not more. Unfortunately, of all the criteria, proportionality is the most subjective to define or to "nail-down" with any certainty. The future is seen through a glass-darkly

---

[52] *See* John Finnis, Joseph M. Boyle, Jr., and Germain Grisez, *Nuclear Deterrence, Morality and Realism.* (Oxford, UK: Clarendon Press, 1987).

[53] Erik Ritter von Kuehnelt-Leddihn, *The Menace of the Herd, Or Procrustes at Large*, 112.

[54] Carroll Quigley, *Tragedy and Hope: A History of the World in Our Time*, 255.

(1 Corinth. 12:13) and who is to say how many will suffer and die in a war? The very possibility of escalation should be enough to add the needed concept of a "presumption against violence," adjudicated by the virtue of prudence, to the doctrinal canon.

Georgetown University political scientist (now deceased) Carroll Quigley further explains the nature of the change in the weapons situation as far as modern warfare is concerned, going all the way back to 1966 when he wrote these following passages. He understood even then that the political leadership of the globe was already on the brink of a universal totalitarian imposed "truce" (as far as the weapons situation went). Quigley candidly puts the case that mass-killing is and will be the predominant political issue for the foreseeable future:

> The danger of such weapons (Weapons of Mass Destruction) becoming common, *or even becoming commonly known*, among the people of the world, including the less developed nations, is very great, opening an opportunity to all kinds of political blackmail or even to merely irresponsible threats. The parallel danger from new weapons of chemical warfare are even more horrifying. One of the nerve gases now currently available in the United States is so potent that a small drop of it on an individual's unbroken skin can cause *death in a few seconds.*[55]

> But the new weapons, in seeking increased range, had become weapons of mass destruction rather than instruments of persuasion. If the victims of such weapons are killed, they can neither obey nor consent. Thus the new weapons have become instruments, not of political power, but of destruction of all power organizations. This explains the growing reluctance by all concerned to use them. Furthermore their range and areas of impact make them most ineffective against individual men and especially against the minds of indi-

---

[55] Carroll Quigley, *Tragedy and Hope: A History of the World in Our Time*, 1210. [emphasis added]

vidual men. And, finally, in an ideological state it is the minds of men that must be the principal targets. Any organization is coordinated both by patterned relationships and by ideology and morale.[56]

The political conditions of the latter half of the twentieth century will continue to be dominated by the weapons situation, for, while politics consists of much more than weapons, the nature, organization, and control of weapons is the most significant of the numerous things that determine what happens in political life.[57]

This is rarely factored into the judgments of the so-called voting citizen (kept ignorant of such things?), especially as concerns the level of risk involved with present day warfare, e.g. since the time of WWI.[58] So, perhaps lesser injustices are necessarily tolerat-

---

[56] Ibid., 1207.

[57] Ibid., 1200.

[58] *See* Christopher Buckley, *Little Green Men: A Novel* (New York: Harper-Perennial, 1999), for a fictional take on the old conspiracy theory that during the Cold War a top secret government propaganda office orchestrated phony alien abductions as a means of psychological warfare. Something so sensitive even those involved all-the-way-up to the President were kept in the dark. This is based on true events after WWII in the Eisenhower years. Even former C.I.A. director George H.W. Bush is said to have had seriously considered the possibility of aliens. Something perhaps like *Invasion of the Body Snatchers* (1956) directed by Walter Wanger. It is most likely a myth either manufactured or otherwise in anticipation of high-level type surveillance technologies that were then in development. *See* Mark Monmonier, *Spying with Maps: Surveillance Technologies and the Future of Privacy* (Chicago: The University of Chicago Press, 2002), esp. the KH satellite program or Big Bird. Developments in KH (Keyhole) satellite technology have been kept secret by a delay of about 10 years. The program has progressed from KH-1,2,3, et cetera, to KH-12 and beyond. The conspiracy about aliens has a distinctively British tinge to it. *See* the MI6 website at www.sis.gov.uk for information on the British secret service. The potential abuses of sci-fi type technologies by government agencies (with little public oversight) is startling and outright bizarre. *See* Jonathan D. Moreno, Ph.D., *Mind Wars: Brain Research and National Defense* (New York: Dana Press, 1982)—things the public cannot and supposedly

ed for the duration in order to account for this reordering of ends in war.

Inevitably this is the price that must be paid if there is to be a balance between morality and political realism. Justice can no longer be the sole aim of war. There are few disinterested parties in a global world and, when there are, they seldom have the power to enforce judgment. International bodies are just as susceptible to political pressure as the rest (even more so) and should not be left with the final and absolute say.

Even Cardinal Ratzinger has noted that, "there is no single rational or ethical or religious 'world formula' that could win acceptance by everyone and could then provide support for the whole."[59] This statement is made *despite* the present-day Vatican's desire for unprecedented control in the hands of coalitions like the United Nations. Still, international bodies or unions are *not* necessarily value-neutral or scientifically-objective parties any more so than the individual nations or persons who comprise them. And, as has been demonstrated in the case of World War I, there is usually no simple dichotomy between "aggressor" and "victim." The aggressor is not always the one who fires the first shot and coercion can take other forms than explicit violence.

Arguing to include a "presumption against violence" is and should be central to the aims of modern just war theory. The logic of this presumption is an indirect argument for neutrality (armed or otherwise). If maintaining peace is more important than resorting, in the name of justice, to *unprovoked* violence, then it stands to reason that remaining neutral in another nation's conflict is the best moral course of action. Wars should only be fought to repel coercion from the outside or, in extreme cases, from inside the political structure.

In the traditional formulation there are only three just causes to go to war. **1)** The first is to gain vindication for an offense, **2)** retake something unjustly taken and **3)** to repel injury. Only the

---

does not need to know in development by DARPA. CIA propagandists have notoriously bribed press, fixed elections, and operated "outside of the law." *See* Tim Weiner, *Legacy of Ashes: The History of the CIA* (New York: Anchor Books, 2007).

[59] Joseph Cardinal Ratzinger, "2. What Keeps the World Together: The Prepolitical Moral Foundations of a Free State," in Joseph Cardinal Ratzinger, *Values in a Time of Upheaval*, trans. Brian McNeil (New York: The Crossroad Publishing Company, 2006), 31-44.

latter one **(3)** can be said to have validity anymore. To this end, in recent statements from the Vatican the first two reasons are rejected in authoritative statements, leaving only self-defense.[60] However, a statement can only eliminate the first two rationales of war on paper. They are not so easily expelled in reality. The third cause allows for defense against overt "acts of aggression" in the sense of violent acts, but the first two causes are typically what lead to an overt violent act in the first place.

Once blood has been shed, diplomacy becomes stifled. It remains a possibility that, at certain times, it may be necessary to curb the danger before it reaches the point of violence. *But*, violence breeds violence and the use of force is too deeply woven into the fabric of society to eliminate it altogether. Thus we are back at the same conundrum of when to go to war and how to prevent it. Order, let alone justice and liberty, are sometimes difficult to maintain, even with the best intentions. A "presumption against violence" is a welcome addition to the Just War Doctrine. There remain no easy black and white answers.

9. *The Conservation of Civilization*
and the Destruction of War in the Present:
The Pope's Regensburg Lecture on September 12, 2006

The "bottom-line" perhaps, as to hammering-out the Just War ethic, is that it is impossible to create an objective ideology of warfare that fits all circumstances or every historical epoch (Christian, Catholic or otherwise). In the end, justice is reliant on the virtue of leaders, the vigilance of citizens and the moral fabric of civilization. Religion has traditionally been the steward of these ultimate checks against violence. The Just War Doctrine itself cannot be uprooted from the church and tradition from which it came, that is, without *loosing* that critical element of the popular support necessary to implement it. Randolph Bourne, a progressive writer during the First World War, was made famous for his refrain "war

---

[60] *See* James Turner Johnson, *Just War Tradition and the Restraint of War: A Moral and Historical Inquiry* (Princeton, NJ: Princeton University Press, 1981).

is the health of the state."[61] He was somewhat mistaken by the word "health" though. Religion is the real *health* or good of the state, and of society, if that religion is integral, moral and rooted firmly in its customary traditions.

And so, even our wars today, the world over, are often mere cover for ancient conflicts underlying oft-denied, but irrevocable religious bulwarks. As Cardinal Manning once said, "All human differences are ultimately religious ones."

An important present case in point of this is the religious significance of the calendar date of 9/11 to America's interventions in the Middle East—that is, to the history of the West's relation to the war with Mohammadanism. Rarely if ever is it publicized that this date of attack had had great importance in history long *before* the present day; a significance that in fact bears directly on the essential religious meaning of the conflict (much to the dismay of secular ideologues—one can imagine).[62]

No less of an authority than Arnold Toynbee, decades before the terrorist attacks on 9/11, took as well-established truth the significance of (the other) September 11th in 17th century Austria. Toynbee explains in certain terms (in his magisterial *A Study of History*) that the unification brought about by the Austrian Empire with Hungary, after the *Battle of Mohacz*, is, by general impartial agreement (in the 1940s) *the most* significant event in all of Europe's conflict against the Middle Eastern invasion since the Crusades or after.

Toynbee then shows that (along with Mohacz) the turning-point of "hugest" significance (in all of World-History) is *The Battle of Vienna*. Now, there seems to be nothing spectacular about this in itself. However, what is rarely commented on is that the famous *Battle of Vienna* (as a matter of great historical importance) had accomplished the absolute defeat of all Moslem aggression in Europe—for more than 300 years afterwards—in a victory led by the King of Poland (John III Sobieski) on September 11th (1683). During the reign of Louis XIV, King of France, and Emperor Leopold I, the Grand Vezir Kara Mustafa of the Sultan Mehmed IV led more than 100,000 Turks in a siege against Vienna in a battle com-

---

[61] Randolph Bourne, "The State," in *We Who Dared To Say No To War: American Antiwar Writing From 1812 To Now*, 135.

[62] *See* John Denson, ed., *The Costs of War: America's Pyrrhic Victories.*

parable to such world-turning events as the Spanish Armada or Napoleon's defeat at Waterloo.[63]

To put this in perspective, it has been a long-recognized fact of history (but little known nowadays) that Islam suffered its final death-blow in the Western World on September 11th—that is, until now. So, what this means is that war with the Islamic states has incontrovertibly re-established itself in the modern era . . . on the very same date that it had ended more than three centuries ago!

For every historian worth his or her salt, the decisive *Battle of Vienna* was (and is) nearly universally understood to have issued the decisive blow to Islam as concerns conflicts going all the way back to the Crusades. Exempla gratia: Bishop Fulton J. Sheen here with the traditional retelling of it:

> The Christian European West barely escaped destruction at the hands of the Moslems. At one point they were stopped near Tours, and at another point, later on in time, outside the gates of Vienna. The Church throughout northern Africa was practically destroyed by Moslem power, and at the present hour the Moslems are beginning to rise again.[64]

So, again, what this means is that *The Battle of Vienna* has been accepted by historians, for hundreds of years, as having marked the end of the "Crusades"—broadly construed—and provided a final lasting victory over Islam. *The Battle of Vienna* was (and is) universally recognized as the major juncture where the Mohammadans centuries-old offensive against Europe and the West—starting with Charles Martel's victory at Tours—ceased, *for good*, until the present day.

To be sure, a good historian can easily enough show that (despite media propaganda to the contrary) present day wars in the Middle East cannot disentangle the religious aspects of the conflict by means of secular ideologies alone.[65] Trying to ignore or down-

---

[63] Warren Carroll, The Revolution Against Christendom, 12.

[64] Fulton J. Sheen, "Mary and the Moslems," in Jacques Jomier, O.P, *The Bible and the Qur'an*, trans. Edward P. Arbez (San Francisco: Ignatius Press, 1959), Appendix Five, 121.

[65] *See* Jason Stanley, *How Propaganda Works* (Princeton, NJ: Princeton University Press, 2015).

play the religious dimension of present wars is just another pervasive attempt to rewrite history (as in World War I).

So, in the (now long forgotten) history, the Austrian Empire stood firm for hundreds of years in heroic victory against her enemies in the East only *after* Mohacs, The Battle of Vienna, and to a lesser extent Lepanto (1571). Toynbee, a rather dry historian not prone to overstatement, puts the importance in no small terms. He states here in unequivocal language, as matter of fact, that:

> Indeed, from the moment of the Danubian Hapsburg Monarchy's foundation its fortunes followed those of the hostile Power whose pressure had called it into existence. The heroic age of the Danubian Monarchy coincided chronologically with the period during which the Ottoman pressure was felt by the Western World most severely.

> This heroic age may be taken as beginning with the first abortive Ottoman siege of Vienna in 1529 and the *ending with the second* [September 11-12] in 1683.

> In these supreme ordeals the Austrian capital played the same role in the desperate resistance of the Western World to the Ottoman assault *as Verdun played in the French resistance to the German assault in the war of 1914-18*. Both sieges of Vienna were turning-points in Ottoman military history. The failure of the first brought to a standstill the tide of Ottoman conquest which had been flooding up the Danube Valley for a century past—and the map shows, what many will find hard to believe without verification, that Vienna is more than half-way from Constantinople to the Straits of Dover.

> The failure of the second siege [9/11/1683] was followed by an ebb *which continued thereafter*, in spite of all pauses and fluctuations, until the Turkish frontier had been pushed back from the Southeastern outskirts of Vienna, where it had stood

from 1529 to 1683, to the Northwestern outskirts
of Adrianople.[66]

To see this in perspective, it was estimated at the time—during these final years of the establishment of the modern Austrian Empire—that more than 500,000 "Austrians" were killed by Ottomans in less than a ten year period.[67] This is a huge percentage of people, especially given the population numbers of that region during the last decades of the 17th Century. *Vienna* was the decisive battle that permanently ended the blood-letting after hundreds of years of Ottoman invasions. "Without much exaggeration, the war of 1683-1699 against the Sultan can be called the last of the crusades."[68]

We often forget that these modern wars being fought now (since the very beginnings of modern Total War in the 20th century) can in fact be traced *deep* into the fading recesses of history's annals. Perhaps it could be mere coincidence of timing or an intentional directive by the terrorists who carried out the attacks on New York in 2001; that is, in reference to this date in World-History. However, that few know this parallel is bizarre and unsettling.[69]

The Ottoman siege of Vienna on September 11-12, 1683, "evoked a Western counter-attack which continued, *with no serious check, from 1683 to 1922*, by which date the 'Osmanlis had been bereft of the whole of their empire and confined once more to their Anatolian homelands."[70] For any but the trained historian, uncovering this history is not easy to see (just as in the case of the sinking of the *Lusitania*).

However, it *is* easy to see why this would be suppressed if more commonly known. In fact, it *has been* more widely known by nearly every Middle Eastern historian since the 1600s. So one suspects that what is of greater importance here, than the historical

---

[66] Arnold J. Toynbee, *A Study of History* (Oxford, UK: Oxford University Press, 1946), 119. [emphasis added]

[67] John Stoyle, *The Siege of Vienna* (London: Collins, 1964).

[68] Ibid., 284.

[69] There have of course been stranger coincidences that perhaps have no alignment other than sheer coincidence; such as John Adams and Thomas Jefferson both dying on July 4th. A treatment of this phenomenon in is George William Rutler, *Coincidently* (New York: The Crossroad Publishing Company, 2006).

[70] Arnold Toynbee, *A Study of History*, 536-537. [emphasis added]

reality of religious war, is the cover of political self-interest and/or the propagandistic commandeering of present day wars to suit ideological purposes.[71] Toynbee further explains in *A Study of History*:

> The *only* semblance of an effective external challenge to our society since the 'Osmanlis' second failure to take Vienna [9/11/1683] has been the challenge of *Bolshevism* which has confronted the Western World since Lenin and his associates made themselves masters of the Russian Empire in A.D. 1917.[72]

So, the only external military threat comparable for more than 300 years after *Vienna* is Communism! Now this would raise an eye if televised on 5 o'clock news chatter for a year of National news cycles. Yet, the only place where this history has even been alluded to in a public medium outside of dusty-history-textbooks is in Pope Benedict XVI's (Joseph Ratzinger) September 12th, 2006 Regensburg Lecture—at the University of Regensburg where he once had served as professor.[73] And, of course Ratzinger was immediately castigated and censured by World Press authorities for beginning to address, with the power of his office, (even in remote or indirect terms) the deeper religious dimensions of wars issuing against Islamic terror. Heaven forbid the opportunity for internationalist ideologues—who control the majority of world-media outlets—to exploit the conflict for secular political agendas be lost because of it.

Nonetheless, modern theorists of war *cannot* dishonestly continue to hide the vexing complexities that arise throughout history without significant consequences, one way or another. Ignorance of history because of "chronological" arrogance by the present political powers is sheer barbarism plain and simple. Even the radical-left who desire to eradicate history completely as precedent for anything but denunciation of racism, sexism, or economic exploitation, cannot theorize absolutely in their pretention that history

---

[71] *See* Henry A. Lee, *Why They Hate Us: September 11, 2001: And justice for none* (Scarborough Sta., NY: Pastime Publications, 2002).

[72] Arnold Toynbee, *A Study of History*, 203. [emphasis added]

[73] *See* Tracy Rowland, *Ratzinger's Faith: The Theology of Pope Benedict XVI* (Oxford, UK: Oxford University Press, 2008).

no longer "exists."[74] Purported causes of current events are more than usually the mere echoes of things long forgotten.[75] That the date of the defeat of Islamic aggression is traceable to September 11th and that no more serious threats plagued Western civilization until the start of the Cold War *is important*, albeit what "use" this would be to the hopelessly propagandized mass machinery of public opinion is another story.

To be sure, there *are* reasons, of course, to not make too much of this, e.g., aside from its questionable importance to present objectives and/or any intentional dishonesty about the history involved. Political sensitives today run high and history is inherently "politically incorrect" to tell straight out via the channels of mainstream-media propaganda. And, like understanding foreign languages, fragments of history are incomprehensible to the public unless fluency with the greater contexts is prevalent in the majority's popular imagination already.

Moreover, as to *why* this would be an unpopular "spin" added to the reporting of world events, Georgetown Professor Fr. James Schall provides the un-PC take on Pope Benedict XVI's controversial Regensburg Lecture. He writes as to the "dumbed-down" religious dimensions of September 11:

> The argument goes: All religions are "peaceful." Islam is a religion. Therefore, Islam is peaceful. This is not a historical syllogism that explains the actual record of the expansion of Islam from its beginning in Arabia till its reaching Tours in the eighth century and Vienna (on September 11th,) 1683. Nor does it explain the violence and law used within Muslim states to prevent any expression of faith or philosophy that does not conform to their own understanding of the Koran. This earlier expansion was almost exclusively by military conquest, often extremely brutal, against Christian, Persian, Hindoo, or other lands.[76]

---

[74] Noam Chomsky, *Media Control: The Spectacular Achievements of Propaganda*.
[75] Hilaire Belloc, *The Great Heresies* (New York: Sheed & Ward, 1938), 123.
[76] James Schall, *The Regensburg Lecture* (South Bend, IN: St. Augustine's Press, 2007), 152. The lectures were delivered Sept 9-14, 2006. The controversial statements were made on the 12th.

And so, who today can tolerate obscure military history lectures outside of the specialist engineers of the war itself? It is better to say "they" hate us and attack us because we are the "good guys." Who has patience for anything else in the daily barrage of sports statistics, celebrity gossip, and cosmetics commercials?

Still, the facts are *all* relevant. *But* it takes a historian's eye to see the relevance. That is the problem. That is why the "big-lies" go unchallenged. And so, the lies and historical revisionism of World War I continue to be present in the here and now.[77] Nonetheless, the lesson should be learned. After the history of *this* time comes out in the future, and once the propaganda of the present has dissipated in the public memory, the story of wars instigated by 9/11 will appear much the same as the distortions told about the *Lusitania* or American involvement in the First World War—or Pearl Harbor or the Tet Offensive for that matter.

In the end, Catholic Moral Theology and Just War Principles will *not* provide a final definitive answer to the vexing question of war. But these principles (incarnate in religion and cultures) *can be* a powerful force for peace in the hands of the right people at the right time. They (the Just War principles) are more perennial than the passing tide of current events or the self-interested parties who control how events are perceived.

Once again, here Fr. Schall quotes Friedrich Nietzsche in the epigraph to his book on The Regensburg Lecture in that: "The greatest events and thoughts—but the greatest thoughts are the greatest events—are comprehended last: the generations which are

---

[77] Paul Fussell, *The Great War and Modern Memory* (New York and London: Oxford University Press, 1975). Fussell relates with great insight the literary and artistic means by which World War I has been portrayed. It is always a distortion to show history as an ideal-type in an artistic medium, but often with war it becomes intentionally dishonest—how we are made to remember it. Some of the more interesting renderings include the award-winning classic film based on the novel, *All Quiet on the Western Front* (1930). And, in literature, Thomas Pynchon's over-the-top novel *Gravity's Rainbow*, which goes into lurid description of WWII's "White Visitation" (based loosely on activities of the SOE—Special Operations Executive). *See*, Thomas Pynchon, *Gravity's Rainbow* (New York: Penguin Books, 2006).

their contemporaries do not experience such events—they live past them."[78]

They live past them. Often the least comprehensible history is the history of the times in which you live. Nietzsche famously decried that we are not knowers of ourselves. In fact, we know ourselves least of all.

> We knowers are unknown to ourselves, and for a good reason: how can we ever hope to find what we have never looked for? There is a sound adage which runs: 'Where a man's treasure lies, there lies his heart.' Our treasure lies in the beehives of our knowledge. We are perpetually on our way thither, being by nature winged insects and honey gatherers of the mind. The only thing that lies close to our heart is the desire to bring something home to the hive.
>
> The sad truth is that we remain necessarily strangers to ourselves, we don't understand our own substance, we *must* mistake ourselves; the axiom, 'Each man is furthest from himself,' will hold for us to all eternity. Of ourselves we are not 'knowers' . . . .[79]

And we can't know what is of crucial importance in the here and now because it won't be widely seen or understood until long after those in the present are gone.

The Just War Doctrine is not anachronistic as some would have it. However, the decisive idea (or key) needed to absolutize it is still missing and perhaps always will be. History is complex. The complexity of world events is always difficult to truly see, and especially while a "hot" war is what is at stake. Or, in the more jocular words of Buchanan's polemic, "We love the old republic,

---

[78] Friedrich Nietzsche, *Beyond Good and Evil: Prelude to a Philosophy of the Future* (Mineola, NY: Dover Publications, 1997), 142, as quoted in James V. Schall, *The Regensburg Lecture*, i.

[79] Friedrich Nietzsche, "The Genealogy of Morals," in Friedrich Nietzsche, *The Birth of Tragedy and The Genealogy of Morals*, trans. Francis Golffing (Garden City, NY: Doubleday Anchor Books, 1956), 149.

and when we hear phrases like 'New World Order,' we release the safety catches on our revolvers."[80]

10. *The Antiwar Movement in America during WWI*

To return to the topic of a CONSERVATIVE's constitution, the most atrocious conflicts of the twentieth century were all perpetrated by leaders of a leftist bent. [81] Hitler, Stalin and Mao, racked up death tolls equal to that of all previous centuries combined. Even the moderate leftist idealists of the West dissolved their dreams in a river of blood during two world wars that disintegrated civilization like an acid bath. Taking aim at this myth of modern ideological warfare, we note here Kirk's reaction to Mr George Herbert Walker Bush's betrayal of "conservative ideals" in Kuwait:

> A war for Kuwait? A war for an oil-can! The rest is vanity; the rest is crime. A Republican administration in Washington contrived entry into the Spanish-American War. Since then, until 1991, it was Democratic governments of the United States that propelled the United States to war, if sometimes through the back door: the First World War, the second World War, the Korean War, the Indo-Chinese wars. But an unimaginative, "democratic capitalist" Republican regime, early in 1991, committed the United States, very possibly, to a new imperialism. For Mr. Bush's "New World Order" may make the United States detested—beginning with the Arab peoples—more than even the Soviet empire was. Mr. Bush's people hinted at their intention of station-

---

[80] As quoted in Justin Raimondo, *Reclaiming the American Right: The Lost Legacy of the Conservative Movement* (Wilmington, DE: ISI Books, 2008), 263.
[81] Justin Raimondo, *Reclaiming the American Right: The Lost Legacy of the Conservative Movement*. Here is provided the in-part censored history of the American Right's traditional anti-warism. Raimondo shows that it is the Leftists in America, driven by zealous foreign policy ideologies, who have promoted endless wars of intervention.

ing an American army "presence" permanently on the Persian Gulf, to insure the steady flow of petroleum to the consumers of the United States. Increasingly, the states of Europe and the Levant may suspect that in rejecting Russian domination, they exchanged King Log for King Stork. President Bush's assembling of half a million men in the deserts of Arabia, and then bullying and enticing Congress into authorizing him to make war, sufficiently suggests that *conservative views are not identical with the measures of the Republican party*. We learn from the saturation-bombing in Iraq that genuine conservatives—as distinguished from arrogant nationalists—have a hard row to hoe when they endeavor to teach the American democracy prudence in foreign relations;[82]

It remains for those who still revere The Permanent Things of civilization to defend what is actually worth defending. Arrogant Nationalists seeking only almighty political-power can be greater enemies to civilization than the worst of petty tyrants. It is for those who succumb to the temptation of an "armed ideology" to impose perdition on the fragile accomplishment of ordered liberty. Peace is not simply a justification to maintain the status quo, nor is war simply politics "by other means."[83]

Both doctrinaire pacifism and amoral militarism are inadequate solutions to the problem of war.[84] There are real moral absolutes, derived from the Biblical text and the Natural Law, which must be combined with the prudent judgment of cautious and noble statesmen who revere such things in the first place. A final and grave decision to take a people to war is never a simple moral equation. But peace is the prerogative, as Christ taught us. In the life of Christ is the certain detachment from the ways of the world and the spirit of "leadership" through example and sacrifice, not

---

[82] Russell Kirk, "Toward a Prudent Foreign Policy," in *The Politics of Prudence*, 221-222.

[83] Carl von Clausewitz, *On War*, ed. and trans. Michael Howard and Peter Paret (Princeton, NJ: Princeton University Press, 1976). "Politics by other means" is a phrase "coined" by von Clausewitz.

[84] *See* Brian V. Johnstone, "Pope John Paul II and the War in Iraq," *Studia Moralia* 41 (2003) 309-330.

political force or desire for gain [libido dominandi].[85] It is only the neutral party (armed-neutrality or otherwise) in a conflict which can embody both these ideals.

Turn of the century man of letters Gilbert Keith Chesterton once wrote that "the supreme psychological fact about patriotism is that the patriot never under any circumstances boasts of the largeness of his country, but always, and of necessity, boasts of the smallness of it."[86] In this vein, Kuenhelt-Leddihn goes on to say that:

> in respect to World War I, the issue was national-
> ism rather than patriotism. Patriotism is never ag-
> gressive vis-à-vis other nations, but nationalism,
> which was reborn in the French Revolution, curi-
> ously enough 'knows no borders.' It incites na-
> tions to force other nations to adopt their pattern
> of political 'happiness.'[87]

It comes as no surprise then that in America during WWI, "the opposition to the war came mostly from farmers, old-school classical liberals, pacifists, Main Street Republican isolationists, and socialists."[88] Support for the war, on the other hand, was manufactured in New York and Washington, DC. Characters as disparate as perennial socialist presidential candidate Eugene Debs to titans of industry Henry Ford and Andrew Carnegie were all united in their loathing of the War.[89] Ironically, Eugene Debs was impris-oned by Wilson under the unconstitutional *Espionage and Sedition Acts* for speaking out against the War. But he still received one million votes for president with the campaign slogan "For Presi-dent: Convict No. 9653."[90] Strange behavior for a country that was

---

[85] *See* John H. Yoder, *The Politics of Jesus: Vicit Agnus Noster* (Grand Rapids, MI: William B. Eerdman's Publishing, 1972).

[86] G. K. Chesterton, *The Napoleon of Notting Hill* (London: Jane Lane, 1928 [1904]), 134.

[87] Erik von Kuehnelt-Leddihn, *Leftism Revisited: From de Sade and Marx to Hitler and Pol Pot*, 208.

[88] Bill Kauffman, *Ain't My America: The Long, Noble History of Antiwar Con-servatism and Middle-American Anti-Imperialism*, 68.

[89] *See* Eugene Debs, *Debs: His Life, Writing and Speeches*, ed. Bruce Rogers (Girard, Kansas: The Appeal to Reason, 1908).

[90] Ibid.

warring for liberty abroad. Ford, who knew better than most, went on record saying that:

> for months the people of the United States have had fear pounded into their brains by magazines, newspapers and motion pictures. No enemy has been pointed out. All the wild cry for the spending of billions, the piling up of armament and the saddling of the country with a military caste has been based on nothing but fiction.[91]

Of all the newspapers, only mogul William Randolph Hearst was against the War. The rest of the press easily succumbed to jingoism. Congress likewise folded under the pressure. The heart of America, however, still beat for peace and the antiwar movement would remain strong throughout both wars. The "hard left" controlled the dominant sentiment in the first war and the "Old Right" in the second with the country's most influential antiwar movement to date; America First.[92]

> The AFC [America First Committee] was founded in September 1940 at Yale Law School, of all places, by a set of men who went on to great establishment success. They included Potter Stewart (Supreme Court justice), Sargent Striver (George McGovern's running mate in 1972), Gerald Ford (!), Kingman Brewster Jr. (Yale president), and the aforementioned Bob Stuart (Quaker Oats CEO and Reagan's ambassador to Norway). Ford, amusingly, was the first to drop off the executive committee: he was afraid that being involved with an antiwar group might cost him his job as assistant football coach. Courage sharpens its profile!

[91] Walter Millis, *Road to War: America, 1914-1917* (Boston: Houghton Mifflin, 1935), 303, as quoted in Bill Kauffman, *Ain't My America: The Long, Noble History of Antiwar Conservatism and Middle-American Anti-Imperialism*, 68.

[92] Bill Kauffman, *America First: Its History, Culture, and Politics* (Amherst, New York: Prometheus Books, 1995).

The America First Committee was the largest (eight hundred thousand members) antiwar organization in U.S. history. Its members ranged from Iowa Republicans to Wyoming socialists. John F. Kennedy was a donor, as was his reptilian father.[93]

People lined up on different sides of the fence for a variety of reasons and more than a few were inspired by their religious beliefs. Others were driven by ethnic or national loyalties. None agreed on everything, but the cause of peace sometimes makes for unusual bedfellows. The Pope was staunchly and courageously neutral, although the Roman Catholic Church in America slanted toward war. A powerful presence, there should have been a powerful mobilization of Catholics under Benedict's banner, but the American Church at that time was not in a position to challenge the government outright.[94] Nevertheless, Benedict XV stands out as a lone sane voice in this age of mass-insanity.

11. *Conclusion:*
William Jennings Bryan, Pope Benedict XV, Neutrality and Peace

The moral case for neutrality in World War I is best embodied by Benedict XV, who was *the only* neutral party asking and praying for peace from the outset. The key role of a neutral party, and the most important role in war, is that of *peacemaker*. Benedict stood firm for peace and never wavered from this stance. He also never violated his neutrality. Nevertheless, warding off despair with prayerful petitions, Benedict was incapable of putting an end to the conflict. In the beginning, when Wilson spoke of peace, there was a diplomatic effort by these two neutral parties to negotiate for "peace without victory." However, in 1917 Wilson brusquely dismissed the Pope.[95] Likewise, Emperor Charles genu-

---

[93] Ibid., 80-81.

[94] *See* John F. Piper, Jr., *The American Churches in World War I* (Athens, Ohio: Ohio University Press, 1985).

[95] *See* the Papal encyclical of Benedict XV *Ad Beatissimi*, issued November 1, 1914. And, Walter H. Peters, *The Life of Benedict XV* (Milwaukee: The

inely sought peace and was rejected. A deeply religious man, Charles sought peace not only because of a "military condition," but above all "as his solemn duty, before God, towards the people of the Empire and all the belligerents."[96] Austria-Hungary would suffer the most in the aftermath.

In America it was William Jennings Bryan who stood out most courageously for the cause of peace. This was not splendid isolation in the old-line sense. [97]He had in fact made friends with the great pacifist Tolstoy in Russia. Empowered as the Secretary of State, he could not countenance the dishonesty to the public by Wilson and his administration about its ends in the war. History is uncontestable that Wilson had been planning to enter the war privately with his shadowy partner Edward Mandell House long before the fact was made public.[98] He and House had been maneuvering to do so *before* and at the time of the *Lusitania's* attack. This of course became the opportune moment to provide the reason needed. Bryan immediately, sensing what could transpire, recommended the normal conservative protocol of international relations after the sinking, but he soon realized that Wilson had other ideas.

Bryan and Wilson did in fact show each other the utmost cordiality once having decided to go separate ways politically. However, Bryan was decidedly tight-lipped for the sake of the party he served, while in private he had felt betrayed by Wilson and House. Wilson had had House keep much of their foreign activities secret from Bryan, even while Bryan was occupying the higher

---

Bruce Publishing Company, 1959), Chapter XI: "*The First Encyclical*, Ad Beatissimi," 102-110.

[96] Warren H. Carroll, *1917: Red Banners, White Mantle* (Front Royal, VA: Christendom Press, 1981), 42.

[97] An important part of the agenda of Cultural Marxism is uninhibited open borders to immigrants. There is no faster means to undermine the institutions necessary for non-State intermediary bodies of culture. Of course, this leads directly to more dependence on the Nation-State for all social welfare, which then issues in a vicious circle that can, hopefully for the Marxists, enable a Communist *coup d'etat*. *See* Antonio Gramsci, *Selections from the Prison Notebooks of Antonio Gramsci*, eds. and trans. Quintin Hoare and Geoffrey Nowell Smith (New York: International Publishers, 1971).

[98] *See* George Sylvester Viereck, *The Strangest Friendship in History: Woodrow Wilson and Colonel House* (New York: Liveright Inc Publishers, 1932).

office and had the right to be made aware of the negotiations House was carrying-on abroad.

So, Bryan resigned in dignity with the moral high ground. Bryan's was the more noble argument in retrospect too—that is, *despite* being the lost and forgotten side of the case now . . . because of dominant boosters of the victory (after the fact). In his first address to the press after resigning, Bryan spells-out clearly what he sees as the lack of adequate justifications for entering Europe's war:

> Two of the points on which we differ, each con-
> scientious in conviction, are:
>
> First, as to the suggestion of investigation by an
> international commission, and,
> Second, as to warning Americans against traveling
> on belligerent vessels or with cargoes of ammuni-
> tion.
>
> I believe that this nation should frankly state to
> Germany that we are willing to apply in this case
> the principle which we are bound by treaty to ap-
> ply to disputes between the United States and
> thirty countries with which we have made treaties
> providing for investigation of all disputes of every
> character and nature.
>
> These treaties, negotiated under this administra-
> tion, make war practically impossible between this
> country and these thirty governments, represent-
> ing nearly three-fourths of all the people of the
> world.
>
> Among the nations with which we have these
> treaties are Great Britain, France, and Russia. No
> matter what disputes may arise between us and
> these treaty nations, we agree that there shall be
> no declaration of war and no commencement of
> hostilities until the matters in dispute have been
> investigated by an international commission and a
> year's time is allowed for investigation and report.
> This plan was offered to all the nations without

any exception whatever, and Germany was one of the nations that accepted the principle, being the twelfth, I think, to accept. No treaty was actually entered into with Germany, but I cannot see that that should stand in the way when both nations endorsed the principle. I do not know whether Germany would accept the offer, but our country should, in my judgment, make the offer.

Such an offer, if accepted, would at once relieve the tension and silence all the jingoes who are demanding war. Germany has always been a friendly nation, and a great many of our people are of German ancestry. Why should we not deal with Germany according to this plan to which the nation has pledged its support?

The second point of difference is as to the course which should be pursued in regard to Americans traveling on belligerent ships or with cargoes of ammunition.

Why should an American citizen be permitted to involve his country in war by traveling upon a belligerent ship when he knows that the ship will pass through a danger zone? The question is not whether an American citizen has a right under international law to travel on a belligerent ship; the question is whether he ought not, out of consideration for his country, if not for his own safety, avoid danger when avoidance is possible.

It is a very one-sided citizenship that compels a government to go to war over a citizen's rights, and yet relieves the citizen of all obligations to consider his nation's welfare . . .

I think, too, that American passenger ships should be prohibited from carrying ammunition. The lives of passengers ought not to be endangered by cargoes of ammunition, whether that danger comes from possible explosions within or from possible attacks from without. Passengers and ammunition should not travel together. The attempt to prevent American citizens from incurring these risks is entirely consistent with the effort which our Government is making to prevent attacks from submarines.

The use of one remedy does not exclude the use of the other. The most familiar illustration is to be found in the action taken by municipal authorities during a riot. It is the duty of the mayor to suppress the mob and to prevent violence, but he does not hesitate to warn citizens to keep off the streets, but, for their own protection and in the interest of order, he warns them not to incur the risks involved in going upon the streets when men are shooting at each other.

The President does not feel justified in taking the action above suggested. That is, he does not feel justified, first, in suggesting the submission of the controversy to investigation, or, second, in warning the people not to incur the extra hazards in traveling on belligerent ships or on ships carrying ammunition.[99]

There is no doubt that Bryan is holding a stronger case in many respects; a moral case that cannot be dismissed, but was. Americans were not enthusiastic about the war. The sinking of the *Lusitania* was *not* an attack on the United States. There were numerous international agreements that America would not violate her neutrality without due process of investigation first. This included Germany, Britain, and nearly every other country involved. Our entry into the war was *unprovoked* and history attests that it was Wilson's agenda to get us involved already before it happened. The actual reasons were less noble than the official ones. The push to war had more to do with financial interests or vain ideological

---

[99] William Jennings Bryan and Mary Baird Bryan, *The Memoirs of William Jennings Bryan*, 410-412.

dreams of worldwide democracy, than justice or defense. Bryan was a principled politician who listened to his own conscience and sometimes marched to his own drummer, but he was insufferably popular no less. His resignation letter to Wilson is this:

My Dear Mr. President,

It is with sincere regret that I have reached the conclusion that I should return to you the commission of Secretary of State with which you honored me at the beginning of your administration.

Obedient to your sense of duty and actuated by the highest motives, you have prepared for transmission to the German Government a note in which I cannot join without violating what I deem to be an obligation to my country, and the issue involved is of such moment that to remain a member of the Cabinet would be as unfair to you as it would be to the cause which is nearest my heart, namely, the prevention of war.

I, therefore, respectfully tender my resignation, to take effect when the note is sent, unless you prefer an earlier hour. Alike desirous of reaching a peaceful solution of the problems arising out of the use of the submarines against merchantmen, we find ourselves differing irreconcilably as to the methods which should be employed.

It falls to your lot to speak officially for the nation; I consider it to be none the less my duty to endeavor as a private citizen to promote the end which you have in view by means which you do not feel at liberty to use.

In severing the intimate and pleasant relations which have existed between us during the past two years, permit me to acknowledge the profound satisfaction which it has given me to be as-

sociated with you in the important work which
has come before the State Department, and to
thank you for the courtesies extended.

With the heartiest good wishes for your personal
welfare and for the success of your administration,
I am, my dear Mr. President,

Very truly yours,

W. J. Bryan[100]

Wilson could not know at first what this would do to his administration's support, political ambitions, or other such things.
One can imagine he was surprised, but glad to have an opportunity
to appoint a war-time Secretary who did not share Bryan's scruples.
Bryan and Wilson were said to have gotten along moderately well,
but Bryan was very much a political appointee, being used from
the start to gain his political constituency for Wilson. He was never
a part of Wilson's inner circle of lofty academics and intellectuals.
A lawyer from Lincoln, Nebraska, Bryan was worlds apart from
the millionaire capitalists of the East Coast establishment.[101]

Bryan does in fact note in his memoirs that being excluded
from the party's inner circle of decision-making is one of the major
reasons he stepped-down. House and Wilson were too deceptive
in their activities and Bryan was a God-fearing man.[102] Wilson accepted the resignation cordially.[103] Again, the former governor of

---

[100] Ibid., 406-407.

[101] Many of the budding elites of Yale, Harvard, Princeton—the scions of
industrialist families—were gung-ho for the war as an opportunity for
military adventurism. Future political leaders often want, need, or desire
the opportunity of war to establish a military "right" for their aspiring
political authority. Men like old-time Yalies Rob Lovett and Kenney
MacLeish in WWI. *See* Marc Wortman, *The Millionaire's Unit: The Aristocratic Flyboys Who Fought The Great War And Invented American Air Power*
(New York: PublicAffairs, 2006).

[102] Stephen Vincent Benét. *The Devil and Daniel Webster* (New York: Farrar
& Rinehart, 1937). Classic American folk tale about a political deal with
the devil.

[103] For a more favorable portrait of Wilson *see* Louis Auchincloss, *Woodrow Wilson: A Penguin Life* (New York: Penguin Group, 2000).

New Jersey and president of Princeton would not see reason and he was unapologetically undeterred in his crusade.

Washington, June 8, 1915.

RESIGNATION ACCEPTED

My Dear Mr. Bryan,

I accept your resignation only because you insist upon its acceptance; and I accept it with much more than deep regret, with a feeling of personal sorrow. Our two years of close association have been very delightful to me. Our judgments have accorded in practically every matter of official duty and of public policy until now; your support of the work and purposes of the administration has been generous and loyal beyond praise; your devotion to the duties of our great office and your eagerness to take advantage of every opportunity for service it offered has been an example to the rest of us; you have earned our affectionate admiration and friendship. Even now we are not separated in the object we seek but only in the method by which we seek it.

It is for these reasons my feeling about your retirement from the Secretaryship of State goes much deeper than regret. I sincerely deplore it. Our objects are the same and we ought to pursue them together. I yield to your desire only because I must and wish to bid you Godspeed in the parting. We shall continue to work for the same causes even when we do not work in the same way.

With affectionate regard, sincerely yours,

Woodrow Wilson[104]

---

[104] William Jennings Bryan and Mary Baird Bryan, *The Memoirs of William Jennings Bryan*, 407-408.

The Democratic Party let Bryan go in peace. There was no talk of calling him a traitor. But, the decision to set America on an irreversible course of international intervention had been made for good at this point. Some think for ill, others not. There can be no doubt however that Jesus Christ is for peace, against the violent or greedy, and an impartial judge of nations.

In the end, *peacemaker* and *warmaker* are contradictory postures. In war, belligerents, on all sides, easily lose their heads and harden their hearts. Conflicts escalate, blood is shed and the wounds become impossible to heal by acts of mercy. The demand for an elusive justice overtakes the desire for peace. The moral role of neutrality is, therefore, noble and just and good. Neutrality is, practicably, the only means to open the road to reconciliation short of extraction of penalty by a victor party.

Across the Atlantic in Rome, the year before Bryan issued his resignation, America having chosen sides, the Pope continued to pray for peace. On Christmas Eve, 1914, Benedict XV, refusing to take sides, passionately appealed to the nations of the world to let "the fratricidal weapons fall to the ground! Already they are too bloodstained; let them at last fall! And may the hands of those who have to wield them return to the labors of industry and commerce, to the works of civilization and peace!"[105] Words that spoke truth then. Words that still echo now. Words that can (should) echo even to today.

---

[105] Walter H. Peters, *The Life of Benedict XV*.

BIBLIOGRAPHY

Auchincloss, Louis. Woodrow Wilson: A Penguin Life. New York: Penguin Group, 2000.

Belloc, Hilaire. The Great Heresies. New York: Sheed & Ward, 1938.

Benét, Stephen Vincent. The Devil and Daniel Webster. New York: Farrar & Rinehart, 1937.

Bierce, Ambrose. The Unabridged Devil's Dictionary, eds. David S. Schultz and S. T. Joshi. Athens & London: The University of Georgia Press, 2000.

Boyle, Jr. Joseph, John Finnis, and Germain Grisez. Nuclear Deterrence, Morality and Realism. Oxford, UK: Clarendon Press, 1987.

Buckley, Christopher. Little Green Men: A Novel. New York: HarperPerennial, 1999.

Bryan, William Jennings and Mary Baird. The Memoirs of William Jennings Bryan. Chicago, Philadelphia, and Toronto: The John C. Winston Company, 1925.

Buchanan, Patrick J. Churchill, Hitler, and the Unnecessary War: How Britain Lost Its Empire and the West Lost the World. New York: Three Rivers Press, 2008.

Burke, Edmund. Reflections on the Revolution in France. New York: Penguin Books, 2004.

Cahill, Lisa Sowle. Love Your Enemies: Discipleship, Pacifism, and Just War Theory. Minneapolis: Augsburg Fortress, 1994.

Camus, Albert. The Plague. trans. Stuart Gilbert. New York: Vintage International, 1948.

Carroll, Warren H. and Anne W. Carroll. The Crisis of Christendom: A History of Christendom, Vol. 6. Front Royal, VA: Christendom Press, 2013.

Carroll, Warren H. 1917: Red Banners, White Mantle. Front Royal, VA: Christendom Press, 1981.

Carroll, Warren H. The Revolution Against Christendom: A History of Christendom, vol. 5. Front Royal, VA: Christendom Press, 2005.

Chesterton, G. K. Lepanto. San Francisco: Ignatius Press, 2003.

Chesterton, G. K. The Napoleon of Notting Hill. London: Jane Lane, 1928 [1904].

Chomsky, Noam. Media Control: The Spectacular Achievements of Propaganda CD-ROM. New York: Seven Stories Press, 2004.

Clausewitz, Carl von. On War. eds. and trans. Michael Howard and Peter Paret. Princeton, NJ: Princeton University Press, 1976.

Conrad, Joseph. Heart of Darkness: A Norton Critical Edition. ed. Paul B. Armstrong. New York: W. W. Norton & Company, 2006 [1899].

Corey, David D. and Charles, J. Daryl. The Just War Tradition: An Introduction. Wilmington, DE: ISI Books, 2012.

Debs, Eugene. Debs: His Life, Writing and Speeches. ed. Bruce Rogers. Girard, Kansas: The Appeal to Reason, 1908.

Denson, John, ed. The Costs of War: America's Pyrrhic Victories. Edison, NJ: Transaction Publishers, 1999.

Fleming, Thomas. The Illusion of Victory: America in World War I. New York: Basic Books, 2003.

Fussell, Paul. The Great War and Modern Memory. New York and London: Oxford University Press, 1975.

Gramsci, Antonio. Selections from the Prison Notebooks of Antonio Gramsci. eds. and trans. Quintin Hoare and Geoffrey Nowell Smith. New York: International Publishers, 1971.

Griffin, G. Edward. The Creature from Jekyll Island: A Second Look at the Federal Reserve. Westlake, CA: American Media, 2001.

Grotius, Hugo. The Rights of War and Peace: Including the Law of Nature and of Nations. trans. A. C. Campell, A.M. New York and London: M. Walter Dunne, Publisher, 1901.

Hammond, Bray. Banks and Politics in America: From the Revolution to the Civil War. Princeton, NJ: Princeton University Press, 1957.

Johnson, James Turner. Just War Tradition and the Restraint of War: A Moral and Historical Inquiry. Princeton, NJ: Princeton University Press, 1981.

Jomier, O.P., Jacques. The Bible and the Qur'an. trans. Edward P. Arbez. San Francisco: Ignatius Press, 1959.

Kauffman, Bill. Ain't My America: The Long, Noble History of Antiwar Conservatism and Middle-American Anti-Imperialism. New York: Metropolitan Books, 2008.

Kauffman, Bill. America First: Its History, Culture, and Politics. Amherst, NY: Prometheus Books, 1995.

Kennan, George. American Diplomacy, 1900-1950. Chicago: The University of Chicago Press, 1951.

Kipling, Rudyard. A Choice of Kipling's Verse. ed. T. S. Eliot. London: Faber and Faber, 1941.

Kirk, Russell. The Conservative Mind: From Burke to Eliot. Washington, DC: Regnery Publishing, 1985.

Kirk, Russell. The Politics of Prudence. Wilmington, DE: ISI Books, 1993.

Kirk, Russell. Redeeming the Time. ed. Jeffrey O. Nelson. Wilmington, DE: ISI Books, 1999.

Kirk, Russell. The Roots of American Order. Wilmington, DE: ISI Books, 2003.

Kuehnelt-Leddihn, Erik von. Leftism Revisited: From de Sade and Marx to Hitler and Pol Pot. Washington, DC: Regnery Gateway, 1990.

Kuehnelt-Leddihn, Erik von. The Menace of the Herd, Or Procrustes at Large. Milwaukee, MN: The Bruce Publishing Company, 1943.

Lee, Henry A. Why They Hate Us: September 11, 2001: And justice for none. Scarborough Sta., NY: Pastime Publications, 2002.

Mills, C. Wright. The Power Elite. Oxford, UK: Oxford University Press, 1956.

Monmonier, Mark. Spying with Maps: Surveillance Technologies and the Future of Privacy. Chicago: The University of Chicago Press, 2002.

Moreno, Jonathan D. Mind Wars: Brain Research and National Defense. New York: Dana Press, 1982.

Nash, George H. The Conservative Intellectual Movement in America Since 1945, Thirtieth-Anniversary Edition. Wilmington, DE: ISI Books, 2008.

Nietzsche, Friedrich. Beyond Good and Evil: Prelude to a Philosophy of the Future. Mineola, NY: Dover Publications, 1997.

Nietzsche, Friedrich. The Birth of Tragedy and The Genealogy of Morals. trans. Francis Golffing. Garden City, NY: Doubleday Anchor Books, 1956.

O'Donovan, Oliver. The Just War Revisited. Cambridge, UK: Cambridge University Press, 2003.

Peters, Walter H. The Life of Benedict XV. Milwaukee: The Bruce Publishing Company, 1959.

Piper, Jr., John F. The American Churches in World War I. Athens, Ohio: Ohio University Press, 1985.

Pynchon, Thomas. Gravity's Rainbow. New York: Penguin Books, 2006.

Quigley, Carroll. Tragedy and Hope: A History of the World in Our Time. New York: The Macmillan Company, 1966.

Raimondo, Justin. Reclaiming the American Right: The Lost Legacy of the Conservative Movement. Wilmington, DE: ISI Books, 2008.

Ramsay, Paul. The Just War: Force and Political Responsibility. New York: Charles Scribner's Sons, 1968.

Ratzinger, Joseph Cardinal. Values in a Time of Upheaval. trans. Brian McNeil. New York: The Crossroad Publishing Company, 2006.

Rowland, Tracy. Ratzinger's Faith: The Theology of Pope Benedict XVI. Oxford, UK: Oxford University Press, 2008.

Rutler, George William. Coincidently. New York: The Crossroads Publishing Company, 2006.

Schall, S.J. James V. The Regensburg Lecture. South Bend, IN: St. Augustine's Press, 2007.

Stanley, Jason. How Propaganda Works. Princeton, NJ: Princeton University Press, 2015.

Stoyle, John. The Siege of Vienna. London: Collins, 1964.

Tolkein, J.R.R. The Two Towers. New York: Ballantine Books, 1954.

Toynbee, Arnold J. A Study of History. Oxford, UK: Oxford University Press, 1946.

Vidal, Gore. Perpetual War for Perpetual Peace: How We Got To Be So Hated. New York: Thunder's Mouth Press/Nation Books, 2002.

Viereck, George Sylvester. The Strangest Friendship in History: Woodrow Wilson and Colonel House. New York: Liveright Inc Publishers, 1932.

Weiner, Tim. Legacy of Ashes: The History of the CIA. New York: Anchor Books, 2007.

Woods, Jr., Thomas E. How the Catholic Church Built Western Civilization. Washington, DC: Regnery Publishing, 2005.

Woods, Thomas E. and Murray Polner, eds. We Who Dared To Say No To War: American Antiwar Writing From 1812 To Now. Philadelphia: Basic Books, 2008.

Wortman, Marc. The Millionaire's Unit: The Aristocratic Flyboys Who Fought The Great War And Invented American Air Power. New York: PublicAffairs, 2006.

Yoder, John H. The Politics of Jesus: Vicit Agnus Noster. Grand Rapids, MI: William B. Eerdman's Publishing, 1972.

V.

LAW, VIRTUE OR HEAVEN:

IMMANENT INSTANTIATION OR ULTIMATE FULFILLMENT IN THOMAS AQUINAS' WRITTEN *CORPUS*

cujus regni non erit finis, CREDO

Acepta con serenidad el consejo de los años, renunciando sin reservas a las cosas de juventud. Fortalece tu espíritu para que no te destruyan desgracias inesperadas. Pero no te angusties con oscuros pensamientos. Muchos temores nacen de la fatiga y la soledad. Sin olvidar la disciplina, sé amable contigo mismo.

Max Ehrmann, DESIDERATA

dwelling on visions,

puffed up without cause by a human way of thinking (COLOSSIANS 2:18)

9. That we can know God by His essence in this mortal life.

171. That a man who is [well-]ordered as far as [his] understanding and emotions are concerned, to the extent that the intellectual virtues and other, moral [virtues], about which the Philosopher speaks in the Ethics, are suffi-cient to bring this about, is well-enough disposed for eternal happiness.

172. That happiness is had in this life and not in another.

177. That raptures and visions are caused only by nature.

Etienne Tempier, THE CONDEMNATION OF 1277

1. *Introduction*

In this research essay are presented three alternative interpretations of *The Metaphysical Good*. First, the ordered hierarchy of human fulfillment Thomas Aquinas presents in the *Treatise on Happiness* will be explained to demonstrate the conclusion that there is no complete fulfillment in this life. Happiness [felicitas] lies in the eternal hereafter. Second, John Finnis is discussed in lieu of his scholastic refinement of the ordering of human goods in Aquinas' natural law theory, namely, the *summum bonum* of Heaven as well as the "relative-relativity" immanent human flourishing has in this respect. Finally, Alasdair MacIntyre is addressed to re-examine the highest immanent good in Aquinas' hierarchy; virtue. In sum, the admissibility of the latter two approaches to the more traditional Thomistic approach is considered as to the rout of scholastic philosophical tradition in the present age.[1]

2. *Thomas Aquinas and the Hierarchy of Fulfillment*

Thomas Aquinas in the *Treatise on Happiness*—along with lengthy deliberations *in abstracto* about the meaning of *The Good in itself*—lists the varying ends that rational creatures seek in order to instantiate the quality of *goodness* in their lives. Honor, pleasure, health, power, money, Aquinas concludes do not satisfy the person eternally.[2] Rather, even the highest goods of, for instance, virtue and knowledge, are not completely satisfactory. Instead, Aquinas concludes, being that the human person is made for life everlasting, then, the fleeting satisfactions of immanent goods never fully satis-

---

[1] Moral philosopher Prof. Charles Taylor is also cited here to contextualize the revisions of Aquinas' moral philosophy in secular cultures. Charles Taylor, *A Secular Age* (Cambridge, MA, and London, UK: The Belknap Press of Harvard University Press, 2007).

[2] Thomas Aquinas, *The Treatise on Happiness • The Treatise on Human Acts: Summa Theologiae I-II: 1-21*, trans. Thomas Williams (Indianapolis, IN: Hackett Publishing Company, 2016), Question 2: 'Of Those Things in Which Man's Happiness Consists': Articles 1-8.

fy the *beatitudo* of the individual made in the *image and likeness* of God [imago dei].[3]

On the contrary to Aquinas, it can be said that the real instantiation of *The Good* [bonum universale] is not the God who is the Creator of life everlasting. It might very well be the case that resting in *The Good* in this life is the ultimate end [telos] of purposeful action.

Using the pursuit of immanent enjoyment for a first "premise" of practical reason, however, only two primary alternatives for achieving *The-Good*-as-such remain open possibilities for the end in question (immanent satisfaction).

1) that desire is directed toward an end that is "objective" whether or not it satisfies in delight [delectation], which means that *The Good* can be enjoyed, not for pleasure, but rather for satisfaction [frutio] in knowing that the action aimed at is good in itself. Hence here we have Aristotle in the *Nicomachean Ethics*:

> One is led to believe that all men have a desire for pleasure, because all strive to live. Life is an activity, and each man actively exercises his favorite faculties upon the objects he loves most. A man who is musical, for example, exercises his hearing upon tunes, an intellectual his thinking upon the subjects of his study, and so forth. But pleasure completes the activities, and consequently life, which they desire. No wonder, then, that men also aim at pleasure: each man finds that it completes his life, and his life is desirable. [4]

2) The other alternative is that the end being sought is relative to the satisfaction of desire, there being no "objectively good" quality to direct the will toward one end rather than another. This means that all "good" then is simply the feeling of satisfaction in whatev-

---

[3] *See* Thomas Aquinas, *Treatise on Human Acts:* Question 11, Article 3: 'Is Enjoyment Only Of The Ultimate End?'

[4] Aristotle, *Nicomachean Ethics*, trans. Martin Oswald (Upper Saddle River, NJ: The Library of Liberal Arts, 1999), 282.

er, so long as it leads to pleasure—that is, in contrast to an objective criterion of fulfillment.[5]

In the former case **(1)** objective goods might or might not satisfy in terms of pleasure or "feeling good."[6] In the latter case **(2)** of subjective preference, the underlying measure of *The Good* is reduced to subjective satisfaction irrespective of objective fulfillment. In other words, with no "objective" measure in the ordering of moral goods, whatever delivers pleasure to the individual is eligible for satisfaction of *The Good* of the good life; this being the most reductive measure of what *The Good* is.[7] In Bertrand Russell *The Pursuit of Happiness* he explains this, this way: "Animals are happy so long as they have health and enough to eat."[8]

Notching down the hierarchy a little more, it is easy enough to see that there can be a slippery slope involved in abandoning the rigoristic form of Aquinas' philosophy here. Aquinas, in protecting the absolute of Heavenly reward, as well as the *beatitudo* of God (who provides it in the afterlife), is defending in principle that which, in effect, orders all other ends relative to the absolute endpoint [finis] of God—beatitude and Heaven—and not the other way around. Purity of heart is to *will one thing* (Luke 10:42). The Absolute is not relative to multiplicities of "relative goods."[9]

When Aquinas is abandoned in the case of thinking *The Good* is human fulfillment directed toward multiplicities of immanent goods, each with an "equal" measure of goodness, the objective quality of *The Good* is sustained **(1)**, but the question of the relation between various objective goods, one to another, is a question that then is still subjectively difficult to settle.[10]

---

[5] This is moral relativism *á la* Jeremy Bentham's push-pin.

[6] "IV Fulfilment and Morality," in John Finnis, *Aquinas: Moral, Political, and Legal Theory* (Oxford, UK: Oxford University Press, 1998), 103-131.

[7] Even Sigmund Freud admits that pleasure (intellectual or carnal) is ultimately unsatisfying. *See* Sigmund Freud, *Civilization and Its Discontents: With a Biographical Introduction by Peter Gay* (New York & London: W. W. Norton & Company, 1989).

[8] Bertrand Russell, *The Conquest of Happiness* (New York: Liveright Publishing Corporation, 1930), 13.

[9] Søren Kierkegaard, *Purity of Heart Is To Will One Thing: Spiritual Preparation for the Office of Confession*. trans. Douglas V. Steere (New York: Harper & Row, Publishers, 1948).

[10] Much of Finnis' natural law theory is intended to prevent Thomistic ethics from devolving into "proportionalism." The defense of "objective"

Is knowledge greater than honor? Or, is health better than money? Finally, when character virtue is by admission the instrumental means to the end of knowing (the virtue of Practical Reason or *phronesis*) which good is which good and in what proportion, then, perhaps virtue is indeed truly *the* one indisputable "Supreme Good" of *all* moral striving and/or happiness. Even in the both/and approach of thinking that immanent human flourishing is just as important as the transcendent glory of *beatitude* in Heaven, virtue is still the most fundamental means to both kinds of ends here (immanent and/or transcendent).[11]

As stated, **(A)** removing virtue, **(B)** removing "objective immanent goods," or **(C)** removing the Final End of Heaven, leaves only the satisfaction of desire as the sole measure of human happiness **(2)**. However, satisfaction of desire is, in the end, nothing but the maximization of pleasure, either refined (intellectual delight) or base (carnal appetite).[12] Aquinas, in the Sixth Article of Question 2, *Whether Man's Happiness Consists in Pleasure?* writes:

> On the Contrary, Boethius says (De Consul. iii): Anyone that chooses to look back on his past excesses, will perceive that pleasures [typically] have a sad ending: and if they can render a man happy, there is no reason why we should not say that the very beasts are happy too.[13]

Ut voluntas satietur—"to seek happiness is nothing but to seek the satiation of the will." This cynical maxim is as old as philoso-

---

moral absolutes is in John Finnis, *Moral Absolutes: Tradition, Revision, and Truth* (Washington, DC: Catholic University Press, 1991.) Also, for the more theological interpretation *see* Germain Grisez, *The Way of the Lord Jesus: Volume 1: Christian Moral Principles* (Quincy, IL: Franciscan Press, 1997), "6: Critique of the Proportionalist Method of Moral Judgement."

[11] Alasdair MacIntyre concluded, therefore, that virtue is the best measure of moral perfection, rather than obedience to universal rules of moral behavior deduced from natural law. Alasdair MacIntyre, *Whose Justice? Which Rationality?* (Notre Dame, IN: University of Notre Dame Press, 1988).

[12] *See* Thomas Aquinas, *Treatise on Happiness*: Question 2, "Of Those Things Which Man's Happiness Consists," Sixth Article: "Whether Man's Happiness Consists in Pleasure?"

[13] Ibid.

phy itself. A poetic litany of this conclusion can be seen in Kierkegaard's famous admonition of the The Æsthete in *Either/Or II*—
deeply informed by an ancient Greek epicureanism:

> As far as enjoyment goes, you have an absolutely
> aristocratic pride . . . compared with those who
> are chasing after satisfaction, you are satisfied, but
> that in which you find your satisfaction is abso-
> lute dissatisfaction. To see all the glories of the
> world is no concern of yours, for in thought you
> are beyond them, and if they were offered to you,
> you would very likely say, as always: Well, maybe
> one could spend a day on that. You do not care
> that you have not become a millionaire, and if the
> chance were offered to you, you would very likely
> answer: Well, it could really be interesting to have
> been a millionaire, and one could probably spend
> a month on it. If you could be offered the love of
> the most beautiful of girls, you would neverthe-
> less answer: Yes, it would be all right for half a
> year. At this point I shall not add my voice to the
> frequent heard lament about you that you are in-
> satiable; I shall rather say: In a certain sense you
> are right, for nothing that is finite, not even the
> whole world, can satisfy the soul of a person who
> feels the need of the eternal.[14]

So, in seeing that this is where the *reduction ad absurdum* termi-
nates the argument about human fulfillment (in this life), the re-
fortification of the other three approaches [namely, that of Thomas Aquinas (*beatitudo*), John Finnis (objective immanent flourishing),
and Alasdair MacIntyre (virtue)], in defining *The Good of happiness*, is
a necessary and fruitful academic exercise.

Otherwise, the adequate defense of the more stringent stance
of Aquinas—that the only ultimate fulfillment of the human person is beatitude with God (in the afterlife)—is impossible. The
relevance of this debate is hard to deny once it is admitted that, in

---

[14] Søren Kierkegaard, *Either/Or II*, trans. Howard V. Hong and Edna H.
Hong (Princeton: Princeton University Press, 1987), 202-203.

the current state of things, popular ethical culture in the Western World is vehemently anti-Thomistic in nearly every respect.[15]

No less, Aquinas remains one of the greatest philosophers of all time. He continues to exert a tremendous influence to this day. That amendments, improvements or corrections, to his philosophy of happiness/human action deserve careful consideration in the present day is apparent however.

3. *John Finnis & Immanent Human Flourishing*

Thomas Aquinas' framework of moral philosophy is mapped and refined by British Legal Philosopher John Finnis, concurrently with fellow scholars Germain Grisez, Joseph Boyle and Robert P. George.[16] In particular, the *New Natural Law Theory* that they floated into the academic discourse of the 1980s is a sophisticated defense of Thomas Aquinas' action theory.

Aquinas in the Mediæval World was, to be sure, *not* in conversation with the "melting-pot" of contemporary academic philosophies—which, for the most part, leave no "doubting-stone" unturned.[17] Many of these epistemological skepticisms dissolve much of the philosophical foundation underlying Aquinas' *faith seeking understanding* mode of Mediæval Realism, that is, often without good reason to.[18] Nevertheless, Aquinas' systematic philosophy is an integral whole which contains within itself the seeds of defense against modernist critics (even after centuries of challenge). Be-

---

[15] The long drawn-out narrative of secularization is well documented in Charles Taylor, *A Secular Age*, esp. Part IV: "Narratives of Secularization."
[16] For an appraisal of the "new" natural law theory *see* Robert P. George, *In Defense of Natural Law* (Oxford, UK: Oxford University Press, 2001). And George's broader outlook on the culture is in Robert. P. George, *The Clash of Orthodoxies: Law, Religion, and Morality in Crisis* (Wilmington, DE: ISI Books, 2001).

[17] The best appraisal of the current place of Thomism in the university *see* Alasdair MacIntyre, *God, Philosophy, Universities: A Selective History of the Catholic Philosophical Tradition* (Lanham, MD: Rowman & Littlefield, 2011).
[18] *See* Anselm, *Basic Writings*, ed. and trans. Thomas Williams (Indianapolis, IN: Hackett Publishing Company, 2007). "Faith Seeking Understanding" is the maxim of St. Anslem of Canterbury more than a century before, of course.

cause of this, the historical viability of the Mediæval system is all the more impressive (in retrospect).[19]

That being said, what the philosophical revisions of John Finnis *et al* accomplish is the necessary and earnest reinterpretation of the Thomistic tradition in light of more recent historical developments.[20] Finnis, in summoning Aquinas into conversation with the present fashion of epistemic threats—that often take aim at the very validity of the *Summa Theologiæ* as such—is addressing the relevance of Aquinas' philosophy to modern skepticisms like, for instance, the so-called "naturalistic fallacy" (is/ought dilemma) or Legal Positivism.[21]

Much of Aquinas' philosophy can be seen as somewhat vulnerable to critics who think that the context in which it arose invalidates its continuing truth. The old political elevation of the First Estate of the Catholic clerisy to positions of power has been, more or less, torn-down since the Middle Ages. This indeed has precipitated the call for rear-guard type actions against continued antagonisms to the living legacy of Aquinas' philosophical tradition; in the Roman Catholic Church especially. This is true of the philosophers inside the modern academies as well as clerics in the churches outside.[22] In this respect, John Finnis is particularly successful at addressing the practical aspects of Aquinas' moral philosophy, namely, decisive actions concerning Basic Goods.

"The First Principle" of practical reason is stated in Thomas Aquinas quite clearly, e.g. will *what is good* and avoid evil—*bonum est*

---

[19] A good defense of moderate scientific realism is Hilary Putnam, *The Many Faces of Realism: Paul Carus Lectures* (LaSalle, IL: Open Court, 1987). For an introduction to traditional Aristotelian realism, *see* Mortimer J. Adler, *Ten Philosophical Mistakes* (New York: Touchstone, 1985).

[20] The theory of the development of tradition is in John Henry Newman, *An Essay on the Development of Christian Doctrine* (Notre Dame, IN: University of Notre Dame Press, 1989).

[21] These are the stated purposes of Finnis' *Natural Law and Natural Rights*. John Finnis, *Natural Law and Natural Rights: Clarendon Law Series* (Oxford, UK: Clarendon Press, 1980), Part One, 3-50.

[22] The sacking of the First Estate during the French Revolution, and the subsequent destruction of the Mediæval structure, is historically well described in Christopher Dawson, *The Gods of the Revolution, Introduction by Arnold Toynbee* (New York: NYU Press, 1972).

faciendum et prosequendum, et malum vitandum.[23] However, the content of *The Good* in Aquinas is not so well defined, as many Thomists admit. As a matter of history, it is very possible that Aquinas, being a Mendicant Friar with the decidedly *otherworldly* vocation that that entails, perhaps places less emphasis on worldly pursuits in "seeing-through" the immanent transient nature of this life by means of ascetic religious disciplines.

In having supposedly the full abundance of supernatural virtues (faith/hope/charity) Aquinas' vision of the hereafter was probably graced with an uncommon perfection that, outside of a few rare exceptions, does not exist.

Aquinas' dogmatism regarding the Final End or absolute *Good* being God alone (who is the true beatitudo of life), and no other, creates, in practice, certain degrees of relativity amongst good(s) lower in the hierarchy.[24] In the Eighth Article of Question 2, *Whether Any Created Good Constitutes Man's Happiness?* Aquinas writes:

> I answer that: It is impossible for any created good to constitute man's happiness. For happiness is the perfect good, which lulls [satisfies] the appetite altogether; else it would not be the last end, if something yet remains to be desired. Now the object of the will, i.e., of man's appetite, is the universal good; just as the object of the intellect is the universal true. Hence it is evident that naught can lull man's will, save the universal good. This is to be found, not in any creature, but in God alone; because every creature has goodness by participate. Wherefore God alone can satisfy the will of man, according to the words of Psalm 102:5:

---

[23] By this is meant *synderesis* (basic apprehension of "good and evil"), rather than *conscientia* (the objective content of both). However, it remains possible to question the traditional Thomistic interpretation of synderesis in some contexts. *See* Alasdair MacIntyre, *Whose Justice? Which Rationality?* 188-189.

[24] Thomas Aquinas, *Treatise on Happiness*, Question 2: "Of Those Things Which Man's Happiness Consist," Eighth Article: "Whether Any Created Good Constitutes Man's Happiness?"

Who satisfieth thy desire with good things. Therefore God alone constitutes man's happiness.[25]

So, for Aquinas it is all or nothing. No Heaven means no
happiness. This being the case, immanent goods of human flourishing naturally assume an inferior place in Aquinas' ordering. In
theory, Aquinas sees truly only three absolutely basic natural ends
to human existence—life, procreation and *Rationality*.[26] Of course,
the third here (Rationality) is what all other goods depend upon as
a matter of deduction.

Rationality, being the end specifically natural to Human Nature (versus plant or animal life), supposedly leads perfected intel-
lects infused "in" the minds of supremely rational persons to conclude, with Aquinas, that the Final End in life is God, Heaven in
addition to beatitude, not immanent goods or satisfaction in pleasure.[27] Therefore, all other ends are appropriated, discerned or
judged, by the proximity of the specific good in question to the
Final End, not vice versa.

Individual goods, once being deemed less than fully satisfactory, are then ultimately relegated to a realm of lower goods—or
even outright evisl. Every good that is not the Final End is judged
relative to whether the specific good, indeed, leads toward the Final End or away from it.[28]

---

[25] Ibid.

[26] *See* John Finnis, *Aquinas: Moral, Political, and Legal Theory* (Oxford, UK: Oxford University Press, 1998), "The Basic Reason for Action," 79-86.

[27] Thomas Aquinas, *Treatise on Happiness*, Question 2: "Of Those Things in Which Man's Happiness Consists," Eighth Article: "Whether Any Cre-ated Good Constitutes Man's Happiness?"

[28] *See* the ecclesiastical "Prayer to Obtain the Grace of a Devout Life" composed by Thomas Aquinas in the Middle Ages:

> "Let all things that pass away
> seem base in my eyes,
> and let all things that are eternal
> be dear to me.
> Let me turn away from that joy
> that is without You,
> neither permit me to desire anything
> that is outside You.
> Let me take delight in the labor
> that is for You;

Seeing that the renunciation of The World [le monde] is less desirable today, perhaps; The World having more opportunities for pleasure as well as Heaven being more commonly doubted, then, defending the absolute *Good* of Aquinas is more difficult in present circumstances.[29]

It seems that Aquinas is saying that "happiness means death" to (post)-modern ways of thinking. Technically speaking, for Aquinas happiness means perfection, so, there *can be* terrestrial happiness, but it is absolutely contingent on perfect happiness in Heaven. The ordering *cannot* be reversed for any reason; that is, or the essence of happiness is lost.

Even after having admitted the centrality of Heaven in Aquinas' philosophical system, though, there remain significant questions as to the status of the lower goods (health, wealth, power, money, honor, procreation, marriage, et cetera), esp. in practical moral decisions of choice and judgment.

More along these lines, Finnis, in placing the category of *Religion* amongst incommensurable self-evident Basic Goods, does re-order Aquinas, while, at the same time elicits conclusions implicit in the original natural law ethic of the *Summa Theologica*. The revision that Finnis offers is, possibly, more beneficial with respect to

---

and let me find all repose tiresome
that is without You.
My God,
give me the grace
to direct my heart toward You
and to grieve continually at all my failures,
together with a firm purpose of amendment."

Thomas Aquinas, "[716] Prayer to Obtain the Grace of a Devout Life," in *Favorite Indulgenced Prayers: Containing Some of the Finest Prayers from both New and Old Editions of the Enchiridion of Indulgences*, ed. Anthony M. Buono (New Jersey: Catholic Book Publishing Corp., 2006), 182-185.

[29] For recent approaches to the question of heaven in an age of empirical science *see*, Hans Küng, *Eternal Life? Life After Death as a Medical, Philosophical, and Theological Problem*, trans. Edward Quinn (Garden City, NY: Doubleday, 1984). And, for a more diverse multicultural account *see* Mircea Eliade, *Death, Afterlife, and Eschatology: A Thematic Source Book of the History of Religions, Part 3 of From Primitives to Zen* (New York: Harper & Row, Publishers, 1974). An exploration of the possibility of miracle is in Stanley L. Jaki, *Miracles and Physics*, 2nd Edition (Front Royal, VA: Christendom Press, 1999).

the worldly sphere of human flourishing than to that of ascetic religious vocations, *á la* Aquinas in Middle Ages.[30]

In taking Practical Reason [phronesis] for the "first premise" of Finnis' ethic, the rule of moral behaviour can be deduced like in Aquinas by identifying *real* goods from *apparent* goods; goods which Aquinas partially dismissed—having already identified human fulfillment relative to eternal beatitude as square one.

The place of immanent human flourishing in honors, riches, bodily health, pleasure, power, even virtue itself, or any created good for that matter, is relegated to a less important sphere of action in the *Treatise on Happiness*.

So, Finnis, in denoting *Religion* to a more moderate standing, in practice defines the Final End in terms of the desire for answers to ultimate questions, rather than the actual satisfaction of those answers once known (or the praxis which leads to this).[31] It follows that the "conclusions" of the New Natural Law Theory are then arrived at irrespective of the Final End (Heaven) Aquinas identifies as being the sole highest good that is *The Good* in itself. Finnis—

> there is the value of what, since Cicero, we summarily and lamely call 'religion.' For, as there is the order of means to ends, and the pursuit of life, truth, play, and aesthetic experience in some individually selected order of priorities and pattern of specialization, and the order that can be brought into human relations through collaboration, community, and friendship, and the order that is to be brought into one's character and activity through inner integrity and outer authenticity, so, finally there arise questions as: *(a)* How are all these orders, which have their immediate origin in human initiative and pass away in death, related to the lasting order of the whole cosmos and to the origin, if any, of that order? *(b)* Is it not perhaps the case that human freedom, in which one rises above the determinism of instinct and impulse to an intelligent grasp of worthwhile forms of good,

---

[30] John Finnis, *Natural Law and Natural Rights*, 85-97.

[31] Ibid., 89-90.

and through which one shapes and masters one's environment but also one's own character, is itself somehow subordinate to something which makes that human freedom, human intelligence, and human mastery possible (not just 'originally' but from moment to moment) and which is free, intelligent, and sovereign in a way (and over a range) no human being can be?

Misgivings may be aroused by the notion that one of the basic human values is the establishment and maintenance of proper relationships between oneself (and the order one can create and maintain) and the divine.[32]

Does not even a Sarte, taking as his *point de départ* that God does not exist (and that therefore 'everything is permitted'), none the less appreciate that he is 'responsible'—obligated to act with freedom and authenticity, and to will the liberty of other persons equally with his own—in choosing what he is to be; and all this, because, *prior to* any choice of his, 'man' is and is-to-be free? And is this not a recognition (however residual) of, and concern about, an order of things 'beyond' each and every man? And so, without wishing to beg the question, may we not for convenience call that concern, which is concern for a good consisting in an irreducibly distinct form of order, 'religious'?[33]

On the contrary to Finnis, say that the ultimate answer to "Religion" is that Thomas Aquinas is right. God alone is the Final End and higher than any created good, absolutely. Then, Basic Goods like "religion" are not so incommensurable after all . . . as Finnis would have it.

Still, in desiring rational reasons for action (in this life), those who fail *to see* the divine "illumination" [gratia illuminans] of Aqui-

---

32 Ibid., 89.
33 Ibid., 90.

nas' reasoning, let alone the Faith of his evangelical counsels (poverty/chastity/obedience), can indeed salvage ethical prescriptions for decision-making with the ethical theories of John Finnis.

To sum up; using the revisions of the New Natural Law Theory in addition to the *Summa* is valuable as a prescriptive framework so long as the above "caveat" on "religion" as a mere Basic Good is observed or acknowledged. In the Roman Catholic Church the *Summa* continues to serve as a valuable resource with which systematic moral "manuals" of moral or religious instruction (across historical time periods) are provided to close to a billion faithful the world over. This, ideally, is where John Finnis can contribute most to the further development of Aquinas' doctrinal system as a relevant practical matter.[34]

Finally, having now listed "objectively" specific human goods ("basic" because "self-evident" or intelligible in their own right) the moral principles of Thomas Aquinas do have, contrary to critics, a wider range as well as greater practical applicability in Finnis' recent revision. To serve as simple examples, that an individual can choose to golf (play), read Chaucer (knowledge), appreciate the beauty of the Mona Lisa (æsthetic appreciation), see some friends for cocktails (sociability), or procreate in marriage (life), is fully *Rational* (e.g. moral) so long as the doing of such things is not contrary to eternal salvation or practical reason.[35]

Derivative of human *Rationality* are *8 modes of responsibility* further developed by Finnis' colleague Germain Grisez. These general rules prohibit what is considered an objectively direct action against integral human flourishing prescribed by the Basic Goods. Moreover, what is not contrary to a Basic Good is then by these "rules of thumb" licit. Theologian Benedict Ashley outlines the modes of responsibility here:

> 1. One should not be deterred by felt inertia from acting for intelligible goods.

---

[34] A description of the way in which Thomistic ethics can lead to the practical manuals of Moral Theology or religious praxis *see* John Mahoney, *The Making of Moral Theology: A Study in Roman Catholic Tradition* (Oxford, UK: Clarendon Press, 1987).

[35] John Finnis, *Natural Law and Natural Right*, "V. The Basic Requirements of Practical Reasonableness," 100-127.

2. One should not be pressed by enthusiasm or impatience to act individualistically for intelligible goods.

3. One should not choose to satisfy an emotional desire except as part of one's pursuit and/or attainment of an intelligible good other than the satisfaction of the desire itself.

4. One should not choose to act out of an emotional aversion except as part of one's avoidance of some intelligible evil other than the inner tension experienced in enduring that aversion.

5. One should not, in response to different feelings toward different persons, willingly proceed with a preference for anyone unless the preference is required by intelligible goods themselves.

6. One should not choose on the basis of emotions which bear upon empirical aspects of intelligible goods (or bads) in a way which interferes with a more perfect sharing of the good or avoidance of the bad.

7. One should not be moved by hostility to freely accept or choose the destruction, damaging, or impeding of any intelligible human good.

8. One should not be moved by a stronger desire for one instance of an intelligible good to act for it by choosing to destroy, damage, or impede some other instance of an intelligible good.[36]

Another important piece of this schema is the nature of the Basic Goods themselves. The 7 Basic Goods outlined by Finnis (play, knowledge, life, sociability, æsthetic appreciation, practical

---

[36] *See* Benedict M. Ashley, "The Scriptual Basis of Grisez's Revision of Moral Theology," in *Natural Law and Moral Inquiry: Ethics, Metaphysics, and Politics in the Work of Germain Grisez*, 39-40.

reason, religion) are each independently irreducible and incommensurable as immanent goods. All other immanent goods of human flourishing are, then, by this reasoning, merely instrumental to these ends alone.[37] *Practical Reason* as one of the 7 self-evident and irreducible Basic Goods is the means by which the above *modes of responsibility* originate. That is the key basis of the New Natural Law's theory of action.

The elevation of immanent flourishing to a greater place of importance in the Natural Law of Finnis is relevant for a number of reasons. As a purely shallow matter of reaching the predominant cultural attitude of "this-worldliness" today, the revision is welcome. Global life expectancies being more than 78 some odd years *the world over*, sitting around waiting for Heaven may not suit the rational moral agent (in contemporary times) the very same way it did, say, the Mediæval Friars during Aquinas' age.[38]

Aquinas himself in all likelihood *could* very well have worked to save the poor alongside Francis of Assisi; that is, instead of taking all that solitary time in writing the *Summa* that it took. No doubt, the *Summa* did need writing at some point in history, or something like it. Perhaps St. Thomas was providentially predestined to be the man for the job.

Hypothetically at least, the *Summa* now written, what can it be thought would Aquinas do instead by his own reckoning? Com-

---

[37] Ibid., 85-97.

[38] It seems that people today are more inclined to have it all. The travel-itch, especially, seems to consume a lot of time and energy. Yet, Aquinas would likely agree with Horace in that "travel narrows the mind" and is just another thing vainly conceived to distract (often unhappy) people. Nowadays, books that outsell the *Summa* include Patricia Schultz, *1,000 Places to See Before You Die: A Traveler's Life List* (New York: Workman Publishing, 2003). A very "teleological" series that betrays present-day immanent desires. Or, a more articulate demonstration of this sentiment about the meaning of what's behind the *travel-itch*, Gilbert K. Chesterton in *What I Saw in America*: "I have never managed to lose my old conviction that travel narrows the mind. At least a man must make a double effort of moral humility and imaginative energy to prevent it from narrowing the mind. Indeed there is something touching or even tragic about the thought of the thoughtless tourist, who might have stayed at home loving Laplanders, embracing Chinamen, and clasping Patagonians to his heart in Hampstead or Surbiton, but for his blind and suicidal impulse to go and see what they looked like." G. K. Chesterton, *What I Saw in America* (New York: Dodd, Mead & Co., 1923), 1.

ment on the person who wrote it before he did? No, probably not. For Finnis at least, Aquinas may see fit to try a Par 5 on a golf course, train his dog Rex to fetch, sit or lie-down, or look for something interesting to look at in and around Mediæval Rome (should such things fulfill his better immanent nature).[39]

So, that Heaven is the last end [finis] for Aquinas there is no doubt. Only that it seems Heaven, in being sought solely in the pursuit of *immanent* goods, is possibly lost sight of when relegated too much to the realm of legitimate rational pursuits in an architectonic system of deductive moral principles and/or prescriptive rules (as in Finnis). Perhaps, the "New" Natural Law, once taken out of the Mediæval context of origination with Aquinas, is, in some respects, actually contrary to the more eschatological revelations of Christ Aquinas truly believed.

Aquinas, steeped in the theology of Christianity prior to his philosophical enquiries, would no doubt have more Scriptural evidences for his more purist-stance on happiness as the Final End.

For instance, the *beatitudes* or the *Sermon on the Mount* have a decidedly otherworldly cast that do not seem so much concerned with immanent human flourishing as *the* end or meaning of life:

> Blessed are the poor in spirit, for theirs is the kingdom of heaven.
>
> Blessed are those who mourn, for they shall be comforted.
>
> Blessed are the meek, for they shall inherit the earth.

---

[39] The question is, once having identified "objectively" evil acts, then, how is the choice made among the relative proportionate "goods," that is, after seeing the complexity of possible actions and consequent outcomes? This is chiefly where virtue is more adequate than rational rule-based moral systems. The following section addresses this question by means of Alasdair MacIntyre's understanding of virtue. For instance, Aristotle: "Thus we can experience fear, confidence, desire, anger, pity, and generally any kind of pleasure and pain either too much or too little, and in either case not properly. But to experience all this at the right time, toward the right objects, toward the right people, for the right reason, and in the right manner—that is the median and best course, the course that is the mark of virtue." Aristotle, *Nicomachean Ethics*, 43.

> Blessed are those who hunger and thirst for righteousness, for they shall be satisfied.
>
> Blessed are the merciful, for they shall obtain mercy.
>
> Blessed are the pure in heart, for they shall see God.
>
> Blessed are the peacemakers, for they shall be called sons of God.
>
> Blessed are those who are persecuted for righteousness' sake, for theirs is the kingdom of heaven.
>
> Blessed are you when men revile you and persecute you and utter all kinds of evil against you falsely on my account. Rejoice and be glad, for your reward is great in heaven, for so men persecuted the prophets who were before you. (Mttw: 5:1-12)

Taken to be "normative" prescriptions, the above telling of salvation contradicts Basic Goods theory at least in part. In light of the prophetic witness of Revelation Aquinas cites authoritatively, Saint Thomas' philosophy is closer to the Gospel, no doubt, than present revisions of it.

So, say, on the contrary here that to choose to browse around a museum (aesthetic appreciation) or to play tennis (play) is *not* the fulfillment of beatitude. Still, Finnis' system is finally valuable insofar as his revision is truly informative toward the objective measure of instantiation, namely, ultimate fulfillment or Happiness (capital H), *and* the attainment of eternal salvation, not contrary to it.

To be sure, *beatitudo*, *blessedness*, as well as the Greek idea of *eudaimonia* [felicitas or *real* happiness], speak more to an objective *state of being* irrespective of subjective satisfactions. That aside, there is little reason to suspect that Heaven is made more (or less) likely while viewed solely under the auspices of the more traditional framework of Thomas Aquinas—that is, than while also taking into consideration the re-structuring of Finnis.[40]

As a practical matter the contradiction is an issue of degree and not of kind. It is an important ongoing concern for Thomisitc scholarship, but, by admission, the majority of Thomists have not ruled out the New Natural Law as such—e.g., as fundamentally contrary to the "spirit" of Thomism itself. There is nothing explicitly anathema per se. Finnis *is* a Catholic scholar.

Finnis' colleague at Princeton Robert P. George explains—as to the criticism that the New Natural Law Theory is a deontological ethic—

> Whether or not Aquinas himself supposed that sound practical philosophy necessarily depends upon a methodologically antecedent speculative philosophy of nature, this supposition has long prevailed among those who have understood themselves to be working within the Thomistic tradition of natural law theorizing. It is hardly surprising therefore that the Grisez-Finnis theory, inasmuch as it dispenses with this supposition, strikes many thinkers who are sympathetic to natural law theory as woefully inadequate. It seems 'obvious' to them that natural law theory must be about deriving norms of conduct from nature. To deny that moral norms can be so derived is, they assume, to embrace Kantian formalism, at best, and moral relativism or even skepticism at worst.[41]

There are many other acknowledgments or defenses against the varying criticisms of this sort that have been leveled at Finnis,

---

[40] No deductive system is fully satisfactory until it is "subjectively appropriated" in ways in which an individual's virtue can never be fully objectified as propositional knowledge.

[41] Robert P. George, "Recent Criticism of Natural Law Theory," in Robert P. George, *In Defense of Natural Law*, 75. And, for arguments pro and con *see* this excellent collection of essays on the New Natural Law Theory—Robert P. George, ed. *Natural Law and Moral Inquiry: Ethics, Meta physics and Politics in the Work of Germain Grisez* (Washington, DC: Georgetown University Press, 1998).

George, Grisez, Boyle, and company. Too many to go into in a short essay of pointed appraisal. Safe to say however that The New Natural Law Theory does provide useful practical interpretive rules for ethical behavior by protecting the human sphere of objective goods; that is, from the threat of present moral disintegration.

Seeing that Finnis' re-structured system of Natural Law remains in conversation with other systems, which then can refer back to the Thomistic and/or Mediæval ethical tradition, there is no reason to doubt that Finnis' contribution can be (and is) admitted as an important reform of Aquinas' theories of happiness and human action—for just the above reasons.

4. *Alasdair MacIntyre: Aristotle and Virtue*

Thomas Aquinas, while asking the question *Whether in Happiness Vision Ranks before Delight?* answers that: "On the contrary: The cause is greater than its effect. But vision is the cause of delight. Therefore vision ranks before delight . . ."[42]

Here Thomas is explaining that the cause of something is "greater" than the effects. Delight (meaning instantiation of something good) is the last effect and therefore the least good, relative to *The Good itself* who is God. The instantiation of *The Good* is "lower" than the good action that causes enjoyment.

Aquinas further understood that pleasure is the basest satisfaction because pleasure is the enjoyment of enjoyment for its own sake. Instead, real enjoyment is the enjoyment of something that is actually an imperfect part of the perfect *Good*.

In Aquinas, mere satisfaction is low, pleasure lower, whereas delight in enjoying *The Good* is higher than either. In Aquinas it is Heaven as the summum bonum which draws everything unto itself. To reiterate, remove the faith in Heaven in the ordering (being the indisputable "first premise" of Aquinas' *faith seeking understanding*) and it falls to immanent goods to account for *The Good*. Even here though, objective rules and moral prescriptions can be nonetheless

---

[42] Thomas Aquinas, *Treatise on Happiness*: Question 4, Second Article: "Whether Happiness of Vision Ranks before Delight?" Seventh Article: "Whether Some Good of the Soul Constitutes Man's Happiness?"

salvaged from the immanent sphere of Aquinas' ethical system, like in Finnis as we have shown.[43]

Virtue is intrinsically less tangible than most moral prescriptions. Often virtue is all the more difficult to qualify, regulate, or determine the operation thereof, because of this. Scottish moral philosopher Alasdair MacIntyre has gone to great lengths in order to objectify the science of virtue in this regard. In *After Virtue*, for instance, the case is made that the contextualization of virtue in *living philosophical traditions* is necessary so as to keep the rule of virtue from becoming "dead letter by default." That virtue is not an external rule imposed from writ alone, but rather the very power of the soul to perform a moral action, discern moral good, or fulfill the moral life, means that virtue itself can be possibly the very "lynchpin" to the immanent sphere of flourishing happiness in Aquinas' ethical thought.[44]

As in Finnis, much of the New Natural Law's prescription is determined by the virtue of *phronesis* [practical reason]—the only Basic Good that is also a traditional virtue—or the modes of responsibility that reason deduces. However, knowing when to perform an action, in what measure, finding the "golden mean" of virtue as in Aristotle, appropriating tradition to historical context as in MacIntyre, each require certain degrees of subjective virtue outside of what the moral prescriptions of natural law can provide.

MacIntyre is bold to state in his various writings that the questions of *whose justice?* or *which rationality?* are inevitable after the disintegration of traditional modes of belief. For him, the system of Aquinas taken in its entirety is lived, practically, with significant difference in the present age (i.e. for the individuals who desire to become the living embodiment of Mediæval Catholic "reaction") than, say, the communities which thrived around the University of Paris during the Middle Ages.

So, protecting the integrity of Thomism is almost more consuming as an academic project (for the elite few given the privilege

---

[43] Noted before, John Finnis' project is in part a working-out of this kind of system. To see how the New Natural Law Theory is applied to specific moral cases *see* Germain Grisez, *The Way of the Lord Jesus, Vol. 3: Difficult Moral Questions* (Quincy, IL: Franciscan Press, 1997).

[44] Arguments for the immateriality of an intellectual soul or power *see* Mortimer Adler, *Intellect: Mind over Matter* (New York: MacMillan Publishing, 1990). Or, William Barrett, *Death of the Soul: From Descartes to the Computer* (Garden City, New York: Anchor Books, 1987).

and means like Macintyre) than actually seeing as well as acting upon the veracity of it.

Underlying the "theory of virtue" is the original question in Aquinas *"what is the highest good?"*—or what is the *summum bonum*. Resurrecting Aquinas in the present world, who would be nearest to the answer amongst contemporaries? Taking away the absolute definition that *beatitudo* in the otherworldly Heaven is *The Good* itself, where would Aquinas' judgments now lie?

To see the answer, first the exhaustive ordering of the goods in the *Treatise on Happiness* must be addressed once more. The ordering of goods in the *Summa* is loosely a rating from lowest to low, to higher, to high, to highest. The full ranking of articles **1-9** is, in order: **(1)** wealth, **(2)** honors, **(3)** fame or glory, **(4)** power, **(5)** health, **(6)** pleasure, **(7)** virtue, **(8)** *any created good whatsoever* **(9)** Heaven.

Now, virtue being second only to "any created good" whatsoever, if you remove the importance of Heaven, what then is *The Good* fallen to next in terms of satisfying goodness and happiness?

It seems that Finnis would be more closely aligned with the order of *created goods*, as well as identifying what an intrinsic evil is.[45] On the other hand, MacIntyre is more interested in the "goods of the soul"—virtues. On an overall appraisal here, these two (created goods or virtue) are really the only viable options left outside of purely subjective pleasure in one form or another. So, what is the greatest good or in what does happiness consist, second to Heaven, outside of mere satisfaction?

Aristotle is the best "clue" to see what Aquinas' philosophy naturally "turns into" once leaving Heaven aside; that is, for the sake of re-ordering morality toward "This World." Aristotle is clearly the source that MacIntyre stands on. And, of course, he is in good company. "The Philosopher" (Aristotle) was Aquinas' preferred authority in philosophy as well.[46] Nevertheless, Aquinas in the *Seventh Article of Question 2* identifies the lacunae of virtue this way:

---

[45] *See* John Finnis, *Moral Absolutes: Tradition, Revision and Truth*.

[46] Aquinas' commentary on Aristotle's *Physics* is in Thomas Aquinas, *St. Thomas Aquinas' Commentary on Aristotle's Physics*, trans. Blackwell, Richard J. Richard J. Spath, and W. Edmund Thirlkel (New Haven, CT: Yale University Press, 1963).

If, then, we speak of man's last end, as to the thing itself which we desire as last end, it is impossible for man's last end to be the soul itself or something belonging to it. Because the soul, considered in itself, is as something existing in potentiality: for it becomes knowing actually, from being potentially knowing; and actually virtuous, from being potentially virtuous. Now since potentiality is for the sake of act as for its fulfillment, that which in itself is in potentiality cannot be the last end. Therefore the soul itself cannot be its own last end . . . But if we speak of man's last end, as to the attainment or possession thereof, or as to any use whatever of the thing itself desired as an end, thus does something of man, in respect of his soul, belong to his last end: since man attains happiness through his soul.[47]

Aristotle, not believing in Heaven, and using the *goods of the soul* for the Final End of the Good Life, came to a similar conclusion that Aquinas concludes as to unhappiness in this life. Finally dissatisfied with the shadows of this existence (having supposedly missed the supernatural virtues of faith, hope or charity), stoically, Aristotle advises, "Call man no happy until he is dead."[48]

And so, in Book I:10 of the *Nicomachean Ethics* Aristotle addresses this question like Aquinas: *Can a man be called "happy" during his lifetime?*:

Suppose we do not call a dead man happy, and interpret *Solon's* words to mean that only when a man is dead can we safely say that he has been happy, since he is now beyond the reach of evil and misfortune—this view, too, is open to objection. For it seems that to some extent good and evil really exist for a dead man, just as they may exist for a man who lives without being conscious

---

[47] Thomas Aquinas, *Treatise on Happiness*: Question 2, "Of Those Things in Which Man's Happiness Consists," Seventh Article: "Whether Some Good of the Soul Constitutes Man's Happiness."

[48] Aristotle, *Nicomachean Ethics*, Book I:10.

of them, for example, honors and disgraces, and generally the successes and failures of his children and descendants.[49]

no function of man possesses as much stability as do activities in conformity with virtue: these seem to be even more durable than scientific knowledge. And the higher the virtuous activities, the more durable they are, because men who are supremely happy spend their lives in these activities most intensely and most continuously, and this seems to be the reason why such activities cannot be forgotten.[50]

Is there anything to prevent us, then, from defining the happy man as one whose activities are an expression of complete virtue, and who is sufficiently equipped with external goods, not simply at a given moment but to the end of his life? Or should we add that he must die as well as live in the manner which we have defined? For we cannot foresee the future, and happiness, we maintain, is an end which is absolutely final and complete in every respect. If this be granted, we shall define as "supremely happy" those living men who fulfill and continue to fulfill these requirements, but blissful only as human beings. So much for this question.[51]

So Aristotle believes that happiness can be had with perfect virtue and abundant created goods in life and in posterity. But this quality of happiness cannot be known for sure until a man is dead. Aristotle's meaning is that *The Good Life* can be possibly ruined in the last act of life, or before. Cæsar Augustus disgraced on his death bed perishes in the thought that the public memory of his great conquests will be overshadowed posthumously in history by

---

49 Ibid., 23.

50 Ibid., 25.

51 Ibid., 26.

losing what was won, in the end. In the end his success would be in vain.

Now, Aquinas believes this too, however, for different reasons. Compounding God's judgment at the hour of death creates cause to fear (even more so) the loss of virtue, especially at the final moments on earth. For Aquinas, this life is only an *inchoate vitae aeternae* [foretaste of eternal beatitude].

For Aristotle, happiness can be had here through virtues or material goods—had till the end of life and then even after by way of posterity. And Aristotle agrees with Aquinas in that one would be a fool to rest absolutely in any momentary pleasures, satisfactions, or to be duped by any seemingly permanent transitory happiness in this existence. Along these lines it is not too hard to see that Aquinas in fact "transfigures" the Aristotelian philosophy— that is, by the addition of the revealed truth of Heaven.

Is this Aristotelian Virtue Ethic—of which Alasdair MacIntyre has contributed so much to its modern development— "better" than Finnis' interpretation of Aquinas, or does it still fall short of the original notion that Heaven-Is-The-Final-End-Of-Happiness? Perhaps it is best to answer that all three approaches can, properly understood, be complementary rather than mutually-exclusive of one another.

Satisfaction, enjoyment and delight, being derivative of *The Good*, *The Good* being the "cause" of virtue, virtue leading to objective goods in this life, Moral Law protecting objective good, can be said to mean that *goodness* as such in effect is caused by the ultimate *Good* God . . . then virtue, then created good, then moral law.

So, in the end, God in Heaven (Aquinas) who provides everlasting beatitude is higher than the happiness which is virtue alone (MacIntyre)—which is nevertheless the only *means to* the goods that satisfy—as well as the necessary basis to attain the objectivity and universality "moral law" provides to *Right* actions (Finnis).

5. *Conclusion*

Having described, in part, the philosophy of happiness that originated with Thomas Aquinas, it is (or now can be) seen for what it is; the basis of the Mediæval moral code's most purist form.

Thomistic theologian Josef Pieper relates—in nicely succinct language—Aquinas' understanding here, in that:

> When it is said that man by nature seeks happiness, the statement obviously implies that by nature he does not already possess it. 'In the present life perfect happiness cannot be.' Man is not happy by virtue of his being. Rather, his whole existence is determined precisely by the nonpossession of ultimate gratification. That, after all, is the significance of the concept of *status viatoris*. To exist as man means to be "on the way" and therefore to be nonhappy. Naturally, man does not cease to be man when he reaches the goal of his way. But it remains true that the concept of an Eternal Life, which simultaneously is Eternal Rest, cannot be grasped by our limited minds.[52]

And so, Finnis' revision can be said to be significant in protecting the deeper conclusions of the moral code Aquinas has provided for us. Moreover, MacIntyre is even closer to the mark in seeing that virtue is perhaps the best place where Aquinas is left to reign morally in the contemporary world—that is, as to the philosophy of humankind's seeking after happiness (the meaning of it all).

However, it is still more Aquinas who seems to understand in full that the only real measure of happiness is God. He, unlike Aristotle, locates the truth of happiness in the contemplative soul and *not* the active life of virtue or human flourishing.

In the end it is Aquinas who sees that happiness—in this life or hereafter—is the contemplation [contemplatio] of God. It is, to be sure, only the man who fixes his gaze on a transcendent heaven, as the perfection of his existence, who will see the foretaste of perfect happiness to come . . . *ubi amor, ibi oculus*—where love is, there is the eye. So, *advéniat regnum tuum*—Thy kingdom come.

---

[52] Josef Pieper, *Happiness and Contemplation*, trans. Richard and Clara Winston (New York: Pantheon, 1958), 27.

SUPPLEMENTUM

Q. THOMAS AQUINAS recognizes both *imperfect* and *perfect* happiness. Discuss his account of each and of the relationship between the two. Do any problems, tensions, or inconsistencies arise in other areas of his thought (e.g. action theory, account of virtue) as a consequence of his acknowledging both sorts of happiness?[53]

A. St. Thomas Aquinas in the *Summa Theologiæ* addresses the question of human happiness in the *Treatise on Happiness*. Parts of the definitions he provides or systematic explanations contained therein can perhaps appear at first to be counter-intuitive when seen through the worldly fashion of "common" sense. For instance, Aquinas is uncompromising on the notion of perfect happiness necessitating the Last End of human existence, namely, God. God, for Aquinas, is an uncreated perfection [beatitudo increata] that cannot be fully possessed short of the perfection of the human person in Heaven. Therefore, Aquinas reasons that no created good can satisfy the desire for ultimate fulfillment. Only the perfect Creator can grace the human creature with the perfect happiness that Aquinas en-visions in the *Summa* (I-II, q. 5. a. 3).[54]

Aquinas further reasons, by examining the nature of the world in which he lives, that the perfection of human happiness is not in this life. By way of deduction he concludes that perfect happiness can therefore only potentially lie in the hereafter, that is, dependent on the just deserts of Heaven or Hell or Purgatory. For Aquinas, suffering or the inherent imperfections of human nature (sin) as well as the natural imperfections of lesser created "goods" will be replaced with the ultimate satisfaction of "the Good" itself through, with or in, God in Heaven. Aquinas concludes in the *Treatise on Happiness* that the perfection of human fulfillment is the *uncreated* God who is not or cannot be satisfactorily had in earthly existence (I-II, q. 5 a. 1).

---

[53] This question is worded by Prof. Thomas Williams, (Phd, Notre Dame) for the qualifying examination* of *Artium Magister* in philosophy at the University of South Florida. *Dec. 2013

[54] All in-text citations of the *Summa* in this SUPPLEMENTUM are taken from the Dominican Fathers' translation. *See* Thomas Aquinas. *Summa Theologiæ.* trans. The Fathers of the Dominican Province (New York: Benzinger Brothers, 1920).

Aquinas spells-out in the *Treatise on Human Happiness* his position with respect to the various rival goods of life. He hierarchically orders created goods from the least fulfilling goods to those that in this life begin to approximate the eternal perfection of human happiness in Heaven. Goods that Aquinas lists in the *Treatise on Happiness* include the following: wealth, honors, fame or glory, power, bodily goods (health), pleasure (carnal), goods of the soul (virtue), or created goods in general (immanent human flourishing). Each is dealt with in turn, then relegated to the realm of imperfect goods by way of identifying faults that leave the good ultimately imperfectly satisfying for the human person (I-II, q. 2 a. 1-8). Aquinas deduces with what is essentially a "process of elimination" that perfect happiness is nothing other than God. There is no perfect happiness with God here, so perfect happiness is in Heaven.

Tension arises in Aquinas' account as to the prominence of the Last End of human happiness being placed in an altogether different category from immanent human flourishing. A prudent question of Aquinas' position on human happiness is whether he is right to finalize imperfect happiness relative to his overriding concern with absolute fulfillment that is not here, but rather with God in an essentially different mode of existence in Heaven. God in Heaven is the sole means by which the human person is made perfectly fulfilled. However, that Heaven is "perfect" happiness via the uncreated "Good" that is God means that Aquinas' vision of the afterlife is contingent on the uncreated grace of God being inaccessible to the finite human person in this world in the same manner that Aquinas imagines happiness in Heaven to be perfect with it (I-II, q. 3. a. 1).

Labeling imperfect the happiness of immanent human flourishing, or the excellence of virtue, or the enjoyment of created goods, is contingent on whether Aquinas is *right* about the essence of Heaven's qualitative distinction from the known world's happiness. What Aquinas calls imperfect goods can be aspects of the perfect Good when the perfect Good is present in this life in the same way here that it is in Heaven—via the uncreated grace that Aquinas believes distinguishes Heaven. Aquinas is often interpreted to understand created goods of imperfect earthly happiness in terms of created graces [beatitudo creata] that perfect the imperfections of human nature (I-II q. 112 a. 1). For Aquinas, human nature exists apart from the grace that God creates, while the grace that God creates is not God Himself in His essence (which is reserved for the perfection of Heaven) but rather another mode of participation in the created world that remains fundamentally imperfect without the Final End.

Division into perfect or imperfect happiness in Aquinas is highly speculative. There is admittedly no intrinsic error with speculative philosophy, especially regarding the Scholastic project. Nevertheless, tension does arise when a fundamental part of Aquinas' *Treatise on Happiness* is contestable or problematic. For example, Aquinas holds that final or perfect happiness is "nothing else" than the vision of the divine essence (I-II q. 3. a. 8). That perfect happiness is rare albeit possible in this life is denied by Aquinas based on the conclusion that human nature cannot see or have the divine essence. The divine essence is the uncreated grace that for Aquinas is God's perfection unencumbered by the imperfections of the finite creation.

One can test Aquinas' position by the same means of deduction by which the conclusion that perfect happiness is only in Heaven is reached. In other words, using Aquinas' own criterion of judgment, the ideal of perfection being possible in this life can be examined when the field of happiness is narrowed to essential imperfections—that Aquinas believes cannot be surpassed without first altering the world into another realm that permits perfect human happiness. The list of imperfect goods is worth summarizing to demonstrate the point.

First, Aquinas discounts wealth for being an instrumental means to other ends. Hoarding money is essentially dissatisfying when considered apart from usage (I-II q. 2. a. 1). Moreover, Aquinas eliminates honors, fame or glory, for being contingent on the opinions of others in much the same way. Favor from others is relatively desirable but cannot fulfill the person in the ultimate manner that Aquinas means (I-II q. 2. a. 2-3). Likewise, power is rejected for having no intrinsic perfection beyond the uses toward which the power is used. Similar to money, power is satisfying or dis-satisfying relative to what you do with power or the honor you receive from having power (I-II q. 2 a. 4). Health (bodily good) is necessary for happiness in the same vein that ideal bodily perfection is necessary for happiness. No health means an imperfect physical body with which to perform virtue or enjoy goods (I-II q. 2 a. 5). Moreover, bodily pleasure is the instantiation of this or that good, not "the Good" in and of itself. An instantiation of pleasure is transient by definition, not ultimately fulfilling (I-II q. 2 a. 6).

Virtue or the "good of the soul" is the habit of human excellence. For Aquinas virtue is almost ultimate fulfillment, but falls short for being an essentially instrumental perfection for the achievement of some other created good. However, virtue, unlike the other imperfect instrumental goods, can have every created good or the perfection of happiness in Heaven for an object. Hence, virtue is one of the highest goods for Aquinas (I-II q. 2 a. 7). Finally, Aquinas questions whether any created good whatsoever can provide the perfect happiness that he sees missing from the above. His answer is no (I-II q. 2 a. 8). Created goods cannot be the source of their own perfections but rather only an imperfect part or transient aspect of an uncreated (immutable) transcendent Good, meaning the essence God Himself. The *Summum Bonum* is God. God is the *Summum Bonum*. Perfect happiness is in seeing the divine essence or in being perfected by the divine essence by seeing the vision of the divine essence (according to Aquinas' understanding of the divine). Perfect happiness is nowhere but in Heaven. That that is so is the key question that is being addressed here.

Aquinas can be challenged on the above when his notion of Heavenly perfection is considered more closely. For example, created goods (imperfect aspects of perfect satisfaction) can be perfectly maintained for the duration of terrestrial existence or even into the afterlife. Whether the person knows this or not during the course of his or her life is not the matter. For Aquinas, when death comes or Heaven is reached the attainment of earthly perfection is not lost, but finalized. Ultimate finalization in no way necessitates that perfect happiness is not possible while living in an imperfect world. Perfect satisfaction of every desire can be potentially fulfilled in this life with the possible exception of the desire for God Himself. Absence of the Final End causes Aquinas to disallow perfect happiness short of Heaven. Still, the desire for Heaven can be satisfied in this life by perfect faith. The certainty of Heaven can be attained by perfect grace.

Now, an objection to Aquinas on this vital issue is that there is nothing in the constitution of God's creation that eliminates the potential for perfect happiness amidst imperfect happiness. Aquinas' metaphysical notion of the vision of the divine essence in Heaven differs from the way in which the divine essence can be potentially en-visioned here. Aquinas believes that perfect happiness is not possible when there is an unsatisfied immanent or "transcendent" desire. An assumption is made by Aquinas that

desire causes unhappiness so that there can be no unfulfilled desire
or will in Heaven. Furthermore, Aquinas states that the observance
of God's effects leads the person to desire to know the cause of
the effects, who can be known only insofar that He exists, but not
in His essence. Still, God reveals His essence by way of revelation,
which is then known or seen with the eyes of faith. The essence of
God's goodness, truth or beauty, is known by finite creatures with
finite measure here as well as in Heaven.

There is no reason by which Aquinas can absolutely reject the
notion that human persons who remain finite creatures in everlasting Heaven will continue to know God in essentially the same way
that God is known here.[55] Faith can know God here without
doubt provided God's grace. Finite knowing ceases to be finite
knowing in one way when the finite creature can know eternally.
However, eternal finite knowing in no way necessitates some other
means of knowing other than to continue to know the way finite
human persons know now, but without end. Therefore, the same
can be said of human happiness when the potential for human
happiness is not limited by Aquinas' understanding of what necessitates an "imperfect" happiness in this life relative to the perfect
happiness of Heaven.[56] Namely, perfect happiness is possible in
this life when the following conditions have been met: **1)** there is
no privation of imperfect goods **2)** Heaven is known by faith **3)**
Heaven is attained by grace prior to death **4)** God's *uncreated grace*
(His essence) is already present in the same way that He will be
present eternally in Heaven.

An important contention with allowing for the affirmation of
the above conclusion, as to potential perfect happiness contra
Aquinas, is whether the "beatific vision" is what Aquinas means by
vision of the divine essence. The beatific vision is nothing other
than the vision of God Himself, of whom Aquinas believes the
human person can see just the effects. Uncreated grace is used in
Scholastic philosophy technically to name the distinction between
God Himself and the effects of God (created graces) in the human

---

[55] *See* Pierre Duhem, *Medieval Cosmology: Theories of Infinity, Place, Time, Void,
and the Plurality of Worlds*, trans. Roger Ariew (Chicago: The University of
Chicago Press, 1985).

[56] A related question is that of "the best of all possible worlds" made
famous by Leibnitz. *See* Wilhelm Gottfried Leibnitz, *Philosophical Essays*,
trans. Roger Ariew and Daniel Garber (Indianapolis, IN: Hackett Publishing Company, 1989).

soul. The former is God's uncreated essence whereas the latter is the created effect that God's uncreated essence creates in terms of *supernatural grace* added onto human nature. Aquinas' system does not permit knowledge of the *uncreated* in this life apart from rational deductions about theoretical aspects of the nature of God's essence or by partaking in God's image.

God is not, for Aquinas, directly knowable. Rather, God is logically understood by His effects on the soul or through understanding His creation. The main contention with condition **(4)** above is just this distinction. Nonetheless, various authorities who accept the theology of Aquinas have defended God's *uncreated presence*. Challengers of Aquinas have pointed out that grace is not some-"thing" added onto human nature, but instead known already in human nature (supernaturally constituted in direct union with the divine essence).[57] Distinguishing super-nature from human nature is just one Scholastic interpretation which happens to support Aquinas' position on perfect happiness. That the beatific vision or *uncreated grace* is structurally impossible in this world, but communicated all the same through the effects of God on the soul is not settled matter in Scholastic philosophy. It is possible that there is more than just a *foretaste of eternal beatitude* [inchoatio vitae aeternae] here.

Aquinas is right insofar as perfect happiness is by definition not possible without knowledge of God. Knowledge of God beyond theoretical reason or even divine revelation is necessary to fulfill the person with divine beatitude the way Aquinas means. The question is, is that already potentially in human experience now? The added perfection of the beatific vision is potentially not an actual qualitative transformation in Heaven. Beatific vision can be just the temporal everlasting extension or moral re-ordering or ontological perfection of what is already known. That leaves the first three conditions listed above for open consideration while

---

[57] Karl Rahner pioneered this notion of the *Supernatural Existential*. Or rather, that *uncreated* grace is structurally fundamental to human nature, e.g. not added on to it or as an effect of created grace. The divine essence is self-communication of *God the Holy Spirit* that is made present here. *See* Karl Rahner. *Spirit in the World*, trans. William Dych, S.J. (New York: Continuum, 1994 [1968]). Henri de Lubac laid the groundwork for this rendering. *See* Henri de Lubac, S.J. *The Mystery of the Supernatural*, trans. Rosemary Sheed (New York: Herder and Herder, 1967).

attempting to discount the possibility of a perfect happiness in this life qualitatively akin to Heaven.

That there can be potentially no privation of imperfect goods is without doubt **(1)**. Wealth, power, bodily goods, pleasure, honor, virtue, every created good for that matter, can be abundantly had with respect to God's ends. Still, temporal existence is plagued in this life by physical corruption, so the above condition is admittedly rare in history. That the rarefied state of perfect grace can ever be true for everyone in this life is another important issue. Nevertheless, hope that that will be the case in Heaven is sufficient to accept the condition for the individual who succeeds by the grace of God in fulfilling (without fear of loss) the satisfaction of imperfect goods.

As to condition **(2)** Aquinas is contrary to the position that perfect faith in Heaven means the same for happiness when contrasted with the *experience* of Heaven. His objection is more about condition **(4)** in this case since for Aquinas the added experience of Heaven is the vision of the divine essence instead of the continuation of human happiness with how the divine essence is now experienced (in terms of uncreated grace). Albeit the absence of threat of evil is one condition that is never satisfied in this life, faith can make evil absent in the present as well as in the future. Heaven knows evil, but does not fear or is not tempted. That same condition can exist for the exceptional individual in this life.

Finally, as to condition **(3)** Aquinas is opposed based on condition **(4)** once more. According to Aquinas grace can predestine Heaven, but not in the temporal consciousness of the individual who is not yet there. When Heaven is known in this way there is no detraction from perfect human happiness. Confidence in winning the race leaves the happiness of the participant intact prior to the race as well as after having won. The possibility of losing might be material fact. However, grace transforms the impediment similar to danger that cannot harm or evil that cannot effectively tempt. The runner who knows by God's grace that he will win the race is not necessarily more or less happy before or after having won. Imperfect happiness is only the consequence of the loss that never comes when the win is doubted.

Even having satisfied the four conditions outlined in the preceding, the problems of sin and human misery remain. In Aquinas' Catholic philosophy no man is without sin save Christ, who is like man "in all things but sin." However, the reality of historical sin is not necessarily an absolute cause for further sin or impediment to perfection. A person who has sinned is still potentially perfect or actually perfect when the sin is repented of or forgiven and/or God's grace repairs the damage left from the marks former sins have left on the soul. Actual divine transformation is present in Eastern Christianity more so than in Western Christianity—where vicarious legal atonement predominates with the more pessimistic view of human nature based on original sin. Nevertheless, there is plentiful precedent in Christianity East or West for the notion that sin is absolutely repaired by divine grace or perfection potentially attained by virtue. For Aquinas then, the issue still remains the same irrespective of sin regarding the possibility of a human perfection without the added aspect of direct union with the divine essence.

Last of all, the human misery that is separation from God is an inescapable constituent of earthly existence that, according to Aquinas, negates the possibility for perfect happiness in this life. Similar to the attainment of imperfect human goods, rarely is the individual permanently perfect in each of the measures of imperfect perfections from perfect health to perfect virtue to perfect power or perfect wealth. For example, even with perfect health, physical death remains necessary. Here one important distinction is made as to the word happiness, which then contradicts Aquinas' conceptual requirements for "perfect" happiness in the purist form. When happiness implies absolute freedom from terrestrial miseries by definition, Aquinas is then correct in that perfect happiness excludes human misery. However, shifting to the Greek word *Eudaimonia*, instead, leaves the possibility open for objective happiness amidst subjective suffering.

Moreover, the Christian word *beatitudo* is even more closely aligned with Aquinas' meaning but very definitely contradicts Aquinas' position in admitting perfect blessedness while suffering. No Christian philosopher doubts the absolute blessedness of Christ who suffered. Christ was blessed to suffer instrumentally for the end of Redemption. Aquinas tellingly cites *The Book of Job* instead of the New Testament when addressing the question "whether one can be happy in this life?" Human suffering potentially prevents human happiness, but not necessarily so. Just the same that one can know evil without fear or temptation on earth or in Heaven, there is no reason to doubt that the blessed can know suffering either in the past, present, future or even eternally in Heaven, by seeing or remembering suffering in Hell or Purgatory. Aquinas believes that the miseries specifically inherent to finite creatures will be necessarily altered in Heaven, or Heaven is not Heaven. Nonetheless, finite (created) creatures remain finite eternal creatures in Heaven as on earth, so Aquinas is possibly incorrect in this respect.

To sum up; yes problems or tensions arise from Aquinas' recognition of imperfect versus perfect happiness in the *Treatise on Happiness*. Most significantly, there is a problem as to whether perfect happiness is recognizable in the first place, since Aquinas' cognition of "nonconceptual" divine essence in Heaven is based on Aquinas' conceptual cognition of Heaven in this life. Imperfect happiness is known by the ideal of perfect happiness, but Aquinas can only speculate about what the ideal is. He cannot re-"cognize" what he cannot know by cognition. Aquinas can know the ideal in theory, which means that the ideal can be potential in this life however rare in actuality.

Uncreated grace is possibly "pre-conceptual" in the here and now, meaning that the divine vision is latent but potentially actual in this life. For instance, Aquinas states that Heaven or perfect happiness is imagined with phantasms, but the world prevents the phantasm from being realized. Aquinas is unnecessarily limiting the potential for perfect happiness in comparison with the speculative perfect happiness that he thinks Heaven is.

In conclusion, why is the question of Aquinas' version of happiness an important matter in the first place? Aquinas' ethical system situates every known good of existence relative to an unknown Absolute Good someplace else. Moreover, the practical consequence of Aquinas being mistaken in this is no small issue, but shifts the entire ethical focus from Heaven to virtue or immanent human flourishing and created goods. When the perfect happiness of earth is possible, the perfect happiness of Heaven will not then subordinate the importance of relatively "imperfect" created goods to the attainment of speculative Heavenly rewards. The ethic of Aquinas is then more attuned to "this-worldly" happiness instead of the "other-worldly" ideal that is a logical consequence of his vision of what this world is in relation to the afterlife.

Some contemporary Thomistic scholars have admitted this—without compromising religious belief—seeing full well that the hierarchy Aquinas proposes in the *Treatise on Happiness* hinges on his theory that the vision of God's uncreated essence is *added onto* human nature only after the Final End.

When the vision of the divine essence is potentially already here in the finite manner in which the vision will be present in Heaven everlastingly, then the division of imperfect happiness from perfect happiness is simply a matter of degree rather than an altogether different kind of object to be attained. Questioning Aquinas on happiness in this way need not necessitate acceptance of the contrary view. Importance lies rather in the fact that settling the issue finally in favor of Aquinas' use of the imperfect/perfect categories is hasty or detrimental to the very salvation or truth that Aquinas sought with his philosophizing. In the end, the categories ought to be optionally dispensed with or re-considered once this is made necessary by historical shifts and needful realignments to other relevant parts of the *Summa Theologiæ*.

BIBLIOGRAPHY

Adler, Mortimer. Aristotle for Everybody. New York: Touchstone, 1978.

Adler, Mortimer. Intellect: Mind over Matter. New York: MacMillan Publishing, 1990.

Adler, Mortimer J. Ten Philosophical Mistakes. New York: Touchstone, 1985.

Anselm. Basic Writings. ed. and trans. Thomas Williams. Indianapolis, IN: Hackett Publishing Company, 2007.

Aquinas, Thomas. St. Thomas Aquinas' Commentary on Aristotle's Physics. trans. Blackwell, Richard J. Richard J. Spath, and W. Edmund Thirlkel. New Haven, CT: Yale University Press, 1963.

Aquinas, Thomas. On Evil. Notre Dame, IN: University of Notre Dame Press, 1995.

Aquinas, Thomas. Summa Theologiæ. trans. The Fathers of the Dominican Province. New York: Benzinger Brothers, 1920.

Aquinas, Thomas. The Treatise on Happiness • The Treatise on Human Acts: Summa Theologiae I-II: 1-21. trans. Thomas Williams. Indianapolis, IN: Hackett Publishing Company, 2016.

Aquinas, Thomas. Treatise on Law. trans. Richard J. Regan. Indianapolis, IN: Hackett Publishing Company, Inc., 2000.

Aristotle. Aristotle's Psychology: A Treatise on the Principle of Life (De Anima and Parva Naturalia, trans. William Alexander Hammond, M.A., Ph.D. London: Swan Sonnenschein & Co., 1902.

Aristotle. Nicomachean Ethics. trans. Martin Oswald. Upper Saddle River, New Jersey: The Library of Liberal Arts, 1999.

Aristotle. Physics. trans. Robin Waterfield. Oxford, UK: Oxford University Press, 2008.

Aurelius, Marcus. Meditations. trans. Martin Hammond. New York: Penguin Books, 2006.

Barrett, William. Death of the Soul: From Descartes to the Computer. Garden City, New York: Anchor Books, 1987.

Boethius. The Consolation of Philosophy, Revised Edition. trans. Victor Watts. New York: Penguin Books, 1999.

Buono, Anthony M. Favorite Indulgenced Prayers: Containing Some of the Finest Prayers from both New and Old Editions of the Enchiridion of Indulgences. New Jersey: Catholic Book Publishing Corp, 2006.

Chesterton, G. K. What I Saw in America. New York: Dodd, Mead & Co., 1923.

Clarke, W. Norris. The One and the Many: A Contemporary Thomistic Metaphysics. Notre Dame, IN: University of Notre Dame Press, 2011.

Dawson, Christopher. The Gods of the Revolution. Introduction by Arnold Toynbee. New York: NYU Press, 1972.

Duhem, Pierre. Medieval Cosmology: Theories of Infinity, Place, Time, Void, and the Plurality of Worlds. trans. Roger Ariew. Chicago: The University of Chicago Press, 1985.

Ehrmann, Max. Desiderata: Palabras de Vida. León, España: Everest, 2003.

Eliade, Mircea. Death, Afterlife, and Eschatology: A Thematic Source Book of the History of Religions, Part 3 of From Primitives to Zen. New York: Harper & Row, Publishers, 1974.

Finnis, John. Aquinas: Moral, Political, and Legal Theory. Oxford, UK: Oxford University Press, 1998.

Finnis, John. Fundamentals of Ethics. Washington, DC: Georgetown University Press, 1983.

Finnis, John. Moral Absolutes: Tradition, Revision, and Truth. Washington, DC: Catholic University Press, 1991.

Finnis, John. Natural Law and Natural Rights. Oxford, UK: Clarendon Press, 1980.

Freud, Sigmund. Civilization and Its Discontents: With a Biographical Introduction by Peter Gay. New York & London: W. W. Norton & Company, 1989.

George, Robert. P. The Clash of Orthodoxies: Law, Religion, and Morality in Crisis. Wilmington, DE: ISI Books, 2001.

George, Robert P. In Defense of Natural Law. Oxford, UK: Oxford University Press, 2001.

George, Robert P., ed. Natural Law and Moral Inquiry: Ethics, Metaphysics and Politics in the Work of Germain Grisez. Washington, DC: Georgetown University Press, 1998.

Gilson, Etienne. The Christian Philosophy of St. Thomas Aquinas. New York: Octogon Books, 1988.

Grisez, Germain. The Way of the Lord Jesus: Volume 1: Christian Moral Principles. Quincy, IL: Franciscan Press, 1997.

Grisez, Germain. The Way of the Lord Jesus, Vol. 3: Difficult Moral Questions. Quincy, IL: Franciscan Press, 1997.

Hyman, Arthur, James J. Walsh, and Thomas Williams, eds. Philosophy in the Middle Ages: The Christian, Islamic, and Jewish Traditions, Third Edition. Indianapolis, IN: Hackett Publishing Group, 2010.

Jaki, Stanley L. Miracles and Physics, Second Edition. Front Royal, VA: Christendom Press, 1999.

Kierkegaard, Søren. Either/Or II: A Fragment of Life. trans. Howard V. Hong and Edna H. Hong. Princeton, NJ: Princeton University Press, 1987.

Kreeft, Peter. A Summa of the Summa: The Essential Philosophical Passages of St. Thomas Aquinas' Summa Theologica Edited and Explained for Beginnners. San Francisco: Ignatius Press, 1990.

Küng, Hans. Eternal Life? Life After Death as a Medical, Philosophical, and Theological Problem. trans. Edward Quinn. Garden City, NY: Doubleday, 1984.

Leibnitz, Wilhelm Gottfried. Philosophical Essays. trans. Roger Ariew and Daniel Garber. Indianapolis, IN: Hackett Publishing Company, 1989.

Lubac, S.J. Henri de. The Mystery of the Supernatural. trans. Rosemary Sheed. New York: Herder and Herder, 1967.

MacIntrye, Alasdair. After Virtue: A Study in Moral Theory. Second Edition. London, UK: Duckworth, 1985.

MacIntyre, Alasdair. Dependent Rational Animals: Why Human Beings Need the Virtues. Chicago: Open Court, 2012 [1999].

MacIntyre, Alasdair. God, philosophy, universities: A Selective History of the Catholic Philosophical Tradition. Lanham, MD: Rowman & Littlefield Publishers, 2009.

MacIntyre, Alasdair. Whose Justice? Which Rationality? Notre Dame, IN: University of Notre Dame Press, 1988.

Mahoney, John. The Making of Moral Theology: A Study in the Roman Catholic Tradition. Oxford, UK: Clarendon Press, 1987.

Pieper, Josef. Guide to Thomas Aquinas. trans. Richard and Clara Winston. San Francisco: Ignatius Press, 1991.

Pieper, Josef. Happiness and Contemplation. trans. Richard and Clara Winston. New York: Pantheon, 1958.

Putnam, Hilary. The Many Faces of Realism: Paul Carus Lectures. LaSalle, IL: Open Court, 1987.

Rahner, Karl. Foundation of the Christian Faith: An Introduction to the Idea of Christianity, trans. William V. Dych. New York: The Seabury Press, 1978.

Rahner, Karl. Spirit in the World. trans. William Dych, S.J. New York: Continuum, 1994 [1968].

Russell, Bertrand. The Conquest of Happiness. New York: Liveright Publishing Corporation, 1930.

Schultz, Patricia. 1,000 Places to See Before You Die: A Traveler's Life List. New York: Workman Publishing, 2003.

Southern, R. W. The Making of the Middle Ages. New Haven: Yale University Press, August 1953.

Taylor, Charles. A Secular Age. Cambridge, MA, and London, UK: The Belknap Press of Harvard University Press, 2007.

Taylor, Charles. Sources of Self. Cambridge: Harvard University Press, 1989.

VI.

FUN, LOVE & PASSION

A THOMISTIC INTERPRETATION OF AUGUSTINE'S SIN

The pursuit turned out to be long and tortuous, leading at last into the vast forests of scholastic science. From Zeno to Descartes, hand in hand with Thomas Aquinas, Montaigne, and Pascal, one stumbled as stupidly as though one were still a German student of 1860. Only with the instinct of despair could one force one's self into this old thicket of ignorance after having been repulsed at a score of entrances more promising and popular. This far, no path had led anywhere, unless perhaps to an exceedingly modest living.

Henry Adams, THE EDUCATION OF HENRY ADAMS

This fire before us, said the dean, will be pleasing to the eye. Will it therefore be beautiful?

In so far as it is apprehended by the sight, which I suppose means here esthetic intellection, it will be beautiful. But Aquinas also says Bonum est in quod tendit appetitus (I: a. 5 q. 4). In so far as it satisfies the animal craving for warmth fire is good. In hell however it is an evil.

Quite so, said the dean, you have certainly hit the nail on the head.

James Joyce,
A PORTRAIT OF THE ARTIST AS A YOUNG MAN

—Enters Augustinian monastery of the strict observance on July 16, 1505.

1. *Introduction*

Saint Augustine in the *Confessions* charts the course of his life from sinful youth into the ambitions of worldly careerism, then finally conversion to Christ Jesus. The heart's search for solace for Augustine comes only at the cost of profound battle with inner demons. Historically, Augustine's *Confessions* is without doubt wholly unique when considered in the context of Western literature.[1] For the first time in the Ancient World an unapologetically introspective Christian voice left an eternal testament that still echoes down through the ages.[2] Some of the best received passages in the *Confessions* come from Augustine's discernment of youthful sin as well as (perhaps) an over-reaction to the depth of his habitual transgressions.[3] The temptations that plagued Augustine's hard-fought conversion riddled his conscience with guilt [reatus] throughout his years.

By contrast, the written *corpus* of Thomas Aquinas is exceedingly beneficial while clarifying or more sharply defining an authoritative Catholic interpretation of Augustine's sin.[4] Aquinas is the other great giant of Catholic philosophy. After the theological convictions of Patristic times settled or solidified into Mediæval order, the discipline of philosophy developed in new directions while in no way compromising the key doctrines Augustine believed. In particular, Aquinas adds many detached insights of value to the passions [passio] Augustine poetically divulges in retrospect. Aquinas' more strictly rational system provides an opportunity *to see* the rightness inherent in Augustine's introspective self-

---

[1] No other book of its kind has had anything close to the same import on Western Civilization, save some fictional works like John Bunyan, *The Pilgrim's Progress: From This World To That Which Is To Come* (Chicago: Moody Classics, 2007), which is one of the most highly read books of religion after the Bible, or, William Shakespeare, *The Tragedy of Hamlet Prince of Denmark*, ed. Sylvan Barnet (New York: Signet Classics, 1998), which has the same sort of dramatic rendering of existential searching in it.

[2] James Hitchcock, *History of the Catholic Church* (San Francisco: Ignatius Press, 2012), 91.

[3] Oliver O'Donovan, *The Problem of Self-Love in St. Augustine* (New Haven, CT: Yale University Press, 1980).

[4] Thomas Aquinas, *Summa Theologica*, trans. The Fathers of the Dominican Province (New York: Benzinger Brothers, 1920).

judgment—that is, in terms of an over-arching judgment of Christian history.

Aquinas' theoretical refinements of the human passions contribute important nuances missing from Augustine's philosophical train of vision in the *Confessions*.[5] Aquinas thoroughly systematizes Augustinian themes in an altogether different historical key. The thesis here, therefore, is that Aquinas can helpfully augment "gaps" that Augustine (through no fault of his own) cannot see in examining his own individual conscience, that is, without later Mediæval Catholic thought. Since Augustine is consumed by fixating on the sinfulness of his passions for the duration of the narrative, Aquinas' view of the passions provides an added supplement in order to address whether Augustine is entirely correct in imagining human sinfulness the way in which he does see it in his conscience.[6]

2. *Context*

Augustine wrote near the close of the Roman Empire once the barbarians had pressed in upon the gates of civilization in the known world.[7] Dreary circumstance that caused Augustine to develop his vision of the *City of God*—15 years after the *Confessions*—in opposition to the *City of Man*, also led Augustine to stoutly defend in uncompromising manner against accusations leveled by practitioners of former rites.[8] The charge that there is a curse wrought when abandoning pagan deities (to worship Christ) heavily informed Augustine's later world-view. One significant reason

---

[5] The "turn to the subject" that practically began with Augustine is explained and argued in Charles Taylor, *Sources of Self* (Cambridge: Harvard University Press, 1989).

[6] Ibid., I-II: q. 22 - 48 & II-II: q. 166-170.

[7] A comparable example where a great work of literature was written in a time of great turmoil could be *The Decameron*, which was written during the plague of the Black Death. The siege of Rome and the onset of the so-called Dark Age is similar in terms of decline. By comparison Aquinas lived during a time of relative security and unity of belief. *See* Giovanni Boccaccio, *The Decameron*, trans. Mark Musa and Peter Bondanella (New York: Signet Classics, 2002).

[8] See Augustine, *The City of God*, trans. Marcus Dods, D.D. (New York: Barnes & Noble, 2006).

for the pessimism about human sin so ingrained in Augustine's psyche is that the world-civilization in which he lived in fact teetered on the brink of an abyss.[9]

"Fun" (love or happiness) is less prevalent to be sure for Augustine in his later years than in his youth. When he gazes back into the subjective experiences that marked his memory from early childhood or adolescence, Augustine's mind is troubled by the worldly pleasures sought to satisfy transient appetites.[10] When the sober picture of his later years emerges in the *Confessions*, Augustine is humbled in spirit with contrition of heart. He muses on the temptations that drove him to commit acts of disrepute or partake in base pleasures of fickle enjoyment.[11]

Toward the end of the *Confessions*, Augustine is found abstaining from every sin involved with the flesh, the eyes, or the pride of life (1 John 2: 16-17).[12] His harsh reaction against all illicit sins of youthful mischief is driven in part by how he frames his individual narrative of the *Confessions* via the "the signs of the times" that he reads in history. In other words, the pervasive sin Augustine sees tearing apart his hope for life in a world free from human wretchedness is correlated to the deteriorating Roman world around him. The dark picture of human nature emerges from the bleak point of history Augustine inhabited in the shadow of looming Roman decline.[13]

When Christianity conquered the West prior to the birth of the Mediæval, former traces of various religious cults rooted in the deep recesses of human history had been routed in most respects.[14] Fertile soil for the seeds of Catholic Christianity to grow existed free from many of the "weeds" of Roman times that some-

---

[9] Christopher Dawson, *Dynamics of World History*, ed. John J. Mulloy (Wilmington, DE: ISI Books, 2002), 311-341, "St. Augustine and the City of God."

[10] Augustine of Hippo, *Confessions*, trans. F. J. Sheed (Indianapolis, IN: Hackett Publishing, 2006), 63-66.

[11] Ibid., Book X.

[12] Ibid., Book VII Chapters 7-17.

[13] Christopher Dawson, *Dynamics of World History*, 283-299, "The Kingdom of God and History."

[14] Gilbert Keith Chesterton, *Saint Francis of Assisi* (London, UK: Image Books, 1989), "Chapter II: The World St. Francis Found," eloquently narrates the re-birth of Christian civilization free from Roman influences during The Middle Ages.

times maliciously invaded the delicate tree of Christianity during the time of Augustine.[15]

In the Middle Ages Thomas Aquinas often viewed life (in general) in more friendly terms regarding the potential for absolute dominion through moral obedience or the potential for goodness or virtue in human nature. Peace in the universities supported by the unified faith of civilization in the so-called "Age of Faith" provided Aquinas the contemplative leisure to rest assured that the light of the ages could be hammered out in systematic form without error.[16] Of course, this is a somewhat prosaic picture of the Middle Ages that can be often over-emphasized in scholarship. Josef Pieper notes: "There exits the romantic notion that the thirteenth century was an era of harmonious balance, of stable order, and of the free flowering of Christianity. Especially in the realm of thought, this was not so."[17]

Still, whether the appraisal of the respective ages of Augustine or Aquinas were better or worse than is thought, there is no doubting that they were different. Much insight can be seen in how these the great philosophers of each epoch approach the similar themes of the same religion. And that is the intention here in using Aquinas to interpret Augustine in the *Confessions*.

3. *Fun, Love & Passion*

Seeing Augustine in light of historical development is an important exercise. Aquinas is probably the most fitting counterpart for relative definition. Another comparison can be made here with the two great thinkers of the Reformation. In some ways Martin Luther is like the passionate and emotional Augustine and John

---

[15] Harold Berman, *Law and Revolution: The Formation of the Western Legal Tradition* (Cambridge, MA: Harvard University Press, 1993), argues that Catholicism is radically altered from the Patristic civilization after the Gregorian Reforms, effectively marking the beginning of distinctly Medieval forms of Christian religion characterized by wholly unique Western church philosophies.

[16] Will Durant, *The Age of Faith* (New York: Simon & Schuster, 1950), "Book V: The Climax of Christianity A.D. 1095-1300."

[17] Josef Pieper, *Guide to Thomas Aquinas*, trans. Richard and Clara Winston (San Francisco: Ignatius Press, 1991), 3.

Calvin more detached and systematic like Aquinas. This is a loose juxtaposition, but it illustrates why it can be important to bring out the difference by contrast.[18]

Aquinas' rendering of sinful passion is worth reciting in sum in order to place Augustine's self-criticism in proper context. Most importantly, Saint Thomas cites Augustine in the *Summa Theologica* to the effect that: "All the passions are caused by love: since love yearning for the beloved object is desire and having and enjoying it is joy."[19] Love is the most important passion. Love is the essence of God. That love is a passion is the key.

In *Question 25* Aquinas then charts a schema by which the course of the passions can be understood. The map of passion is as follows: 1) Love & Hatred 2) Desire & Aversion 3) Fear & Daring 4) Anger 5) Joy & Sadness.[20] There is no surprise that the theme of this movement runs throughout Augustine's *Confessions*. *Passio* is without doubt center stage.

Desire, joy, sadness, the gravity of love, fear, hope, despair, circumscribe the language of repentance on Augustine's literary palette (from beginning to end). However, one missing aspect of Augustine's account is the systematization Aquinas provides of how the passions actually fit together in the moral order of the human person.

For example, every passion originates in love for the desired object.[21] Love generates desire while hatred is opposed to love by creating aversion in the human heart.[22] Hope [spes] or despair [desperatio] can often nourish or deprive love, that is, whether or not the object of desire is believed to be attainable.[23] When an object of desires arises, fear can regress into despair, but daring propels the person into action braced by fortitude against the irascible appetite.[24] Anger results when the desire is frustrated, which is not

---

[18] *See* John Calvin, *Institutes of the Christian Religion*, trans. Henry Beveridge. (Peabody, MA: Hendrickson Publishers, 2008). *See* Martin Luther. *The Ninety-Five Theses, On Christian Liberty, and Address to the Christian Nobility*, trans. R. S. Grignon and C. A. Buchheim (Overland Park, KS: Digireads.com Publishing, 2009).

[19] Thomas Aquinas, *Summa Theologica*, I-II: q. 25.

[20] Ibid.

[21] Ibid., I-II: q. 26-28.

[22] Ibid., I-II: q. 29.

[23] Ibid., I-II: q. 40.

[24] Ibid., I-II: q. 45.

sinful in proportion to the rational rightness of the object.[25] Then, finally, joy is the resting in satisfaction, but sadness comes from falling short of the mark.[26] Love is the beginning and the end—*Alpha and Omega.*

In the beginning of the *Confessions*, Augustine is storm-tossed by the passions of youth. Filled with tremendous love that would inspire magnificent achievements of truthful devotion, Augustine effectively altered the direction of history with the gravitas of his passion. Still, the very weightiness of Augustine's desire operated for much of his early life in terms of love seeking an object unknown in darkness. For Aquinas, "love demands some apprehension of the good that is loved."[27] This lacunae of apprehension is wrestled with in Augustine's spirit until God finally calms the aggravated desire with the eternal peace of immutable divine satisfaction.[28] Then, and only then, is the desire of Augustine's love instantiated beyond the temporary pleasures vainly sought in his youth.

Much of Augustine's pre-conversion experience was spent wandering in the thick forest of mysticism or occult doctrines or seeking meaning in vain pleasures. Toward the end of his soul-searching Augustine can be said to have concluded with the Preacher of Ecclesiastes: "Vanity of vanities. All is vanity" (Ecclesiastes 1: 2). Final reckoning with the ultimate futility of searching for fulfillment in the conceits of pride, greed, ambition, lust or esoteric Gnostic doctrines, opened the eyes of Augustine to the naught that is worldly dissipation or final dissolution.[29]

---

[25] Ibid., I-II: q. 46-48.

[26] Ibid., I-II: q. 31-39.

[27] Ibid., I-II: q. 26.

[28] Augustine of Hippo, *Confessions*, Book X: Chapter 27.

[29] This is a prevalent theme in all religious autobiography esp. see 3 of the more classic twentieth century versions in Thomas Merton, *The Seven Storey Mountain: An Autobiography of Faith* (New York: Harcourt, Inc., 1948); C. S. Lewis, *Surprised by Joy: The Shape Of My Early Life* (Orlando, FL: Harcourt, 1955); & John Henry Newman, *Apologia Pro Vita Sua* (New York: Penguin Books, 2004). No doubt, it is still one of the more popular genres in religious literature. Lesser known, but a contemporary examplar is Episcopal priest, Ian Morgan Cron, *Jesus, My Father, the CIA, and Me: A memoir . . . of sorts* (Nashville, TN: Thomas Nelson, 2011). And even pseudo-religious psychologist C. G. Jung seems more convincing in his spiritual autobiography. *See* C. G. Jung, *Memories, Dreams, Reflections*, ed. Aniela

Desirous love that drove Augustine into the vortex of Roman politics or propelled his intellect to the heights of sophisticated fancy is effectively "re-channeled" after his conversion. The voracious appetite of his drive toward final meaning develops into the extreme kind of ascetic discipline that shapes Christianity's humility or brokenness. Augustine's dark vision of the human condition is reflected in the world-renouncing piety that precipitated the occasion of Augustine's absolute conversion to Christ.[30]

Augustine in these moments of reflection is responding to the world of his former years with an individualized ethic that seeks to discern universal Truth in "fear and trembling" (Phil. 2:12) provided the introspective events of his memory.[31] Nonetheless, Augustine's chastisement of the "old man" (Romans 6:6) of his adolescence is burdened by peculiar aspects of his personality that are wholly unique—"We know that our former man was crucified with him so that the sinful body might be destroyed, and we might no longer be enslaved to sin."

Augustine's narrative is irreparably embedded in the concrete particularity of history. Causing Augustine's guilt or longing in the *Confessions* is not just the guilt of universal sin. Rather, Augustine's sin is tied to an individual understanding of himself that exists solely in the personality of his deeply reflective intellect.

Augustine renounces everything that is a barrier to the worship of God who reconciles his soul. His withdrawal is similar to the early Christian hermits such as St. Antony of Egypt whose ascetic desert-dwelling made an impression on Augustine's spiritual formation.[32] Ambrose's humility in the flux of decadent Roman politics likewise inspired Augustine's sense of Christian spirituality amidst temptations.[33] Moreover, the ascetic world-denial that consoled Augustine's restless heart laid the foundation for the mysticism of vital monastic orders, or, even the Mediæval mendicants

---

Jaffe. trans. Richard and Clara Winston. (New York: Vintage Books, 1989 [1963]). For a good religious-political version of this (in the Henry Adams third person) *see* Russell Kirk, *The Sword of Imagination: Memoirs of a Half-Century of Literary Conflict* (Grand Rapids, MI: William B. Eerdmans Publishing Company, 1995).

[30] Augustine of Hippo, *Confessions*, Book X: Chapter 27.

[31] Ibid., Book X: Chapters 8-25.

[32] Ibid., Book VIII: Chapter 6.

[33] Ibid., Book VI: Chapters 3.

who followed in the spirit of Augustine by the eventual succession of historic development.[34]

Is the "fun" of life simply the vain desire of cupidity or the conceited diversion of curiosity? Or, is the Augustinian spirituality just one amongst many passionate responses to human sinfulness?[35]

The potential universal interpretive Truth contained in the *Confessions* cannot be entirely abstracted beyond the inspiration of Augustine's individual conscience.[36] So, it is Saint Thomas Aquinas' blueprint that is more appropriate for discerning universal truths about human selfhood, than the vivid rhetoric of Augustine's personal narrative. Augustine's deeply entrenched desires, along with his heavy guilt or heady intellectual groping in the dark shadowy mists of his inner psyche, can be fruitfully re-imagined in the more "objectively-minded" rational system of Aquinas. Through the lens of Saint Thomas' succinct conclusions regarding fun, love, or the movement of passion, the yearnings or austere judgments of Augustine can be better seen in the eyes of the other great brilliant light of Catholic thinking.

For example, "fun" is dealt with in Thomas Aquinas in *Question 168*: "modesty as consisting in outward movements of the body."[37] The wording here is somewhat misleading for the subtext includes the articles: "whether there can be a virtue about games?" "whether there can be sin in the excess of play?" or "whether there is a sin in lack of mirth?"[38] On the contrary, Augustine, who "panted for honors, for money, for marriage" while God laughed at him, comes to the conclusion that "life is a misery

---

[34] Christopher Dawson, *Religion and the Rise of Western Culture* (New York: Sheed & Ward, 1950), provides descriptions of Augustine's influence over Mediæval monasticism.

[35] Scott MacDonald, "Petit Larceny: The Beginning of All Sin," in *Augustine's Confessions: Critical Essays*, ed. William E. Mann (Lanham, MD: Rowman & Littlefield, 2006).

[36] Conversion experiences have some universal descriptive factors, but Augustine's is decidedly unique. *See* William James, "LECTURE IX: Conversion," and "LECTURE X: Conversion-concluded," in William James, *The Varieties of Religious Experience: A Study in Human Nature Being the Gifford Lectures on Natural Religion Delivered At Edinburgh in 1901-1902* (New York: Signet Classic, 1983), 171-224.

[37] Thomas Aquinas, *Summa Theologica*, II-II: q. 168.

[38] Ibid.

and death an uncertainty."[39] Augustine's mood toward the end of the *Confessions* is solemn as well as highly critical of diversions that detract from the regiment of ascetic discipline he practices. Perhaps, Augustine is here reacting to the sins of his former years with an excess of guilt to compensate for the turmoil of mistaken belief that in retrospect causes him so much internal anguish.

An appropriate place to find the content of Augustine's thoughts on the theme of lingering worldliness is *Book X* of the *Confessions*. Augustine recites an exhaustive litany of earthly delights running the full gamut of pleasures derived from appetite: lust of the eyes, lust of the flesh, worldly ambitions, immoderate curiosity for knowledge, vain speculations of astrology, the enchantments of music, the enticements of games, hunger in the belly, violations of continence that haunt Augustine's sleep, or even the simplest trivialities that consume his peers. In the end, Augustine is left in the spirit of longing for final release from the shadowy distractions that corrupt the contemplation of the only Truth he re-cognizes. Aquinas expresses the same sentiment when he famously said that life's work is just "straw" after having heard the voice of God speak directly into his heart.[40]

Augustine is possessed in the narrative of the *Confessions* by an overriding concern for Platonic Truth in the intellect apart from the sinful shadows of creation. In *Book X*, Augustine explicitly denies the value of each organ of sensate life.[41] Important to note is that Christians have throughout history assumed the attitude of Augustine's ascetic suspicion toward sensate pleasure, believing that that is God's will. However, most forms of Catholic Christianity rarely preach the austerity of world-denial that churchmen, monks, mendicants or saints, often practice, that is, in terms of the only viable mode of life excluding more worldly vocations. [42] Granted, Augustine does not advocate the far extreme (on the spectrum of world-denial), but he is certainly more in line with

---

[39] Augustine of Hippo, *Confessions*, Book VI: Chapter 6-11.

[40] Gilbert Keith Chesterton, *Saint Thomas Aquinas: "The Dumb Ox"* (London, UK: Image Books, 1956), colorfully narrates the story.

[41] Augustine of Hippo, *Confessions*, Book X.

[42] Like in different rules of the religious life. See the most ancient monastic rule in The Benedictine Monks of St. Meinrad's Abbey, eds. *The Holy Rule of Our Most Holy Father Saint Benedict* (St. Meinrad, IN: A Grail Publication, 1950). And, a rule of the "early" modern era in St. Francis de Sales, *Introduction to a Devout Life* (Ratisbon: Frederick Pustet & Co., 1900 [1609]).

emphasizing ascetic virtue than, say, the flamboyant lifestyles of Baroque Catholicism that relished the savor of "cheap grace" or La Dolce Vita.[43]

Although Augustine is cited by Aquinas in order to authorize the goodness of moderate leisure in games, Augustine in the *Confessions* harshly criticizes every delight—that is not in direct service to God—by rendering every pleasure merely instrumental for the end of replenishment, similar to eating for nourishment or health rather than enjoyment.[44] Augustine goes so far as to rebuke the appetite in the belly for being sinful, betraying an over-zealous suspicion of the material body.[45] He then chastises in *Book X* every organ of sensate existence effectively seeing potential enemies of pure contemplation [contemplatio] in the sight of the eyes, the touch of the flesh, the smell of the nose, the taste of the mouth, the sound of the ears or the appetite in the gut.[46] Tellingly, Augustine frames human sin absolutely in terms of *concupiscence*, rather than *irascible* appetites with which he does not struggle nearly so much.

Aquinas likewise places intellect over will or will over appetite in the classical tripartite ordering of the soul. Intellect controlling sensate appetite generates the "rational" appetite of will in the Thomistic system much the same that Augustine learned the classical ordering from Plato.[47] Nevertheless, Aquinas relaxes the hierarchy by placing love in the sensate appetite, then seeing love in terms of integral importance to the divine plan. Love is to suffer the divine, for Aquinas.[48] Therefore, love is the source and summit of all passion in the *Summa*. "Passion implies that the patient is drawn to that which belongs to the agent."[49] God who draws out love in the human person is sought after in direct proportion to

---

[43] Charles Taylor, *A Secular Age* (Cambridge, MA: The Belknap Press of Harvard University Press, 2007), Chapter 2 "The Rise of the Disciplinary Society," exhaustively explains the Catholic spirit of openness toward worldliness from seasonal "feasts of misrule" to the "multi-speed" order of Catholic hierarchy.

[44] Thomas Aquinas, *Summa Theologica*, II-II: q. 168.

[45] Augustine of Hippo, *Confessions*, Book X: Chapter 31.

[46] Ibid., Book X: Chapters 32-43.

[47] *See* Plato, *The Republic*, trans. Desmond Lee (London, UK: Penguin Books, 2003).

[48] Thomas Aquinas, *Summa Theologica*, I-II: q. 26. a. 1.

[49] Ibid., I-II: q. 22. a. 2.

love's gravity in the heart. To find God in the intellect in terms of rational belief is a far cry from the passionate aspect of Christianity that can be in some ways opposed to the spirit of Greek philosophy, that is, when the ancient distrust of bodily creation assumes too much importance.[50]

4. *Conclusion*

Augustine's sin is essentially the sin of misplaced desire. Love misdirected knotted the heart of Augustine in such a way that absolute retreat into the intellect suited Augustine's pre-disposition more so than Aquinas, who had no personal experience of radically untamed passion absent faith. Aquinas's intellectual system is more balanced after centuries of deliberation, whereas Augustine's passion-filled heart is victim to polarities that create an over-reaction to the sins of concupiscence. Nevertheless, Augustine *embodies* passion in the *Confessions* in a way that Aquinas is hard pressed to replicate.

No doubt, Augustine remained *in the world* while not *of the world* amidst performing priestly duties or retiring into cloistered seclusion after conversion. Still, Augustine's beliefs about human wretchedness (Pascal) drawn from the heart-break of his own experiences led him to paint an overly black picture of the human condition, that is, by the historical standard of Catholic philosophy. Mirth is missing from Augustine's somber tonality. Joy in nothing other than disembodied intellect feels inadequate when contrasted with the vibrancy of Augustine's youthful longing. Augustine's humility is crushed humility of human brokenness in the face of worldly despair, rather than the irony of mirth.[51]

---

[50] Like in the *Confessions*, compendiums of the life of Christ often read with the more of the moving appeal of religious autobiography. Three of the better 20th century ones are: Romano Gaurdini, *The Lord*, trans. Elinor Castendyk Briefs (Henry Regnery Company, 1954); Frank Sheed, *To Know Christ Jesus* (San Francisco: Ignatius Press, 1980 [1962]); & Fulton J. Sheen, *Life of Christ* (New York: Doubleday, 1990 [1977]). Compendiums of the Gospels told in chronological order can serve as narratives which serve a similar role as religious autobiography.

[51] Gilbert K. Chesterton, *Orthodoxy* (New York: Dodd, Mead and Company, 1936 [1908]), "Chapter 9: Authority of the Adventurer," provides

In one of the great 20th century spiritual autobiographies, Gilbert K. Chesterton ends on this very note of the human *mirth* (humor) of God in Christ Jesus. He writes in these famous last lines of *Orthodoxy* (1908) as to Jesus:

> I say it with reverence; there was in that shattering personality a thread that must be called shyness. There was something that He hid from all men when He went up a mountain to pray. There was something that He covered constantly by abrupt silence or impetuous isolation. There was some one thing that was too great for God to show us when He walked upon our earth; and I have sometimes fancied that it was His mirth.[52]

And so, in sum—laughter, fun, rejoicing in the goodness of God's material creation, the love of life apart from contemplative searching, have little place in Augustine's heart after God calls him away from the vanity of living in the immanence of created pleasure. Still, the mirth that can humbly share fun, love, or passion, never fully disappear from the spirit of Augustine's life, nor (attested by Aquinas) from the life of the Church.

---

another passionate spiritual auto-biography akin to Augustine's *Confessions*, beautifully ended by Chesterton on the note of Jesus' mirth. Chesterton's own official autobiography is also yet another outstanding example of the perennial influence of the genre of religious writing Augustine did so much to create. *See* G.K. Chesterton, *The Autobiography of G.K Chesterton* (San Francisco: Ignatius Press, 2006).

[52] Gilbert K. Chesterton, *Orthodoxy*, 298-299.

BIBLIOGRAPHY

Adams, Henry. The Education of Henry Adams: An Autobiography. Boston and New York: Houghton Mifflin Company, 1918.

Augustine of Hippo. The City of God. trans. Marcus Dods, D.D. New York: Barnes & Noble, 2006.

Augustine of Hippo. Confessions. trans. F.J. Sheed. Indianapolis, IN: Hackett Publishing Group, 2006.

Augustine of Hippo. The Confessions of Saint Augustine. trans. Rex Warner. New York: Signet Classics, 2009.

Aquinas, Thomas. The De Malo of Thomas Aquinas. ed. Brian Davies. trans. Richard Regan. Oxford, UK: Oxford University Press, 2001.

Aquinas, Thomas. The Summa Theologica. trans. The Fathers of the Dominican Province. New York: Benzinger Brothers, 1920.

The Benedictine Monks of St. Meinrad's Abbey, eds. The Holy Rule of Our Most Holy Father Saint Benedict. St. Meinrad, IN: A Grail Publication, 1950.

Berman, Harold J. Law and Revolution: The Formation of the Western Legal Tradition. Cambridge, MA: Harvard University Press, 1997.

Boccachio, Giovanni. The Decameron. trans. Mark Musa and Peter Bondanella. New York: Signet Classics, 2002.

Bonhoeffer, Dietrich. The Cost of Discipleship. New York: The Macmillan Company, 1963.

Bunyan, John. The Pilgrim's Progress: From This World To that Which Is To Come. Chicago: Moody Classics, 2007.

Calvin, John. Institutes of the Christian Religion. trans. Henry Beve-ridge. Peabody, MA: Hendrickson Publishers, 2008.

Chesterton, Gilbert Keith. The Autobiography of G. K Chesterton. San Francisco: Ignatius Press, 2006.

Chesterton, Gilbert Keith. Orthodoxy. London, UK: Image Books, 1991.

Chesterton, Gilbert Keith. Saint Francis of Assisi. London, UK: Image Books, 1989.

Chesterton, Gilbert Keith. Saint Thomas Aquinas: "The Dumb Ox." London, UK: Image Books, 1956.

Cron, Ian Morgan. Jesus, My Father, the CIA, and Me: A memoir . . . of sorts. Nashville, TN: Thomas Nelson, 2011.

Dawson, Christopher. Dynamics of World History. ed. John J. Mulloy. Wilmington, DE: ISI Books, 2007.

Dawson, Christopher. Religion and the Rise of Western Culture. New York: Sheed & Ward, 1950.

Day, Dorothy. The Long Loneliness: The Autobiography of Dorothy Day. New York: Harper & Row, 1997 [1952].

Durant, Will. The Age of Faith. New York: Simon & Schuster, 1950.

Gaurdini, Romano. The Lord. trans. Elinor Castendyk Briefs. Henry Regnery Company, 1954.

Hitchcock, James. History of the Catholic Church. San Francisco: Ignatius Press, 2012.

Hyman, Arthur, James J. Walsh and Thomas Williams, eds. Philosophy in the Middle Ages: The Christian, Islamic, and Jewish Traditions. Third Edition. Indianapolis, IN: Hackett Publishing Company, Inc., 2010.

James, William. The Varieties of Religious Experience: A Study in Human Nature Being the Gifford Lectures on Natural Religion Delivered At Edinburgh in 1901-1902. New York: Signet Classic, 1983.

Joyce, James. A Portrait of the Artist as a Young Man. ed. Seamus Deane. London, UK: Penguin Books, 2003.

Jung, Carl Gustav. Memories, Dreams, Reflections. ed. Aniela Jaffe. trans. Richard and Clara Winston. New York: Vintage Books, 1989 [1963].

Kirk, Russell. The Sword of Imagination: Memoirs of a Half-Century of Literary Conflict. Grand Rapids, MI: William B. Eerdmans Publishing Company, 1995.

Lewis, C. S. Surprised by Joy: The Shape Of My Early Life. Orlando, FL: Harcourt, 1955.

Lomardo, O.P., Nicholas E. The Logic of Desire: Aquinas on Emotion. Washington, DC: The Catholic University of America Press, 2011.

Luther, Martin. The Ninety-Five Theses, On Christian Liberty, and Address to the Christian Nobility. trans. R. S. Grignon and C. A. Buchheim. Overland Park, KS: Digireads.com Publishing, 2009.

Mann, William E., ed. Augustine's Confessions: Critical Essays. Lanham, MD: Rowman & Littlefield, 2006.

Merton, Thomas. The Seven Storey Mountain: An Autobiography of Faith. New York: Harcourt, Inc., 1948.

Newman, John Henry. Apologia Pro Vita Sua. New York: Penguin Books, 2004.

O'Donovan, Oliver. The Problem of Self-Love in St. Augustine. New Haven, CT: Yale University Press, 1980.

Pieper, Josef. Guide to Thomas Aquinas. trans. Richard and Clara Winston. San Francisco: Ignatius Press, 1991.

Plato, The Republic. trans. Desmond Lee. London, UK: Penguin Books, 2003.

Russell, Bertrand. The Conquest of Happiness. New York: Liveright Publishing Corporation, 1930.

Sales, St. Francis de. Introduction to a Devout Life. Ratisbon: Frederick Pustet & Co., 1900 [1609].

Shakespeare, William. The Tragedy of Hamlet Prince of Denmark. ed. Sylvan Barnet. New York: Signet Classics, 1998.

Sheed, Frank. To Know Christ Jesus. San Francisco: Ignatius Press, 1980 [1962].

Sheen, Fulton J. Life of Christ. New York: Doubleday, 1990 [1977].

Taylor, Charles. A Secular Age. Cambridge, MA: The Belknap Press of Harvard University Press, 2007.

Taylor, Charles. Sources of Self. Cambridge: Harvard University Press, 1989.

VII.

THE DEVELOPMENT OF JOHN HENRY NEWMAN'S MARIAN THEOLOGY:

THE CULT OF THE SAINTS IN VICTORIAN ENGLAND

In Western Europe, after the fall of the Roman Empire, the one powerful and universal association was the Church. Membership in that association was theoretically voluntary and practically obligatory.

Even today, the Church of Rome, which dominated Western Europe for a thousand years, with its peculiar combination of authoritarian centralization, Roman absolutism, local autonomy, political resilience, and theoretic moral rigor, remains in operation on the dogmatic basis of the theology of Thomas Aquinas, within the political framework of Gregory the Great: still holding itself the sole repository of a truth and a faith essential to human salvation.

Lewis Mumford, THE CITY IN HISTORY

I planted, Apollos watered, but God caused the growth. Therefore, neither the one who plants nor the one who waters is anything, but only God, who causes the growth. (1 CORINTH. 3:6-7)

Quæ est ista quæ progreditur quasi aurora consurgens, pulchra ut luna, electa ut sol, terribilis ut castrorum acies ordinata?

CANTICUM CANTICORUM SOLOMONIS (CAP. VI. 10)

1. *Introduction:*

This essay is an exploration of the question of how John Henry Newman reconciled himself to Marian doctrines and popular devotions, using his theory of development as articulated in *An Essay on the Development of Christian Doctrine*. For Newman, growth is the very essence of spiritual life, both in community and as an individual. Newman's own theory of institutional growth is closely related to his personal growth and experience of conversion.

It is with this in mind that Newman's notional theories will be placed in the context of his personal development and his *real assent* to Catholic dogma.[1] Admittedly, Marian doctrines were a central difficulty for Newman. However, his theoretical reservations eventually dissolved and Marian theology became a cornerstone of both his doctrinal understanding and spirituality. How this happened, both in theory and practice, is the main focus of this essay.

2. *The Virgin Mary in Newman's Life*

After a lifetime of writing, John Henry Newman created a vast body of work covering a wide range of subjects. It is therefore necessary to narrow the focus to only the most relevant texts. The primary works under consideration are the *Apologia Pro Vita Sua*, *An Essay on the Development of Christian Doctrine*, and the *Letter to E. B. Pusey on Occasion of His Eirenicon*. The *Apologia Pro Vita Sua* is the most intimate portrait available of Newman's religious thoughts and will be used for the purpose of gaining insight into Newman's spiritual path; esp. as to devotion to Mary in particular and the invocation of Saints in general.

In the *Apologia Pro Vita Sua* Cardinal Newman confesses that the excessive honour paid to Our Lady was the "great crux as regards Catholicism."[2] A distinguishing mark of the Roman Catholic Church is that the most recent and most definitive *ex cathedra* "infallible statements," namely, the *Immaculate Conception* and the *As-*

---

[1] *See* John Henry Newman, *An Essay in Aid of a Grammar of Assent* (London: Longmans, Green, and Co., 1903).

[2] John Henry Newman, *Apologia Pro Vita Sua* (New York: Penguin Books, 2004), 179.

sumption, both concern Marian doctrine. Much can be learned from J. H. Newman's own transition—from an outspoken critic of Marian beliefs and practices—to a thoughtful seeker, and then finally to a Catholic convert devoted to the Virgin Mary.

The surest path to understanding Newman's individual growth is through his theory of institutional growth in *An Essay on the Development of Christian Doctrine. An Essay on the Development of Christian Doctrine* was written during a critical turning point in Newman's life, after he had moved from a "conservative" idea of church development to what can be considered the more "additive" approach of the Roman Catholic Church. For Newman, the key question was how to recognize authentic developments, beyond the time of primitive Christianity, from corruptions.

Once Newman settled into the Roman Catholic communion he became one of the ablest defenders of Marian theology among his former Anglican colleagues.[3] The popularity of his writings and his reputation for integrity of character did much to heal the tensions over the Immaculate Conception and the delicate subject of Papal Infallibility, which were two key fault lines in England at the time.[4]

This is best illustrated in the *Letter to E. B. Pusey*, which was written in response to the *Eirenicon*, an ecumenical, if somewhat polemical apologetic for the Anglican Church's positions. Again, the focus was on Mary mostly because of the recent infallible statement from the Pope on the Immaculate Conception and the fact that many Anglicans considered Marian devotion to be "Mariolatry," and the very essence of Rome's theological errors.

A central theme of Newman's defense is the idea that Mary is "the New Eve" as a complement to Christ "the New Adam" (Romans 5:17). In the *Letter to E. B. Pusey* he makes the case that this

---

[3] Newman was by most critical standards one of the great modern day reformers of Catholicism. *See* C. Colt Anderson, *The Great Catholic Reformers: From Gregory the Great to Dorothy Day* (New York: Paulist Press, 2007).
[4] *See* for instance these contemporary pieces on the Catholic understanding of the Virgin Mary: Hugo Rahner, S.J. *Our Lady and the Church*, trans. Sebastian Bullough, O.P. (New York: Pantheon Books, 1961); Karl Rahner, *Mary: Mother of God, Theological Meditations* (New York: Herder and Herder, 1963); Joseph Cardinal Ratzinger and Hans Urs von Balthazar, *Mary: The Church at The Source*, trans. Adrian Walker (San Francisco: Ignatius Press, 1997); Fulton J. Sheen, *The World's First Love* (Garden City, NY: Image Books, 1956).

was an honoured, documented, and almost universal tradition in the writings of the Church Fathers themselves.

3. *John Henry Newman:*
   Early Development and Conversion Experience

Newman was brought up in a devout Anglican family of good social standing. He was taught to fear God and to have high moral standards. He had little contact with Catholics, although at one point he recalls discovering a drawing he did as a child of an up-right cross with what appear to be rosary beads; something he had picked-up from he knows not where. His religious training consisted of church attendance, family-based Scripture readings and household prayer. As he describes it, he had a "perfect knowledge of his catechism."[5]

However, during his adolescence, he began (as many young men do) to question his beliefs and to doubt the religious sense ingrained in him from his upbringing. The young Newman became tempted by the "spirit of the age" [zeitgeist] to conform to the society around him, a society that was swiftly drifting off into what later in life he would term liberalism. It was the liberal's position in England at the time to doubt both authority and tradition and to replace each with private judgment alone. There were many contenders for Newman's intellect and heart. He read the likes of such fashionable Enlightenment thinkers as Voltaire, Thomas Paine and David Hume. In response to Voltaire's denial of the immortality of the soul he was to say to himself, "how dreadful, yet how plausible."[6] Like all good Englishmen he wanted to be a respectable gentleman, but not particularly devout.[7]

His self-described "first conversion" came about after he was stricken with illness in 1816. Around this time he was given several theological books by a pious clergyman by the name of Rev. Walter Mayers, whom he credits with the "beginning of divine faith in

---

[5] John Henry Newman, *Apologia Pro Vita Sua*, 23-24.

[6] Ibid., 25.

[7] Philip Boyce, ed., *Mary: The Virgin Mary in the Life and Writings of John Henry Newman* (Grand Rapids, MI: William B. Eerdmans Publishing Company, 2001), 4.

me."[8] At the tender age of fifteen, Newman became convinced of his "election," or rather, that he was predestined for "eternal glory." Unfortunately, at this time he also became convinced that the Pope was, in fact, the antichrist of Biblical implication.[9] Through his many readings he had adopted several other Calvinist ideas in this vein.[10] His early prejudices would "stick with him" throughout his years as an Anglican clergyman.

The most lasting impression from these formative years was to create in Newman an internal disposition of turning away from material reality to a reverent concern for the invisible world he believed there to be. He realized that life is an unending battle between the powers of good and evil and that he was called to fight for the good. He resolved to seek "holiness rather than peace" and to engage the conflict with the daily practice of prayer and life-long commitment. He knew very early on that "growth is the only evidence of life," and, with this in mind, he began his quest for truth and holiness.[11] These early seeds would eventually blossom into Newman's Catholic faith.

At Oxford, Newman was a key player in what became known as the Oxford Movement (a group of Anglicans seeking legitimacy for the English Church in primitive Christianity). After an initial reading of the Church Fathers Newman became convinced of the notion that the Anglican Church was a *via media*, or middle way of sorts, between the errors of Protestantism and the excesses of Rome.[12]

However, after digging deeper into history, he could not escape the eventual conclusion that "to be deep in history is to cease to be Protestant," and that Anglicans were in fact Protestants in the ancient sense of the Arians and Monophysites (as he would

---

[8] John Henry Newman, *Apologia Pro Vita Sua*, 25.

[9] *See* John Calvin, *Institutes of the Christian Religion*, trans. Henry Beveridge (Peabody, MA: Hendrickson Publishers, 2008), "Book Fourth: Chapter 7: Of the Beginning and Rise of the Romish Papacy, till It Attained a Height by Which the Liberty of the Church Was Destroyed, and All True Rule Overthrown"; and *see* Martin Luther, *The Ninety-Five Theses, On Christian Liberty, and Address to the Christian Nobility*, trans. R. S. Grignon and C. A. Buchheim (Overland Park, KS: Digireads.com Publishing, 2009).

[10] John Henry Newman, *Apologia Pro Vita Sua*, 25.

[11] Ibid., 26-27.

[12] Ibid, 77.

later come to discover).[13] These discoveries eventually opened up Newman's mind to the complementary idea that the Roman Catholic Church is what it has forever claimed to be: the visible and Apostolic Church of Christ. At the time, all of this dismayed Newman tremendously. In 1843 he resigned his Anglican offices and retired to Littlemore for three years of study and prayer. During this time he wrote *An Essay on the Development of Christian Doctrine*, for which *section 5* here is devoted.

4. *Anglican Period:* Development Concerning Mary and the Invocation of Saints

Newman from an early breeding had a strong prejudice against the cult of the Saints and the invocation of the Virgin Mary in particular. He grew up in an anti-Catholic milieux. The excessive honour paid to Mary, which was from a historical and cultural context much different from his own, seemed to Newman the very hallmark of idolatry. Newman's first religious instinct was, rightfully so, toward Christ. He discovered early in his religious growth that the doctrine of the Incarnation belongs at the center of Christianity and was on guard against any doctrine that would water-down this sublime revelation.

When learning the ways of Catholics for the first time, he was most struck by the seeming elevation of Mary to the stature of Christ. His first impression was that this was a direct affront to the Incarnation itself and, therefore, harshly criticized the practice of invoking Mary instead of Christ (which he took to be Catholic dogma). He was not in dialogue during this time with someone who could explain the careful distinction between the excesses of the practice and what the Catholic Church actually teaches.[14]

In *Tract 71* written during these years before his conversion, Newman makes several charges against Catholics based on biased sources. The chief charge was that Catholics attributed omnipo-

---

[13] John Henry Newman, *An Essay on the Development of Christian Doctrine* (Notre Dame, Indiana: University of Notre Dame Press, 1989), 8. And, John Henry Newman, *Apologia Pro Vita Sua*, 134. Also, *see* John Henry Newman, *The Arians of the Fourth Century* (London: Longmans, Green, and Co., 1895).

[14] John Henry Newman, *Apologia Pro Vita Sua*, 179.

tence to Mary, which he understood to be an attribute of God alone. It was popularly believed that on account of her office she could command her son with a mother's authority and that Christ could not refuse her requests. This seemingly presented Mary as having the same power as Christ. Newman believed that Catholics treated Mary as interchangeable with the Son of God as an object of worship.[15] Or, as Pusey would later charge in the *Eirenicon*: "her intercession is held to be coextensive with his."[16]

It was also held by many Anglicans that there was no Scriptural evidence for Mary being exempted from Original Sin and that the testimony of the Church Fathers provided little evidence to justify the current beliefs of Roman Catholics. They even alleged that in some places Catholics worshiped the Virgin Mary as a goddess.[17] Worst of all perhaps, they charged that the Roman Catholic Church sought to impose these grave errors universally through the exercise of infallible authority. However misguided these accusations were, Newman himself after his conversion would come to the acknowledgement that "in truth, the honour of our Lady is dearer to them (the Catholic Church) than the conversion of England."[18]

In the controversial *Tract 90* of these same years Newman attempted to give a Catholic interpretation of the *39 Articles*. There were several glaring obstacles to this endeavor. The invocation of saints is explicitly condemned in *Article XXII* here—"The Romish Doctrine concerning purgatory, Pardons, Worshipping and Adoration, as well as Images as of Relics, and also Invocation of Saints, is a fond thing, vainly invented, and grounded upon no warranty of Scripture, but rather repugnant to the Word of God."[19] This is the

---

[15] John Henry Newman, "On the Controversy with Romanists," in John Henry Newman. *Tracts for the Times*. ed. James Tolhurst D.D. (Notre Dame, IN: University of Notre Dame Press, 2013).

[16] Edward Bouverie Pusey, *An Eirenicon, In a Letter to the Author of "The Christian Year,"* (New York: D. Appleton and Company, 1866), 44.

[17] John Henry Newman, "On the Controversy with Romanists," in John Henry Newman. *Tracts for the Times*.

[18] John Henry Newman, "A Letter Addressed to Rev. E. B. Pusey, D.D., On Occasion of His Eirenicon," in John Henry Newman, *Certain Difficulties Felt by Anglicans in Catholic Teaching, Vol. II* (London: Longmans, Green, and Co., 1896), 116.

[19] Oliver O'Donovan, *On The Thirty-Nine Articles: A Conversation with Tudor Christianity* (London: SCM Press, 2011), Appendix 1.

most blatant contradiction on this account between the Anglican and Catholic churches.

There are also several other problems with the *Articles* as well, but *Article XXII* is the biggest (at least in relation to Mariology). In one sentence the *Article* denounces the whole practice of popular devotion in the Catholic Church. This was, of course, written long before the irreformable definitions on the Immaculate Conception [1854] and the Assumption [1950], but it is easy enough to see how the honour paid to Our Lady is clearly implicated.

In 1841 Newman himself wrote that the Catholic Church "goes very far indeed to substitute another Gospel for the true one. Instead of setting before the soul the Holy Trinity, and heaven and hell; it does seem to me, as a popular system, to preach the Blessed Virgin and the Saints, and Purgatory."[20] Still,. with these misgivings in mind, Newman was to admit that:

> in spite of my ingrained fears of Rome, and the decision of my reason and conscience against her usages, in spite of my affection for Oxford and Oriel, yet I had a secret longing love of Rome, the Mother of English Christianity, and I had a true devotion to the Blessed Virgin, in whose College I lived, whose Altar I served, and whose Immaculate Purity I had in one of my earliest Sermons made much of.[21]

This above passage is from a sermon preached in Newman's last year as an Anglican. *The Reverence due to the Virgin Mary* was preached on the feast of the Annunciation in 1832. It provides the best portrait of Newman's inclinations while still an Anglican about Mary. In the sermon Newman's belief in the doctrine of Mary as "the New Eve" makes one of its first appearances in his public ministry.[22] He had begun to deduce from this idea the vari-

---

[20] John Henry Newman, "Letter to Dr. Jelf in Explanation of the Remarks, 1841," in John Henry Newman, *The Via Media*: Vol. II (London: Longmans, Green, and Co., 1901), 369.

[21] John Henry Newman, *Apologia Pro Vita Sua*, 155.

[22] John Henry Newman, "Sermon XII: The Reverence Due the Virgin Mary," in John Henry Newman, B.D., *Parochial and Plain Sermons, Vol. II* (London: Longmans, Green, and Co., 1902), 127-133.

ous implications of Mary's office for which he had built a strong documentary case from the Church Fathers.

If indeed the curse pronounced on Eve was reversed through Mary's fiat, then, as Newman hints here, Mary's importance could *not* be overestimated short of making her equal with Christ and worshiping her as divine. Newman also quotes the words of the Archangel Gabriel in order to show the Scriptural basis for the importance of Mary in the economy of salvation.[23] Newman in this sermon was beginning to realize that the role of Mary does not detract from the role of her divine son, but rather complements it. Beyond this, Newman would come to see that Marian doctrines actually protect the dogma of the Incarnation. Mary, by nature of her closeness to the Savior (the closest of all creatures) was called to a special kind of Holiness; a Holiness that all God's creatures should aspire to and pay the highest reverence to.

Newman hesitates to call Mary the "Mother of God," although he most likely accepted this title personally as fitting for her. He was wary of the reaction of his fellow Anglicans and was careful not to offend his audience. He was right in this intuition. Once Newman began making strong statements about the role of Mary, he was soon accused by some of secretly holding the doctrine of the Immaculate Conception, which was something he at this time neither admits nor denies.[24] In one such remark Newman rhetorically asks a question concerning the perfection of Mary and then goes on to say that:

> this contemplation runs to a higher subject, did
> we dare follow it; for what, think you, was the
> sanctified state of that human nature, of which
> God formed His sinless Son; knowing as we do,
> 'that which is born of the flesh is flesh,' and that
> 'none can bring a clean thing out of an unclean?'[25]

A major "sticking-point" for Newman was the distinction between intercession and invocation. Newman in his Oxford years realized that the doctrine of the *Communion of Saints* meant that all

---

[23] Ibid.,127.

[24] Philip Boyce, ed., *Mary: The Virgin Mary in the Life and Writings of John Henry Newman*, 22.

[25] Ibid, 132.

members of the Body of Christ, living and departed, can intercede and pray for one another. Invocation, on the other hand, was a vexing practice for Newman. Invoking a Saint seemed to imply that Saints could achieve what praying to God directly could not. He was under the impression that to invoke a Saint in order to persuade God to do something that God otherwise would not do was doctrinally unsound. It seemed to imply that praying to a Saint was somehow superior to praying to God directly.[26]

Furthermore, he could not find a record of the practice in the early Church Fathers, which caused him even more distress. He saw the popular practice of invocation, if carried too far, as leading to and sometimes constituting idolatry. One of the last hurdles for Newman was this fear that the *Invocation of Saints* would obscure rather than complement his commitment to the Incarnation and the unique mediation of Christ.[27] In fact, scrupulosity kept Newman from invoking Mary until he was received into the Catholic Church. He continued to struggle with the distinction until the very end of his life.[28]

5. *The Turning Point:*
An Essay on the Development of Christian Doctrine

When Newman retired to Littlemore he wrote *An Essay on the Development of Christian Doctrine*. During the process of writing he resolved many of his remaining difficulties with Catholic doctrine, among them the invocation of the Saints and the nature of Mary's office. In the *Apologia Pro Vita Sua* Newman alludes that reconciling himself to these doctrines was actually instrumental in his coming to a proper understanding of doctrinal development.

A central idea underlying *An Essay on the Development of Christian Doctrine* is the notion that dogmatic development did not end with the close of the primitive age, but rather continued throughout the history of the living and visible Catholic Church and is

---

[26] John Henry Newman, "On the Controversy with Romanists," in John Henry Newman. *Tracts for the Times.*

[27] John Henry Newman, *Apologia Pro Vita Sua*, 179.

[28] Philip Boyce, ed., *Mary: The Virgin Mary in the Life and Writings of John Henry Newman*, 29.

magnified through it. The key question in *An Essay on the Development of Christian Doctrine* is how to distinguish genuine developments from corruptions.[29] For Newman, if the promised action of the Holy Ghost is operative in the Catholic Church beyond ancient times, and that Church alone, then he desired to be in full communion with that Church. The question remained as to the nature of this "action" and how to discern it.

The promise of the Holy Ghost in the New Testament is, practically speaking, more mystical than actual. It is difficult to understand apart from the concrete of historical fact. In other words, the authority of inspiration often does not justify itself. One must first know how to identify the true Church, *then* the knowledge of authority follows. It was the historical fact of authentic development (and hence of inspiration) that Newman was primarily after in writing *An Essay on the Development of Christian Doctrine*.

The notes Newman outlines are a careful weaving of "conservative" and "progressive" forces. The categories of "conservative" and "progressive" are not meant to impose a black and white picture on a nuanced work of theology. Admittedly, the "notes" themselves were not necessarily conceived by Newman in this way. In the balance, however, Newman's notes (or "marks" of development) allow for measured development without losing sight of tradition. This measured aspect is one of the strongest features of the 7 notes as marks of development.

Distinguishing between the notes that move the tradition forward from the ones that mostly preserve the integrity of the existing tradition is of value for understanding how Newman's theory of development is operative in the dynamic movement of history. It is also helpful when situating Marian doctrines within the Catholic Tradition and defending them against the charge of being mere innovations or worldly "traditions of men" (Mark 7:8)—"You leave the commandment of God, and hold fast the traditions of men." Contemporary debates about theological development as such have a tendency to be framed in a similar way. The categories "progressive"/ "conservative" are used here simply as a hermeneutical key for understanding Newman's complex theory of development.

---

[29] John Henry Newman, *An Essay on the Development of Christian Doctrine*, 4.

And so, the notes that are chiefly conservative in nature are **1)** "preservation of type," **2)** "continuity of principles," **3)** "conservative action on the past," and **4)** "chronic vigor." These notes recognize that Christianity is a historic religion and must develop along historical lines. Fashions do not necessarily become truths (the mark of *chronic vigor*) and Christian principles are objective, lasting and universal (the mark *continuity of principles*).[30]

Adherence to these notes insures that the essential form of the early Church is kept intact (the mark *preservation of type*) and that continuity is regarded as an essential quality of doctrinal development (the mark of *conservative action on the past*).[31] Newman believed that, contrary to liberalism, the true Church of God has to remain what it was from the beginning and what it was ordained by God to be forever.

However, the "deposit of Faith" must also grow as the living Church proceeds through the centuries and adapts to different problems and circumstances. The notes of **5)** "logical sequence," **6)** "assimilative power" and **7)** "anticipation of future," are more progressive by nature and provide the main characteristics of healthy growth in history. False developments can be sorted out from genuine additions in accord with the tests of *logic, assimilation* and *anticipation*.

Logic (the organization of thought) is an abstract scientific means used to evaluate consistency in development. "Assimilative power" sets its face to the future as new developments outside the tradition arise—"In Christianity, opinion, while a raw material, is called philosophy or scholasticism; when a rejected refuse, it is called heresy." And, an "anticipation of future"[32] can be considered a kind of assimilation by hindsight. All three notes are principles of progress that are "on guard" against arbitrary innovation, but still move the tradition forward—"Ideas are more open to external bias in their commencement than afterwards; hence the great majority of writers who consider the Medieval Church corrupt, trace its corruption to the first four centuries, not to what are called the dark ages."[33]

---

[30] Ibid., 178-179 & 204.

[31] Ibid., 172 & 200.

[32] Ibid., 187.

[33] Ibid.

Along with the other four notes, they balance to create a nuanced and largely effective means of identifying authentic developments and, hence, the *true* Church. Newman admits that the 7 notes taken together are not meant to be wholly systematic, nor are they meant to be exhaustive. In other words, there is room according to Newman's theory of development for the further development of Newman's theory of development. But, these are the most exhaustive and systematic treatment of theological development written (practically ever). It was in addressing a specific time and place in history that the nature of this project became necessary to begin with and more relevant for Newman.

In *An Essay on the Development of Christian Doctrine*, the section on the Office of the Virgin Mary is placed under the mark Newman identifies as "anticipation of future."[34] Each note/mark has a bearing on each relevant doctrinal development (i.e. relics, the office of the Pope, icons, sacramentals, holy water, indulgences, purgatory, the seven sacraments, et cetera), but that the Office of the Virgin Mary as a development is covered under note 7 is indicative of the greater doctrinal growth at stake here.

Of the progressive notes, "anticipation of future" and "assimilative power" both make use of the *illative sense*, or rather, what Newman defines as "converging antecedent probabilities and intuitive judgment."[35] "Logical sequence" is more reliant on formal reason. With the Office of the Virgin Mary all three are relevant. Every note, "conservative" or "progressive," must be brought to bear in order to evaluate authentic developments. If all the criteria are not met, then a development is likely to be invalid. Although there is no fixed method to decide this. It is for Newman a matter of judgment and discernment.

Newman held that the doctrines concerning Mary were not essentially new, but instead a result of growth in the understanding of the Church over time.[36] They came about in part by following earlier beliefs concerning Mary to their natural consummation. As to the Office of the Virgin Mary, "anticipation of future" was most likely chosen in order to emphasize the presence of Marian doctrines in the early Church and to de-emphasize their absence.

---

[34] Ibid., 415-418.

[35] *See* John Henry Newman, *An Essay in Aid of a Grammar of Assent*.

[36] John Henry Newman, *An Essay on the Development of Christian Doctrine*, 400.

Unfortunately, there is not enough documentation of early Church beliefs and practices to deduce Marian doctrines such as the Immaculate Conception—that is, purely with logic . . . from primary sources. In the discernment of these developments it is necessary to use the illative sense. As for anticipation of future development, Newman states that:

> the records indeed of those times are scanty, and we have little means of determining what daily Christian life then was: we know little of the thoughts, and the prayers, and the meditations, and the discourses of the early disciples of Christ, at a time when these professed developments were not recognized and duly located in the theological system; yet it appears, even from what remains, that the atmosphere of the Church was, as it were, charged with them from the first, and delivered itself of them from time to time, in this way or that, in various places and persons, as occasion elicited them, testifying to the presence of a vast body of thought within it, which one day would take shape and position.[37]

Although various Marian practices were assimilative of later popular devotions, and the later doctrines were defined with the help of logical inference, the doctrines themselves do not have their origin in later periods and therefore seeds of growth are located in an anticipation. The doctrines and practices were present in seed form during the first centuries. In the particular case of the Office of the Virgin Mary "anticipation" is the most accurate principle of development, but, again, assimilation and logic both have an important part to play in continued growth of doctrine—as do the more conservative notes of *preservation of type*, *continuity of principles*, *conservative action on the past*, and *chronic vigor*.

Newman provides a heavily researched case for the practice of Marian devotion and the dignity of her office. He traces the idea of mediation to the intercession of angels in the Old Testament and the relevant appeals to created beings for assistance (2 Macca-

---

[37] Ibid.

bees 12:38, 41-46, and 15:12-16).[38] The earliest Patristic writings available testify that Mary was certainly the *New Eve* and that she holds a uniquely important place in the economy of salvation.

Newman relies on Patristic writers to support his case. He quotes the authority of St. Justin Martyr in saying that, "Eve being a virgin and incorrupt, having conceived the word from the serpent, bore disobedience and death; but Mary the Virgin, receiving faith and joy, when Gabriel the Angel evangelized her, answered."[39] This statement clearly indicates the parallel between Mary and Eve and their relevant roles in salvation.

Likewise, Tertullian wrote that "the fault of Eve in believing [the Serpent], Mary by believing hath blotted out."[40] Tertullian dissented from the Church on some issues, but he was in agreement on this important point. Furthermore, St. Irenaeus, who was a disciple of St. Polycarp (who in turn was supposedly a disciple of St. John the Evangelist himself) is actually the most direct here: "As Eve becoming disobedient became the cause of death to herself and to all mankind, so Mary too, having the predestined Man, and yet a Virgin, being obedient, became cause of salvation both to herself and to all mankind."[41]

"Cause of salvation" is powerful language and shows that Mary was not only the mere complement to Christ, but truly instrumental in the salvation of mankind. These are some of the earliest writings from Patristic times and carry considerable weight as evidence. Mary, according to those closest to the time of Christ, had a very special part to play in the redemption, that is, to the point where many of the supposed exaggerations seem nearer to the truth than the stark practices and beliefs of many Protestant sects.

Going all the way back to the time of the Christians hiding in catacombs, there can be found depictions of the Virgin and Child in early Christian art.[42] Given the prevalence of this ancient symbol, that a popular devotion to the Virgin Mary should have grown-up in the Church is hardly surprising. The authoritative statements

---

[38] Ibid., 138-139.

[39] Ibid., 416.

[40] Ibid.

[41] Ibid., 417.

[42] John Henry Newman, "A Letter Addressed to Rev. E. B. Pusey, D.D., On Occasion of His Eirenicon," in John Henry Newman, *Certain Difficulties Felt by Anglicans in Catholic Teaching, Vol. II*, 55.

concerning the nature and implications of her office are clearly *anticipated* from the very beginnings of Christianity.[43] Scripture itself bears witness to the special favor Mary is shown by God and testifies that she is "blessed among women" (Luke 1:28-38).

As to Newman's earlier hesitancy concerning devotion to Mary coming at the cost of the worship owed to Christ alone, he eventually takes the stand that devotion to Mary is precisely the guarantor of proper worship. The title *Mother of God* is inseparable from the correct theological understanding of the Incarnation and a protection against error. He admits that in practice Marian devotion can be abused, but he states that "carnal minds will ever create carnal worship for themselves; and to forbid them the service of the Saints will have no tendency to teach them to worship God."[44] Newman does not consider it a valid line of argument to take away the tender spirituality of Marian devotion (which complements the awe-ful worship of God) for the sake of possible misuse by untutored minds. Rather, he believes the necessary distinction is made clear enough in history for everyone to comprehend.[45]

---

[43] Even in the religions arising from Muhammad we see an elevation of Mary to an (at least) equal status to Christ, and in some respects greater. This Islamic interpretation is doctrinally wrong of course, but much of Islamic belief about these matters originates in the popular understandings, heresies, or misunderstandings of the ancient world. By the 8th century the conflicts about the title *Theotokos* had already pre-dated the birth of Muhammadanism. There is in fact a genealogy of the Virgin Mary in the Koran that traces her origin back through Abraham and Noah to Adam. There are also verses on the Annunciation, Visitation, and Nativity. In the nineteenth chapter alone there are forty-one verses on Jesus and Mary. The Koran is actually stronger on the perpetual virginity of Mary, ever virgin, than what many protestants believe. She is seen as the blessed mother of the prophet Jesus—who prepares the way for Muhammad. The Virgin Mary is the true *Sayyida* [Lady]. *See* Muhammad, *The Qur'an*, trans. M. A. S. Abdel Haleem (Oxford, UK: Oxford University Press, 2010). And, Jacques Jomier, O.P. *The Bible and the Qur'an*, trans. Edward P. Arbez (San Francisco: Ignatius Press, 1959).

[44] John Henry Newman, *An Essay on the Development of Christian Doctrine*, 428.

[45] Some of the doctrinally sound but more popularly misunderstood Marian devotions include the piety of St. Louis Mary de Montfort. *See* St. Louis Mary de Montfort, *True Devotion to the Blessed Virgin Mary*, trans. Frederick William Faber, D.D (Bay Shore, NY: The Montfort Fathers' Publication, 1950). Also, the scapular devotion of St. Simon Stock and

6. *Catholic Period: Letter To E. B. Pusey On Occasion Of His Eirenicon*

John Henry Newman further develops these ideas in the *Letter to E. B. Pusey.* In 1866 Newman's friend and renowned Anglican clergyman E. B. Pusey published an *Eirenicon.* Pusey's *Eirenicon* is a systematic chronicle of Anglican grievances against Rome. It had become popular among the intelligentsia of England at the time of its publication. It was written a decade after the Pope's solemn definition of the Immaculate Conception in 1854. Mary figures prominently in it.

Newman in reply wrote his most systematic account of Marian theology to date (during his Catholic period) and perhaps one of the best ever formulated. In order to defend against the charges leveled by Pusey, Newman's method was to use Scripture and Patristic writings, both of which were common ground with Anglicans. Many of the charges against Mariology Newman was already more than familiar with, having had reflected deeply on them in the process of his own personal growth and conversion from Anglican to Catholic. However, he was now fully equipped with a veritable treasury of documentary evidence and a strong spiritual conviction for this civil, though combative, exchange with his old friend.

Pusey could not contest the titles given to Mary by the Church Fathers, and most especially Mary the New Eve. What he did dispute was the perceived excesses of Roman doctrine and popular practice. He was concerned that the Roman Catholic Church had made Mary co-equal with Christ and that in practice she was worshiped as He. Like Newman before him, Pusey felt that elevating Mary would come at the cost of the worship owed to God alone. He put forth both the title co-redemptress and the doctrine of Immaculate Conception as the key examples of this kind of quasi-idolatry and dogmatic innovation.[46] As to the title

---

the Carmelites is often seen as an overtly embellished Marian Devotion. *See* Leopold Glueckert, O. Carm., *Desert Springs in the City: A Concise History of the Carmelites* (Darien, IL: Carmelite Media, 2012), 61-62. And of course there are the modern day apparitions of the Virgin Mary at Lourdes and Fatima which have led to popular devotions. *See* William Thomas Walsh, *Our Lady of Fatima* (New York: The MacMillan Company, 1951).

[46] Edward Bouverie Pusey, *An Eirenicon, In a Letter to the Author of "The Christian Year,"* 67-68.

co-redemptress, Newman only mentions it once directly in reply. He states that,

> When they found you with the Fathers calling her Mother of God, Second Eve, and Mother of all Living, the Mother of Life, the Morning Star, the Mystical New Heaven, the Sceptre of Orthodoxy, the All-undefiled Mother of Holiness, and the like, they would have deemed it a poor compensation for such language, that you protested against her being called a co-redemptress or a Priestess.[47]

Newman is using the Church Fathers here against Pusey. He does this to illustrate the fact that the alleged excess of devotion was already present in the early tradition. The elevation of Mary is not a new development as supposed. Simply because *co-redemptress* is a relatively new title does not mean that it is not consistent with what came before. *Second Eve* and *Mother of God* are hardly less reverent in terms of the implications of her importance to salvation.

That Mary's fiat reversed Eve's sin assigns to Mary a special role in the Redemption no other creature can lay claim to. That she should be deemed first among God's creatures is perfectly fitting. As first among creatures, to attach special devotion to her [hyperdulia] is a natural development even if the practice was not wholly present in the early Church in explicitly the same way.

Many Anglicans already hold to "high notions of the Blessed Virgin" and are, therefore, not in the same position as other Protestant churches in their accusations.[48] They also lay claim to the name Catholic as a (the?) universal church.[49] These complaints seem rather like quibbling, which Newman saw-through as Pusey's polemic. Ian Ker comments on this here:

---

[47] John Henry Newman, "A Letter Addressed to Rev. E. B. Pusey, D.D., On Occasion of His Eirenicon," 78.

[48] Ibid.

[49] The piety of Lancelot Andrewes gives an exemplar of the more traditional Anglican devotion. *See* Launcelot Andrewes, *The Private Devotions of Lancelot Andrewes [Preces Privatae]*, trans. F. E. Brightman (Gloucester, MA: Peter Smith, 1983). And for a history of the Reformation *see* Philip Hughes, *The Reformation in England*, Revised Edition: Three Volumes in One (London: Burns and Oates, 1962 [1950]).

not surprisingly he [Pusey] had been reticent about the contents of his so-called Eirenicon, which was calculated to make Catholics 'very angry—and justly angry'. He had quoted indiscriminately and from extreme writers, some of whom Newman had never even heard of. Newman agreed that it was 'a mere doctrinaire view to enter a Church without taking up its practical system', but it was not necessary to accept every detail and emphasis of it 'as represented by its popular catechisms and books of devotion'. Using St Alfonso Liguouri's moral theology and spirituality, for example, did not necessarily imply accepting his theory of equivocation and his particular Marian piety.[50]

Newman believed that what the Roman Catholic Church teaches is thoroughly *orthodox* [right-belief], although at various times and places there have been those who have held heterodox views. For the "common religious man" (both Anglican and Catholic) these arguments for the most part make little difference. Pusey was seizing on a popular ignorance and exploited it for controversy.

In rebuttal, Newman makes another important distinction. Christ is Divine and the Second Person of the Trinity: "He alone has an entrance into our soul, reads our secret thoughts, speaks to our heart, applies to us spiritual pardon and strength." By contrast:

> Mary is only our mother by divine appointment, given us from the Cross; her presence is above, not on earth; her office is external, not within us. Her name is not heard in the administration of the Sacraments. Her work is not one of ministration towards us; her power is indirect. It is her prayers that avail, and her prayers are effectual by the fiat of Him who is our all in all.[51]

---

[50] Ian Ker, *John Henry Newman: A Biography* (Oxford: Clarendon Press, 1988), 579.

[51] John Henry Newman, "A Letter Addressed to Rev. E. B. Pusey, D.D., On Occasion of His Eirenicon," 84.

The distinction between creature and Creator is not confused. The modes of prayer, be that of worship [adoration] or veneration [dulia], are clearly distinct. As for the Immaculate Conception, Newman turns back to the role of Mary as the New Eve once again. He states that this title is "the great rudimental teaching of Antiquity from the earliest date concerning her." He goes on, then, to tell Pusey that this teaching:

> is simply and literally the doctrine of the Immaculate Conception. I say the doctrine of the Immaculate Conception is in its substance this, and nothing more or less than this (putting aside the question of degrees of grace). And it really does seem to me bound up with the doctrine of the Father that Mary is the Second Eve . . . I have drawn the doctrine of the Immaculate Conception as an immediate inference . . . This argument seems to me conclusive.[52]

Newman is bringing his theory of development to bear and drawing out from the tradition of the Fathers, using both formal and informal reason, what is implicitly already there. Newman in his *Letter to Pusey* is urging his old friend to follow the path of development that he himself had trod personally *and* theologically. He sympathizes with the continuing difficulties of Anglicans, but is strong in his final conviction that:

> The Catholic Church allows no image of any sort, material or immaterial, no dogmatic symbol, no rite, no sacrament, no saint, not even the Blessed Virgin herself, to come between the soul and its Creator. It is face to face, 'solus cum solo,' in all matters between man and his God. He alone creates; He alone has redeemed; before His awful eyes we go to death; in the vision of Him is our eternal beatitude.[53]

---

[52] Ibid., 31-32.
[53] John Henry Newman, *Apologia Pro Vita Sua*, 179.

7. *Conclusion*

John Henry Newman's life and works attest to the fact that
the doctrine of the Catholic Church is a unified and indivisible
whole. The mediation of the Saints, and of Mary especially, are of
fundamental and indispensable importance. In *An Essay on the Development of Christian Doctrine* he states his conclusion here:

> The Incarnation is the antecedent of the doctrine
> of Mediation, the archetype both of the Sacra-
> mental principle and of the doctrine of the merits
> of the Saints. From the doctrine of Mediation fol-
> lows the Atonement, the Mass, the merits of the
> Martyrs and Saints, their invocation and cultus.
> From the Sacramental principle come the Sacra-
> ments properly so called; the unity of the Church,
> and the Holy See as its type and centre; authority
> of Councils, the sanctity of the rites; the venera-
> tion of holy places, shrines, images, vessels, furni-
> ture, and vestments.[54]

It all holds together. Newman had come to accept the entirety
of Catholic beliefs and practices. He saw clearly that all of the
Church's teachings are all-of-one-piece. The most important point
for Newman was to find the true Church and to be in full communion with it. After a long period of rigorous study and spiritual
reflection, Newman finally came to recognize the Catholic to be
that Church. His theory of doctrinal development followed closely
upon his own personal conversion and cannot be separated from it.
Just as the individual comes to grow in understanding, the Church
of Jesus Christ grows in history as it comes to know Him.

Newman developed a strong devotion to Mary during his lifetime and became one of her ablest defenders. He more than conquered his numerous reservations concerning Marian beliefs and
practices. After his Catholic conversion he came to truly embody
his popular saying that "ten thousand difficulties do not make one
doubt."[55] Toward the end of his life he continued to grapple with

---

[54] John Henry Newman, *An Essay on the Development of Christian Doctrine*,
93-94.

[55] John Henry Newman, *Apologia Pro Vita Sua*, 214.

difficulties, but he was far beyond the point of seeing doubt as a reason against faith. As he grew old in faith and weak in strength, he was no longer capable of saying Mass or even reading his breviary, but he still had his rosary beads and the Virgin Mary's gentle consolation, which he took with him to his grave.[56]

Newman died on August 11, 1890.[57] He was beatified by Pope Benedict XVI at Cofton Park of Rednal, Birmingham, on September 19, 2010. Saint Newman's festal celebration of canonization is on the 9th of October each year.

---

[56] Philip Boyce, ed., *Mary: The Virgin Mary in the Life and Writings of John Henry Newman*, 25.

[57] Ian Ker, *John Henry Newman: A Biography*, 745.

BIBLIOGRAPHY

Adomnán of Iona. Life of St Columba. trans. Richard Sharpe. New York: Penguin Books, 1995.

Anderson, C. Colt. The Great Catholic Reformers: From Gregory the Great to Dorothy Day. New York: Paulist Press, 2007.

Andrewes, Launcelot. The Private Devotions of Lancelot Andrewes [Preces Privatae]. trans. F. E. Brightman. Gloucester, MA: Peter Smith, 1983.

De Montfort, St. Louis Mary. True Devotion to the Blessed Virgin Mary. trans. Frederick William Faber, D.D. Bay Shore, NY: The Montfort Fathers' Publication, 1950.

Glueckert, O. Carm., Leopold. Desert Springs in the City: A Concise History of the Carmelites. Darien, IL: Carmelite Media, 2012.

Hughes, Philip. The Reformation in England. Revised Edition: Three Volumes in One. London: Burns and Oates, 1962 [1950].

Jomier, O.P., Jacques. The Bible and the Qur'an. trans. Edward P. Arbez. San Francisco: Ignatius Press, 1959.

Keller, Theo, ed. The Little Office of the Blessed Virgin Mary: In Latin and English. London: Baronius Press, MMXV.

Ker, Ian. John Henry Newman: A Biography. Oxford: Clarendon Press, 1988.

Kinkead, Rev. Thomas L. Baltimore Catechism Four. Charlotte, NC: Saint Benedict Press, 2010 [1891].

Lewis, C. S. The Discarded Image: An Introduction to Medieval and Renaissance Literature. Cambridge, UK: Cambridge University Press, 1964.

Luther, Martin. The Ninety-Five Theses, On Christian Liberty, and Address to the Christian Nobility. trans. R. S. Grignon and C. A. Buchheim. Overland Park, KS: Digireads.com Publishing, 2009.

Muhammad. The Qur'an. trans. M. A. S. Abdel Haleem. Oxford, UK: Oxford University Press, 2010.

John Henry Cardinal Newman. The Arians of the Fourth Century. London: Longmans, Green, and Co., 1895.

Newman, John Henry. Mary: The Virgin Mary in the Life and Writings of John Henry Newman. ed. Philip Boyce. Grand Rapids, MI: William B. Eerdmans Publishing Company, 2001.

Newman, John Henry. An Essay on the Development of Christian Doctrine. Notre Dame, Indiana: University of Notre Dame Press, 1989.

Newman, John Henry. Apologia Pro Vita Sua. New York: Penguin Books, 2004.

Newman, John Henry. An Essay in Aid of a Grammar of Assent. London: Longmans, Green, and Co., 1903.

Newman, John Henry. Certain Difficulties Felt by Anglicans in Catholic Teaching, Vol. II. London: Longmans, Green, and Co., 1896.

Newman, John Henry. Mary: The Second Eve. ed. Sister Eileen Breen, F.M.A. Rockford, IL: TAN Books and Publishers, 1982.

Newman, John Henry. Mary: The Virgin Mary in the Life and Writings of John Henry Newman. ed. Philip Boyce. Leominster, Herefordshire: Gracewing Publishing, 2001.

Newman, John Henry. Parochial and Plain Sermons: Vol. II. London: Longmans, Green, and Co., 1902.

Newman, John Henry. Tracts for the Times. ed. James Tolhurst D.D. Notre Dame, IN: University of Notre Dame Press, 2013.

Newman, John Henry. The Via Media: Vol. II. London: Longmans, Green, and Co., 1901.

O'Donovan, Oliver. On The Thirty-Nine Articles: A Conversation with Tudor Christianity. London: SCM Press, 2011.

Pusey, Edward Bouverie. An Eirenicon, In a Letter to the Author of "The Christian Year." New York: D. Appleton and Company, 1866.

Rahner, S.J. Hugo. Our Lady and the Church. trans. Sebastian Bullough, O.P. New York: Pantheon Books, 1961.

Rahner, Karl. Mary: Mother of God, Theological Meditations. New York: Herder and Herder, 1963.

Ratzinger, Joseph Cardinal, and Hans Urs von Balthazar. Mary: The Church at The Source. trans. Adrian Walker. San Francisco: Ignatius Press, 1997.

Sheen, Fulton. The World's First Love. Garden City, NY: Image Books, 1956.

Walsh, William Thomas. Our Lady of Fatima. New York: The MacMillan Company, 1951.

WHY, IT'S A LOOKING-GLASS BOOK, OF COURSE!

LEWIS CARROLL, Through the Looking-Glass

'Beware the Jabberwock, my son!
The jaws that bite, the claws that catch!
Beware the Jubjub bird, and shun
The frumious Bandersnatch!'

He took his vorpal sword in hand:
Long time the manxome foe he sought—
So rested he by the Tumtum tree,
And stood awhile in thought.

And, as in uffish thought he stood,
The Jabberwock, with eyes of flame,
Came whiffling through the tulgey wood,
And burbled as it came!

One, two! One, two! And through and through
The vorpal blade went snicker-snack!
He left it dead, and with its head
He went galumphing back.

And has thou slain the Jabberwock?
Come to my arms, beamish boy!
O frabjous day! Callooh! Callay!'
He chortled in his joy.

PART II
CONCLUSION:

Why write? There is no doubt—in this 'day and age'—a massive overproduction of words that cannot consumed persists. Thankfully, good writers need not fear in that almost everything written to wider audiences is pretty *bloodless*, like the times. So buyer beware. "He's college but not Ivy."

That said, one needs to earn a living—make money, as it were. So often we unfortunately make an idol of what is done for work in the tick-tock time of work-a-day selfs. Karl Marx reminds us that we as *homo economicus* are doers before we are knowers. It has been this way for some time, I can imagine.

Our pre-industrial forbearers, of religious or philosophical persuasions especially, could not (as a majority) have been more contrary to us on this account though. Our friend C. Wright Mills tells us the story of productive money-getting here:

> To the ancient Greeks, in whose society mechanical labor was done by slaves, work brutalized the mind, made man unfit for the practice of virtue. It was a necessary material evil, which the elite, in their search for changeless vision, should avoid. The Hebrews also looked upon work as 'painful drudgery,' to which, they added, man is condemned by sin. In so far as work atoned for sin, however, it was worthwhile, yet Ecclesiastes, for example, asserts that 'The labor of man does not satisfy the soul.'

> In primitive Christianity, work was seen as punishment for sin but also as serving the ulterior ends of charity, health of body and soul, warding off the evil thoughts of idleness. But work, being of this world, was of no worth in itself. St. Augustine, when pressed by organizational problems of the church, carried the issue further: for monks, work is obligatory, although it should alternate with prayer, and should engage them only enough to supply the real needs of the establishment. The church fathers placed pure meditation on divine

matters above even intellectual work of reading
and copying in the monastery.

With Luther, work was first established in the
modern mind as 'the base and key of life.'[1]

So much for that. Thanks Martin Luther. Thanks Jean Cauvin.
Thanks Adam Smith. It is good to write, think, pray, for pleasure
(?). Work for fun is good I think. Work for a higher religious call-
ing is better. Work because you have to is a bore.

No doubt, I have been alienated from the pressing needs of
laboring for my keep by being *spoil'd* in graduate studies of larger
aspiration. Even to write for some other end outside of a deeper
knowledge of Truth (there being such a thing) seems a prostitution
of sorts. Perhaps, especially on religion. I've thought it awkward at
times in observing the paid workers of religion taking their slice of
alms to support their secure middle-class lifestyle. I couldn't do it
in good conscience. Better to join the labor pool of honest workers. But, then again, here we have the ever-zealous Saint Paul re-
minding us of the *Rights Of An Apostle* quite clearly:

> *Do we not have the right to our food and drink? Do we
> not have the right to be accompanied by a wife, as the other
> apostles and the brethren of the Lord and Cephas? Or is it
> only Barnabas and I who have no right to refrain from
> working for a living? Who serves as a soldier at his own
> expense? Who plants a vineyard without eating any of its
> fruit? Who tends a flock without getting some of the milk?*

> *the plowman should plow in hope and the thresher thresh
> in hope of a share in the crop. If we have sown spiritual
> good among you, is it too much if we reap your material
> benefits? If others share this rightful claim upon you, do
> not we still more?*

> *Nevertheless, we have not made use of this right, but we
> endure anything rather than put an obstacle in the way of*

---

[1] C. Wright Mills, *White Collar: The American Middle Classes*, Fiftieth Anniversary Edition (Oxford, UK: Oxford University Press, 2002 [1951]),
215-216.

the gospel of Christ. Do you not know that those who are
employed in the temple service get their food from the temple,
and those who serve at the altar share in the sacrificed of-
ferings? In the same way, the Lord commanded that those
who proclaim the gospel should get their living by the gospel.

Woe to me if I do not preach the gospel! For if I do this of
my own will, I have a reward; but if not of my own will, I
am entrusted with a commission. What then is my reward?
Just this: that in my preaching I may make the gospel free
of charge, not making full use of my right in the gospel (1
Corinthians 9:4-7, 10-14, 16-18).

So there you have it. What is good enough for Saint Paul
should be good enough for me. Even the apostles need to eat. The
Rabbi Saul pre-conversion is known, of course, to have made his
trade as a tent-maker. He was a student under the Rabbi Gamaliel.
Perhaps this was sort of like equivalency to a Phd in religion.
Probably not, but it doesn't matter. We all know too that Saint
Paul was a Roman citizen of, for a Jew, fairly prominent standing
in the Empire. That he knew how to argue for his fair share, using
his normal fervor of articulation, we can be sure.

Moving right along . . . in this brief analyzing conclusion of
the work of writing (why, for what reason, et cetera), I look to the
great twentieth century "class-thinker" Professor Paul Fussell to
gain a sliver of insight into the current context of our era's wordi-
ness. The essays in this the *secunda* part of my book were maybe
properly over-worded. I can't tell. I wrote them for graduate spe-
cialization on the things that I like to write about. Or, the things
that I know to write about. That I fall into this pompous trap of
middle-class cliché at certain junctures is a given. For example, my
interposing words like *penultimate* [really ultimate] or *indubitably* [?].
See Fussell here:

The passive voice is a great help to the middle
class in multiplying syllables. Thus the TV news-
man will say "No injuries were reported" (eight
syllables) when he means "No one was hurt"
(four). Pseudo-Latinism is another useful technique. *In colleges* has a measly four syllables, but *in*
academia has six, just as *in the suburbs* has four but

in suburbia five, and in addition conveys the sug-
gestion that the speaker is familiar with the classical tongues. (A real Latinist would honor the ac-
cusative case and say *in suburbiam*, but let that
pass.)

We can infer the middle-class (rather than prole
[lumpen proletariat]) origins of most terrorist
groups by their habit of leaving behind, after their
outrages, *communiqués* rather than *notes*, or even
messages. A benign, all-wise, and all-powerful editor and supervisor of expression among the middle class would have a busy time wielding his blue
pencil. One man asked by Coleman and Rainwa-
ter if he's better off than his father answers yes,
and explains: 'I have an M.A. and my father just
finished high school. This has meant that I am
able to engage in higher-paying areas of employment.' Here the editor would strike out all (twenty
syllables) after *meant*, replacing those words with
the four syllables of I can earn more money.[2]

I am happy to say, however, that not once does the word *dis-
combobulated* appear anywhere in this book. I am tempted to start
academic essays with *once upon a time* though. Try as I might, I am a
creature of my social construction. I can't help thinking that I was
raised being one of those *petite* middling Americans, who, "feel that
they live in a time of big decisions, but they know they are not
making any."[3] I chewed on this reflection of myself for a while,
then got passed it. Fearful of the fierce ideological Marxist, consti-
pated and alone in the British Museum, seeing-through everything
with the shrewd eye of a class-struggler, there can be still great
kernels of insight in looking through a sociological lens.

The powers of the present age are weird and unsettling. The
principles that we are being made to live are even perverser still.
To get a footing as to where things are headed, one must be something of the mad hatter these days, trying-on all sorts of twisting

---

[2] Paul Fussell, *Class: A Guide Through the American Status System* (New York:
Summit Books, 1983), 164.
[3] Ibid.

ideological world-views for size—to see behind what's really going on, that is.

I've ceased trying to social-climb (wrong word perhaps) into the top tiers of power beyond my station of birth. I once thought maybe it is possible, like the kid who wants to be U.S. President when he or she "grows up," then ends up the janitor or a school teacher. The typical question of the American businessman that is sometimes used to point right at it—if you're so smart . . . why aren't *you* rich and powerful? Touché. Well, at least I'm smart enough to recognize that this question is a bowel-movement issuing from a rotting decay of our "civilization."

Very true . . . for the would-be members of the top status levels,

> There are several ways to become rich. By the middle of the twentieth century in the United States, it has become increasingly difficult to earn and to keep enough money so as to accumulate your way to the top. Marriage involving money is at all times a delicate matter, and when it involves big money, it is often inconvenient and sometimes insecure. Stealing, if you do not already have much money, is a perilous undertaking. If you are gambling for money, and do so long enough, your capital will, in the end, balance out; if the game is fixed, you are really earning it or stealing it, or both, depending on which side of the table you sit. It is not usual, and it never has been the dominant fact, to create a great American fortune merely by nursing a little business into a big one. It is not usual and never has been the fact carefully to accumulate your way to the top, and many who try fall by the way. It is easier and much safer to be born there.[4]

Sound financial advice, no? Words that should be taken to heart. This is the big secret in fact. In the old days, "the main chance, usually with other people's money, was the key; in later

---

[4] C. Wright Mills, *The Power Elite*, Fiftieth Anniversary Edition (Oxford, UK: Oxford University Press, 1956), 115.

generations the accumulation of corporate advantages, based on grandfathers' and father's position, replaces the main chance."[5] Not so much anymore? Seems kind of a fixed thing either way—a game of unjust profits, in a sense, where no one gets too far from the social place they are born into. American dream? Not so much anymore.

For some time, the corporation has been the "organized center of the propertied classes." And the type of experience needed to get there is tightly controlled.

> One often hears that practical experience is what counts, but this is very short-sighted, for those on top control the chances to have practical experience of the sort that would be counted for the higher tasks of sound judgment and careful maneuver. This fact is often hidden by reference to an abstract, transferrable quality called 'managerial ability,' but many of those who have been up close to the higher circles (but not of them) have been led to suspect that there probably is no such thing.[6]

It's a sham a little. That's the big secret. "Most chief executives take much pride in their ability 'to judge men'; but what are the standards by which they judge? The standards that prevail are not clear-cut and objective; they seem quite intangible, they are often quite subjective, and they are often perceived by those below as ambiguous."[7]

OK. So? How do we get to be one these *The One Who Decides* people? What does it take?—"The only answer we can find anywhere is: the sound judgment, as gauged by the men of sound judgment who select them."[8]

In the end, "The fit survive, and fitness means, not formal competence—there probably is no such thing for top executive positions—but conformity with the criteria of those who have already succeeded. To be compatible with the top men is to act like

---

[5] Ibid., 115-116.

[6] Ibid., 140.

[7] Ibid., 140.

[8] Ibid., 141.

them, to look like them: to be of and for them."⁹ *And*, "Those who have had low beginnings must think all the harder before taking a risk of being thought unsound."¹⁰ *Because*, "Those chosen are picked, not so much for strictly personal characteristics—as for qualities judged useful to 'the team.' On this team, the prideful grace of individuality is not at a premium."¹¹

Hard logic? OK. So it's not nearly so much like that anymore. People are free now to do as they please, sort of sans the old social stigmas. But I think it holds true that the ways "in" (the inside track/whatever) are the same. Wanting to be successful we must remember:

> The upper management of U.S. business may be recruited from among (1) insiders in the administrative hierarchy; (2) insiders in the firm's financial or clique structure; (3) outsiders who have proved themselves able at managing smaller firms and are thus viewed as promising men on the management market; or (4) younger outsiders, fresh from technical or business training, who are usually taken in at lower levels with the expectation that their promotion will be unencumbered and rapid.¹²

That's about it. Yay Goldman Sachs. Yay J.P. Morgan. I don't think this is really any different now than it was in the 1950s when C. Wright Mills wrote it. Maybe back then it was just some other banking establishment like Kuhn, Loeb & Co.? Or another industrial giant like I.G. Farben. I might be wrong. The shadowy powers still hold the day. The occasional prodigy can find a road less traveled perhaps. I am sure that there is no way to read (or be read) your way into the commanding heights of power though. Like with God himself, you must be kind of "called" as the elect by those who already have the beneficences to bestow.

Maybe it's just my poverty of spirit. Or burning envy. I can't tell. 400 pages later I should probably find a day job. Anyone who

---

⁹ Ibid., 141.

¹⁰ Ibid. 142.

¹¹ Ibid., 142

¹² C. Wright Mills, *White Collar: The American Middle Classes*, 84

takes too much career advice from Karl Marx maybe ought to seek out a humanist therapist like Abraham Maslow as well.[13] Doom and gloom. Doom and gloom. Is what I say.

Nevertheless, Marx or no Marx, there is something to this idea that there is no real freedom to be anything other than what you are already. The dreaded possibility that we are to ourselves no more than a pair of Chinese handcuffs to be revealed as such to our future posterity. The more I tug the greater trap I'm in.

Know Thyself the temple inscription of Apollo told us for centuries. The more I try the tighter the handcuff tightens. And then . . . ouch! left with ourselves once again "man the measure of all things." I can look on the bright side, though, of certain things of course. The GDP is not too shabby, last time I checked about 5 years ago. *BUT*—for most of us:

> Alienation in work means that the most alert hours of one's life are sacrificed to the making of money with which to 'live.' Alienation means boredom and the frustration of potentially creative effort, of the productive sides of personality. It means that while men must seek all values that matter to them outside of work, they must be serious during work: they may not laugh or sing or even talk, they must follow the rules and not violate the fetish of 'the enterprise.' In short, they must be serious and steady about something that does not mean anything to them, and moreover during the best hours of their day, the best hours of their life. Leisure time thus comes to mean an unserious freedom from the authoritarian seriousness of the job.[14]

Get a life. Get a job. Work to work. Live. Die. Most people, as they used to say, live lives of quiet desperation. Philosophy *is* a

---

[13] *See* Karl Marx, *Das Kapital: Kritik der politischen Oekonomie*, 3 Vols. ed. Frederick Engels (New York: International Publishers, 1984 [1894]). Of course, Cultural Marxism is no long-term alternative to Corporate Fascism.

[14] C. Wright Mills, *White Collar: The American Middle Classes*, 236.

hard-headed science—whatever detractors say. It just doesn't give much of the sound judgment for getting ahead.

There is a certain maliciousness at times on the dryer side of writing things down for public consumption. A "deconstuctor" of the written word puts all the onus on the writer nowadays, not the reader. The writer is never understood, no matter what. So, the reader is free to make of it what he or she will. There is no set meaning to anything. Meaning? What is that? Words twist, evolve, devolve, do nothing at all. It's a language game of interpretation, no more. Or a play for power, easily seen through. Me, not you. That sort of thing.[15]

You never can see the real writer behind the mask of the written words anyway. Who knows what type of a guy Plato really was? Some things about him we'd never know about would probably shock us if we did. But we buy his writings still—more than 2000 years later. So, why not make of it what the "feeling" of interpretation tells us it is.

What does this here book "feel like"? To the reader of it? Not sure. I can only say, given the looseness of it, maybe this project is a little unique, nay, individual even. Nonsense verse? I can't remember.

Yeah, yeah, yeah. [Sic]

That being said, *I am* an autodidactic reader and writer. My mastery of the weasel word is prodigious. I am the metaphorical Luddite by analogy. One thing I can say is that I have tried my best to abstain of all things that make our modern scholarship so sterile and dull. Computers for one are the bane of this. I don't think computers actually improve writing one bit. The opposite in fact is true. The *feel* of writings written on type-writers, or with a quill, or chiseled onto stones with blood and sweat, or dyed into papyrus scrolls then aged in the sun, is a wholly other league in comparison to the tin-eared Microsoft auto-spell check, thesaurus and word count. Double for the internet lookup.

I've used every bell and whistle of digital props as minimally as possible—looking things up in good old-fashioned library stacks or leaving it out. My spelling is practically flawless, so I can count the times I've pressed the Spelling & Grammar button on two

---

[15] *See* Michel Foucault, *Les Mots es les choses: An Archaeology of the Human Sciences* (New York: Vintage Books, 1994 [197]).

hands. I am convinced that my grammar is actually better than the computer's. I have to turn off the auto-correct to write what I want. I can somehow sense the Microsoft Word program getting angry at me while I write this. Computers and the death of the soul?

I am not alone I imagine. Carl Gustav Jung backs me up. In his memoirs, retiring to his esoteric Swiss abode in a part of his house he calls *The Tower*, in this reflection he sees the impending failure of our blooming hurry-and-get-it-fast new stuff culture:

> Reforms by advances, that is, by new methods or gadgets, are of course impressive at first, but in the long run they are dubious and in any case dearly paid for. They by no means increase the contentment or happiness of people on the whole. Mostly, they are deceptive sweetenings of exist-ence, like speedier communications which un-pleasantly accelerate the tempo of life and leave us with less time than ever before. *Omnis festinatio ex parte diabolic est*—all haste is of the devil, as the old masters used to say.
>
> Reforms by retrogressions, on the other hand, are as a rule less expensive and in addition more last-ing, for they return to the simpler, tried and tested ways of the past and make sparsest use of news-papers, radio, television, and all supposedly time-saving innovations.[16]

Thank you for that Dr. Jung. Breath of fresh air. I have not watched a single television program of any kind for more than 5 minutes in over 6 years. Probably more. I don't read the news ever. My brain is free and pure of most advertising schlock. It has taken years to unlearn the garbage of the media infused into my psyche since childhood—growing up in 1980s New York (the lowest of the low for that sort of thing).

I wouldn't drive a car if I didn't have to. I quite honestly be-lieve that it would take no more than a year or two for the whole

---

[16] C. G. Jung, *Memories, Dreams, Reflections*, Revised Edition, ed. Aniela Jaffé, trans. Richard and Clara Winston (New York: Vintage Books, 1989 [1961]), 236-237.

economy to shift to a carless infrastructure. It would solve the obesity problem in America by making people walk to places. And I'm not even an environmental fanatic. I'd prefer a carless society purely for æshtetic reasons. I think life is better without cell phones or the internet too.

OK, so this book should have been an interesting read. I had fun writing these essays. This book. I've been a good student about the things that I like. A fierce independence of mind has led me at times to the attitude of "what do teachers know." I love to learn no less. Strictly speaking I am not armchair philosophy or rote religion. I draw upon, I think, many many interesting experiences in my 34 years on this earth.

As to the nature of present-day academic success I can't help citing the former chairman of the Harvard admissions committee Wilbur Bender. It's a spot-on juicy quotation. In his experience at screening Harvard hopefuls, Mr Bender explains that—

> The student who ranks first in his class may be genuinely brilliant or he may be a compulsive worker or instrument of domineering parents' ambitions or a conformist or a self-centered careerist who has shrewdly calculated his teachers' prejudices and expectations and discovered how to regurgitate efficiently what they want. Or he may have focused narrowly on grade-getting as compensation for his inadequacies in other areas, because he lacks other interests or talents or lacks passion and warmth or normal healthy instincts or is afraid of life. The top high school student is often, frankly, a pretty dull and bloodless, or peculiar fellow. The adolescent with wide-ranging curiosity and stubborn independence, with a vivid imagination and desire to explore fascinating by-paths, to follow his own interests, to contemplate, to read non-required books, the boy filled with sheer love for life and exuberance, may well seem to his teachers troublesome, undisciplined, a rebel, may not conform to their stereotype, and may not get the top grades and the highest rank in class. He may not even score the highest level on standard multiple choice admission tests, which may

> very well reward a glib, facile mind at the expense
> of the questioning, independent, or slower but
> more powerful, more subtle, and more interesting
> and original mind.[17]

Very true Mr. Bender. Very true. You're no Solzhenitsyn, but very true. OK. So I can be glib and facile once in a while. However, I am very much the second type of Wilbur Bender's description. I've never regurgitated efficiently as far as I can tell. My imagination *is* terribly vivid. I have read *all* the non-required books I can. Powerful, subtle, interesting *and* original may be a stretch for me, but I'm very much in the running for these things. A sophomoric sentence ever so often is de rigueur for my type, but that is to be expected as coming with the territory.

Of course, there is no need to worry about "measuring up" to Harvard or Princeton or even Yale I think. Most honest scholars I come across can readily admit our age is a cultural wasteland. The great Aldous Huxley saw this with great lucidity. I can't agree more that—in our disgustingly pretentious aspirations to lay claim to being "the best of all possible cultures" historically—advances in our technological prowess have really, as Aldous Huxley tells us, led to nothing but a higher *"vulgarity"* . . . when all is said and done.

It takes a deep artistic eye like Huxley to see that—

> Process reproduction and the rotary press have
> made possible the indefinite multiplication of
> writing and pictures. Universal education and
> relatively high wages have created an enormous
> public who know how to read and can afford to
> buy reading and pictorial matter. A great industry
> has been called into existence in order to supply
> these commodities. Now artistic talent is a very
> rare phenomenon; whence it follows . . . that, at
> every epoch and in all countries, most art has
> been bad. But the proportion of trash in the total

---

[17] As quoted in Carroll Quigley, *Tragedy and Hope: A History of the World in Our Time* (New York: The Macmillan Company, 1966), 1274.

artistic output is greater now than at any other period.[18]

So be it. If this book is more present day trash it's trash. Scholarship isn't technically an artistic thing anyhow, so I guess I'm not pretending there. Gave it a whirl. A shot, so they say. That somebody somewhere might get a thing or two out of it more the better, my reader. 'Twas a pleasure to write it.

Another story comes to mind for some reason. Thinking on the homogenous mass of people out there (?) living dreary lives of oppressed post-industrial humanity . . . I grow vengeful.

Rex Tenebris. A ghost story by Russell Kirk about Mr S. G. W. Barner, Planning Officer—"a thick-chested, hairy man, forever carrying a dispatch case, stooping and heavy of tread, rather like a large, earnest ape." This resolute and soulless corporate bureaucrat rezones an ancient little village named Low Wentford in Scotland, then proceeds to displace all the residents to a State planned community called Gorst.[19] In the village there is isolated an old woman named Mrs. Oliver—"an ancient little woman with a nose that very nearly meets her chin"—living in the last sound cottage there.

It is disconcerting to Barner that a "doddering old creature like the obdurate Mrs. Oliver should prefer living in this unhealthy rurality." He thinks it better that she should be served a compulsory purchase order to move to the council-flat made available to her in Gorst. S. G. W. Barner, Planning Officer, with his State credentials, pays her a visit to force her exit. She is repulsed by him as a detestable little man.

Barner then proceeds with his plans for demolition of her tiny home as well as the abandoned old church All Saints parish nearby—there is no church in the planned community of Gorst.

There was once buried in this church's graveyard a village schoolmaster. A nasty story is told about him—an atheist by the name of Mr Reddy, he was cursed and denounced by the vicar of All Saints continually from the pulpit. One day, during the first

---

[18] Aldous Huxley, "Beyond the Mexique Bay. A Traveller's Journal," as quoted in Walter Benjamin, "The Work of Art in the Age of Mechanical Reproduction," *Illuminations*, trans. Harry Zohn. ed. Hannah Arendt (New York: Schocken Books, 2007 [1955]), 217-252.

[19] "Ex Tenebris," in Russell Kirk, *Ancestral Shadows: An Anthology of Ghostly Tales* (Grand Rapids, MI: William B. Eerdmans Publishing Company, 2004), 3-17.

week of Lent, Reddy is found in a brook with his neck broken. It was thought an accident at the time. He has been buried in the church graveyard ever since. Six months later the last vicar of the now abandoned church himself was found drowned in the Low Wentford quarry. The village did not know what to make of it and the church was closed soon thereafter.

Now, in Low Wentford there is a respected hereditary "nobility," the Ogham family, who try to resist Barner in the town council and to protect Mrs. Oliver from eviction. *But*, Mr. S. G. W. Barner, Planning Officer "had made up his mind that not one stone *is* to be left upon another in Low Wentford." Removing every last personage from the little town, Mr Barner, Planning Officer, is confident that . . .

> advanced planning, within a few years, surely would liberate progressive societies from dependence upon old-fashioned farming. He disliked the whole notion of agriculture, with its rude earthiness, its reactionary views of life and labor, its subservience to tradition. The agricultural classes would be absorbed into the centers of population, or otherwise disposed of; the land thus placed at the public command would be converted to garden cities, or state holiday-camps, or proving grounds for industrial and military experiment.[20]

> With proper employment of scientific methodology, one day society would plan its weather, perhaps eliminating the seasons. But for the stupidity of entrenched interests, the thing would have been accomplished already. Superstition!

On the evening of Ash Wednesday, S. G. W. Barner, Planning Officer, is paid a phone call by one Mr. Hargreaves, who says that he is the vicar of All Saints church in Low Wentford. He wishes to speak with Barner about Mrs. Oliver. They arrange a meeting in the graveyard near her cottage. They confront each other. The right reverend Hargreaves warns Barner to show her and the town mercy.

---

[20] Ibid.

Barner is obstinate. He is unmoved and agitated by the ghostly vicar's waxy face—a laugh "nearer the braying of a mule than anything from a man's throat." Pallid skin, red beaming eyes, and distended nostrils, Hargreaves issues his last warning:

Cursed is he that perverteth the judgment of the stranger, the fatherless and the widow.[21]

Cursed is he that smiteth his neighbor secretly.[22]

For now is the ax put to the root of the trees, so that every tree that bringeth forth not good fruit, is hewn down and cast into the fire.[23]

The story ends. The town is puzzled. The curious death of Mr S. G. W. Barner is a topic of conversation even beyond the town of Gorst . . . "the *Review of Collective Planning* observed that in Barner, pragmatic social reconstruction had lost one its most promising younger advocates."[24]

There is controversy about S. G. W. Barner, Planning Officer's cremation. Unfortunately, the clean new town of Gorst is outspoken in opposing the 'barbarous practice' of scattering ashes over unconsecrated grounds; public grounds that have *not* been zoned for a church building yet (or perhaps ever). And Miss Harris of Holy Trinity church in Old Gorst refuses his ashes there too.

So . . . in a twist of fate Mr Barner's remains end up in the graveyard of the abandoned All Saints church in Low Wentford. Close by of course is Mrs. Oliver's cottage, who is now secure in her home. No more social planners attempt to approach her with eviction business. And so, she is often found visiting the church grounds, "she weeds her garden, and bakes her scones, and often sweeps the gravestones clean: thus she continues surprisingly vigorous for a woman of her years."

Mr Hargreaves the purported vicar is never heard from again. Turns out to be a *ghost* who killed Barner. The only person to actually attest to the vicar Hargreaves' existence is Mrs. Oliver, who says to the authorties that she has not seen him since. She explains

---

[21] Ibid.

[22] Ibid.

[23] Ibid.

[24] Ibid.

to Sir Ogham of the Ogham family, though, that she *does* have a new visitor from time to time—"a Mr. Reddy, highly opinionated, given to denying the existence of Heaven, and suffering dreadfully from some old injury to his neck." Another ghost we now know.

The death of S. G. W. Barner, Planning Officer, is talked about then passed over soon after. The occurrence is officially explained by the Gorst authorities here:

> Apparently Barner had been making a brief inspection of the derelict church of All Saints, which he intended to persuade ecclesiastical authorities to demolish, when the roof of the north porch, weakened by incompetent restorers near the end of the eighteenth century and further imperiled by neglect, fell upon him. His body was not discovered until the following afternoon.[25]

Writing is a ghostly business. Leave a testament of yourself behind, who knows where it will end up a long, long time from now. Wasn't that the secret of the Hebrew prophets. Feels like *time* bending time a little. Would-be members of the top status levels, "students are, if the truth be known, a bad lot. En masse they're as fickle as a mob, manipulable by any professor who'll stoop to it. They have, moreover, an infinite capacity for repeating dull truths and old lies with all the insistence of self-discovery. Nothing is drearier than the ideology of students, left or right.

A stranger kissed me,
    and I cried.
My rich, old aunt kissed me,
    and I shied.
A pretty girl kissed me,
    and I sighed.

Truman Capote, REACTIONS TO A KISS

where—not in dim mysteries, as in this dark world of ours, but—face to face

---

[25] Ibid.

POSTSCRIPTUM

But the person who is neither cold nor hot is an abomination, and God is no more served by dud individualists than a rifleman is served by a rifle that in the moment of decision clicks instead of firing.

Søren Kierkegaard, CONCLUDING UNSCIENTIFIC POSTSCRIPT TO THE PHILOSOPHICAL FRAGMENTS: A MIMICAL-PATHETICAL-DIALECTICAL COMPILATION, AN EXISTENTIAL CONTRIBUTION

No one can lay claim to omniscient status. Our thoughts and ideas originate with who we are *even before* we are aware of what we have become. I owe a quick autobiographical family sketching, I think, to—at the very least—establish my "right" to write on things of importance. We all know that there is a difference between *power* and *authority*. My worldly power is not so great, so I might try to give an accounting of the nature of my authority by means of the written word. I understand it can be distasteful to some to write on politics, war, religion, et cetera —if it is thought that you have "no right" to.

A sharp anecdote—as to piece *IV. The Just War Tradition In Mundo Huius Temporis* of my essays—is that my grandfather Bryan Clinton Hammond was in fact named after William Jennings Bryan. I cannot see that I would have come to research WJB for any other reason. A lot of what *I have* written about in this book is occasional in much the same way.

Good writers, I am told, know how to massage the "right-brain" by conjuring thoughts or ideas using what is "in" the deeper regions of the subjective consciousness. This, of course, does not invalidate anything scientific or factual, but only means that it is better to write *what you know*, and *know* deeply, even while writing on something objective-empirical-scholarship, et cetera.

And so, in some of my "left-over" tidbits or loose-ends of research I turned up this amusing parallel. We have in our family a letter from William Jennings Bryan written to my great grandfather Browne Clinton Hammond in 1897. Browne, as my Dad would tell it, was a "soapbox" politician in King's County, Brooklyn. He ran on the Socialist ballot in New York in numerous elections and befriended W. J. Bryan and Eugene Debs.

This great grandfather of mine placed third for U.S. Congressman (1892) King's County 11th district to Amos J. Cummings (Democrat) and runner-up Abraham H. Sarasohn (Republican). He placed third again in his second bid for U.S. Congressman (1912) King's County 6th district to William M. Calder (Democrat) and runner-up Robert H. Roy (Republican). He also ran on the Socialist or Prohibition tickets for New York state senator (1910, 1924), and state assembly (1909, 1920, 1922). . . . so, it can be seen, I believe, why my grandfather was then named Bryan Clinton.

My great grandfather Browne Hammond was also the first of our family to have arrived in New York from Virginia—after the loss of the Civil War—where the Hammonds had settled some time around the American War of Independence in the late 1700s. In fact, I am the seventh generation of this line bearing the Hammond name.

That being said, this is a letter that I have from William Jennings Bryan sent in reply to Browne on the birth of my grandfather. It reads:

Lincoln, Neb., Feb. 1897

My Dear Sir,

I write to thank you for the honor you do me in giving my name to your son. It is a high compliment and I appreciate it. That the child my grow up to be a comfort and a blessing to his parents is the wish of

Yours Truly,

W. J. Bryan

Nothing extraordinary, I think. A common courtesy, but a gentleman's acknowledgement no less. William Jennings Bryan, to be sure, had written thousands of letters a year. What is more interesting, however, is the context of this letter. It comes just one year before Bryan's offer to serve in the Spanish-American War. In Bryan's memoirs there is this letter to then President McKinley:

Lincoln, Neb., April 25, 1898

Hon. William McKinley
President

My Dear Sir—

I hereby place my services at your command during the war with Spain and assure you of my willingness to perform to the best of my ability any duty to which you, as the commander in chief of the army and navy, may see fit to assign me.

Respectfully Yours,

W. J. Bryan

I think this an interesting parallel no doubt. I don't know what relevance it would have to others, only that it demonstrates where political dispositions can originate. As far as Bryan's political importance goes, the part he played is by consensus a key to American history in World War I. It is of note that he here had not yet come to the full realization of his antiwar convictions—and I'm sure that there could be other sidebars added or more footnotes to endlessly dig into the weaving twists and turns of history's annals.

On the political end of things, we Hammonds have been participants in nearly every American war since our founding. My great great great grandfather John Hammond (who bore seventeen children) fought in the *War of 1812* around the defenses of Norfolk, VA. The brother of my great great grandfather Peter J.— Samuel Clayton Hammond—was the color-bearer for his regiment under Stonewall Jackson in the Virginia campaigns of the *Civil War*. Another brother of my great great grandfather—Mayberry Hammond—was shot and wounded at Gettysburg, then later killed by Federal soldiers on retreat from Lynchburg after General Hunter's defeat by Jubal A. Early. Yet another brother of this line—Theodore Buchanan Hammond—was shot and killed in 1862 during the *Battle of Seven Pines*. And, another brother—Rev. Wesley Hammond—served as a Methodist chaplain.

In *World War I*, my grandfather's brother-in-law served with distinction with the American Expeditionary Forces in France. My grandfather's cousin—Charles Galloway Hammond—was awarded by General Pershing the Distinguished Service Cross for exceptional valor in the battle of July 15th, 1918; while he was serving in France with the 42nd (Rainbow) Division. My great grandfather's nephew—Gerald Webb Follin of Bryan, TX—married Grace Cleveland in 1914, a niece of ex-President Grover Cleveland and Frances Folsom.

My own father Robert George Hammond was a Seaman First Class in the Navy during *World War II* (July 5, 1944–June 3, 1946). At age 18-years-old, and stationed in New York harbor, he had to see the War upfront aboard ammunition vessels in the Atlantic, Indian, and Pacific oceans. After the War, he was awarded the European Theatre Medal, Asiatic Theatre Medal, Pacific Theatre Medal, and a Victory Medal, under President Harry Truman.

My Dad and his brother managed my grandfather's Depression-era business after World War II—Bryan Elliott and Company. They operated in New York City for 40+ years. Bryan-Elliott began as a printing-broker and had commissions from the military to make war-maps at one point. It became largely a trade-show and design (POP) business, introducing foreign products into the United States through a post-war office in Paris in the 1950s—launching products like Bon Bel, Germaine Monteil, Biscuit—and, domestically IBM, Kodak, Timex, etc. Some of the original clients included famous industrialists like James Cash Penney.

My Dad's company designed the bicentennial exhibition for the United States Navy in 1975. His biggest clients were foreign governments for the 1964 New York World's Fair, organized in Queens by Robert Moses and John F. Kennedy. He designed the Lebanese pavilion (and others) for the Fair at the Flushing Meadows fairgrounds—now home of the U. S. Open and the NY Mets—and then at the Montreal Expo in 1967. In the 50s, 60s, 70s, he did business with various governments in the Middle East and behind the "Iron Curtain," (Romania, Hungary), at the height of the Cold War. He continued to do work for the French and Italian Trade Commissions in New York and retired to Sutton Place on the Eastside of Manhattan.

This book was dedicated to him, so I'll end on that note.

ACKNOWLEDGEMENTS

First of everyone, I thank my mother for all of her love and support. I'd also like to thank the faculty members at the graduate schools where I studied: *Washington Theological Union, University of South Florida, The Catholic University of America, The Dominican House of Studies*, and *Christendom College*—and in particular, my Master's Thesis Director Rev. Dr. Kevin O'Neil, C.Ss.R, and Thesis Reader Rev. Dr. Donald Buggert, O.Carm. Also, each individual professor in whose courses my seven research essays were written deserves a special nod: In the ordering of *"& Other Essays"* they are: *I.* Dr. Joanne Waugh (USF), *II.* Dr. James Strange (USF), *III.* Dr. Stephen Turner (USF), *IV.* Rev. Dr. Brian V. Johnstone, C.Ss.R. (CUA) *V.* Dr. Thomas Williams (USF), *VI.* Ibid., Dr. Thomas Williams (USF), *VII.* Rev. Dr. John T. Ford, C.S.C., S.T.D. (CUA)—as well as all others with whom I took courses or through whom I have learned the relevant material in these pages—esp. Rev. Dr. John Corbett, O.P. (DHS), Dr. Roger Ariew (USF), Dr. Angela Senander (WTU), Dr. Michael DeJonge (USF), Dr. Hunt Hawkins (USF), Rev. Dr. Joseph Mindling O.F.M. Cap. (WTU), Dr. Theresa Koernke, I.H.M. (WTU), Rev. Dr. Joseph Wimmer, O.S.A. (WTU), and Rev. Dr. Leopold Glueckert, O.Carm (WTU).

I would also like to thank Rev. Anita Keire for the idea to self-publish this with Createspace. And I thank Carrie Scupholm for her assistance during graduate school, esp. in proof-reading thesis drafts. I'd like to thank Dr. Winthrop Adkins for his encouragement to pursue academia as a career path. And I thank Rev. Anthony Penachio for introducing Catholicism to me—to which I converted in 2007. Moreover, I'd like to acknowledge the other schools in whose libraries research was done for this project—specifically: *New College of Florida, Eckerd College, Stetson Law School, University of Tampa, Fairfield University, Manhattanville College, Northeastern University*, and *Yale*. Similarly, I acknowledge all that I have learned in worship services as well as the graces I have received through the numerous churches attended the last nine years or so—Catholic, Presbyterian, Episcopal, Orthodox, Lutheran, Nondenominational, or otherwise. In particular, the *Shrine of the Immaculate Conception* in DC, *St. Mary's Parish* Greenwich, and *Round Hill Community Church*. I don't think I've missed more than one or two Sundays of church in nearly ten-years.

Made in the USA
Columbia, SC
26 October 2017

SMOKESCREEN

Edward Lincoln may be a worldwide superstar who plays
daring detectives on the big screen, but in reality he's just
an ordinary man. Unfortunately, his ailing friend doesn't
seem to think so—and now he's come to South Africa to
investigate who's been tampering with her racehorses. But
it isn't long before he realizes he must go face-to-face with
a killer—and give the performance of his life to *save* his
life . . .

continued . . .